THE STEPHEN LAWRENCE INQUIRY

Appendices

Presented to Parliament by the Secretary of State for the Home Department
by Command of Her Majesty
February 1999

CM 4262-II   £24.00

APPENDICES

CONTENTS

1. Brief history of the Inquiry

2. Report by the Police Complaints Authority on the Investigation of a Complaint against the Metropolitan Police Service by Mr N and Mrs D Lawrence

3. Transcript of the Inquiry's Preliminary Hearing in Woolwich, 8 October 1997

4. Transcript of the Inquiry's opening day, 16 March 1998, including the application by Mr Michael Mansfield QC for an adjournment

5. Transcript of the resumption of the Inquiry, 24 March 1998, including opening remarks by the Chairman and his Advisers; and opening statements on behalf of the Inquiry, Mr and Mrs Lawrence and the Metropolitan Police Service

6. Statements to the Inquiry of Mrs Lawrence

7. Statements to the Inquiry of Mr Lawrence

8. Statements to the Inquiry of Mr Brooks

9. Transcript of the apology on 17 June 1998 to Mr and Mrs Lawrence by Assistant Commissioner Johnston

10. Transcript of a compilation video of intrusive surveillance conducted on the five "suspects", as seen by the Inquiry

11. Kent County Constabulary Calendar List

12. Extract from the MPS Policy File

13. The Report by Detective Chief Superintendent Barker of his Review

14. Witnesses who appeared before Part 1 of the Inquiry

15. Legal representatives of the parties to the Inquiry

16. Persons who appeared before Part 2 of the Inquiry

17. Those who provided written submissions to Part 2 of the Inquiry

18. Publications seen by the Inquiry

BRIEF HISTORY OF THE INQUIRY

Background

1. On 24 June 1997, the Home Secretary (the Rt Hon Jack Straw MP) met with Mr & Mrs Lawrence to discuss their application, made via their solicitor Mr Imran Khan, for a judicial inquiry into the death of their son, Stephen. They were accompanied by Mr Khan and Michael Mansfield QC, Bernie Grant MP, John Austin-Walker MP and supporters of the Lawrence family. Mr Straw and his Ministers had been considering for some weeks their concern about this matter.

2. After that meeting, a news release in these terms was issued by Mr Straw:

    > *"I am glad to have been able to meet Mr & Mrs Lawrence today and have been deeply moved listening to the tragic circumstances surrounding the death of their son, Stephen.*
    >
    > *Whilst in opposition I met Mrs Lawrence and was impressed by her determination and courage in such difficult circumstances. This meeting was my first opportunity to meet Mr & Mrs Lawrence in my capacity as Home Secretary and another chance for me to discuss with them the distressing details of their son's case. We have also had the chance to discuss broader issues, including racially motivated crime and the relationship between the police and ethnic minority communities.*
    >
    > *It is not an option to let this matter rest.*
    >
    > *I recognise that a strong case has been made by Mrs Lawrence for some form of an inquiry and I am actively considering what she put to me.*
    >
    > *I will also carefully consider the other issues that were raised during our meeting and reflect on the best way to address the widespread concern resulting from this case.*
    >
    > *I hope to make an announcement soon."*

Appointment

3. On 31 July 1997, the Home Secretary gave written answers to Parliamentary Questions from Clive Efford MP and John Austin-Walker MP, saying that he had decided to establish an inquiry under section 49 of the Police Act 1996. The terms of reference of the inquiry were to be:

    > *"To inquire into the matters arising from the death of Stephen Lawrence on 22 April 1993 to date, in order particularly to identify the lessons to be learned for the investigation and prosecution of racially motivated crimes."*

4.   Sir William Macpherson of Cluny, formerly a High Court Judge, was appointed to conduct the inquiry, being supported as Advisers by Mr Tom Cook, formerly Deputy Chief Constable, West Yorkshire Police; Dr Richard Stone, Chairman, Jewish Council for Racial Equality; and the Rt Revd Dr John Sentamu, the Bishop for Stepney.

First steps

5.   Stephen Wells and Alison Foulds from the Home Office's Operational Policing Policy Unit were appointed Secretary and Assistant Secretary in August 1997; and Peter Whitehurst, from the Treasury Solicitor's Department, was appointed Solicitor to the Inquiry in the same month. Linda Dann joined as the Assistant Solicitor in November; with Janet Crowl and Gerry Ranson, as the Personal Secretary and Documents Officer respectively in the Secretariat, arriving in December. Jayne Wiltshire, Personal Secretary, joined the Treasury Solicitors team also in December. Mike Booker acted as Inquiry Press Officer from February to December 1998. Maureen Puttnam joined as a Personal Secretary in December 1998.

6.   The Attorney General instructed David Penry-Davey QC as Counsel to the Inquiry, with Anesta Weekes as second counsel. Unfortunately, the Inquiry very quickly was denied the services of Mr Penry-Davey upon his appointment to the High Court Bench: Edmund Lawson QC was appointed as successor in November 1997. John Gibson joined as junior Counsel in December.

7.   Separate, short and informal meetings with Mr & Mrs Lawrence, and their Counsel and Solicitor; and with the Chairman and Deputy Chairman of the Police Complaints Authority; the Commissioner and Deputy Commissioner of the Metropolitan Police; the Director of Public Prosecutions; and officials from the Commission for Racial Equality, were held very soon after the Inquiry was formed. These were the obvious initial main parties to the Inquiry; and the purpose behind the meetings was for them and the Inquiry to discuss any immediate problems and concerns.

Background reading

8.   Ahead of, during, and after the formal proceedings of the Inquiry, a number of sources of background information - reports and other publications, videos, press articles - were seen and read by the Chairman, Advisers and support staff. A bibliography is given in Appendix 18.

Accommodation and services

9.   In accordance with convention, the Inquiry quickly sought to establish itself locally, in premises within the London Borough of Greenwich. Unfortunately, given the nature of the Inquiry and its need for sufficient space, privacy and security, appropriate premises could not be found in the Borough, although a number of alternatives were examined. Premises were ultimately found in Hannibal House in the Elephant & Castle area of Southwark, South East London, and these were converted to the Inquiry's requirements. The search for accommodation was an arduous one, and the Inquiry expresses its thanks, in particular, to the London Borough of Greenwich; ISD7 Branch of the Department of Health; and the Buildings and Estate Management Unit in the Home Office for their help, the latter also for their management of the necessary building works. The Inquiry moved to Hannibal House on 1 December 1997.

10.   It soon became clear that the volume of papers likely to come before the Inquiry would be vast, and could only properly be managed, both in terms of their use as a resource and an archive as well as their handling during hearings, by use of sophisticated information technology. Other Inquiries were visited - including the North Wales Child Abuse and the Ashworth Special Hospital tribunals - to discern an appropriate solution. With the help of the Home Office Central Information Systems Unit, a specification was devised. Contractors were invited to submit competitive tenders for meeting this requirement, Sellers Imago being successful. The Inquiry therefore was able to operate without recourse to masses of paper copies of documentary evidence: instead, as is increasingly customary in public inquiries, material was scanned into the system (by Legal Technologies Limited), and then called up (by Grace Vaughan, from Sellers Imago) and viewed, on screens, in the Inquiry chamber. As evidence was given, a contemporaneous note of the proceedings was prepared and shown on screen. This service was also provided by Sellers Imago, a contract being awarded after competitive tendering.

11.   Copies of the transcript were available for consultation in Hannibal House. A copy was also sent each day to the public library closest to Hannibal House, and to the central library of the London Borough of Greenwich.

The site of the murder

12.   The Chairman, Mr Cook, Secretary and Assistant Secretary, and Solicitor visited the site of Stephen Lawrence's murder, on 7 October 1997. Counsel, junior Counsel and Secretary returned to the site the next day. A night-hours visit by the junior Counsel, and Secretary and Assistant Secretary was made to the site and surrounding locality on 3 November. Mr Cook and the Assistant Secretary visited the site again during November. The Secretary and Dr Sentamu made a night hours visit on 1 December.

13.   Other visits to the site by Inquiry staff took place. The Secretary attended vigils held at the place where Stephen died, led by Dr Sentamu on 15 March and 22 April 1998.

Immunity

14.   The Attorney General authorised the Chairman to give the following undertaking in respect of immunity:

> *"In respect of any person who provides evidence to this Inquiry, that no evidence he or she may give before the Inquiry, whether orally or by written statement, nor any written statement made preparatory to giving evidence nor any documents produced by that person to the Inquiry, will be used in evidence against him or her in any criminal proceedings, except in proceedings where he or she is charged with having given false evidence in the course of this Inquiry or having conspired with or procured others so to do."*

15.   A similar immunity in respect of disciplinary matters was provided by the Police Complaints Authority and the Commissioner of the Metropolitan Police.

Preliminary hearing

16.   The Chairman held a preliminary public hearing at Woolwich Public Hall, Market Street, Woolwich on 8 October 1997. At this meeting, the Chairman dealt with some procedural aspects of the Inquiry, and invited applications from parties to be legally represented. Extracts from the transcript of the hearing are at Appendix 3.

17.   This hearing was advertised by Public Notice in newspapers circulating in the locality, in the London Borough of Greenwich's own newspaper, and in four newspapers printed by the ethnic minority press. The principal parties to the case and the Greenwich Council for Racial Equality were given separate notice of the hearing. The print media were allowed to be present throughout, but the broadcast media were not permitted to film the proceedings.

18.   Further preliminary hearings were held at Hannibal House, with limited attendance. These were, for instance, to explore formally matters of public interest immunity relating to documents in the hands of the Metropolitan Police.

Report from the Police Complaints Authority into Mr & Mrs Lawrence's complaints against the Metropolitan Police Service

19.   A report under section 97(2) of the Police and Criminal Evidence Act 1984 was presented to the Home Secretary by the Police Complaints Authority, and this was placed before Parliament on 15 December 1997. It is reproduced at Appendix 2. After some necessary deletions, the report by the Investigating Officer, and the supporting evidence, was in due course made available, without precedent, to the parties to the Inquiry.

Collection of evidence

20.   The represented parties to the Inquiry were required by section 250 of the Local Government Act 1972 to provide documents to the Inquiry. The first major batch of documents was received by the Inquiry on 9 October 1997, from the Metropolitan Police Service. All evidence was placed in secure storage in Hannibal House, while agreement to share individual batches of documents with the other represented parties was obtained. In some cases, particularly so as to protect the identities of witnesses and informants, or so as not to hinder the continuing police investigation into the case, steps were taken to "redact", that is to say, censor, relevant content in documents.

21.   During February 1998, the Inquiry produced a schedule of issues emerging from the evidence, and this was shared and agreed with the represented parties to the Inquiry. Documents were entered onto several CD ROMs, so that the evidence could be viewed by the parties, with viewing software, away from Hannibal House. In all, about 100,000 pages of evidence were received by the Inquiry.

22.   At this time, advertisements were placed in local newspapers, calling for witnesses to Stephen's murder, or those who had other evidence, to come forward to the Inquiry.

The Media

23.   Representatives of the media were invited to meet the Chairman, and view the Inquiry's facilities, in February 1998. They were also invited to photograph the Chairman visiting the site of Stephen's murder, shortly before the public hearings began.

Part 1 Hearings

24. A number of adjournments were agreed by the Chairman, so that the first formal public hearing of the Inquiry did not take place until 16 March 1998. On that day, the Chairman agreed to a further application for an adjournment on behalf of Mr & Mrs Lawrence, so that they might consult the Home Secretary about the contents of a critical article which had appeared in the Observer newspaper the day before. Having being reassured by the Home Secretary, Mr & Mrs Lawrence were present when the Inquiry reopened on 24 March. The relevant extracts from the transcripts of the hearings are at Appendices 4 and 5.

25. A full list of the witnesses who gave evidence at the Inquiry is given at Appendix 14. All witnesses were given advance notice of the issues proposed to be raised with them: these notices are known colloquially as "Salmon" letters.

26. Hearings were conducted formally. The Inquiry had powers to call for witnesses to attend, under section 250 of the Local Government Act 1972. Witnesses were sworn, and Counsel for the Inquiry examined each witness, relevant cross examination from each party following. Witnesses were also required to answer questions from the Chairman and his Advisers.

27. Notices announcing the opening of the Inquiry were placed in local, minority and national newspapers. The public and the media were given free and open access to the Inquiry. There was no recording or broadcasting of the Inquiry. Proceedings were relayed by closed circuit television to an assembly and waiting area in Hannibal House, so that those unable to gain a seat in the Chamber could nevertheless witness proceedings; and so that those who found themselves distressed by the proceedings could nevertheless also share in the work of the Inquiry. Closed circuit television monitors were also provided in a press room; and basic fax, telephone and photocopying facilities were provided for the public and for the media.

28. Civilian security staff acted as receptionists and as general supervisors of the Inquiry floor, but the day to day supervision of the Inquiry Chamber was undertaken by the Secretary and Assistant Secretary. Information packs for the media and for the general public were provided. Private rooms were provided for the parties to the Inquiry.

29. Enhanced safety measures were put in place on 29 and 30 June, and on 1 October. On those days proceedings were also broadcast by video link to overflow accommodation in the Elephant & Castle shopping centre.

30. Closing submissions to Part 1 of the Inquiry were made in September 1998, followed almost immediately by oral submissions to Part 2 of the Inquiry.

Hearings "in chambers"

31. From time to time, the Chairman of the Inquiry was required to rule on applications which needed to be made, in the interests of avoiding prejudice or maintaining the safety of individuals, in private. On such occasions, the public and media were invited back into the Inquiry Chamber to hear the Chairman's rulings.

The 5 "Suspects"

32. Once the decision had been taken to call as witnesses the five men previously charged with Stephen's murder, a hearing in chambers took place on 14 May 1998. This was to discuss the range of questions to be put, and the procedure to be adopted for their examination and cross-examination. In the light of that, a notice of leave to apply for judicial review of the Inquiry's decision to call the men was made.

33. The application was heard before Mr Justice Laws on 12 June. He held that the draft questions proposed to be put to the men could raise matters outside of the proper terms of remit of the Inquiry, and the application was granted. The substantive hearing was held before Lord Justice Simon Brown and Mr Justice Hooper on 18 June. It was held that the five men could not properly be asked questions as to their guilt or innocence; but reaffirmed the Chairman's discretion, other than that, to allow questions to be put to them.

34. The five men gave evidence on 29 and 30 June. Proceedings were disrupted on 29 June, but evidence was resumed once order had been restored.

35. A video showing extracts from recordings made by a video/audio surveillance probe of Gary Dobson's premises had been shown on 15 June. The transcript of that video is at Appendix 10.

Part 2 Hearings

36. In May 1998, the Secretary wrote to a range of organisation and individuals, inviting written submissions about their concerns in respect of racially motivated crime, and ideas for the future handling of such cases. Advertisements were also placed in a range of newspapers. A total of 148 submissions was received, as listed in Appendix 17.

37. So that its terms of reference might be met in full, the Inquiry undertook to take oral evidence in Hannibal House from those organisations best placed to implement any recommendations which the Inquiry might ultimately put forward. These hearings took place in late September and early October 1998, and a full list of those making such submissions is given in Appendix 16.

38. In order to test the temperature of opinion outside South East London, meetings in public were also held at six locations away from the Elephant & Castle. These were held in Ealing and Tower Hamlets in West and East London respectively; and in Manchester, Bradford, Bristol and Birmingham. The dates of these meetings are also given in Appendix 16, together with a full list of those appearing before the Inquiry on those days.

39. During this period the Press Officer issued newsletters to interested parties so that they could keep abreast of the work of the Inquiry.

Provisional criticism by the Inquiry

40. In accordance with principles of completeness, those individuals who were likely to face criticism by the Inquiry were, in December 1998, given advanced notice of the substance of those criticisms. This process, known colloquially as "Maxwellisation", invited witnesses to respond to the criticisms proposed to be made, and to provide any further representations about the proposed criticism. Those responses were considered by the Inquiry during January 1999, and have been reflected in the Inquiry's Report.

Cost of the Inquiry

41. The final cost of the Inquiry was not certain at the time of printing this Report, but is likely to be in excess of £3m.

42. The Chairman recommended to the Home Secretary that the Metropolitan Police Service should, in accordance with section 49(5) of the Police Act 1996, meet the full costs of setting up and establishing the Inquiry, together with all those costs which directly accrued from Part 1 of the Inquiry. The costs of Part 2 of the Inquiry, establishing the future handling of cases of racially motivated crime, should, the Chairman believes, be met by the Home Office as the findings were of more general application.

Report by the Police Complaints Authority on the Investigation of a Complaint against the Metropolitan Police Service by Mr N and Mrs D Lawrence

Presented to Parliament by the Secretary of State for the
Home Department by Command of Her Majesty
December 1997

Cm 3822

£3.55

Complaint against the Metropolitan Police Service

Mr N and Mrs D Lawrence

Introduction

This report prepared by the Police Complaints Authority is one of two which result from the Kent County Constabulary investigation into the way in which the Metropolitan Police Service handled the murder of Stephen Lawrence.

It is presented under Section 97(2) of the Police and Criminal Evidence Act 1984. This enables the Authority to report on any matters which it considers should be drawn to the Secretary of State's attention "by reason of their gravity or of other exceptional circumstances". It should be considered against the fully detailed report of the Authority supervised inquiry and its associated evidence.

The final report by the Investigating Officer, Deputy Chief Constable Robert Ayling, is, as a result of a judgment by the Court of Appeal, subject to public interest immunity and may therefore only be disclosed on the orders of a court. Copies will, however, be made available to the Secretary of State under Section 98 of the Act and to the public inquiry chaired by Sir William Macpherson of Cluny.

This PCA report sets out the main events and chronology. It describes the key elements of the complaint investigation and the main findings. It evaluates the quality of the first murder investigation. It also suggests some issues to be considered by the Metropolitan Police and by the police service as a whole.

Section 1: Main Events

Stephen Lawrence was returning home on the night of 22 April 1993 accompanied by a friend. They were intending to catch a bus and were some 20 yards from the bus stop at the junction of Dickson Road and Well Hall Road, SE9. Without warning, they were attacked by a group of white youths who had run across the road. His friend managed to evade the attack but within seconds Stephen Lawrence sustained two major life-threatening wounds inflicted by a large knife. No evidence has ever been produced to suggest this was anything other than an entirely unprovoked racially motivated attack.

The friend ran along Well Hall Road away from the scene of the attack. Despite bleeding heavily, Stephen Lawrence followed and managed to run 255 yards before collapsing. Witnesses say that the white youths ran off down Dickson Road. However, none of the three people at the bus stop were aware at that time of the extent of Stephen Lawrence's injuries. This was due to the speed of the attack, the number of youths around him and the fact that he was able to get up and run along the road.

The friend called the emergency services from a phone box near the spot where Stephen Lawrence had collapsed. Two members of the public went to his aid, joined shortly afterwards by an off-duty police officer and his wife who were passing in their car. Uniformed police officers then arrived followed by a police carrier from the Territorial Support Group (TSG) which responded to the emergency call. Local residents came to the scene and Stephen Lawrence was then conveyed by ambulance to the Brook Hospital. Efforts to save him failed and he was declared dead at 23:17 hours.

An investigation led by officers from the Metropolitan Police Service Area Major Investigation Pool (AMIP) led to the arrest of three white youths after fifteen days and a fourth three days later. A fifth youth was arrested on 3 June 1993.

A report was sent to the Crown Prosecution Service in July 1993. However, they subsequently decided to discontinue the prosecution on the grounds that there was insufficient evidence to provide a realistic prospect of conviction.

In August 1993 the Metropolitan Police Service conducted an internal review of the case under the direction of a detective chief superintendent. This was recommended procedure in major crime inquiries which had thus far not led to a prosecution.

This professional scrutiny reported in November 1993. It concluded that "the investigation has been progressed satisfactorily and all lines of inquiry correctly pursued". The report recommended changes in the way in which liaison was maintained with the families of victims. It also commented on the exceptional circumstances faced by this murder investigation team in view of the degree of community anger and the public reactions to this appalling crime.

The Lawrence family had begun to lose confidence in the conduct of police officers with whom they came into contact at an early stage of the first murder investigation. As time went on they also began to doubt the effectiveness of the inquiry.

The first murder investigation team continued their efforts to no avail and in June 1994 a decision was taken to reinvigorate the inquiry by taking a fresh approach. An experienced detective superintendent was appointed with a brief to consider innovative and creative means of investigating the murder since traditional approaches had not been successful. This investigation worked closely with the Lawrence family and their legal representatives. It provided much of the material that formed the basis of the subsequent private prosecution of the five white youths originally arrested.

Following committal proceedings, three of these youths were sent for trial at the Old Bailey in April 1996. However, important identification evidence was disallowed by the judge and the case collapsed. Much of the evidence acquired by the second investigation team was therefore never put before a jury.

The inquest into Stephen Lawrence's death was conducted by Sir Montague Levine at Southwark Coroner's Court in February 1997. The purpose of an inquest is to determine the cause of death. However, the effectiveness of the police operation, both on the night of the murder and in the days that followed, was brought into question by the Lawrence family's legal representatives. Responses from police officers giving evidence did not satisfy the family. If anything they strengthened the impression that there had been serious failings by police officers at key stages on the night of the attack and during the first murder investigation.

The family made a statement to the inquest outlining their concerns in strong terms. They suggested that the failure to detect the crime and bring the murderers of their son to justice was due to racism on the part of the Metropolitan Police Service. At the conclusion of the inquest they lodged a formal complaint about the conduct of the first murder investigation.

The independent Police Complaints Authority approved the appointment of Robert Ayling, Deputy Chief Constable of Kent County Constabulary, to lead the investigation into the complaint under the supervision of Authority Member James Elliott. The investigation began in March 1997 and the final report by the Investigating Officer is nearing completion.

On 31 July, following representations from the Lawrence family, the Secretary of State announced the setting up of a Public Inquiry under Section 49 of the Police Act 1996 to "inquire into matters arising from the death of Stephen Lawrence" and to "identify the lessons to be learned for the investigation and prosecution of racially motivated crimes".

The Investigating Officer's report and supporting evidence will be made available to the Inquiry prior to the opening of its public hearings. The PCA has already supplied members of the Inquiry with a substantial amount of background material.

Section 2: The Complaint made by the Lawrence Family

The family's complaint can be summarised into six main areas:

First aid

As a result of evidence given at the inquest, the family felt that police officers either lacked the training necessary to give their son first aid prior to the arrival of the ambulance or "did not want to get their hands dirty with a black man's blood".

Management of the murder scene

They believed that insufficient action had been taken early enough to search for suspects in the area or to cordon off the scene of the attack in order to preserve evidence. An example of what they felt to be a casual approach was provided by an officer who gave evidence at the inquest that she had written her notes when sitting on a bench near the scene. In the family's view she should have been deployed with all urgency searching the area for suspects or evidence.

Mr and Mrs Lawrence also felt that information on racial attacks held at local police stations should have been accessed during that night to try and identify likely suspects.

Police liaison with the family

Within days of the murder, relations between police liaison officers and the family began to break down. The Lawrence family felt they were treated in a patronising manner and were not being kept informed as to what was happening. They also felt that the liaison officers did not live up to undertakings that had been given. Eventually they asked for the liaison officers to be removed.

Conduct of the murder investigation

The Lawrence family were aware that information about possible suspects was being passed to the police. Some of that information had been received directly by the family and then conveyed to the police. Mr and Mrs Lawrence became concerned that this information was not being taken seriously, not properly acted upon, or only pursued when it was too late to secure vital evidence.

They also came to believe that witnesses had not been handled properly and that the investigation had given undue attention to their son's background and associates. The police appeared to believe that Stephen Lawrence might have had criminal associations which had some bearing on the reasons for his murder. The Lawrence family felt that while such inappropriate inquiries were being pursued, key evidence and opportunities to detect those responsible for their son's death were slipping away.

The Richard Everett case

The Lawrence family complained at the inquest that the case of Richard Everett, a white boy stabbed to death by a gang of Asian youths in Kings Cross, contrasted sharply with the police handling of their son's case. The manner of Richard Everett's death bore similarities to their son's murder. However, in the former case, early arrests were made and ultimately a conviction was achieved. To the Lawrence family this illustrated a clear difference in treatment and a lack of commitment by the police to solving their son's murder.

Possible corruption or collusion

In September 1997 the Lawrence family expressed concern to the complaint investigating team that there might have been corrupt relationships between police officers in the first murder investigation and some of the suspects or their relatives. Alternatively, they felt that the first investigation into their son's death might have been given lower priority than police inquiries into the activities of major criminals in the area who had links with those suspected of killing their son.

Section 3: Complaint Investigation

Introduction

The Investigating Officer, Deputy Chief Constable Ayling, and his deputy, Detective Superintendent Clapperton, have between them considerable experience of investigating major crime including murder cases. They have been supported by a team of six detectives together with a civilian crime analyst and administrative and clerical support staff. This team has been solely dedicated to the complaint investigation since March 1997.

There has been extensive contact with the supervising Member throughout. In addition, Superintendent Hope, formerly Chair of the Black Police Association, has been consulted by the supervising Member on aspects of the investigation. A number of experts in particular fields relevant to the investigation have also contributed independent assessments.

The complaint investigation team has to date undertaken 523 actions or tasks related to a line of inquiry, taken 160 statements, conducted seventeen major interviews, some of several days' duration, and have, in total, spent 16,000 working hours on the inquiry.

Virtually all serving police officers involved in the case at the time have either provided witness statements or have been interviewed. Where appropriate such interviews have been under disciplinary regulations. It is noteworthy that virtually all officers have given their full co-operation to the Investigating Officer in providing information, giving statements or answering questions during in-depth interviews. Six of the senior officers involved in the case are now retired but have co-operated fully with the Investigating Officer.

When evaluating the work of these officers, consideration has been given, where appropriate, to doing so against standards prevailing in the Metropolitan Police Service at that time.

First aid

Police officers were at the scene within minutes of the assault on Stephen Lawrence. All officers, who were present prior to the ambulance arriving or who gave statements at the time, were interviewed by the Investigating Officer under disciplinary regulations. Statements were taken from all members of the public who had been at the scene. Some were interviewed as witnesses by the complaint investigation team. Evidence related to the care given to Stephen Lawrence by police officers has been examined and evaluated by a medical expert in accident and emergency treatment and first aid.

Findings

The available evidence indicates that the first police officers to arrive at the scene did what they could for Stephen Lawrence. For example, desperate attempts were made to speed the arrival of the ambulance. But the severity of his injuries was not fully appreciated and incorrect assumptions were made about the appropriate first aid measures required. This was partly due to misleading information about the nature of his injuries and the cause of his collapse. The investigation has not produced any evidence to support the allegation that the police officers were indifferent to his plight or that they did not attempt to care for him. However, the issue of first aid training for police officers will be the subject of recommendations by the Investigating Officer in his final report.

Management of the murder scene

The family has alleged that the police failed to take the assault on their son seriously. As a result, they did not act quickly enough to search for possible suspects and to secure the crime scene. Mr and Mrs Lawrence came close to the scene on their way to the hospital shortly after the murder. They had been alerted by a neighbour's son who had been at the bus stop. They did not see any police activity and this later fuelled their concerns that there had been a slow and inadequate response to the attack on their son.

The complaint investigation has traced approximately 50 officers up to and including the rank of chief superintendent who were present at the scene in the hours following the murder. Statements have been taken and interviews conducted. All records of police messages have been traced together with the majority of relevant vehicle use logs, officers' notebooks and records of actions. This material has been evaluated to identify the nature and timing of police activity at the scene of the murder.

Where house to house inquiries were made on the night in question, local residents have been contacted and interviewed in order to compare their recollections with those of police officers.

Findings

The complaint investigation has uncovered a substantial amount of evidence to show that the police response at the scene was prompt and professional. Three police vehicles arrived (not including the off-duty officer's vehicle) shortly after the attack. However, they had departed by the time that Mr and Mrs Lawrence drove through the area. Two cars had accompanied the ambulance to the hospital and the TSG carrier was deployed to search the area for suspects shortly after its arrival. Officers who remained took steps to preserve the crime scene, assisted by the off-duty police officer and his wife.

Stephen Lawrence was declared dead at the hospital at 23:17 hours. After examining all available information an analyst has concluded that seven police road blocks were in place by that time. They covered both the site of the assault and the spot where he fell. This was at a time when the police were under the impression that they were responding only to a serious assault.

Relatives of Mr and Mrs Lawrence have subsequently confirmed they were diverted by the police road blocks on their way to the hospital.

Substantial numbers of officers then arrived. They came from the Commissioner's Reserve (TSG), the detective branch, uniform duty and specialist services such as dog handlers and forensic and scenes of crime officers.

The evidence shows that officers were deployed to search the immediate area for a murder weapon using portable lighting. House to house inquiries were also undertaken. This was confirmed by the recollections of ten local residents contacted by the complaint investigation team.

Various senior officers attended the scene including two chief superintendents. One in particular has given a comprehensive account of his actions. Having arrived approximately fifteen minutes after Stephen Lawrence was declared dead at the hospital, he directed all the steps taken from then on to secure the scene and to continue the search for evidence.

The officer writing up notes on a bench had been instructed to guard the crime scene while other officers were searching the area. She had been advised by a detective officer to write her report at the earliest opportunity since she had been one of the first uniformed officers at the scene and her recollections might have provided important material for the crime investigation.

The inquest was the first public opportunity to examine what happened on the night of the murder. However, most of the police evidence was given by junior officers who were not in a position to provide a full account of police activity on the night, nor is an inquest the most appropriate means to consider these issues since its purpose is to determine the cause of death.

Nevertheless, the Lawrence family saw it as an important arena in which their concerns could be raised. It showed them how little they knew about what actually happened on the night of their son's death and during the subsequent murder investigation. They were understandably angered and disillusioned by the limited answers they received. As a result they lost the limited confidence which had been retrieved by the efforts of some police officers.

From the point of view of the Metropolitan Police Service the inquest was a lost opportunity to provide a full account of their actions on the night of Stephen Lawrence's murder. Senior officers who had been present at the time did not give evidence. If they had, it is at least possible that many of the questions raised by the Lawrence family would have received satisfactory answers, particularly in relation to the management of the crime scene on the night in question.

The investigation has concluded that the management of the scene was of a high standard. Appropriate resources were deployed quickly. Decisions were taken to exploit, as far as was reasonable, the potential for house to house inquiries and searches in the immediate area. Unfortunately, none of these details were recorded in a scene log. If such a document had been created it would have been a straightforward task to establish the extent of police activity on the night of the murder and so to answer some of the Lawrence family's concerns.

Family liaison

Several members of the Lawrence family have been interviewed about their recollections of the contact with the family liaison officers. The officers involved have been interviewed at length under disciplinary regulations.

Findings

Conflicting accounts make it difficult to establish precisely what happened. Nevertheless, it is clear that the officers concerned lost the confidence of the Lawrence family at an early stage and were unable to regain it.

Attempts by senior officers to retrieve the position were unsuccessful and the need to deal with the family of a crime victim through a solicitor created a situation with which they were unfamiliar. Much of the tension was caused by the inevitable conflict between the need to protect the integrity of the investigation while at the same time providing the family with the information they needed.

It is clear that the Metropolitan Police failed to acknowledge how they were going wrong in their relations with the Lawrence family. As a result, they were unable to take sufficient creative and flexible action to retrieve the loss of faith the family had suffered. Tried and tested methods had failed, but the responsible officers seemed to have little idea of what to put in their place.

Conduct of the murder investigation

The murder investigation began on the night when Stephen Lawrence was murdered. It was led initially by the duty detective superintendent from the Area Major Investigation Pool. Because of this officer's other commitments responsibility was handed over four days later to a second detective superintendent. This officer retained responsibility for the investigation until the following year. In relative terms the inquiry was well resourced and at no stage of the complaint investigation has it been suggested that it was hampered by a lack of resources.

One of the first tasks of the complaint investigation was to obtain from the Metropolitan Police Service all records, information and evidence relevant to the first murder investigation and to convey this material to a secure location at Kent County Constabulary Headquarters. Every assistance was given by the Metropolitan Police Service in completing this task.

Officers from the first murder investigation team who are still serving have co-operated fully with the complaint investigation. Where appropriate they have been interviewed under disciplinary regulations. Most of the senior officers involved with the case have now retired. Nevertheless, they have co-operated fully with the complaint investigation and have been interviewed at length. They included two former detective superintendents, two former chief superintendents, a former commander and former deputy assistant commissioner.

Through painstaking assessment of the available information, records of actions and interviews with police officers and witnesses, the complaint investigation has reconstructed the process of the murder team and critically evaluated how it carried out its task. This includes identifying what strategies were adopted and why and how effectively the murder investigation was co-ordinated and managed.

The matching of information available to the senior officers on a day by day basis from the date of the murder and its relationship to the taking of key decisions was thoroughly explored. The complaint investigation also examined critically the preparation for the arrests and the quality of the events that followed. This included the interviewing of suspects, searches for evidence, handling of witnesses and the use of identification parades.

Important elements of the murder investigation were traced back to the beginning. Many original witnesses and sources of information were interviewed during the complaint investigation including some individuals never seen by the first murder investigation team. All exhibits were re-examined and some were subjected to additional forensic testing. Others were tested for the first time.

Solving this crime depended heavily on identification evidence from various witnesses. How the available evidence was acquired, analysed and put to use was thoroughly examined.

Particular aspects of the murder investigation and the complaint have been examined by national experts in the relevant fields and their reports will form part of the evidence submitted by the Investigating Officer with his report.

Anonymous information

The first investigation failed to produce sufficient evidence to support a criminal prosecution. There has been comment ever since that the murder investigation was hampered because it received only anonymous information. It has frequently been suggested that the police had met a "wall of silence" within the community based on fear and intimidation. This has remained the public position of the Metropolitan Police Service to date but the evidence from the complaint investigation does not support this position.

There is considerable evidence that the people of Eltham came forward with valuable information albeit in some cases reluctantly. The early information was vital. It could only have come from sources close to the suspects since street rumour and gossip would not have had time to develop. Responding to information in order to produce evidence should have been a primary focus of the murder investigation. Numerous weaknesses in this area have been identified by the complaint investigation.

For example, information received by the murder incident room very soon after the murder included two anonymous notes and several anonymous telephone calls naming four of the suspects who were eventually arrested. The complaint investigation four years later has been able to identify several of the "anonymous" telephone callers, and has established the means by which the identity of the anonymous letter writer can be confirmed. Greater effort at the time might have identified the sources of the information and produced crucial evidence.

A further example of this type of failure is the fact that within an hour of a national television broadcast on the day after the murder, a person went into Eltham police station with a substantial amount of information about possible suspects. This included details of serious assaults apart from the attack on Stephen Lawrence.

The evidence shows that the potential of this person, coming forward so soon after the murder, was not appreciated by senior officers. In fact this individual was never seen by officers above the rank of detective sergeant. Although the murder investigation eventually attempted to follow it up, the evidence shows that this information and the directions in which it might have led the murder team were never properly exploited.

This informant's identity was known to some officers, but the records of the murder investigation show him as being "anonymous". His identity and his possible value were not identified by the Metropolitan Police Service review carried out four months later. The second murder investigation, which began in June 1994, remained under the impression that this person's identity was not known. So did the Metropolitan Police Service team which continued inquiries on the case until recently. The complaint investigation was able to establish this person's identity and has confirmed that his information came from a vital witness.

Attention to Stephen Lawrence's background

The Lawrence family felt that undue attention was being given to their son's background and associates because the police were not treating the case as one of a racist attack. In fact the records of the murder investigation show that senior officers did regard the assault on him as a racist attack from the beginning. However, they do not seem to have been successful in communicating this to the Lawrence family.

Exploring a victim's background is a normal police practice in murder investigations. In 85% of cases there is some link between the murderer and the victim. This may be an important source of information and all possible lines of inquiry should be explored.

The Investigating Officer has examined whether the amount of time devoted to this line of inquiry and the approach taken was appropriate in this case. The evidence shows that although inquiries were made, the time taken occupied a very small proportion of the overall time spent on the murder investigation. This line of inquiry was curtailed early on in the investigation.

Arrest Decisions

The Lawrence family has criticised the murder investigation for failing to arrest the suspects early enough to acquire vital forensic evidence. Both detective superintendents chose not to arrest early because they felt that they had only anonymous or hearsay information which did not provide reasonable grounds for arrest.

Their judgment has been tested against the records of the murder investigation. These show that, four days after the murder, twenty pieces of information pointed to the suspects who were eventually arrested. Some came from known sources and the complaint investigation has established that some of the anonymous sources could have been identified if appropriate action had been taken.

Information acquired from a local resident and available during the first weekend after the murder might have produced evidence placing the suspects at the scene on the night of the murder. However, this was not followed up until six days later.

Racial incident databases and informants

During the inquest the Lawrence family suggested that information held locally on racial incident databases could have been accessed on the night of the murder and might have led to the identification of suspects. The complaint investigation has examined these files. In addition, it has reviewed Metropolitan Police Service records on other racial attacks and murders committed around the same time to establish whether there were any potential links which might have assisted the murder investigation. In fact, no evidence has been found to suggest that these records held information of value to the investigation of Stephen Lawrence's murder.

However, the complaint investigation has shown that within the first few weeks information from a number of sources, including other police informants, would have corroborated information linking four of the suspects to a number of assaults with knives. This information might have provided a valuable source of evidence. This opportunity was not taken.

Over the initial weekend evidence was acquired which provided an opportunity to arrest two of the suspects for a separate offence of attempted murder. This might have assisted the investigation of Stephen Lawrence's murder. However, the detective superintendents responsible did not take this opportunity although they were aware that it was available. Their reasons for this decision will be one of a number of professional judgments to be commented upon in the Investigating Officer's final report.

Identification evidence

Turning to identification evidence, an evaluation of the material shows that the murder investigation failed to analyse available information effectively by confusing a distinguishing feature of the suspects. It remains a possibility that one offender who played a primary role in the attack has never been identified.

Use of surveillance

Four days after the murder took place, several suspects were put under surveillance. This operation has been scrutinised by an independent expert in surveillance techniques who has concluded that the operation lacked clear objectives and proper guidance. Any benefit accruing from this operation was not fully exploited. Indeed, evidence shows that the surveillance operation missed an opportunity to prevent the loss of potential evidence.

Where it did produce information relevant to the identification of possible suspects this was not properly followed up. Information acquired by the surveillance operation which established an association between the suspects who were subsequently arrested was not used to challenge denials during an interview.

Searches, forensic testing and suspects

Officers making the arrests appeared not to be properly briefed or debriefed. For example, the extent of searches and forensic testing required at the relevant addresses was not made clear to the arresting officers. It was simply assumed that they would take the necessary action. The evidence shows that forensic testing at the homes of those arrested was not carried out to the standards required in this investigation.

In addition, a number of sources of potential forensic evidence from the murder scene were overlooked and some items that were acquired were not subject to forensic testing and therefore not properly eliminated. Where appropriate the complaint investigation carried out additional forensic testing.

The incident room received information over time about a large number of possible suspects. The complaint investigation has shown that a number of suspects other than those arrested were not properly eliminated. For example, the criteria used to accept alibis were in some cases insufficient.

The treatment of witnesses

The care of witnesses showed important weaknesses. Although identification evidence was crucial to detecting this crime, the first identification parade suffered from a lack of preparation and poor communication. As a result, a key witness withdrew co-operation; not all potential witnesses were given the opportunity to identify suspects; not all the suspects appeared in the parade; and the wrong questions were asked of witnesses. Later identity parades suffered from similar weaknesses although not to the same extent.

Summary of findings about the conduct of the murder investigation

In general, the investigation has identified weaknesses in the leadership, direction and quality of work of the first murder investigation. Available information was not dealt with systematically and lacked the necessary analytical approach to maximise its potential to produce evidence. The quality of supervision of officers was poor and assumptions were made about the standard of work being carried out that would not have withstood proper scrutiny.

Decisions were taken without full appreciation of the available information. The implementation of certain decisions (such as those to make arrests) was rushed and suffered from a lack of proper preparation and planning. The detective superintendent in charge of the investigation was unavoidably absent at a crucial time shortly after the arrests of the main suspects. There was confusion during this period, with two senior officers each insisting that the other was responsible for the conduct of the investigation.

In general, the complaint investigation has identified a large number of oversights and omissions which resulted in the murder investigation failing to operate to an acceptable standard.

The Richard Everett Case

The complaint investigation reviewed the material from the Richard Everett murder to determine whether any comparisons could usefully be drawn with the Stephen Lawrence investigation.

Findings

An analysis of the interviews with the suspects in the Stephen Lawrence case demonstrated a number of weaknesses and raised questions about the lack of preparation for interviews, and the training and skills of the officers involved. The interviews in the Richard Everett case were subjected to the same analysis and similar weaknesses were identified.

However, the major difference is that, in the Richard Everett investigation, the police were able to make an early arrest. This enabled them to obtain crucial forensic evidence leading to a successful prosecution.

Possible corruption or collusion

In response to the further concerns of the Lawrence family, the complaint investigation examined whether any possible links could be found between the suspects and members of their families and those key officers in the murder investigation who were in a position to influence the course of the inquiry.

All Metropolitan Police databases, both local and central, were inspected as were National Criminal Intelligence Service records, Customs and Excise and Prison Service databases.

Findings

No connections could be found between the relevant police officers and the suspects or their families. Nor has anything emerged throughout the course of the complaint investigation to support allegations of collusion or corruption.

Section 4: The Review

Four months after Stephen Lawrence was murdered, a review of the investigation was carried out by the Metropolitan Police Service. The purpose of such a review is to provide a fresh impetus to an investigation and to provide support to the officer in charge in a case which has failed to produce sufficient evidence for a criminal prosecution.

Such a review should consider whether all appropriate action has been taken and all information properly evaluated for its potential to provide evidence. It should also determine whether any new lines of inquiry can be identified or whether existing ones should be revisited. Reviews are now an important element in major crime investigations which recognise the demands and complexities of such cases. However, in 1993 they had only recently been introduced into the police service.

This review was commissioned by the deputy assistant commissioner responsible for the area. It was carried out by a detective chief superintendent who was felt to have the appropriate experience. The complaint investigation has examined the review and compared the findings with its own in order to evaluate the review's effectiveness. It has also considered the effect of the review's conclusions on decisions that followed and the extent to which its conclusions were reflected in public statements on the case made by senior officers of the Metropolitan Police Service.

Findings

The review concluded that "the investigation has been progressed satisfactorily and all lines of inquiry correctly pursued". It made mild criticisms of the strategy undertaken by the detective superintendent in charge. However, it concluded that he had broadly discharged his responsibilities in a professional and competent manner whilst experiencing "pressures and outside influences on an unprecedented scale". The review incorrectly maintained the position that much of the information available to the murder investigation team was based on anonymous or hearsay information only, which had therefore limited their ability to achieve a successful prosecution.

The review makes many constructive recommendations in a real attempt to learn from this case and to improve the Metropolitan Police Service's response in similar situations. However, the recommendations are largely focused on the failure of family liaison, support for the victims of racial attacks and the problems of dealing with the pressures posed by the media, community groups and other interested parties.

The complaint investigation has produced evidence showing that there were a substantial number of errors, omissions and lost opportunities in the first murder investigation. In this respect the review did not fulfil its terms of reference and did not give a fresh impetus to the murder investigation. The reassurance it gave to the officer in charge of the case and to senior Metropolitan Police Service officers was ultimately highly damaging.

Section 5: The Second Murder Investigation

In mid-1994 a new direction was taken following a meeting between the Metropolitan Police Commissioner and the Lawrence family. An experienced detective superintendent was appointed with a brief to pursue creative and original approaches to the murder investigation since the use of more conventional police methods had been unsuccessful. This new departure did produce an innovative strategy, including the use of sophisticated surveillance techniques. It was successful in some respects. Nevertheless, the evidence produced by the second investigation and made available to support the Lawrence family's private prosecution was never put before a jury. Its potential has, therefore, never been tested in court.

Findings

The complaint investigation has shown that the second murder investigation was starved of outstanding sources of information and potential evidence because its attention had been directed elsewhere by the review. Senior officers remained under the impression that the identity of the person entering the police station twenty-one hours after the murder was not known. Nor were they aware of the identity of the author of the anonymous letters naming suspects. The complaint investigation has demonstrated that the means to identify both sources of information was available.

Section 6: Issues for the Police Service

The thorough Kent County Constabulary investigation into the complaints made by Mr and Mrs Lawrence has raised a number of issues which merit consideration by the police service as a whole.

The performance of those officers who tried to care for Stephen Lawrence before the arrival of the ambulance calls into question the standard and frequency of first aid training provided to police officers.

The difficulties experienced by officers who attempted to establish a relationship with the Lawrence family underline the importance of providing the maximum possible amount of information at an early stage of such an investigation. It further identifies the need for flexibility in changing laid down procedures to meet particular circumstances.

The process of reviewing major investigations which have not resulted in a criminal prosecution is now well established throughout the police service. However, the Stephen Lawrence case underlines the absolute necessity for the reviewing officer to be clear about objectives and to be rigorous in carrying them through. A review which fails to conduct a searching examination is of no use to an investigating team. Indeed, as in this case, it can do more harm than good.

The Kent investigation has focused attention on a number of serious professional failings by detective officers responsible for the conduct of the Stephen Lawrence murder inquiry. It is for the Metropolitan Police Service to consider whether these are isolated examples or whether they illustrate a need for improved training, regular performance assessment and more exacting standards of management and supervision in major inquiries.

Conclusions

The Lawrence family has expressed anger and disillusionment at the failure to convict the murderers of their son by means of their formal complaint. They regard this failure as a result of racism on the part of the Metropolitan Police Service.

The Metropolitan Police Service has committed substantial resources over several years to the investigation of this appalling crime, supported by a commitment to the Lawrence family from the highest levels within the Service. There is no doubt that a considerable amount of hard work has been undertaken. It is evident that the failure to bring the murderers to justice remains a source of frustration and regret amongst many Metropolitan Police officers.

The complaint investigation has not produced any evidence to support the allegations of racist conduct by police officers nor has it produced any evidence to support many of the specific allegations made by the Lawrence family in relation to events on the night of the murder. The evidence shows that the police operation undertaken immediately after the assault on Stephen Lawrence was well organised and effective.

Nevertheless, the complaint investigation has produced evidence of significant weaknesses, omissions and lost opportunities during the first murder inquiry. These errors were not identified by the internal review carried out by the Metropolitan Police Service. As a result, subsequent attempts to solve the crime have been misinformed. It has also led to public explanations by senior officers about the police handling of this case which are not supported by the evidence.

The Investigating Officer has concluded that of the many items outstanding from the first investigation, eleven remain potentially fruitful lines of inquiry which have not yet been properly followed up. All the information acquired by the complaint investigation on these items has been passed to the Metropolitan Police Service at a senior level and a new detective team has been established to pursue these lines of inquiry. However, the passage of time must by now have diminished their potential evidential value.

Without the Lawrence family's determination to uncover what happened and to maintain the pressure to bring their son's murderers to justice, the serious shortcomings now identified in the first murder investigation and what then followed are unlikely to have been revealed. Nor would the outstanding lines of inquiry now made available to the Metropolitan Police Service by the complaint investigation have been identified.

Printed in the UK by The Stationery Office Limited on behalf of the
Controller of Her Majesty's Stationery Office.
5067821   12/97   19585   J34079

Published by The Stationery Office Limited
and available from:

The Publications Centre
(Mail, telephone and fax orders only)
PO Box 276, London SW8 5DT
General enquiries 0171 873 0011
Telephone orders 0171 873 9090
Fax orders 0171 873 8200

The Stationery Office Bookshops
59–60 Holborn Viaduct, London EC1A 2FD
(Temporary location until mid-1998)
Fax 0171 831 1326
68–69 Bull Street, Birmingham B4 6AD
0121 236 9696 Fax 0121 236 9699
33 Wine Street, Bristol BS1 2BQ
0117 9264306 Fax 0117 9294515
9–21 Princess Street, Manchester M60 8AS
0161 834 7201 Fax 0161 833 0634
16 Arthur Street, Belfast BT1 4GD
01232 238451 Fax 01232 235401
The Stationery Office Oriel Bookshop
The Friary, Cardiff CF1 4AA
01222 395548 Fax 01222 384347
71 Lothian Road, Edinburgh EH3 9AZ
(counter service only)

In addition customers in Scotland may mail,
telephone or fax their orders to:
Scottish Publication Sales,
South Gyle Crescent, Edinburgh EH12 9EB
0131 479 3141 Fax 0131 479 3142

Accredited Agents
(see Yellow Pages)

and through good booksellers

ISBN 0-10-138222-7

9 780101 382229

APPENDIX 3

A   Woolwich Public Hall

Sitting at: Woolwich Public Hall
Market Street
London SE18 6AN

Wednesday, 8th October 1997

B   Before:

(THE CHAIRMAN)
SIR WILLIAM MACPHERSON OF CLUNY
(ADVISERS)
MR TOM COOK
THE RIGHT REVEREND DR JOHN SENTAMU
DR RICHARD STONE

C

**THE INQUIRY INTO THE MATTERS ARISING FROM THE
DEATH OF STEPHEN LAWRENCE**

D   -------------------------

MR D **PENRY-DAVEY QC** and **MISS A WEEKES** appeared on
behalf of the **INQUIRY**
MR M **MANSFIELD QC** and **MR M SOORJOO** appeared on behalf
of the **LAWRENCE FAMILY**
MR J **BEER** appeared on behalf of **THE METROPOLITAN POLICE**

E   MR R **PHILLIPS** appeared on behalf of **THE POLICE
COMPLAINTS AUTHORITY**
MR **JULIAN** appeared on behalf of the **CROWN PROSECUTION
SERVICE**
MR C **BOOTHMAN** appeared on behalf of the **COMMISSION FOR
RACIAL EQUALITY**
MR H **ALLEYNE** appeared on behalf of the **LONDON BOROUGH
OF GREENWICH**

F   MR **BRANDON, RUSSELL JONES & WALKER** appeared on behalf
of officers of the **FEDERATED RANKS**
MR I **LEWIS, ROWE & COHEN** appeared on behalf of
MESSRS ILSLEY, WEEDEN & CRAMPTON
MS J **DEIGHTON, DEIGHTON GUEDELLA** appeared on behalf of
DUWAYNE BROOKS

G   -------------------------

PROCEEDINGS

Transcript of the Stenographic notes of
Sellers Imago
Suite 1-2, Ludgate House, 107 Fleet Street,
London EC4A 2AB

H   TEL: (0171 427 0089)

A

Wednesday, 8th October 1997

THE CHAIRMAN: Good morning ladies and gentlemen, I

welcome you to this first public hearing of the

Stephen Lawrence Inquiry. It is my hope that we will

B

not be over formal in the conduct of these proceedings

for example, I do not ask to you stand when the members

of the Inquiry come into the room and please address us

seated if you wish. It is entirely a matter for the

C

choice of counsel or solicitor as to how they wish to

address us.

Ladies and gentlemen, what I am going to do now is

D

to read an opening statement. It will take a few

minutes but I think it right that I should do so.

There is no need for anybody to take notes or to write

down or to try and catch a telephone number which is

E

included in what I say because copies of what I am

going to read are available for everybody who wishes to

see them as soon as this hearing is over.

You will all know that we are here today for the

F

first preliminary hearing of the Inquiry established by

the Home Secretary to investigate matters arising from

the violent and tragic death of Stephen Lawrence who

G

was killed in Greenwich on 22nd April 1993.

On 31st July 1997 the Home Secretary said in

Parliament that the terms of reference of this Inquiry

H

A

would be:

"To enquire into the matters arising from the
death of Stephen Lawrence on 22nd April 1993 to date,
in order particularly to identify the lessons to be

B

learned from the investigation and prosecution of
racially motivated crimes."

My name is William Macpherson of Cluny and I have
been appointed by the Home Secretary to hold this

C

Inquiry under the provisions of Section 49 of the
Police Act 1996. Until March 1996 I was a Judge of the
Queen's Bench Division of the High Court, and I have
many years of experience of criminal and civil cases in

D

the High Court and in Crown Courts all over England and
Wales.

I alone have the responsibility for the conduct of

E

this Inquiry; and it is my task to make a report to the
Home Secretary at the end of the Inquiry, within the
terms of reference which I have read out to you.

I have the advantage of being able to rely upon

F

the advice of three advisers appointed by the Home
Secretary to assist me. They are sitting on my left,
Mr Tom Cook. Mr Cook was a police officer in
Lancashire, Greater Manchester and West Yorkshire from

G

1964 until 1996. He served as Deputy Chief Constable
of West Yorkshire from 1993 to 1996. He has thus never

H

A had any connection with the Metropolitan Police Force.

Second on my right, the Right Reverend John Sentamu, the Bishop for Stepney. He will be well known to many of you who live in London; and second to my

B left, Dr Richard Stone, who was for many years a General Practitioner in Notting Hill Gate. He has been involved in many community activities, and he is the Chair of the Jewish Council for Racial Equality.

C Mr Cook's advice will be invaluable to me in connection with all policing matters with which this Inquiry will be concerned. The Bishop for Stepney and Dr Stone will advise me primarily upon the community

D and racial aspects of this Inquiry.

The focus of my terms of reference is first of all upon this killing itself, and in particular upon the

E policing and investigation and prosecutions which followed it. No doubt this first and mainly factual part of the Inquiry will spread into other limited fields. But its focus must be on the death of Stephen

F Lawrence and all that followed it.

Since the Inquiry owes its existence to the Police Act, the Inquiry will cover all relevant matters connected with the policing of the area where Stephen

G Lawrence was killed. Both the investigation of that crime and the prosecutions which followed are plainly

H

3

A

connected with the policing of the area in question.

In this first part of the Inquiry I will no doubt, as I have said, rely particularly upon advice given to me by Mr Tom Cook.

B

Secondly, I am required to identify lessons to be learned in this Inquiry for the investigation and prosecution of racially motivated crimes.

In this part of the Inquiry I will no doubt rely

C

upon the advice given by all my advisers, but perhaps more particularly upon the advice from the Bishop of Stepney and Dr Stone.

The purpose of today's preliminary hearing is

D

threefold:

1. To explain the purpose of the Inquiry.

That I have already done;

E

2. To explain the procedure of the Inquiry, and to deal with practical matters concerning the procedure and the conduct of the Inquiry;

3. To consider applications by persons or by bodies to

F

be legally represented at the Inquiry at public cost.

As to procedure and practical matters there are various points to make today. The procedure to be adopted when full hearings start will of course be

G

explained in more detail later. Broadly however the Inquiry will be inquisitorial. I will myself decide,

H

A   with the help of all persons involved, what lines of investigation shall be followed, and which witnesses will be called in the first part of the Inquiry.

B   The second part of the Inquiry will involve primarily written submission or points to be made in connection with the lessons to be learned from the first part of the Inquiry and generally.

C   I next indicate that the full Inquiry will not take place in this Hall. Suitable premises will be found later to house the Inquiry and those involved in it. Those premises will, we hope, be in Greenwich or Woolwich.

D   It may be that further preliminary hearings will take place. Full details of such hearings will of course be published as and when they are arranged and

E   become necessary. The timing and duration of the Inquiry will be a matter of general concern.

F   As is well known the handling of this case by the Metropolitan Police is at present the subject of complaints made by the Lawrence family. The Police Complaints Authority is supervising the carrying out of an investigation into those complaints.

G   The Home Secretary on 31st July specifically said that this Inquiry will only begin when the Police Complaints Authority report has been completed and has

H

A been submitted to Parliament. The latest information is that that report cannot be completed until the end of November 1997, at the earliest.

B I have therefore decided that it would be pointless to try to start full hearings of this Inquiry before the end of January 1998. Full details will of course be given as soon as possible.

C No sensible estimate of the duration of this Inquiry can be given yet. This Inquiry must of course be carefully and fully carried out but it must not go on forever, or allow itself to lose its momentum. Its scale will be controlled. In all this I will seek

D co-operation from all who are involved. So that at the end everybody will at least accept that their evidence or point of view has been heard, but within a sensible

E time scale.

Next I turn to the question of evidence. Much of the evidence to be considered and digested by the Inquiry is already known. But both I and the public

F believe that witnesses may be able to help those who have not so far come forward or been identified. The next phase of the Inquiry's activity will include our request to those witnesses to come forward. No witness

G shall be called to give evidence unless he or she has given a written statement. Public advertisements will

H

be placed in this connection.

We hope that both the public and the Press and the media will help us to hear and consider all available material which is relevant, so that a fair and full and fearless report can be prepared by ourselves.

If and when any substantial application is to be made against a person or body at the Inquiry, that person or body will be informed of the allegation by our Solicitor. The substance of the evidence supporting the allegation will be given in good time by the Solicitor. If the allegation is to be pursued at the Inquiry, the substance of the allegation will be given to that person or body by the Solicitor so that they have an opportunity to deal with it by cross-examination or by evidence. Counsel to the Inquiry will be responsible for seeing that this aspect of the procedure is followed.

Immunity. I have been authorised by Her Majesty's Attorney General to undertake in respect of any person who provides evidence to this Inquiry that no evidence he or she may give before the Inquiry, whether orally or by written statement, nor any written statement made preparatory to giving evidence nor any documents produced by that person to the Inquiry, will be used in evidence against him or her in any criminal proceedings

A

except in proceedings where he or she is charged with having given false evidence in the course of this Inquiry or with having conspired or procured others so to do.

B

Anyone who comes forward may ask that his or her identity be not disclosed publicly, (that is beyond Counsel and Solicitors to the Inquiry and its Chairman and advisers). We will give the most careful

C

consideration to any such request. We appreciate that some people may wish to approach us in confidence. We will always be prepared to hear any representation as to the need for confidentiality before making any

D

decision to allow publicity. Anonymous information is unlikely to be relied upon. Those who do wish to contribute information to the Inquiry will be

E

interviewed in confidence on our behalf.

Next may I say that what we hope and sincerely wish to do is to establish confidence between ourselves and all those who may have become involved in this

F

matter. So that all of us may learn those lessons which are surely there to be learned for the future.

In all its aims and activity this Inquiry will be assisted by a team which will deal with all

G

administrative and practical day to day matters. Mr Stephen Wells, who sits two away from me on my

H

A

right, is the Secretary to the Inquiry.

Miss Alison Foulds, who sits next to him, and others make up his team. Both of them will be available in the Hall after this hearing for any questions that anyone may have. Also available to answer questions

B

will be Mr Peter Whitehurst, who sits in front of me here, who is Solicitor to the Inquiry.

At present a Post Office Box number, a number

C

which I will not read out, is available for correspondence, and the Inquiries telephone contact number is contained in the written document which anybody may have after the conclusion of this hearing.

D

Later the address and telephone number of the Inquiries headquarters will be publicised and will be available to all who wish to communicate with those

E

involved in the Inquiry.

Lastly I turn to representation. No Inquiry can function properly without its own Counsel and Solicitors. They will help with the exacting task of

F

assembling documents and evidence which the Inquiry will consider.

The Solicitor to the Inquiry has instructed on my behalf two Counsel who will be Counsel to the Inquiry.

G

Like all of us who sit here they are wholly independent and impartial and their sole aim will be to help by

H

A presenting on my behalf the material which we will consider.

B Mr David Penry-Davey QC, who sits straight in front of me here, and Miss Anesta Weekes who also sits at the same table, have kindly accepted instructions to be Counsel for the Inquiry.

I should stress this Inquiry does not involve litigation or claims made between parties. Nor will

C the Inquiry be a trial or re-trial of any person or persons.

But of course various persons and bodies involved will have the right to present their points of view.

D Therefore I shall soon consider any applications made for legal representation, and whether such representation can be made at public costs. A person

E or body wishing to be represented must show good cause. I must be satisfied that a person or body has a reasonably direct interest in some aspect of the Inquiry which as a matter of fairness requires such

F representation. If a number of persons have such an interest but for present purposes there is no discernible difference between their interests, I would not be disposed to grant separate representation. The

G correct course would be for them to be jointly represented by one advocate or team.

H

10

A

Any decision I make today by representation will not be final. I will be prepared to entertain any application for representation at any time. It may be that a party will only wish to be represented at a

B

later stage of the Inquiry. It may be that some parties are undecided whether they wish to be represented or not. They may await to see what emerges. I will deal with later applications in the light of circumstances

C

as they develop.

Please note that the fact that representation by lawyers before the Inquiry may be refused to any person or body involved does not mean that the evidence given

D

or the views represented by that person or body will not be considered. They will still be able to give evidence or to put forward their views in whatever way

E

and to whatever extent I may decide. I emphasise however that all questions as to who may be called as a witness or who may provide information or views for consideration by this Inquiry will be decided by

F

myself. Furthermore all witnesses called will be called on my behalf by Counsel to the Inquiry. Cross-examination will be allowed, but this will be controlled by me. I do ask well in advance that such

G

cross-examination as may be allowed should be short, relevant and carefully aimed.

H

A

(A Short Adjournment)

THE CHAIRMAN: I am now ready to give the Inquiry's decision in respect of representation. It is sensible, I think, to go through them all, although I have given

B

an indication in certain respects already.

First of all, the Lawrence family. Mr Mansfield applied on their behalf and we have granted and hereby grant them legal representation throughout. The

C

solicitor will be Mr Imran Khan of JR Jones, as I understand it, and we will authorise, at public cost, three counsel.

D

Secondly, the Metropolitan Police. We have already indicated and I repeat that the Metropolitan Police will be represented by leading and junior counsel and by their solicitors but not at

E

public costs, in the sense that the Metropolitan Police will meet their own costs.

The same applies to the Crown Prosecution Service and they will be represented throughout and at public

F

costs.

The Police Complaints Authority will be told if there is any need for them to be represented, as I

G

indicated during the hearing.

The Commission for Racial Equality will be represented at public costs.

H

35

A

There is no need for me to indicate the other bodies who come under the umbrella for the Commission for Racial Equality but certainly the Greenwich Race Equality Trust will be covered by that representation.

B

It may be that the Borough Council will bring under their umbrella other organisations for whom they will be able jointly to act.

The London Borough of Greenwich applied for

C

representation. That will be granted to them. Initially the application was for representation at the Borough's own cost. We have been told that the application is that their counsel should be paid out of

D

public funds. That application is granted.

The London Borough will also bring under its umbrella the London Borough of Greenwich Race Equality

E

unit and if it sees fit any other organisations that fits within its representation.

There were separate applications by the Police Federation and by a solicitor representing the ranks of

F

above Chief Inspector who may be involved in this Inquiry.

The Inquiry's decision as to their representation is that that matter will be adjourned until after the

G

Police Complaints Authority have reported. There will then be liaison between those solicitors and the legal

H

A team acting for the Inquiry and the decision will be made in the light of that authority's ruling as to whether separate representation throughout is desirable or not and as to who shall pay for it. They may rest **B** assured, as may anybody else involved, that if any blame is attached individually then certainly while evidence is given or any part of the case that is concerning them is heard, they will be allowed to be **C** represented.

Duwayne Brooks, a vital witness who has been involved in this throughout, will be represented by two counsel and solicitor at public costs.

D The Coroners Society I have already dealt with. I believe, subject to correction from the hall or from any member of the public, that I have dealt with all applications for representation.

E Mr Penry-Davey, does that accord with your view and your memory?

MR PENRY-DAVEY: Yes, Sir.

F THE CHAIRMAN: Thank you very much. Therefore in a moment we will close this preliminary hearing but there are some final remarks that I would like to make that have considerable emphasises. The first is to thank **G** all of you, the legal teams, the press and the public for your attendance today. It is a matter of the

H

A

widest interest of course that this Inquiry should take place. We wish very much to gain the co-operation of the public and individuals who live in this Borough and of anybody who has an interest in this tragic affair

B

and its consequences.

Please rest assured -- and I address perhaps particularly the gentleman who spoke in connection with the difficulty of communication through the Town Hall

C

-- that we will do our utmost to make certain that the request for information and for evidence and for views from the public will be pursued as carefully as possible and with as wide a ranging field as possible

D

so that everyone knows what is happening, so the co-operation of the public can be gained and the confidence of the public can be gained as well. We

E

wish our representatives and our administrative body, to be the channel of communication with the public and particularly with all the citizens of Greenwich and Woolwich.

F

I hope that everyone will be assured that that is our aim and our objective. We want to be receptive and we want anything that anyone wishes to put before us, put before us.

G

do not believe, subject to anyone who represents any party wishing to raise any other matter, that it

H

A

would be useful to say any more. I have already indicated that we hope very much to start the public hearings, not in this place but in our own premises, on 3rd February 1998. Meanwhile, we will be gathering the

B

mammoth documentation. We will probably, in two or three weeks time, be advertising widely and with the assistance of local people to gain the confidence of people here in order to get any information that is

C

available which may be of help to us. With that and with my thanks again, not only to the lawyers but to every person who has attended today, I close this first preliminary hearing of the Stephen Lawrence Inquiry.

D

MR MASTER: Chairman, just a point of clarification which I wish to mention because of legal costs and so forth. Those organisations who are active locally, they want to give their evidence and would like some

E

sort of legal aid or something. Would you like to consider some sort of legal help or legal assistance for them.

F

THE CHAIRMAN: What I am going to ask you simply to do is this: if you have matters which you would wish to raise in connection with other bodies who may wish to be represented in the future, would you approach the

G

secretary, preferably in writing, so that we can see exactly what your argument is and then it will be

H

A

considered.

MR MASTER: Thank you.

THE CHAIRMAN: Thank you very much.

(The Inquiry Adjourned)

B

C

D

E

F

G

H

Sitting at:

Hanibal House
Elephant & Castle
London SE1 6TE

Monday, 16th March 1998

Before:

(THE CHAIRMAN)
SIR WILLIAM MACPHERSON OF CLUNY
(ADVISERS)
MR TOM COOK
THE RIGHT REVEREND DR JOHN SENTAMU
DR RICHARD STONE

THE INQUIRY INTO THE MATTERS ARISING FROM THE DEATH OF STEPHEN LAWRENCE

MR E LAWSON QC, MISS A WEEKES and MR J GIBSON appeared on behalf of the INQUIRY

MR M MANSFIELD QC, MR STEPHEN KAMLISH, MR M SOORJOO and MS M BOYE-ANAWOMA appeared on behalf of the LAWRENCE FAMILY

MR J GOMPERTZ and MR J BEER appeared on behalf of THE METROPOLITAN POLICE

MS S WOODLEY QC and MR P DOYLE appeared on behalf of three SUPERINTENDENTS

MR M EGAN and MR R JORY appeared on behalf of Officers of FEDERATED RANK

MR J YEARWOOD and MS M SIKAND appeared on behalf of the CRE

MR W PANTON appeared on behalf of the LONDON BOROUGH OF GREENWICH

MR I McDONALD QC and MR R MENON appeared on behalf of DUWAYNE BROOKS

MR M CHAWLA appeared on behalf of DCS BARKER

MR B BARKER QC and MS J SPARKS appeared on behalf of the CPS

ALL PROCEEDINGS
DAY 1

Transcript of the Stenographic notes of
Sellers Imago
Suite 1-2, Ludgate House, 107 Fleet Street,
London EC4A 2AB
TEL: (0171 427 0089)

Page 1

1   <Day 1   Monday, 16th March 1998.

2   THE CHAIRMAN: Good morning ladies and gentlemen. I

3   welcome you to the first full session of the Stephen

4   Lawrence Inquiry. I have, unfortunately, to spend

5   two minutes to deal with an article written in

6   yesterday's Observer newspaper, at the eleventh hour

7   before we were due to start this Inquiry. The

8   article attacked my suitability to conduct this

9   Inquiry. I mention it only to dismiss the personal

10   allegations with contempt. I had decided not to

11   refer to them at all, but my family and friends

12   advised me that I must do so otherwise the newspaper

13   might suggest that I accepted their statements.

14   The heart of my complaint is, however, that the

15   article amounted to an attempt to implicate Mr and

16   Mrs Lawrence and to undermine the start of this

17   Inquiry. The facts set out were plainly contributed

18   by others to the journalist involved, and were also

19   plainly not checked. They are either factually

20   untrue or gross misrepresentations of the truth. The

21   instances stem, in any event, from aspects of my

22   judicial career, eight, nine and 10 years ago.

23   Personal attacks of misrepresentations have to

24   be borne by people who take on public duty, so that

25   the details of those matters are between me and the

Page 2

1   newspaper; and I do not wish to give currency to the

2   details which maybe only a few people read in any

3   event.

4   The matter which does disturb me is that which

5   concerns the Inquiry itself, namely, the suggestion

6   that I have denied access to documents to one party

7   or another. That is wholly untrue and is a

8   reflection, not only upon me, but upon my lawyers and

9   staff. I resent and deny the allegation for myself

10   and for them. Indeed, both I and my advisers have

11   worked hard to ensure that, so far as possible, other

12   parties' documents, which are of course their

13   property, are available to all parties. Neither

14   Mr and Mrs Lawrence, nor their legal team have raised

15   my unsuitability over the seven months since I was

16   appointed.

17   I propose simply to say that I and my advisers

18   and staff, and indeed all of us acting here for all

19   parties, will not be put off. We will go ahead as

20   soon as we may here with this Inquiry with the firm

21   intention of conducting a full and evenhanded

22   Inquiry into this affair and into all that followed

23   the tragic death of Stephen Lawrence.

24   Having made that statement, I have been given

25   information that Mr Mansfield wishes to make an

Page 3

1   application to me. Mr Mansfield?

2   MR MANSFIELD: Yes. I am very much obliged. May I

3   apologise for being a few minutes late.

4   THE CHAIRMAN: Not at all. I understand of course the

5   problems. Do not worry. Do you want a little time

6   before you make your application or are you happy to

7   make it now?

8   MR MANSFIELD: No, that is very kind, I am happy to

9   make it at the moment.

10   As you know, I represent both Mr and

11   Mrs Lawrence. For reasons known to the Inquiry,

12   Mrs Lawrence is unable to be here this morning but

13   she is intending to be here by midday today.

14   Mr Lawrence is here, as you see.

15   I have an application which is, and I know I

16   have made it twice before, and on both occasions you

17   very kindly acceded to them. There were for quite

18   legitimate reasons for other proceedings and I do not

19   need to develop the reasons. On this occasion the

20   application is for time on two bases. It is for as

21   much time as you feel able to accord us in the

22   circumstances. One is in relation to a request by

23   both Mr and Mrs Lawrence for an urgent meeting with

24   the Home Secretary, hopefully today. Inquiries have

25   been made and it is understood that he is available

Page 4

1   at some point today. I may say also that no meeting

2   has actually been fixed and no time arranged. We

3   only know in general terms that he is, as it were, in

4   London today.

5   Both Mr and Mrs Lawrence have expressed to those

6   that represent them very legitimate concerns about

7   the Inquiry, and those concerns they wish to

8   discuss. I can develop, but I think it would not be

9   appropriate to develop any of them at the moment,

10   with the Home Secretary prior to any Inquiry actually

11   beginning. They are anxious for this Inquiry to

12   continue. May I say that straight away.

13   They are anxious that there should be a Public

14   Inquiry -- a Judicial Inquiry. In fact, it was their

15   initiative in the very first place, following the

16   inquest almost exactly a year ago from now, that had

17   led to not only a complaints Inquiry but the Home

18   Secretary being persuaded that it would be desirable

19   for there to be a full Public Inquiry. So it is

20   their initiative and they do not wish that there

21   should be any break upon that initiative.

22   However, alongside that initiative, sir, I think

23   you must be aware and that I only need to refer

24   briefly to the statement made on behalf of the

25   Lawrences by Mrs Lawrence at the inquest last year in

Page 5

1 which she gave evidence; and I do not intend to read
2 its full terms. You have the document amongst your
3 papers?
4 THE CHAIRMAN: I am very familiar with it, yes.
5 MR MANSFIELD: Obviously I am not going to belabour
6 it with difficult references, whether they be
7 computerised or otherwise.
8   The gist of what she said to the inquest last
9 year, on behalf of both herself and Neville Lawrence,
10 was that she and her family and many of the members
11 of her community, both the black and white,
12 community, felt that the system, the judicial system,
13 starting with the prosecution investigation, right
14 the way through to what happened at the Old Bailey,
15 had let them down. They felt that there were serious
16 deficiencies at all stages. It is against that
17 background that they are concerned at this stage to
18 ensure that the future of the Inquiry is held under
19 the best possible circumstances that can be, as it
20 were, contrived and put together by both the Home
21 Office and ourselves. It is in that context that
22 they would wish to have the urgent meeting with the
23 Home Secretary to have a final discussion about the
24 context in which it is held.
25   There is a further concern, and I appreciate

Page 7

1 who have tried extremely hard, and may I include in
2 that obviously the Secretariat in the case for the
3 Inquiry, who have bent over backwards to ensure that
4 we should have every facility. It is beyond their
5 control as well that this situation has arisen. I
6 merely mention it that it is a factual situation that
7 pages, hundreds of pages of material, therefore,
8 added to the complications of gaining access, again
9 for technical reasons, to the software and the
10 hardware in the case have meant that the team
11 representing the Lawrences have really had an
12 impossible task to try and get ready for today. It
13 is true, of course, that some of the material may be
14 relevant slightly later, but once one is engaged in a
15 day-to-day Inquiry of this kind of detail, it is
16 extremely difficult to catch up and, beyond the
17 merest of openings, evidence in this case in relation
18 to witnesses alone, where witnesses give evidence on
19 one issue and touch upon another, as you are aware,
20 many of the witnesses being called actually fall
21 under a number of different heads; and, if the
22 procedure is to be, which I understand it will be --
23 again no complaint is made of it -- to provide a
24 certain, as it were, convenience to the witness that
25 they are not recalled many, many times and the issues

Page 6

1 again that it may be thought that this is lawyers
2 complaining, but it is not just lawyers complaining;
3 because the problem that we have also faced is not a
4 denial of documents, and may I make it clear on
5 behalf of the family that any suggestion that we have
6 been denied anything is false; we have been denied
7 nothing. The problem is not in denial, I am afraid,
8 the problem has arisen because of the technical
9 complications that again you are very aware of, and
10 it is an unhappy circumstance that Friday and
11 Saturday of last week was the occasion upon which we
12 were finally provided with the materials, or some of
13 the materials that are necessary for this Inquiry.
14   As you may be aware, in normal circumstances
15 Inquiries of this gravity and some even not of this
16 gravity, are provided with materials usually at least
17 three months before, sometimes as much as up to six
18 months before where it is possible, but certainly
19 three: all the materials that are relevant. One
20 does not obviously expect marginal matters to affect
21 it. However, materials at the centre of the Inquiry,
22 some of them, were only, as it were, provided on
23 Friday or Saturday. Again, I am not making complaint
24 about that or criticising anyone for that. It has
25 been an exigency beyond the control of all of those

Page 8

1 were all canvassed at the one time, the witness first
2 comes in the first segment of issues, there are
3 witnesses who plainly touch upon much more
4 significant issues that come later.
5   So it is a problem, therefore, of interlinking
6 and ensuring before we even begin questioning, or
7 anyone begins questioning a witness, that all of the
8 relevant material has been properly canvassed,
9 absorbed, analysed and we do not waste time going
10 through documents.
11 THE CHAIRMAN: I have the point.
12 MR MANSFIELD: So that is the second basis.
13 THE CHAIRMAN: Yes, yes.
14 MR MANSFIELD: Therefore ----
15 THE CHAIRMAN: I am sorry to interrupt you.
16 MR MANSFIELD: All I was going to say is that in
17 relation, therefore, to those two requests, I would
18 ask for as much time as you feel able to accord us.
19 THE CHAIRMAN: Can you give me any indication of what
20 you mean?
21 MR MANSFIELD: Yes, I can. I would ask
22 realistically, given now -- I have asked carefully
23 about the material that has been provided, we would
24 ask for a week to two weeks to ensure that we have
25 all of the material, as it were, and not only that we

Page 9

1 have it, because some of it in hard copy may not in
2 fact be all of the material as it were in the
3 software. So as far as that is concerned, and with a
4 consultation with the Home Secretary, I would ask for
5 at least a week initially, perhaps two weeks.
6 THE CHAIRMAN: I want to ask two questions: first,
7 have you got information yet as to whether the Home
8 Secretary can see Mr and Mrs Lawrence, or is there
9 speculation that he may be in London?
10 MR MANSFIELD: My understanding is that it is not
11 speculation that he is in London. He is in London,
12 but I was not able and I am not able, though the
13 request was made last night, I did not expect an
14 answer by this morning, but I understand, as I say,
15 he is in London but we have no fixed time at which he
16 might be able to see us.
17 THE CHAIRMAN: Yes.
18 MR MANSFIELD: I have just got some latest
19 information. He is prepared to consider this
20 request. He cannot consider the request before
21 tonight. I do not know what that means.
22 THE CHAIRMAN: Secondly, I suppose I must say that you
23 do not need to answer this if you do not wish to do
24 so, but does this stem from the article produced in
25 the Observer newspaper?

Page 10

1 MR MANSFIELD: In part. Perhaps I could put it
2 fairly. It has in part been triggered by this.
3 THE CHAIRMAN: Surely the matter would have been
4 raised during the seven months since my appointment.
5 MR MANSFIELD: I quite agree.
6 THE CHAIRMAN: It stems from the article written in
7 the Observer newspaper.
8 MR MANSFIELD: In part it is triggered by it.
9 THE CHAIRMAN: In part or in whole?
10 MR MANSFIELD: I said the second basis for requiring
11 time.
12 THE CHAIRMAN: Very well. Thank you very much,
13 Mr Mansfield. I am not going to ask for any
14 contributions from anybody else because its does not
15 seem appropriate or necessary to do so. I had no
16 indication that any other applications were to be
17 made, so we will retire because I need some
18 assistance from my community advisers in particular
19 in reaching a decision as to this delicate matter.
20 If there are any other matters to be raised, can I
21 simply indicate to the parties that it is my
22 intention that applications should always be made at
23 the conclusion of each day's sitting, otherwise our
24 hours are unnecessarily interrupted.
25   I have one other question, Mr Mansfield. Would

Page 11

1 it be acceptable to you that I should deliver my
2 short opening statement and that Mr Lawson should put
3 the basic facts before me? Or are you indicating
4 that you would rather that did not happen at all?
5 MR MANSFIELD: I would rather, in fact, because the
6 Lawrences would themselves like to see the Home
7 Secretary before participating, that nothing further
8 is done.
9 THE CHAIRMAN: I understand. We will retire and
10 consider your application. Thank you very much.
11   <(Short Adjournment)
12 THE CHAIRMAN: Mr Mansfield, I did indicate at an
13 earlier hearing that if people wished to address the
14 Inquiry, so to speak, seated I am perfectly happy for
15 that. I will leave it to anybody to follow their own
16 inclinations. I gather that seated the sound comes
17 across better because the microphones are, what you
18 call, in a seated position. There you are. Thank
19 you very much.
20 MR MANSFIELD: May I remain seated?
21 THE CHAIRMAN: Of course. I suppose I am right in
22 saying that effectively you are without instructions
23 in connection with the conduct of the case at the
24 moment until the Lawrences have seen the Home
25 Secretary.

Page 12

1 MR MANSFIELD: I fear that is the position.
2 THE CHAIRMAN: Yes, thank you.
3   Anybody who hears me will realise that it will
4 be a great blow to have to adjourn this case yet
5 again. I was appointed at the end of July and
6 indications were given that the Inquiry might be
7 complete by Easter 1998 and, yet, we have not
8 started. In connection with the application as to a
9 study of documents, it is most unlikely that an
10 adjournment would have been given. I understand the
11 situation and am sympathetic to the lawyers involved
12 but everybody has been faced with problems of this
13 kind in their career and those would be
14 surmountable. On the other hand -- and particularly
15 with the assistance of my advisers on my right, in
16 relation to community matters and in relation to
17 their connection with Mr and Mrs Lawrence -- I am
18 persuaded that I have to adjourn this Inquiry in
19 order to allow Mr and Mrs Lawrence to see the Home
20 Secretary.
21   In view of the fact that my own position is
22 plainly to be discussed, it would be wise and I hope
23 everybody would agree, sensible, that I say no more.
24 The Lawrences will have as much time as they need to
25 see the Home Secretary because I fully understand

Page 13

1 that they wish to thrash out with him the problems
2 which face them now as they have faced them in the
3 past.
4   Therefore, with the advice of my advisers for
5 which I am most grateful, I have had to decide -- and
6 I stress the verb "had" -- that this Inquiry will be
7 adjourned yet again. To mess about and give two days
8 or three days seems to us to be silly. This Inquiry
9 will now be adjourned until Monday, 23rd March at
10 10.00 am. Thank you very much, indeed. Mr Lawson,
11 do you want to raise something?
12 MR LAWSON: Sir, I am sorry, yes. I should have put
13 you on notice about this before. I am afraid that so
14 far as next Monday is concerned that is a day when I
15 have an unbreakable professional commitment. I would
16 not normally raise that but it will be my function to
17 open the Inquiry, so would you mind saying Tuesday.
18 THE CHAIRMAN: Certainly. We will adjourn, unless
19 anybody has any other contribution to make, until
20 Tuesday morning and we will sit from Tuesday until
21 Friday of that week so that we have four sitting
22 days.
23 MR LAWSON: Thank you.
24 THE CHAIRMAN: I think the best thing would be for me
25 to give nobody else an opportunity to make an

Page 14

1 application and therefore we will retire and we will
2 meet again on Tuesday, 24th March.
3   (The Inquiry Adjourned at 10.25 a.m.)
4
5
6
7
8
9
10
11
12
13
14
15
16
17
18
19
20
21
22
23
24
25

Sitting at: Hannibal House
Elephant & Castle
London SE1 6TE

Tuesday, 24th March, 1998

Before:

**(THE CHAIRMAN)
SIR WILLIAM MACPHERSON OF CLUNY
(ADVISERS)
MR TOM COOK
THE RIGHT REVEREND DR JOHN SENTAMU
DR RICHARD STONE**

**THE INQUIRY INTO THE MATTERS ARISING FROM THE
DEATH OF STEPHEN LAWRENCE**

MR E LAWSON QC, MISS A WEEKES and **MR J GIBSON** appeared
    on behalf of the **INQUIRY**
MR M MANSFIELD QC, MR STEPHEN KAMLISH, MR M SOORJOO and
    MS MARGOT BOYE-ANAWOMA appeared on behalf of the
    LAWRENCE FAMILY
MR J GOMPERTZ QC and **MR J BEER** appeared on behalf of
    THE METROPOLITAN POLICE
MS S WOODLEY QC and **MR P DOYLE** appeared on behalf of
    three superintendents
MR ME EGAN and **MR R JORY** appeared on behalf of **officers
    of federated rank**
MR J YEARWOOD and **MS M SIKAND** appeared on behalf of the
    CRE
MR W PANTON appeared on behalf of the **LONDON BOROUGH OF
    GREENWICH**
MR I MACDONALD QC and **MR R MENON** appeared on behalf of
    DUWAYNE BROOKS
MR M CHAWLA appeared on behalf of **DCS BARKER**
MR B BARKER QC and **MS J SPARKS** appeared on behalf of
    the **CPS**

**ALL PROCEEDINGS
DAY 2**

Transcript of the Stenographic notes of
Sellers Imago,
Suite 1-2, Ludgate House, 107 Fleet Street,
London, EC4A 2AB
TEL: 0171 427 0089

I N D E X

Page 15

1 <DAY 2   Tuesday, 24th March 1998.
2 THE CHAIRMAN: Good morning, ladies and gentlemen.
3 May I welcome you to what I really believe today will
4 be the proper and formal opening of the Inquiry.
5   What is going to happen now is that I shall make
6 a short opening address, not dealing with the facts
7 of the case at all but simply with matters that have
8 to be dealt with by me. Then there will be an
9 introduction by my advisers and then I will hand over
10 to Mr Edmund Lawson who will outline the Inquiry's
11 intentions and approach to you.
12   On 31st July 1997, the Home Secretary said in
13 Parliament that the terms of reference of this
14 Inquiry would be to inquire into the matters arising
15 from the death of Stephen Lawrence on 22nd April 1993
16 to date, in order, particularly, to identify the
17 lessons to be learned for the investigation and
18 prosecution of rationally motivated crimes.
19   My name, as I think most of you know now, is
20 William Macpherson of Cluny, and I have been
21 appointed to hold this Inquiry under the provisions
22 of Section 49 of the Police Act 1996. Until March of
23 1996 I was a judge of the Queen Bench Division of the
24 High Court, and I have had many years of experience
25 of criminal and civil cases in the High Court and in

Page 16

1 Crown Courts all over England and Wales.
2   It is my task to make a report to the Home
3 Secretary at the end of the Inquiry within the terms
4 of reference which I have read out.
5   I hold the great, indeed the inestimable
6 advantage of being able to rely upon the advice of
7 three advisers appointed by the Home Secretary to
8 assist me. They will all introduce themselves to you
9 at the end of my short formal opening statement, but
10 simply for the record, the advisors to the Inquiry
11 are, on the extreme right of the four of us, Mr Tom
12 Cook. Mr Cook was a police officer in Lancashire,
13 Greater Manchester and West Yorkshire from 1964 until
14 1996. He served as Deputy Chief Constable for West
15 Yorkshire from 1993 to 1996, and he has thus never
16 had any connection with the Metropolitan Police
17 Force. The second, nearest to me, the Right Reverend
18 John Semtamu, the Bishop for Stepney. He will be
19 well-known to many of you who live in London. And
20 the third, in the middle of the three advisers,
21 Dr Richard Stone, who was for many years a general
22 practitioner in Notting Hill Gate. He has been
23 involved in many community activities, and he is the
24 Chair of the Jewish Council of Racial Equality.
25   Mr Cook's advice will be invaluable to me in

Page 17

1 connection with all policing matters with which this
2 Inquiry will be concerned. The Bishop for Stepney
3 and Dr Stone will advise me primarily upon community
4 and racial aspects of this Inquiry. All three
5 advisers will then bring their wisdom and experience
6 to bear upon all the issues which arise during and
7 from the Inquiry.
8   Leading counsel to the Inquiry is Mr Edmund
9 Lawson, Queen's Counsel; he is assisted by
10 Miss Anesta Weekes and Mr John Gibson.
11   Further introduction of other representatives
12 will be done shortly by Mr Lawson. The three counsel
13 to the Inquiry have been appointed by the Attorney
14 General and they are in all respects independent.
15   Mr Peter Whitehurst and Miss Linda Dann are the
16 solicitors to the Inquiry. Their office is in this
17 building and they can be contacted at once through
18 any member of the Inquiry's staff, should any person
19 wish to give fresh, relevant information to the
20 Inquiry.
21   Similarly, my administrative staff also work in
22 this building. Mr Stephen Wells, who sits in the
23 chair to my right and has just stood up, is the
24 secretary to the Inquiry; and Miss Alison Foulds is
25 his deputy. Mr Michael Booker is press and

Page 18

1 information officer to the Inquiry. Mr Wells and his
2 staff have greatly helped all of us in the
3 preparatory stages of the Inquiry, and he and his
4 staff are always available and ready to answer any
5 queries which may arise.
6   In October I made decisions as to representation
7 for the purposes of the first part of the Inquiry,
8 which starts today, and which will involve the
9 calling of many witnesses, mostly police officers of
10 all ranks, who were involved in the policing and the
11 activities which followed the murder of Stephen
12 Lawrence. Some further decisions on representation
13 have been made by myself since then.
14   The Inquiry owes its existence to the Police
15 Act, and thus the Inquiry will do its best to cover
16 all relevant matters connected with the policing of
17 the area where and after the murder took place. Both
18 the investigation of that crime and the prosecutions
19 which followed are plainly connected with the
20 policing of the area in question.
21   Furthermore, it must be stressed that the focus
22 of the Inquiry is upon the death of Stephen Lawrence
23 and all that followed it. So that the first part of
24 the Inquiry must not be deflected along avenues which
25 are not properly relevant.

1　The issues and areas to be explored will shortly
2　be introduced by leading counsel to the Inquiry. The
3　teams representing various parties and interests have
4　discussed and defined these issues and areas so that
5　a sensible focus is given to the work of the Inquiry
6　as the evidence is given.
7　　However, I should say that our schedule of
8　issues is a working document and will reflect matters
9　which may arise during the Inquiry. It is not cast
10　in stone, there may well be additional issues and
11　areas which need to be addressed and which arise as
12　the Inquiry does its work. We must all be reasonably
13　flexible in this regard.
14　　Witnesses will all be called on my behalf and
15　there will be cross-examination, which I know will be
16　carefully prepared and executed so that the Inquiry
17　does not get lost in concentration upon the less
18　vital aspects of the case. It is my intention that,
19　subject to the overriding need to get to the heart of
20　the issues in question, all those who appear before
21　me will be treated sensitively and with dignity and
22　compassion.
23　　Details of sitting times and duration of
24　hearings are all set out in the written notes, which
25　are available to everybody who attends these public

1　hearings. The procedure of the hearings will be
2　reasonably informal: nobody need stand to ask
3　questions, unless they wish to do so, indeed, in
4　parenthesis, I believe the acoustic system is better
5　suited if those asking questions remain seated; and
6　of course, people may come and ago exactly as they
7　please.
8　　Inevitably, this room looks rather like a Court,
9　but the stricter rules of procedure and evidence do
10　not apply to us in our search for the truth. The
11　hearings will be public, except that I have the power
12　to hear evidence in private, should this be
13　necessary, in the interests of justice, fairness and
14　good order.
15　　I know that the public, who I welcome warmly
16　here today, will appreciate that concentration and
17　attention to evidence is difficult if there is noise
18　or disturbance, and I am sure that everybody will
19　operate with courtesy and control so that my advisers
20　and I, and all who are involved, can do our best to
21　fathom what happened after the terrible murder of
22　Steven Lawrence and decide what lessons can be
23　learned.
24　　No questions can be asked, nor can points be
25　made by members of the public as we go along, no

1　inquiry could possibly function in that way, but
2　anybody who has questions to raise, or has helpful
3　evidence or points which he or she feel should be
4　considered, can approach a member of the Inquiry team
5　at any time for guidance as to what to do.
6　　The first part of the Inquiry will last for some
7　time. It is truly impossible at this moment to say
8　for how long. My objective is to finish the oral.
9　evidence of this part of the Inquiry by or before the
10　end of May of 1998. When the evidence has all been
11　called, the Inquiry will turn to the second part of
12　the Inquiry and will decide what lessons may be
13　learned for the future investigation and prosecution
14　of racially related and motivated crimes. Most of
15　that part of the Inquiry's work will be done by way
16　of written contributions and submissions.
17　　Representations of parties will largely end when part
18　one of the Inquiry is finished.
19　　I hope that during the autumn of 1998 my report
20　will be made to the Home Secretary. I express my
21　thanks to all who have contributed to the preparation
22　of this case: my staff and all of those who are
23　represented and who have helped with the marshaling
24　of many documents and the consideration of much
25　material which already exists. I am sure that this

1　cooperation will continue as the Inquiry performs its
2　difficult and sensitive task.
3　　As you will all know, the Police Complaints
4　Authority considered this case in detail and in
5　private during last year. We were rightly told by
6　the Home Secretary not to start this Public Inquiry
7　until the Authority made its report, which was
8　finally given in January of 1998. I am in no way
9　bound by the Authority's conclusions, which have been
10　published, but I will be much assisted by the
11　interviews and statements which were before the
12　Authority. I hope that the Authority's work on the
13　facts of the case will enable our investigation to be
14　sensibly shortened.
15　　Our hope is that, at the end of the day, we will
16　establish what happened and what may have gone wrong
17　over these last years in connection with the
18　investigation and management of this case. To Mr and
19　Mrs Lawrence, these years must have been dreadful.
20　We hope sincerely that while nothing can alleviate
21　the pain and loss which they have suffered, they may
22　accept that all of us have done our best to establish
23　what was done or not done so that the future may not
24　see repetition of any errors which may be uncovered
25　during our hearings. I hope also that any

Page 23

1 recommendations made about policy and practice in
2 respect of both parts 1 and part 2 of our Inquiry
3 will have lasting effect.
4   I think it both right and, indeed, necessary to
5 repeat one matter which I dealt with at our first
6 hearing in October 1997 and that concerns the limited
7 immunity offered at this Inquiry. I have been
8 authorised by Her Majesty's Attorney General to
9 undertake in respect of any person who provides
10 evidence to this Inquiry that no evidence he or she
11 may give before the Inquiry, whether orally or by
12 written statement, nor any written statement made
13 preparatory to giving evidence, nor any documents
14 produced by that person to the Inquiry will be used
15 in evidence against him or her in any criminal
16 proceedings, except in proceedings where he or she is
17 charged with having given false evidence in the
18 course of this Inquiry or with having conspired with
19 or procured others so to do.
20   Anyone who comes forward may ask that his or her
21 identity be not disclosed publicly, that is, beyond
22 counsel and solicitors to the Inquiry and its
23 Chairman and advisers. We will give the most careful
24 consideration to any such request. We appreciate
25 that some people may wish to approach us in

Page 24

1 confidence. We will always be prepared to hear any
2 representation as to the need for confidentiality
3 before making any decision to allow publicity.
4 Anonymous information is unlikely to be relied upon.
5 Those who do wish to contribute information for the
6 Inquiry will be interviewed in confidence on our
7 behalf.
8   What we hope and sincerely wish to do is to
9 establish confidence between ourselves and all those
10 who have been or have become involved in this matter,
11 so that all of us may learn those lessons which are
12 surely there to be learned for the future.
13   Mr and Mrs Lawrence, and indeed all of us, have
14 waited a long time for this Inquiry to start, but for
15 our part, we simply ask that everybody will cooperate
16 and work together so that the conduct of the Inquiry
17 and its results can be fairly judged at the end of
18 the day.
19   I will in a moment ask my advisers to introduce
20 themselves to you. Then we will hand over to
21 Mr Lawson who will outline the case and the issues
22 involved.
23   For the benefit of everybody here, no evidence
24 will be given today. The first witness will be
25 called tomorrow.

Page 25

1   Transcripts of all the evidence given in the
2 Inquiry are available by arrangement with the company
3 involved in the transcription and the full daily
4 transcript will be available at Greenwich and
5 Southwark public libraries.
6   With that, probably rather boring and formal
7 opening, ladies and gentlemen, of the Inquiry, I am
8 going to ask the advisers to introduce themselves so
9 that you all have a flavour of the richness of the
10 individuals who will assist me with their advice
11 during this Inquiry and starting on the right I will
12 ask Mr Tom Cook to introduce himself.
13 MR TOM COOK: I do not want to over elaborate on
14 personal details, they have already been given.
15 My name is Tom Cook. I joined the Police Service in
16 1964 and served in the areas of Lancashire,
17 Greater Manchester and West Yorkshire. In
18 Greater Manchester and West Yorkshire Police I had a
19 period in charge as head of community relations in
20 both of those forces. I have also served on the
21 National ACPO, Association of Chief Police Officers,
22 crime committees and was secretary of the Committee
23 on Race Relations until my retirement.
24   What I particularly want to do this morning,
25 rather than introduce myself in any detail, is to

Page 26

1 make a personal statement, partly because of the
2 events which occurred last week. That personal
3 statement is as follows:
4   Following the events of last week, occasioned
5 largely by a misleading article in The Observer
6 newspaper, I wish to make crystal clear my commitment
7 to this Inquiry and to its Chairman,
8 Sir William Macpherson.
9   One needs only the briefest of acquaintances
10 with Sir William to be unequivocally impressed with
11 his objectivity and integrity and with his
12 sensitivity to the issues and personalties involved
13 in this Inquiry. The Inquiry in my view can have no
14 better Chairman.
15   My fellow advisers are robustly independent
16 individuals who bring a range of differing experience
17 to the task in hand. The four of us, the Chairman and
18 the advisers together, have very quickly formed a
19 mutual trust and respect which will, I believe,
20 enable us under Sir William's chairmanship to
21 thoroughly, and I stress, perilously explore the
22 issues involved in and underlying the investigation
23 into the racist murder of Stephen Lawrence and
24 ultimately to make a significant contribution to the
25 improvement of racial harmony in our society.

Page 27

1   I therefore urge the public at large to
2   disregard such things as The Observer article and, as
3   Sir William himself has in the past requested, judge
4   this Inquiry by its results. That is all I wish to
5   say at this moment.
6   THE CHAIRMAN: Dr Richard Stone who sits in the middle
7   will introduce himself to you all.
8   MR RICHARD STONE: I am Richard Stone and as you
9   probably know I spent 20 years as a general
10 practitioner in the Notting Hill and Bayswater parts
11 of London.
12   I suppose it is important to say that inevitably
13 in the Notting Hill community as a local family
14 doctor I did find myself very much involved in my
15 local community which, of course, in that area is the
16 Caribbean community of Notting Hill and the Notting
17 Hill Carnival and the areas around there. At the
18 same time it is also important to recognise that as a
19 local GP I inevitably worked very closely also with
20 the local police forces, particularly in my case in
21 the areas of child protection.
22   What I wanted to just say this morning, rather
23 like Thomas done, is make a bit of a personal
24 statement, remind people that nine days ago there was
25 a moving and passionate vigil for Stephen Lawrence at

Page 28

1   the spot where he died. I was privileged to be
2   allowed by my new friend Bishop John here to read
3   there the ancient kaddish prayer which Jewish people
4   have for over 2000 years have chanted as a memorial
5   for the dead. It was a moving and passionate
6   occasion. For me it was probably the nearest I will
7   ever come to knowing Stephen. From what I have heard
8   about him and from what I have read I think he is
9   someone whose company I would have enjoyed.
10   Now I and the other 20 or more in this Inquiry
11 team have to do what we can to find out all that is
12 possible to find out about how he died. We also have
13 to use every ounce of our passion, our intellects,
14 our instincts to sort out the injustice that no-one
15 has been found responsible for that dreadful murder.
16   In my 20 years as a National Health Service GP I
17 learned from my patients something which has been
18 confirmed by almost all surveys of patients. People
19 do try alternative therapies and the main reason they
20 give is that they want more time and they want to
21 feel they have been listened to. Listening is so
22 important and it is listening which this Inquiry is
23 about to do for 6, 8 or 10 weeks.
24   In addition to our listening I do hope the
25 people from all communities will every day fill the

Page 29

1   185 seats we have provided here for the public. One
2   of my mentors, Rabbi Hugo Gryn, used to say that one
3   of his main hopes in life was to have wall to wall
4   congregations. It will help us to focus our minds if
5   we have wall to wall public presence with us during
6   all of the weeks of the Inquiry.
7   In addition to listening there has to be the
8   capacity of the listener to change his or her mind.
9   I have been spending an average of two days a week
10 for the last seven months in the company of the 15 or
11 so key members of this Inquiry. What has impressed me
12 most is the steely determination of every one of
13 those people, the secretaries, the lawyers, the civil
14 servants, the other two advisers, Bishop John and my
15 other new friend, Tom Cook and our judge, Sir William
16 Macpherson himself. All of these people have that
17 determination to get to the core of the issues raised
18 by this racist murder of Stephen Lawrence. Every
19 single one of these people I have found has a
20 remarkable capacity to listen. Every one not only
21 gives the time to listen, but I have also noticed a
22 rare willingness amongst all of them to change their
23 attitudes. That gives a reasonable hope even to a
24 wary person like me that we will find out most of
25 what we all want to know about the murder and about

Page 30

1   the investigations of it.
2   I do not think we can ever know one hundred
3   percent but I am confident that the Lawrence family
4   and all of those other people who have serious
5   concerns about this case will feel that all that can
6   be done to bring a sense of justice will have been
7   done. Of course more may be revealed in years to come
8   but there will be nothing of real importance left to
9   seek out, all of the major issues at the centre of
10 the case will have been dealt with once and for all.
11 That I think is what is needed to bring peace and to
12 move forward any necessary changes in the judicial
13 process that will make Britain a better place for us
14 all to live in.
15 THE CHAIRMAN: Thank you very much. Lastly, to my
16 right the right Reverend Dr John Sentamu, the Bishop
17 of Stepney.
18 DR JOHN SENTAMU: Thank you very much. John Sentamu,
19 Ugandan, black Christian. I chair the
20 Church of England's Committee for Minority Ethnic
21 Anglican concerns which, at the heart of its main
22 concern, is to root out racism from within the
23 structures of that particular organisation.
24   I just want to say two things and then make one
25 request. In Uganda we have a proverb for every

Page 31

1 conceivable situation, and the one which adequately
2 suits this Inquiry says that, "When two elephants
3 fight, the grass gets hurt." Words, arguments and
4 counter-arguments are going to be vigorously offered
5 throughout this Inquiry. Let us not forget in that
6 combat the really hurting ones: Neville and Doreen
7 Lawrence and Stephen's brother and sister, Stuart and
8 Georgina. For five years they have laboured hard to
9 see truth and justice prevail since Stephen was
10 brutally murdered on 22nd April 1993.
11 Another Ugandan proverb says, "When a toe is
12 hurt the whole body stoops down to attend to the pain
13 and to remove the hurt." So let us all, yes, all of
14 us, bend our powers and energies to bring to light
15 truth and justice that has been hitherto illusory. I
16 have nothing but admiration for the Lawrence's
17 tenacity and perseverance. I know that this gang of
18 four will not betray them and the Home Secretary's
19 sacred trust. We have a duty which I believe is
20 important and this gang of four going, I am sure, are
21 going to make sure that trust is not betrayed.
22 If I may speak personally about my own
23 commitment to and involvement in this Inquiry I can
24 do no better that quote Roy Williamson, who retired
25 as Bishop of Southwark in January. He said: "John

Page 32

1 Sentamu is every bit Ugandan. To any given task he
2 behaves like a Yorkshire Terrier. Never let him go -
3 or at least only letting go in order to get a firmer
4 grip." That is the way I am. I want to say let the
5 listener understand.
6 The second thing I want to say comes out of a
7 warning by Dante in The Divine Comedy. He said: "The
8 hottest places in Hell are reserved for those who in
9 time in great moral crisis maintain their
10 neutrality."
11 I, like the Lord Chancellor and Home Secretary,
12 the Right Honourable Jack Straw, MP have complete
13 confidence in Sir William's ability to conduct this
14 Inquiry with fairness and sensitivity. I have had the
15 privilege of seeing Sir William at work for 8 months
16 and I can honestly say that he is totally committed
17 to this Inquiry. He is not unbending although he is
18 very robust and hides an iron fist in a velvet glove.
19 I know he will use the powers of his discretion to
20 great effect and we three advisers will pull out all
21 the stops to assist him in his conduct of this
22 Inquiry.
23 I am assured by a number of vital decisions
24 Sir William has taken. Let me just name one, which I
25 think is very important. All evidence to the

Page 33

1 Police Complaints Authority have been given to all
2 parties represented at this Inquiry. The first time
3 ever the contents of a Police Complaints Authority
4 report have been given to any party, other than the
5 police.
6 The police initially sought nondisclosure of the
7 whole report. Although the report is the property of
8 the Police Complaints Authority it is Sir William's
9 unshakeable view that all information possible should
10 be made available to those represented at this
11 Inquiry. Knowing that this was Sir William's
12 attitude, the police objection to disclosure was
13 withdrawn.
14 This Inquiry has a wider remit than the
15 Police Complaints Authority and must reach
16 conclusions and make its own recommendations - and I
17 am absolutely confident that Sir William and his
18 advisers assisted by the Inquiry and the legal team
19 will leave no stone unturned. I would not have
20 joined if that was not going to be the case.
21 Whatever anybody else chooses to believe or throw at
22 Sir William, this Inquiry needs to remember that he
23 is a distinguished former High Court Judge who ought
24 to be judged by his conduct of this Inquiry and its
25 results. Listen, wait and see must be the best

Page 34

1 articulation.
2 Finally my request is simple: throughout this
3 Inquiry the name of Stephen Lawrence will be used
4 again and again and again and again. May I ask you
5 please to stand in silence to honour his memory to
6 remember him now and always. Please join me in
7 standing for silence. (Pause).
8 Rest eternal grant unto Stephen Lawrence, O
9 Lord. And let light perpetual shine upon him and may
10 he rise in glory. From the rising of the sun to its
11 setting we will remember him. Amen.
12 THE CHAIRMAN: Ladies and gentlemen, I am quite sure
13 that having listened to that moving prayer from the
14 Bishop and heard the three advisers you will realise
15 that the advice which I get will be robust and
16 valuable, indeed.
17 With those opening statements from that side of
18 the Inquiry we will now turn to Mr Edmund Lawson,
19 Queens Counsel, who will introduce those who are
20 represented and will then present his opening
21 statement to the Inquiry. Mr Lawson?
22 MR LAWSON: Thank you, Sir. In a moment I will
23 introduce those who are represented in this Inquiry.
24 First, let me make these introductory comments, if I
25 may. As the Bishop has just said Stephen Lawrence

Page 35

1 was brutally murdered. It happened on a Thursday
2 night, 22nd April, 1993. The attack upon him was
3 obviously cowardly, was unprovoked and was
4 demonstrably racist. He died in Eltham. He was
5 attacked in the street. He was twice viciously
6 stabbed and left to die in the street. He was
7 black. His attackers were white.
8   Despite prolonged investigations, an aborted
9 public prosecution and an attempt at private
10 prosecution there has been no conviction. No-one has
11 been convicted for his murder or for any involvement
12 in the attack upon him. No adjective is adequate to
13 describe the effect which that and the other emotions
14 must have upon his family. It must be, at least,
15 devastating to them.
16   It is also a matter for real concern that his
17 murderers escaped punishment and are free to kill
18 again or, indeed, are free at all.
19   It would, particularly as we are to have the
20 great benefit of hearing from Mr and Mrs Lawrence
21 early on in this Inquiry - it is, perhaps,
22 presumptuous for me to say anything about their son.
23 They can speak of him, of course, better than any.
24   It might, however, be appropriate just to remind
25 the Inquiry and to inform those who listen of this

Page 36

1 little (inaudible) description of him by someone who
2 knew him, in fact, at the Cambridge Harriers Athletic
3 Club, of which he was an active and successful
4 member. Quite coincidently the someone was a
5 policeman who knew him at the club because his son
6 was also involved:
7   "During the period I knew Stephen", he said, "I
8 found him to be polite and respectful. He was a
9 dedicated athlete, always reliable. By far the best
10 athlete in my group and although he was very aware of
11 this fact he was never big headed about it, on the
12 contrary, he appeared embarrassed about his talent.
13   "I never saw him display any form of aggression
14 and would describe his temperament as the same as his
15 father, quiet and unassuming.
16   "He was of good character, exemplary character.
17 He was a young man who had never come into contact
18 with or the notice of the police."
19   The first part of this Inquiry as the terms of
20 reference, which you have quoted, Sir, indicate,
21 concerns his murder and the matters arising from his
22 death. Your terms of reference require you to
23 consider matters arising to date. We will seek to
24 assist you to consider the adequacy of the police
25 reaction to and their investigation of this murder,

Page 37

1 what attempts were made to bring the suspects, and
2 suspects there were, to justice and to consider to
3 what extent any aspect of this case was affected by
4 racism.
5   I refer to the first part, just as you did,
6 sir. The full terms of reference, of course, require
7 that we consider the lessons to be learnt for the
8 investigation and prosecution of racially motivated
9 crimes. That in particular, as you have indicated,
10 is to be part 2 of this Inquiry. Some of the
11 evidence which I, on behalf of the Inquiry, with the
12 assistance of Miss Weekes and Mr Gibson, will lead
13 will inevitably be relevant to part 2 but the
14 evidence we call will primarily be directed to the
15 important issues: what went wrong and why?
16   When I say, "what went wrong", I do not want to
17 indicate prejudgment. This Inquiry team, you, sir,
18 and the advisers being impartial and not prejudging
19 matters. But, that said, it is plain something did
20 go badly wrong. It makes no sense for us on behalf
21 of the Inquiry to ignore the indications which are
22 already available from the mass of material that has
23 been provided to us. It appears that in a number of
24 very material respects the police conduct of the
25 investigation went badly wrong, not least in the

Page 38

1 decision to delay arrests of the principal suspects,
2 who were identified from various sources immediately
3 after the murder but whose arrests were delayed for
4 two weeks or more.
5   We will be asking and you will be seeking to
6 answer the question: is there evidence or any
7 explanation to contradict the clear impression that
8 things went badly wrong? If not, why did they go
9 wrong? We will be inviting you to consider, and
10 producing evidence to assist you to answer the
11 question: were any of the errors due to simple or,
12 perhaps more accurately, gross incompetence or were
13 some vociferously asserted and, as police officers
14 have vigorously denied, attributable to or
15 contributed to directly or indirectly by racism?
16 Those, we apprehend, are the main issues that arise
17 in this Inquiry.
18   To assist you in reaching a conclusion in
19 respect of those main issues there is substantial
20 representation of interested parties and as this is
21 the first day of the Inquiry proper, so to speak, and
22 for the record and for the information of the public
23 who are in attendance, may I indicate the who's who
24 amongst representation.
25 THE CHAIRMAN: Yes; thank you.

Page 39

1 MR LAWSON: Mr and Mrs Lawrence are represented by
2 those who sit immediately to my left, beyond
3 Mr Gibson, that is: Mr Mansfield, Queen's Counsel,
4 Mr Kamlish and Mr Soorjoo, instructed by J R Jones
5 solicitors, and particularly by Mr Imran Khan who has
6 been involved throughout.
7 　　Behind them sit the representatives of the
8 Metropolitan Police Commissioner: that is
9 Mr Gompertz, Queen's Counsel, and Mr Beer, instructed
10 by the solicitor for the Metropolitan Police.
11 　　Next and in the middle of the row behind me,
12 representing three of the superintendents in the case
13 is Miss Woodley, Queen's Counsel, and Mr Doyle,
14 instructed by Rowe & Cohen.
15 　　Behind me, to the right, are the representatives
16 of what I will call the federated ranks of the police
17 force. I hope they will forgive me; I will not
18 identify each and every officer whom they represent;
19 some officers are represented collectively by the
20 Commissioner and others by Mr Egan, who apologises
21 for his inability to be here today, and Mr Jory,
22 instructed by Russell Jones & Walker.
23 　　If we can go back a row (and there is no
24 significance in the rows) -- can I be heard if I turn
25 my head? I think it is necessary that I just

Page 40

1 identify where people are, which may help -- at the
2 far end of the second row, forgive me pointing at
3 them, there sit the representatives of Mr Duwayne
4 Brooks: that is Mr Ian McDonald, Queen's Counsel,
5 and Rajiv Menon. They are instructed by Miss
6 Deighton of Deighton Guedalla. I should have learned
7 how to pronounce it by now; my apologies; not a very
8 good start, I am afraid.
9 　　We also have representation on the part of the
10 London Borough of Greenwich: Mr William Panton. The
11 Commission for Racial Equality, sitting on this side
12 of the second row: Mr Yearwood and Maya Sikand,
13 instructed by the legal department of the Commission.
14 　　In the back row, on the far side from me, there
15 sit the representatives of the Crown Prosecution
16 Service: that is Mr Brian Barker, Queen's Counsel,
17 and Miss Jocelyn Sparks.
18 　　Finally, I think, in terms of representation
19 today, we have Mr Mukul Chawla, instructed by
20 Reynolds Dawson, who sits in the middle of the back
21 row who represents the interests of Ex-superintendent
22 Barker.
23 　　It may be, I do not know, that until we get
24 familiar, or those who are regularly attending get
25 familiar with who is who, it would be helpful if,

Page 41

1 when individual counsel wish to cross-examine, they
2 can initially indicate who they are and who they
3 represent.
4 　　Having taken a few minutes to introduce the
5 parties, let me proceed with what is to be a brief
6 opening of the facts as we anticipate they may be and
7 the factual issues to be considered. Obviously we
8 have no wish, any more than any other member of the
9 Inquiry team has, to delay this already much delayed
10 Inquiry.
11 　　I am going to identify some but not all of the
12 issues; and I shall pose some of the questions, but
13 not all of the questions, that will demand to be
14 asked and answered. Then we will get on with the
15 evidence. Because the only way, we suggest, that
16 this Inquiry can get at the truth is by reference to
17 evidence, not allegations, informed or ill-informed,
18 but evidence and that is what we will be doing.
19 　　We, all of us, have some documents that I will
20 refer to briefly, if I may, that may assist the
21 Inquiry. There is the issues document, to which you,
22 sir, have already referred. It is but a working
23 document to focus thoughts on the issues arising. It
24 has been formulated after consultation with other
25 interested parties. Inevitably, different parties

Page 42

1 have different emphases on different issues. There
2 is no significance whatsoever in the order in which
3 issues are set out in the Statement of Issues, save
4 only that, perhaps logically, we have sought to
5 start, at least, chronologically by dealing first
6 with the events arising immediately after the murder.
7 　　We will seek to call witnesses to give evidence
8 on an issue by issue basis and as to events as they
9 chronologically occurred. Obviously, some witnesses
10 were involved in more than a single event therefore
11 there is bound to be some moving from issue to
12 issue. We want to avoid, if we can, having to call
13 and recall witnesses as opposed to calling them once
14 -- that may not be possible in every case. Some of
15 the more senior police officers concerned may more
16 conveniently give their evidence later on, because
17 they will be being asked to account for a wide range
18 of issues, events and omissions.
19 　　May I refer to the chronology that has been
20 circulated to all parties? This document, helpfully
21 prepared and worked on over many months by
22 Miss Anesta Weekes, is again a working document. It
23 contains detailed references to events in 1993 and
24 brief reference to subsequent events together with
25 references to source material. As you have said,

1 sir, this is not a trial and so I am not going to
2 seek to prove every fact contained in that
3 chronology. Most of it cannot be controversial. I
4 have previously invited, and I renew the invitation
5 to all parties to contribute further to this document
6 as this Inquiry progresses. We positively welcome
7 any suggestions for amendments or additions to it.
8 By the end of this Inquiry there should, with
9 cooperation from all parties, be in that document a
10 complete chronology of all material events.
11 　　We also have, as you have yourself indicated,
12 the advantage of the Kent Police Report: the
13 investigation carried out under the supervision of
14 the Police Complaints Authority. The full report, in
15 excess of 400 pages in length, became available to us
16 at the end of last year. As has been indicated
17 already (and forgive the repetition) the report would
18 not normally be published -- this is a first -- and
19 we have in large measure, may I emphasise, the
20 Chairman's encouragement for full disclosure. We
21 have that to thank for the production and
22 availability of that report, which would ordinarily
23 be confidential and would ordinarily attract immunity
24 from disclosure. I am sure it is going to be
25 particularly helpful to everyone.

1 　　As you have said, sir, the reports and the views
2 expressed within it are in no way binding upon this
3 Inquiry. We will not ignore those views. For
4 working purposes, as the Inquiry proceeds, it may
5 assist us to consider whether such criticisms as are
6 made in that report are valid and should be adopted,
7 whether they are sufficiently trenchant and whether
8 there are further criticisms which could and should
9 have been made.
10 　　The report contains convenient summaries of
11 facts concerning a number of aspects of the
12 investigation. I am going to refer to some in
13 opening this case; others will be adopted by us
14 during the course of our presentation of the
15 evidence. Again, where it appears that these facts
16 are not contentious, we are not going to distract the
17 Inquiry and take unnecessary time by calling
18 unnecessary witnesses. If, of course, any party
19 contends that any of those factual summaries are
20 inaccurate or incomplete, he or she will have ample
21 opportunity to point that out as the Inquiry
22 proceeds.
23 　　With an apology for a further preliminary, may I
24 just deal with three further points? First,
25 anonymity, a number of witnesses have asked that

1 their identity is protected. In particular
2 informants, registered or otherwise, are referred to
3 in documents that have been copied to all parties by
4 letter rather than by name. I hope the reasons for
5 that are obvious. That type of redaction or editing
6 of the documents, and indeed all of the editing that
7 has been done, has been made with your approval, sir,
8 you being content that nobody can or will be
9 disadvantaged thereby.
10 　　Similarly, some aspects of the case relate to
11 surveillance operations carried out by the police.
12 As is perhaps well-known, surveillance sometimes
13 depends upon securing the cooperation of members of
14 the public who would be at risk if their identities
15 or addresses were known. Steps have been taken,
16 therefore, in editing the documents to avoid that
17 risk.
18 　　Many of those involved in the Inquiry, both on
19 the police side and those acting on behalf of the
20 family, in fact know the identity of informants,
21 other anonymous witnesses and details of
22 surveillance. I hope none of us makes a mistake and
23 blurts out names or addresses that we should not do
24 so. I am afraid I cannot promise not to. I will try
25 to avoid it. I am sure we all will.

1 　　I would ask on behalf of the Inquiry for the
2 cooperation of the press. If a name or address
3 appears to slip out, or if there is any doubt about
4 whether a name or address ought to be published,
5 please consult us or the Secretariat before publicity
6 is given.
7 　　Finally, by way of preliminary, you, sir,
8 referred to the immunity which the Attorney-General
9 has authorised you to give in relation to what is
10 said here not being used in criminal proceedings
11 against the provider, save in perjury proceedings and
12 the like. That is a gloss upon the full terms of the
13 immunity which you recited very recently. It would
14 probably be appropriate, I think, to add that the
15 Commissioner of the Metropolitan Police has given a
16 similar authority in respect of the position of
17 police officers facing any possible disciplinary
18 proceedings. It may be appropriate to mention that
19 in the light of a recent announcement. Thus, nobody,
20 police or civilian, has any proper basis for
21 declining to assist this Inquiry in its quest for the
22 truth; and that includes those who I will be
23 referring to in this opening as the five suspects:
24 Neil and Jamie Acourt, Norris, Dobson and Knight.
25 The terms of reference of this Inquiry do not, of

Page 47

1 course, extend to authorising us to investigate the
2 guilt of any particular suspect as opposed to the
3 police investigation of those suspects, but there are
4 obvious areas, we suggest, in respect of which we
5 think those men should be required to testify to this
6 Tribunal and we are going to seek to ensure that they
7 do so.
8   Proceeding then, if I may, to the opening proper
9 at last, a little background. Although there may be
10 some contentious areas which require to be explored,
11 one thing which is clear beyond peradventure and
12 requires no evidence at all, is that Stephen Lawrence
13 was 18 when he was murdered, was a decent law-abiding
14 young man of exemplary character. Equally there is
15 no doubt but that on 22nd April, 1993 when he was
16 murdered he was doing nothing more than trying to go
17 home. He and his friend, Duwayne Brooks, were picked
18 out because they were black and it seems because they
19 were alone. Cowards do not attack big groups.
20   There is some evidence that the likely attackers
21 were inclined to use violence on anyone, black or
22 white, but this attack was plainly racist.
23   Neither Stephen Lawrence nor Duwayne Brooks did
24 anything to provoke an argument, let alone a fight.
25 Stephen Lawrence had no chance to escape. He was, we

Page 48

1 know, the oldest of three children of a family living
2 in Woolwich.
3   He on the evening of 22nd April had been out
4 with his friend Duwayne Brooks, they had apparently
5 been friends since they had met some seven years
6 previously at school. Making their way home to
7 Woolwich that night they found themselves in Eltham
8 waiting for a bus in a road called Well Hall Road.
9 As they looked for a bus they, having moved away
10 somewhat from the bus stop, where there were some
11 other people, so for a moment critically moving away
12 from the other people at the bus stop probably
13 exposed them to the danger which they then met.
14   They moved away a little way from the bus stop
15 looking to see if there was a bus coming when a group
16 of some five or six white youths approached them.
17 Duwayne Brooks recounted that he heard at least one
18 of them make a reference to "nigger". They were
19 obviously looking for trouble. Duwayne Brooks
20 shouted to his friend to run, but Stephen could not
21 because he was surrounded by the thugs, attacked by
22 one or more of them and knocked to the ground.
23   The attackers immediately ran off, apparently
24 down a road called Dixon Road. There are plans of
25 the area to assist us in due course, I need not take

Page 49

1 you to them at the moment. Stephen Lawrence managed
2 to get up, despite, as it turned out, the mortal
3 injuries which had been inflicted upon him, and run
4 some distance down Well Hall Road but then collapsed
5 bleeding heavily.
6   He was seen to run, and then to collapse, by
7 Mr and Mrs Taaffe who had just, as it happened, left
8 the local church, and Mr Taaffe will be giving
9 evidence to this Inquiry, they went to him. He had
10 fortuitously fallen into something like at least the
11 recovery position, well known to anybody acquainted
12 with elementary first aid, as Mr Taaffe was. There
13 was little or nothing they felt they could do for
14 him. They prayed over him and sought to comfort
15 him.
16   In the meantime Mr Brooks had gone to phone for
17 an ambulance. He was understandably at the time very
18 upset and apparently somewhat confused. He was then
19 and later talking of Stephen Lawrence having been hit
20 over the head with an iron bar. Of course, we know
21 that, in fact, he was viciously stabbed in the body.
22   The police arrived. The first to arrive was an
23 off-duty constable, Mr Geddis, followed by two
24 constables who were on duty, Gleason and Bethel.
25 They were followed by an ambulance. Stephen was

Page 50

1 taken to the nearby hospital in Shooters Hill, the
2 Brook Hospital. He arrived just after eleven showing
3 no vital signs. Attempts to resuscitate him failed
4 and a few minutes later he was certified dead.
5   Now, the issues which are set out in the issue's
6 document for the Inquiry's assistance begin, as I
7 previously indicated, with those that arise
8 immediately after the murder and the first issue to
9 be considered relates to first aid. It appears from
10 the evidence that no police officer sought to
11 administer any first aid. It seems at best that the
12 police officers relied mainly or solely upon the
13 Taaffes looking after Stephen Lawrence. It seems as
14 a matter of tragic fact that Stephen's injuries were
15 so severe that first aid would not, in any event,
16 have helped him. But questions do arise whether any
17 first aid was given and if not why not? Whether it
18 should have been attempted by the police? Whether
19 any adequate check was made by any police officer or
20 anybody else at the scene of his, Stephen's
21 condition, to see if first aid should have been
22 given? To consider the question whether first aid
23 was denied by police because, "they did not want to
24 dirty their hands with a black man's blood", as
25 Mrs Lawrence asked after the inquest into her son's

Page 51

1 death.

2   It will also be necessary to consider the

3 adequacy of the first aid training given to these

4 officers and more generally. We have been provided,

5 as you know, with information by the police as to

6 changes that have taken place in their training

7 policy relating to first aid after 1993. We still

8 need to inquire to some extent what the position then

9 was, the adequacy of the changes to which I have made

10 passing reference might be formed properly in the

11 second part of the Inquiry.

12   Further issues arising and relating to the first

13 24 hours or so after the murder include the adequacy

14 of the initial police response, the apparent failure

15 at all stage to keep proper records at the scene and

16 the questions relating also to other information

17 available on how it was deployed.

18   So far as the adequacy of the initial police

19 response is concerned, there seems little doubt but

20 that large numbers of police officers were deployed;

21 that is, turned up at the scene, and arrived

22 quickly. As we will see, whether there were enough

23 police officers deployed thereafter will be a matter

24 which is seriously in issue. The main question in

25 relation to the police deployment at the scene is

Page 52

1 going to be not so much numbers, but how they were

2 used, and how they were directed. We believe that an

3 inspector, Mr Groves, was the first on the scene as a

4 supervising officer and you and we will wish to know

5 what he did and why.

6   As I have mentioned, the attackers had been seen

7 to run off down Dixon Road moments before. What, if

8 any, attempts were made to find them?

9   We will invite consideration to how effective

10 were any police attempts to obtain evidence from

11 people in the immediate vicinity, including those

12 actually at the bus stop close to where the attack

13 took place. We need to look at house to house

14 inquiries and the way in which they were carried out

15 and the way in which information gleaned from those

16 inquiries was reacted to, if at all, by the

17 investigating officers.

18   Let me give, if I may, an example: an important

19 message in this Inquiry, that is a police Message, to

20 which reference will be made later as well, was one

21 that recorded an allegation or information received

22 on Saturday 24th April. I am going to ask that that

23 is the first document that we see on our screens from

24 the computer database, it is PCA 47/397. I wonder if

25 you could throw the switch, Sir. You have control of

Page 53

1 the system.

2 THE CHAIRMAN: Sorry. You should all know that I

3 have the ability to turn off all of your screens

4 should a document appear which should not be shown

5 publicly. There are some, obviously, containing

6 names of informants and so on so that you will remind

7 me if I have left the screens blank.

8 MR LAWSON: Thank you. This, as we can all see, is a

9 police Message form. A constable whose name you can

10 see appearing on there, Bennett, conducting the house

11 to house inquiries which you see on 24th, the

12 Saturday afternoon at about 5.30, spoke to someone

13 who is referred to as witness DD, this is one of

14 those redactions I spoke of earlier, the editing of

15 names and addresses to protect those who are

16 apprehensive that there may be recrimination.

17   If we can look to see what the Message was; it

18 is of interest. That witness, it is no secret it was

19 a she, witness DD, gave that information that there

20 appears:

21   "During visits to Crossbrook Road area the

22 Acourts has cropped up as youths that carry knives

23 and use them."

24   Witness DD said that another witness, who is

25 called EE for these purposes:

Page 54

1   "On the night of the incident saw" -- "on the

2 night of the incident", it should be, then there is a

3 removal because it identifies the individual, "and

4 told her that Jamie and Neil Acourt were walking

5 around the corner. Apparently one of the Acourt

6 brothers carries a machete down his right hand

7 trouser leg."

8   Also, another witness, walked past the boys,

9 Lawrence and friend, when they were at the bus stop.

10 The address of that person was given. I do not know

11 if she saw anybody else. The witness DD does not

12 want anyone to know that she had been talking about

13 the Acourts.

14   I refer to that for this reason, as we have seen

15 that document, that information came to the police on

16 24th April. Apparently, no action was taken in

17 respect of it at all until a week later. We will

18 want to know why there was such a delay. When action

19 was taken we will be inviting you to consider whether

20 it was effective or was it too late already.

21   It does seem additionally in relation to matters

22 at the scene, perhaps of less significance, but that

23 is not for us to judge, but for you, that no scene

24 log maintained, that is a log of events immediately

25 at the scene and, indeed, no rolling log or CAD log

Page 55

1   was initiated. You may wish to ask whether that
2   omission made any difference to the progress of the
3   Inquiry then or later.
4   It also falls for consideration in relation to
5   early matters in the investigation, what information
6   the police had as to other offences of violence that
7   had occurred in the recent past in the area, in
8   particular those that were racist. Most particularly
9   we will focus attention on information received by
10 police concerning such offences where one or more of
11 the five suspects was or were involved.
12   The Kent Police catalogued a number of previous
13 murders and stabbing incidents, and this is one of
14 those summaries to which I referred that we may
15 conveniently adopt at least for working purposes.
16 One finds it in their report beginning at page 59. I
17 do not suggest we take it up at the moment. The
18 reference for those using the computer system will be
19 PCA 50 at page 60. Helpfully, the computer system is
20 one page on from the internal pagination of the
21 report, as long as we remember that.
22   May I just briefly, and I will do it only
23 briefly, describe those incidents that were there
24 catalogued, because some of these names will crop up
25 again as I open to this Inquiry aspects of the

Page 56

1   information that was received relating to the violent
2   antics of one or more of the five suspects.
3   In particular there has been catalogued
4   reference to the murder Orvill Blair in May of 1991,
5   apparently following an argument relating to an
6   allegation that Blair had burgled the killer's
7   premises.
8   I pass on from that to perhaps a more material
9   case, that is not to dismiss for a moment the
10 Orvill Blair matter but to one which is perhaps of
11 more impact.
12   Rolan Adams was murdered -- he was only 15 -- he
13 was black, a 15 year old black lad was murdered by a
14 white youth in February of 1991.
15   Rohit Duggal, an Asian youth, only 16, stabbed
16 to death by another lad, a white lad, called Thompson
17 in July 1992. We will hear later it was suggested
18 there was some association between Thompson and the
19 Acourts gang.
20   There is reference also to stabbings that
21 mercifully did not result in death. Someone called
22 Lee Pearson, a white youth, as it happens, was
23 attacked by a group of other white youths in December
24 of 1991. When he was seen by this Inquiry team, as
25 he was at the end of April, he asserted that the

Page 57

1   Acourts had been part of the gang that had attacked
2   him. He would not cooperate further with police,
3   apparently for fear of revenge being taken upon him.
4   In May of 1992 two brothers called Terry and
5   Darren Witham were for no apparent reason, as they
6   alleged, set upon in the street by Jamie Acourt,
7   Norris and Knight. That led to Norris being charged
8   with wounding and to Jamie Acourt initially being
9   charged with possessing an offensive weapon. Those
10 charges were not pursued on the CPS advice.
11   We will also hear reference to a knife attack
12 upon a young man called Kevin London, a young 16 year
13 old black boy, who was assaulted or threatened with a
14 knife by, he alleged, Dobson in November of 1992.
15   We will hear of Gurdeep Bhangal, a young Asian
16 man, who in March 1993, that is but a few weeks
17 before Stephen's murder, was the victim of a stabbing
18 by a white youth when he was working in his father's
19 Wimpy Bar in Eltham High Street. We will hear
20 reference to that assault too in the course of the
21 information given.
22   Finally, in this brief catalogue we will hear
23 reference to the stabbing of Stacey Benefield. He
24 complained that in March of 1993, again only a few
25 days or weeks before Stephen's murder, he had been

Page 58

1   stabbed in the chest by Norris. At the time when
2   first seen at the hospital to which he went, not
3   surprisingly, he declined to name those who were
4   responsible. It is a recurrent theme that comes up
5   in this investigation, or that came up in this
6   investigation, that a number of witnesses were
7   plainly frightened to associate themselves with any
8   complaint against any of the suspected five, for
9   reasons that are perhaps obvious; but when he was
10 seen by the police investigating this murder, he
11 asserted and confirmed that he had been the subject
12 of an attack by Norris and Neil Acourt. Curiously,
13 he having made a statement to that effect on 25th
14 April of 1993, which would amply have justified the
15 arrest of both of those youths on that occasion,
16 nothing was done until the 7th May.
17   So, we will come back, I will come back and in
18 the evidence we will come back to aspects of those
19 other incidents which may have some bearing upon what
20 should have been done here, at least by the police,
21 and why they did not do it.
22   In this regard, in respect of the opening period
23 of the murder investigation, just as with all other
24 aspects of the investigation, we will call into
25 question the overall management of the investigation

Page 59

1 that falls clearly to be examined by you and by us.
2 To the extent that errors were made, we will be
3 asking: were they a consequence of poor direction
4 from senior officers, or poor execution by junior
5 officers, or a combination of both? Or was it, as
6 has very recently been suggested to us by our expert
7 advisor in relation to the HOLMES computer system,
8 were the errors caused or contributed to by woeful
9 shortage of resources in the sense of simply not
10 enough policeman being devoted to the investigation?
11 That I will come back to.
12 An important issue that falls for consideration
13 comes under the general heading of: "Family
14 liaison". This is an area of particular concern.
15 There is, so it appears, some dispute as to precisely
16 what happened, both immediately and during the
17 ongoing investigation. What is beyond doubt,
18 however, is that Mr and Mrs Lawrence were and remain
19 dissatisfied with the way in which they were dealt
20 with by the police. Sensitivity in dealing with a
21 family traumatised by the sudden and violent death of
22 a son is obviously demanded, not only for reasons of
23 common humanity, but also, and practically, because
24 the cooperation of a bereaved family is often
25 required to assist in an investigation. We will

Page 60

1 ask: was sufficient or any sensitivity shown?
2 Subject to the evidence that is to be given, the
3 indications are that insufficient attention was paid
4 and insufficient information was given to the family
5 at the hospital on the night of Stephen's death. If
6 that was so, why? Can the junior officer, the
7 constable who was present, be blamed? Or would that
8 be unfair? Should responsibility rest with his
9 supervising officers for failing to ensure that there
10 was any proper and sensitive liaison with the family
11 from the outset?
12 There were appointed two police officers as
13 so-called "family liaison officers" -- I do not use
14 "so-called" in a derogatory matter; that was the
15 title that they had -- Bevan and Holden. They have
16 been the subject of public criticism by Mrs Lawrence
17 as being unsupportive and as being very patronising
18 but they vehemently deny that they are to be
19 criticised in that respect. But we will ask whether
20 they were unsupportive, whether they were
21 patronising; at minimum, did they convey that
22 impression and, if so, why? Was that because, if it
23 was done, either they failed in that respect or they
24 gave the impression, which might just be as bad, of
25 failing in that respect and was that a consequence of

Page 61

1 defective training?
2 At the end of May Detective Chief Superintendent
3 Ilsley himself took over responsibility for the
4 family liaison. He has suggested in terms that
5 attempts by him to foster a close relationship with
6 the family were frustrated by a confrontational
7 attitude adopted by the family's representatives, in
8 particular by Mr Khan. We will need to investigate
9 that. Is that a valid criticism?
10 A suggestion has been made by, in fact, the
11 representative of the Greenwich Action Committee
12 Against Racial Attacks that the Anti-racist Alliance,
13 and I quote from the statement from the Greenwich
14 action committee representative, "had already set up
15 camp in the home of the Lawrence's and began to
16 control their communications with outside parties."
17 So what was the relevance, we will be asking, of the
18 ARA and what, if any, impact it did have upon police
19 relations with the family?
20 Mr Khan has been invited to assist the Inquiry
21 in this and a number of other respects, and has
22 kindly and properly agreed to provide an account of
23 his involvement so as to enable you to assess this
24 issue. At the time of speaking we still await and
25 look forward to receiving this statement.

Page 62

1 A separate issue arises in relation to the
2 handling and treatment of Stephen's friend, Duwayne
3 Brooks. He was obviously a vital witness, and he was
4 obviously and understandably much traumatised by the
5 murder. He failed to be treated, he should have been
6 treated, we suggest, both as a witness and as,
7 himself, a victim. I do not know what, if anything,
8 he can or will be able to tell us now. I earnestly
9 hope that he will be able to help this Inquiry and
10 that we will have an indication through his
11 representative of what his current recollection is.
12 The Inquiry will wish to consider how Duwayne
13 Brooks was dealt with by the police at the hospital
14 and immediately afterwards. Did the police consider
15 that he required support as a traumatised victim? If
16 so, what did they do about it? Appearances are not
17 much, if anything. He, of course, also required
18 careful handling as a main eyewitness. "Was that
19 done?", we will ask.
20 Within a few hours of the murder he, Duwayne
21 Brooks, made his first witness statement. The
22 reference to it, and other references, are in the
23 note to which I am referring. I am not going, as you
24 will have seen, to the majority of these documents:
25 we all know where to find them. He made a statement

Page 63

1 within hours of the murder. He described there at
2 least one of the attackers. That is in the early
3 hours of 23rd April.
4   He was not asked to assist in the preparation of
5 any photo-fit. That is probably an old-fashioned
6 phrase, but photo-fit, E-fit I think it is sometimes
7 called but you know what I mean: an attempt to
8 reconstruct a picture of the person described. No
9 attempt was made apparently to ask him to assist in
10 that respect until nearly two weeks had gone by, the
11 6th May. Why so long? He was not alone in being a
12 witness who had described those who had been involved
13 in the attack or were seen near to the attack who
14 were equally much to blame (those who were asked) in
15 being asked to give assistance in providing photo-fit
16 descriptions or similar. That is a matter of serious
17 concern.
18   He, Mr Brooks, was first asked to attend an
19 identity parade on the 7th May when, as a matter of
20 fact, he did not pick out a Jamie Acourt who was on
21 the parade. On the 13th May he did identify Neil
22 Acourt on another parade, but not Dobson and Norris.
23 The parades themselves were, of course, not being
24 held until two or three weeks after the murder. If
25 there had been, as you may conclude there should have

Page 64

1 been, earlier arrests, there would presumably have
2 been earlier parades while the matters were still
3 fresher in the minds of those who were asked to
4 attempt an identification.
5   On 3rd June, Mr Brooks identified Knight on
6 another parade. Knight had been arrested that day.
7 It was primarily the identifications by Mr Brooks of
8 Neil Acourt and Knight that led to each of those men
9 being charged with the murder of Stephen Lawrence.
10 Unfortunately, there is an issue of fact that arises,
11 and which arose some time ago, relating to Mr Brooks
12 identification of those suspects. A Sergeant Crowley
13 asserts that at the time of the parade when Knight
14 was identified Mr Brooks made some comments to him,
15 suggesting that he had received information before
16 the parade, which may have enabled him to make the
17 identification or prompted him as to who to
18 identify. Those comments, if true, would plainly
19 also have devalued his earlier identification of Neil
20 Acourt.
21   Mr Brooks, in previous accounts that we have
22 seen, disputed that Crowley's account was accurate.
23   We must try to resolve this. The importance of
24 it is obvious. Mr Brook's identification of those
25 suspects was vital. The private prosecution that

Page 65

1 followed much later was forced, in effect, to be
2 abandoned once his, Mr Brook's evidence, was excluded
3 by the judge by reason of the background
4 circumstances, in particular the assertions made by
5 Crowley. There in particular, we will seek the
6 assistance of Mr Brooks, if he is able and willing,
7 and also of Mr Khan, who we know to be both able and
8 willing.
9   Later on Duwayne Brooks was himself arrested and
10 charged -- this happened in October of 1993 -- in
11 respect of allegations of criminal damage and violent
12 disorder at a protest rally that took place at
13 Welling on 8th May 1993. That is, coincidently, the
14 day after the arrests, the first arrests, were made
15 and the day after Duwayne Brooks had attended the
16 first identity parade at the police station.
17   Why his arrest was so delayed is not apparent,
18 because there are indications that a police officer
19 or officers in fact recognised him, Duwayne Brooks,
20 from his having attended at the police station for
21 the parade. But six months or so, five months in
22 fact to be precise, went by and he was arrested.
23 There was protracted correspondence between his
24 solicitors and the Crown Prosecution Service, who
25 rejected representations made by Miss Deighton on his

Page 66

1 behalf that the case should be discontinued on
2 medical and other grounds but in fact a Crown Court
3 judge in December of 1994 stayed the case anyway,
4 describing it as an abuse of process.
5   We have mainly to consider the extent to which
6 those events affected Duwayne Brooks, in particular
7 as a witness in the Stephen Lawrence case, and we
8 will ask whether more regard should have been had,
9 and with what result, as to his status in that case,
10 the Stephen Lawrence case, when the Authorities
11 decided to bring and to continue the Welling
12 prosecution.
13   So the handling and the treatment of Duwayne
14 Brooks is a matter which, in the respects I have
15 identified and perhaps others, will fall for careful
16 consideration; as will the handling by the police of
17 information which they received immediately after the
18 murder; and we will need to consider the reaction, or
19 lack of it, to important information.
20   On the evening of the 23rd April, there first
21 came on to the scene a man who has been given the
22 name "Grant". It is not his real name, but that is
23 what we are all going to refer to him as and the
24 police refer to him as. It is a pseudonym. He came
25 to provide some information at the police station.

Page 67

1 The information he provided accused the Acourts and
2 Norris of Stephen Lawrence's murder. It identified
3 Norris as having allegedly previously stabbed Stacey
4 Benefield, the name I mentioned a little while ago.
5 　He asserted that someone called Thompson, who
6 had just been convicted of a racist murder -- you
7 will remember I mentioned Thompson and Rohit Duggal
8 -- that he was part of the Acourt gang. He asserted
9 that they, the gang, had stabbed a boy called Lee in
10 Woolwich. You may remember I referred briefly and in
11 passing to a young man called Lee Pearson who
12 referred, when seen, to having been the victim of a
13 stabbing attack.
14 　That information, received at the police station
15 desk by a constable, was reported immediately and,
16 not surprisingly, by Budgen, the constable, to
17 Detective Inspector Bullock, who was the deputy
18 senior investigating officer at this stage. It
19 appears to have been greeted with considerable
20 indifference by Bullock. He told Budgen just to
21 record it; so Budgeon did as he was told and he
22 cannot be blamed for that.
23 　We can look, if we may, at the message. You
24 will see it on PCA 47 at 363. You will see at the
25 top the date, the 23rd April, the time is in the

Page 69

1 　He went on to say that a young Pakistani boy was
2 murdered last year in Well Hall, that Peter Thompson,
3 who is serving life, was part of a gang, the Acourt's
4 gang, "but in fact one of the Acourts killed this
5 lad. They also stabbed a young lad at Woolwich Town
6 Centre called Lee. He had a bag placed over his head
7 and was stabbed in his legs and arms in order to
8 torture him."
9 　Then, as you see, descriptions are given of
10 Jamie and Neil Acourt. They are both twins.
11 Apparently the house they live in was occupied by
12 their mum who has since left and, significantly:
13 "Believed identity of informant was established." It
14 appears clear that the police were aware from a very
15 early stage who, in fact, Grant was; and they
16 certainly had the means to contact him.
17 　There one sees, and perhaps one should bear in
18 mind what I referred to a little earlier when we
19 looked at the other message from witness DD on the
20 house to house inquiries on the same day, here one
21 sees yet further and much more specific information
22 being given to the police about those who allegedly
23 had committed the attack on Saturday evening. So far
24 as we can tell, nothing was done in reaction to that
25 vital information until the 27th April.

Page 68

1 early evening. You see the indication is "male,
2 pars" -- particulars, no doubt -- "refused" is in the
3 identity box at the top. This is the contemporaneous
4 note that was taken by DC Budgen, whose name appears
5 on that, he having been instructed by Bullock to
6 record the information being received. There is some
7 crossing out that appears on here that has come
8 about, in part, inadvertently. What I am going to
9 ask, if I may, having seen the original message, so
10 to speak, if we look at PCA 50 at 165, we find that
11 conveniently there is set out in the Kent Report the
12 text of that message in legible form.
13 　If we can start further down at page at 12.2/11
14 please. There you see the message: "A male attended
15 RM" -- that is the police station -- "and stated that
16 the persons responsible for the murder of the black
17 youth are Jamie and Neil Acourt", and the address is
18 given, "together with Norris and two other males,
19 identity unknown. The Acourt brothers call
20 themselves the Krays'. In fact, you can only join
21 their gang if you stab someone. They carry knives
22 and weapons most days. Also Norris stabbed a Stacey
23 Benefield a month ago in order to prove himself.
24 Benefield was taken to Brook Hospital and told police
25 he did not know who had assaulted him."

Page 70

1 　Can we look, please, at PCA/47/403. You will
2 see the name Budgen we have seen before, and a
3 detective sergeant called Davidson. It may be that
4 he is going to suggest that there was some earlier
5 unrecorded contact with Grant but, if so, it was
6 unrecorded and no details are available.
7 　The first recorded further contact with him is
8 this, on the evening of 27th April, and we should
9 look because it is important to see what he said. He
10 met with the informant known as James Grant in a
11 local pub. He states that the person was approached
12 by some blacks to find out the Acourts' address and
13 then was threatened by the Acourts not to tell
14 them. "The lad in question is" -- and is someone we
15 are going to call witness BB -- whose address or
16 whereabouts was given. He also stated that another
17 witness, who we are going to call CC, saw the four
18 assailants run past the house -- the address is
19 given -- after the assault. He was left tasked --
20 that is Grant was left tasked -- to find out any more
21 that he could.
22 　Can we go on to the next page, page 404: "Grant
23 then rang" -- this is the same date -- "to say that
24 he thinks he may have found a witness who" -- I
25 cannot read the next word -- "stated to him that" --

Page 71

1 and then another witness's name is revealed. He said
2 that this witness was on a bus. "He is going to firm
3 up on the information and contact us." He states
4 that the Acourts and Norris will probably say
5 nothing -- I am sorry; my eyes are tired -- would
6 probably say nothing, but that Dobson would crack up
7 and probably tell all. He also said, and this may be
8 significant, that there was a fifth blond, unknown
9 kid present.
10   Looking ahead, we are going to want to know, and
11 I anticipate you are going to want to know, what, if
12 any, inquiry was made about the blond boy. As far as
13 we know, he was not one of the five -- the five
14 suspects, that is, as I have defined them.
15   In relation to that information emanating from
16 the man Grant, it will be necessary to demand an
17 answer to why there was no quicker reaction to the
18 original information given by him on the Saturday
19 evening -- forgive me, on the Friday initially. We
20 will ask whether attempts should have been made to
21 debrief him further to ascertain from him from whom
22 he had got the information.
23   The Kent investigators who looked into this when
24 the PCA Kent investigation was going on discovered
25 from Grant who his informant in turn had been. That

Page 72

1 informant will not be named, for similar reasons to
2 those I have given; but why was that not discovered
3 by the Metropolitan Police if years later it was
4 capable of being discovered with apparent ease by the
5 Kent investigators?
6   There has been some reference to Grant, as being
7 an anonymous informant and, therefore, dismissable as
8 such. Some in the original investigation team so
9 described him and that description, apparently, was
10 adopted by Chief Superintendent Barker, as he was
11 when he conducted his review later on in the year.
12 He was not anonymous. His true identity was known.
13 He was not, at the time, it is right to say, a
14 registered informant, but he became one afterwards.
15   From the outset, the police had the means of
16 contacting him, and it cannot be any excuse of what
17 on its face is the inexcusable failure prompted to
18 follow up that up that his information could be
19 simply dismissed as being anonymous tittle tattle.
20   In addition, there was material which
21 substantially corroborated some of Grant's
22 information also coming in and this was anonymous.
23 On the 23rd April an anonymous caller gave
24 information linking the killers of Stephen Lawrence
25 to those who had attacked Stacey Benefield.

Page 73

1   Just to glance at one of those messages, PCA/47
2 at 360. Do you see the date and the time again? The
3 23rd April, the day after the killing, 9 o'clock in
4 the evening, an anonymous female: "I think I may
5 know the person who committed the murder of the black
6 boy. I don't know their names. May be I can find
7 out. Two white boys who hang around Eltham with
8 knives and I think they are the Krays." "I think they
9 are the Krays." "They stabbed a boy called Stacey in
10 Nottingham, or New Eltham. I will try to find out
11 more and call you back." That dove tails, you may
12 think, very much with the Grant information.
13   The same female later -- I will only deal with
14 one of the other messages -- did call back. Can we
15 look at 47 at 380, please. The following afternoon,
16 as you can see, the 24th; the same female who phoned
17 twice on the 23rd: "The boys who did your murder,
18 there are five of them, not six like the paper said.
19 One is called Dobson", and the address is given,"the
20 two main boys are Neil and Jamie Acourt. They call
21 themselves `the Krays'. They are real nutters. Be
22 careful when you go and arrest them: their house is
23 full of knives."
24   I will pause there. We will be looking later
25 also at the searches of those houses. Having regard

Page 74

1 to the information that was received, it seems
2 curious, to put it at its lowest, that there was not
3 a more thorough search for knives.
4   Their address was given, as you see. "They
5 stabbed Stacey Benefield, who is white, about two
6 months ago." The picture was developing and building
7 up, as we can see, in the hours and days immediately
8 after the murder, pointing to the five suspects, or
9 at least some of them. There was other anonymous
10 information provided. It is referred to in summary
11 form in the Kent Report. We will in due course be
12 looking at it, asking what should have been done and
13 was anything done adequately to follow it up. I am
14 not going to detail that at the moment.
15   It is, however, necessary that I revert to
16 dealings with the DD family, if I may call them that,
17 as I have to because their identity is protected. It
18 may be remembered that DD was the source of the
19 information that is recorded (if we may see it again,
20 please) on PCA 47 at 397.
21   DD had given information, we will remind
22 ourselves, on the Saturday evening. Constable
23 Bennet , which is obviously second-hand, what she had
24 been told of the Acourts and of them being seen in
25 the vicinity that very night. The indications in

Page 75

1　respect of that, as I have previously mentioned, are
2　that no action was raised in the sense of a technical
3　police term -- in lay language, nothing was done
4　about it -- until the 30th April when it was decided
5　that something ought to be done about it; and on 1st
6　May something was done about it insofar as following
7　it up was allocated to a detective Sergeant called
8　Chase. Why so late?
9　　　Why, we will be asking, was no connection
10　apparently made by the investigating officers with
11　the Grant information? It was obviously important
12　since DD was doing no more than passing on what she
13　had learnt from others; it was obviously vitally
14　important that those others be tracked down and seen
15　and sought to be pumped for information just as soon
16　as possible. If the delays that occurred were due to
17　a failure by the incident room staff to bring this
18　information sufficiently quickly to the attention of
19　the SIOs -- that is the senior investigating officers
20　-- was that because of some serious flaw in the
21　system for communication of information? Or was this
22　lapse due to oversight, an error of judgment, or
23　what? We do not know. It needs to be pursued.
24　　　Additionally and associated with the DDs, the
25　EEs and the FFs -- all came from one family, that

Page 76

1　much has to be revealed -- some anonymous letters
2　were recovered. Later on they were tracked down to
3　that same family.
4　　　May we look, please, at PCA 45, 341? This is a
5　letter that was left in a phone box in Eltham on the
6　23rd April and was handed in to the police by some
7　strangers who just happened to come cross it. It
8　says, as you can see in terms: "The people involved
9　in last night's stabbing are", and gives the names of
10　the Acourts, Norris and Dobson. "Names 1 and 2",
11　Neil Acourt and David Norris, "also rumoured with
12　Wimpy Bar stabbing in Eltham." You will remember I
13　told you of the young lad who was stabbed in the
14　Wimpy bar. "Name 1" -- that is Neil Acourt -- "was
15　definitely seen in the area prior to the stabbing.
16　"Names 2 and 1" -- that is Neil Acourt and David
17　Norris -- are ringleaders and are positive knife
18　users. The first three of them", it says,"share a
19　house" -- the address is given, and the address is
20　given of the other.
21　　　Can we go to the next page, page 342: "One of
22　these names stabbed that poor lad. The names 1 and
23　2, Neil Acourt and Norris, are very dangerous knife
24　users who always carry knives and quite like using
25　them. The same two have stabbed before. Stacey

Page 77

1　Benefield was their victim about six weeks ago."
2　Indications are given where he lived. "These bastards
3　were definitely involved and must be stopped because
4　they keep getting away with it. This is not a BNP"
5　-- British National Party, I suppose -- "related
6　incident. I must stress this. Approach these chaps
7　with care. Do us all a favour and prove it. Good
8　luck."
9　　　Later it was established that that came from one
10　of those who had given the information to the lady we
11　are calling DD. If only he had been seen quicker,
12　what was anonymous information in that letter could
13　have been turned, surely, into firm evidence.
14　　　There was another similar letter. I will not
15　trouble you with it at the moment. It is to a very
16　similar effect and, obviously, even to a layman, in
17　much the same handwriting that was left anonymously
18　on a police car the next day. We have got it and we
19　will look at it later. The investigators linked it,
20　properly and sensibly, with the other letter and to
21　the DD family and later they recorded that the
22　witness we are calling FF from that family had
23　admitted the authorship of both letters. Was any
24　effective action taken in following up that letter?
25　If not, why not?

Page 78

1　　　There was other information received. I shall
2　not turn to it in detail. A concerned parent, as he
3　described him or herself, sent a letter to the police
4　which arrived by post in early May, identifying Neil
5　or Jamie Acourt as responsible, with others, for
6　Stephen's murder. Seemingly, nothing was done to try
7　to identify the author or how he or she would know
8　and what, if any, evidence the author could have
9　given.
10　　　There are other instances of information having
11　been received set out in summary in the Kent Report,
12　which identified the Acourts, amongst others, as
13　allegedly involved in the murder. That, too, does
14　not seem to have been followed up with any vigour by
15　the investigating officers. Why not?
16　　　As I indicated initially, one of the crunch or
17　crucial questions for this Inquiry in relation to the
18　police conduct may be to ask: having regard to the
19　wide variety of different sources that purported to
20　identify the culprits and the coincidence of those
21　identifications, why were not arrests and searches
22　carried out much, much more quickly? The police, if
23　they can, must answer the indictment of delay.
24　　　There were other allegations that were made, as
25　I have already indicated, against the main suspects

Page 79

1 apart from their involvement in the murder of Stephen
2 Lawrence. I have referred to a number of those
3 already. Let me just briefly remind you of some
4 aspects of it and of the evidence that will be given.
5   So far as Stacey Benefield was concerned, he was
6 at least seen reasonably promptly on the 25th April
7 and made a statement. As the informants had
8 suggested accurately it had occurred, this incident,
9 only a matter of weeks previously. He said in terms
10 that he had been confronted in the street by Norris
11 and stabbed with something he described as "a
12 miniature sword with about a 9 inch blade". He
13 expressly said that he would willingly support a
14 prosecution. After that Norris and Neil Acourt
15 could, and we suggest should, have been arrested
16 without delay. Why were they not?
17   Instead the police took a statement from his,
18 Benefield's companion, the statement they took on the
19 28th April from someone called Farman. He supported
20 Benefield's account. He, too, was willing to assist
21 in a prosecution of the attackers. Still no arrests
22 were made. In fact no action was taken in relation
23 to the Benefield allegations, which on their face
24 must have appeared to be open and shut, until the
25 13th May when the two, Norris and Neil Acourt, were

Page 80

1 arrested having, of course, previously by then been
2 arrested on the murder matter. This gives cause for
3 consideration whether, if they had been arrested much
4 more promptly, there would have been a better
5 opportunity to gather evidence for forensic
6 scientific examination and for parades to be held
7 more quickly, so that those who were asked to attend
8 could do so while the vision of that awful night
9 remained at its freshest in their memory.
10   As a matter of history, Norris in due course was
11 tried for the assault on Benefield. Before the
12 trial, Benefield alleged that attempts had been made
13 to buy him off by those purporting to represent
14 Norris's interests. There were allegations, serious
15 allegations, of jury knobbling (if I may be forgiven
16 the colloquialism) when Norris was acquitted. It is
17 not to undermine his acquittal, that it is to record
18 a fact in that those allegations were made.
19   It leaves one to wonder whether there was
20 someone behind the scenes protecting Norris and his
21 friends, not only in respect of the Benefield
22 allegation that in respect of this investigation,
23 because we do know of numerous witnesses, actual and
24 potential, who were frightened to come forward. The
25 question that may fall to be answered is whether

Page 81

1 police knowledge of the Norris family should have
2 caused them to take further steps to reassure the
3 actual and the potential witnesses as to their
4 safety.
5   You will recall that Grant made reference to
6 Lee. Lee, I have told you, was apparently Lee
7 Pearson and we have looked at aspects of his case
8 already. We have also looked, when looking through
9 the summary in the Kent Report, at the allegations by
10 the Witham brothers that I will not trouble you with
11 further. Again, it is not to undermine the
12 significance of that incident, but I have dealt with
13 it already in opening.
14   I have also referred passingly to Kevin London,
15 the 16 year old lad. He was drawn to the attention
16 of the police at the end of April. Four weeks later
17 someone got around to taking a statement from him
18 when he complained of having been threatened in the
19 street with a knife by Dobson. There is no apparent
20 reason why he was not seen earlier. His evidence was
21 supported by his girlfriend, who made a similar
22 statement. Both were prepared to support police
23 action, but it does not seem that a prosecution was
24 even contemplated. One is bound to ask: "Why not?"
25   So, overall, looking at this information as

Page 82

1 well, this Inquiry will be asking how, if at all, did
2 the police react to that large volume of
3 information? Was the action that they did take
4 sufficient? And, taken together with the information
5 to which I have already referred relating to the
6 identity of Stephen's murderers, how could the delay
7 and inaction possibly be justified?
8   It seems part of the justification that may be
9 sought to be put forward was that it was deemed
10 appropriate to carry out some surveillance and we
11 will be looking at that as well. Some of the
12 principal suspects were under surveillance from the
13 26th April: firstly, the Acourts and then a few days
14 later Norris. Why, if surveillance was thought to be
15 appropriate, was it not started much earlier? Bear
16 in mind the information received on the 23rd is not
17 explained.
18   What was the object of this surveillance
19 operation? One of the constables, called Smith, had
20 understood that the objective, as he has explained,
21 was to provide evidence of association between the
22 various suspects. If that is right, then it would
23 appear that there had been already numerous sources
24 of information alleging association between them. If
25 those sources had been properly followed up, it is

Page 83

1 difficult to see why this surveillance operation was
2 necessary.
3 　　If the object was to provide evidence of
4 association, then it is another curious and
5 disturbing feature of the conduct of this case that
6 the fact that Dobson and Norris had been seen and
7 photographed together and, thus, that is evidence of
8 association, that that fact was not deployed when
9 Dobson on his arrest on the 7th May denied or
10 declined to admit that there was any association. So
11 arrests were delayed, apparently, in part for
12 surveillance to be carried out so as to provide
13 evidence of association, and then no use was made of
14 it whatsoever. I do not know; perhaps this
15 demonstrates that there was a failure of
16 communication between the surveillance teams and the
17 investigating officers. We will have to look into
18 that.
19 　　There was a particularly crass failure, as it
20 seems to us provisionally, in these respects. A
21 photographer was put in place to keep surveillance on
22 the Acourts. Before he got his camera set up on the
23 26th April, he saw somebody leaving their house with
24 what was, appeared to be, or might have been clothing
25 in a bin bag, get into a car and clear off. He

Page 84

1 actually photographed Neil Acourt doing the same
2 thing the following day. He made no report at the
3 time of either of these events. It is fair to say
4 that he had not been told to do so, and incredibly,
5 even if he had been total to do so, he could not
6 because no-one had had the brainwave of giving him a
7 telephone, so he had no means of communication.
8 　　So what was or might have been (and we can only
9 speculate) important evidence was lost, because
10 no-one knows where they went or what was in the
11 bags. I have described that provisionally as being a
12 crass failure. Is that a justified criticism? And,
13 if so, why did it happen?
14 　　I have already indicated there are sensitivities
15 in relation to the surveillance operations. The
16 photographs themselves will not be produced. You,
17 sir, have seen all of them and are satisfied, as I
18 understand, that the description of their contents
19 accurately and adequately satisfies and will satisfy
20 the evidential requirement. The reason for the
21 photos not being produced is that to which I have
22 already referred: principally for the protection of
23 others.
24 　　We will have in relation to the surveillance
25 operation the advantage of expert evidence from a

Page 85

1 gentleman by the name of Pitham, who is responsible
2 for training Regional Crime Squads and others in
3 surveillance techniques.
4 　　May I deal, please, with a separate issue: the
5 treatment of other important witnesses -- that is in
6 addition to Duwayne Brooks. There were a number of
7 such witnesses, including eyewitnesses or near
8 eyewitnesses, if I may so describe them. The
9 question that will arise is whether opportunities
10 were missed and lost by a failure promptly to follow
11 up the lines of inquiry that were provided by such
12 witnesses. If witnesses had been handled
13 differently, might reluctant or frightened witnesses
14 have been more forthcoming? It should, surely, have
15 been woefully apparent to the investigators that some
16 witnesses would be reluctant, would be frightened.
17 Did they, in fact, appreciate that, the police? What
18 did they do about it, if they did? And how
19 effectively?
20 　　Two of the more important eyewitnesses,
21 gentlemen known as Westbrook and Shepherd -- in some
22 of the documents you will find them referred to as A
23 and C respectively but it is no longer believed
24 necessary to disguise their true identity -- both of
25 those lads had been at the bus stop immediately

Page 86

1 before the murder, so they were obviously vital
2 witnesses. Mr Westbrook made a statement on the 24th
3 April giving a detailed description of one of the
4 attackers. He was never asked to provide any help in
5 producing a photo-fit or artist's impression. Why
6 not?
7 　　Weeden suggested, in his interview by the Kent
8 Constabulary, that Westbrook had been asked and did
9 not think he could identify anybody, of the
10 explanation as to why he was not asked to do that.
11 That seems to be wholly at odds with Westbrook's own
12 statement that he, Westbrook, was "confident about
13 recognising him again".
14 　　Similarly, Mr Shepherd made a statement the
15 morning after the murder, the 23rd. He described
16 four of the men in the attacking group. Nearly two
17 weeks was allowed to go by before, on the 5th May, he
18 was asked to help in providing an artist's
19 description. Why not sooner? There appears to be no
20 sensible explanation for that failure.
21 　　As we will hear, Mr Shepherd got fed up in due
22 course with being mucked about by police and ceased
23 cooperating with them. Might it have been different
24 if he had been seen and dealt with properly and
25 sensitively much earlier?

Page 87

1   There were other witnesses near to the scene,
2 again summarised in the Kent Report, that we can look
3 at later but not in this opening, where we will need
4 to consider whether there was adequate follow up or
5 not.
6   I have already mentioned and questioned the
7 adequacy of the follow-up in relation to the DD
8 family. One witness who had been named early on,
9 Emma Cook, as having been in the vicinity, as
10 actually having walked past the bus stop where this
11 had happened, was not seen immediately. It became
12 obvious that she knew the principle suspect. Could
13 she have been coaxed into being more forthcoming? No
14 statement was actually taken from her but we may, if
15 we can, seek to call her to give evidence in these
16 proceedings.
17   There are two witnesses, important witnesses,
18 whose identity is protected who are witnesses B and
19 K. Much later, in November, the witness known as B
20 admitted to police having seen Norris and at least
21 one of the Acourts running in Rochester Way near the
22 murder scene at about the time of the murder. It is
23 inevitably speculative that, if he had been seen
24 promptly and handled properly, might that information
25 have been gleaned from him at the time? Also, might

Page 88

1 it have been possible to ascertain that K, as Grant's
2 source, was Grant's source and might he have been
3 pumped for further information?
4   Others I have referred to in the note that you
5 have before you, I will simply refer to them briefly
6 and pass on as examples of those who were not
7 followed up promptly. Dean Roughton and his
8 description given to the police on the 26th, of
9 seeing youths near the scene, one wiping a large
10 knife on his trousers, giving descriptions, nothing
11 done about it until 3rd May 1993, over a week later.
12 A lady, Mrs Gooch, reported hearing a conversation
13 between youths after the murder, apparently relating
14 to the murder. When this was put to Mr Bullock in
15 his interview by Kent, he agreed that the description
16 which he had given of one of them was reminiscent of
17 Norris. She did that -- she made that report on the
18 27th. An action was raised -- that is the action was
19 entered into the computer -- the following day, the
20 28th April, and a week then went by before anybody
21 went around to see Mrs Gooch. Why the delay?
22   When the arrests were finally made on the 7th
23 May, that is of the Acourts and of Dobson -- Norris
24 was not home but he was arrested by appointment on
25 the 10th -- the reasons for the arrest, as Weeden

Page 89

1 recorded them, were that they were known associates;
2 that there were artist's impressions from witnesses
3 similar to the Acourts; that there was information
4 from various sources as to their involvement in the
5 murder, allegations in possession of knives;
6 allegations of possession of knives and a strong
7 possibility that they were in the vicinity of the
8 murder.
9   If those were the reasons for the arrest, they
10 would have applied with equal force the weekend
11 almost two weeks previously. We will seek an
12 explanation, if there is one, as to why there was not
13 a more expeditious, not hasty, expeditious arrest
14 effected.
15   Perhaps before leaving the question of
16 information that was being received, perhaps I can
17 add passingly reference to this. From time to time
18 suggestions have been made that police officers were
19 being met with what was described as a wall of
20 silence. That does not seem to be borne out by the
21 sort of information we have been looking at, which
22 are only examples of information that was being
23 received from within the community about the apparent
24 identity of the attackers.
25   May I mention briefly, as I have done before,

Page 90

1 the blonde haired man. He was described, as we saw,
2 or mentioned, by Grant. Others, Mr Brooks, Shepherd,
3 Westbrook, all spoke of a blonde or fair haired man.
4 That would not seem to fit any of those five who were
5 ultimately arrested. So we will ask what effort was
6 made to identify the blonde haired man. If none,
7 then why?
8   You will remember that Duwayne Brooks had
9 originally suggested that there were six attackers in
10 the group. There were a number of other suspects
11 that the police had to look at. One must be balanced
12 about this. Of course they had to consider other
13 suspects. Some attention will be devoted in the
14 course of the Inquiry to the extent to which
15 attention was distracted by having to consider those
16 other suspects and we will look at the criteria that
17 were used to eliminate them.
18   As I have mentioned already, turning to the
19 arrests, the arrests and interviews of the main
20 suspects took place a night apart in May: the two
21 Acourts and Dobson on 7th, arrested Norris on 10th,
22 Knight arrested on 3rd June. All of these dates set
23 out helpfully in Miss Weekes's chronology. It is our
24 chronology, really, Miss Weekes has done all of the
25 hard work on it. As I have already mentioned, Norris

Page 91

1 and Neil Acourt were also arrested on 13th May for
2 the Benefield attack. They were promptly identified
3 on identification parades by Benefield and his friend
4 Farman and were charged then with attempted murder.
5 As I have suggested, they could have been arrested
6 for that matter, if no other, on 24th April.
7   Obviously, an officer in charge of an
8 investigation of this sort has to exercise judgment.
9 If it is to be the case that the delay in effecting
10 the arrests is attributable to the exercise of a
11 judgment by the senior officer then we will
12 respectfully suggest that his judgment was seriously
13 flawed. That is a matter to be considered when the
14 evidence is given. There are areas for concern in
15 relation to the searching of the suspect's premises.
16 It must be acknowledged, and I do not think you need
17 to be a policeman for this, if you leave the search
18 for two weeks it is not likely to be particularly
19 fruitful unless you are particularly thorough in the
20 way in which you, the officer, carry it out. We need
21 to ask how thorough the searches were.
22   At a pre-briefing prior to the searches and
23 arrests there was a suggestion made, according to a
24 police officer, that the Acourts were prone to hide
25 knives under the floorboards in their house. One

Page 92

1 might have thought that would have given some police
2 officer a clue that it might be a good idea to look
3 under the floorboards but apparently nobody did.
4   Whilst instructions were given to seize blood
5 stained clothing the chances of finding which two
6 weeks on must have been remote in the extreme and you
7 remember the opportunities lost when the surveillance
8 man simply watched dumbly as apparent clothing was
9 leaving the premises. No instructions were given to
10 carry out any tests to detect blood otherwise in the
11 premises on other clothing, on soft furnishing,
12 towelling, et cetera. Why not?
13   The interviews that took place of the suspects
14 fall to be considered in examining the police
15 conduct. The police certainly had plenty of time to
16 prepare for the interviews. One consequence at least
17 of the delayed arrests. Only Dobson of the initial
18 group answered questions in interview. As I have
19 said, no association with Norris was admitted by him,
20 but he was not confronted with the surveillance
21 evidence that was available. The Kent officer has
22 suggested that this is the result of a lack of
23 planning and preparation; is that a valid criticism?
24   Similar criticisms were made by the Kent
25 officers of the non-productive Acourt interviews;

Page 93

1 they would not answer questions. Could those
2 interviews have been better structured? Would it
3 have made any difference? Would the Acourts, in any
4 event, have stayed silence?
5   Norris too answered no questions when he was
6 interviewed after his arrest on the 10th. A Kent
7 officer has suggested this might have been because
8 the interview was conducted, "in a shallow manner and
9 showed a lack of structure and lack of objective".
10 You will need to consider whether that is a
11 justifiable criticism.
12   As is the case in respect of Knight, belatedly
13 arrested on 3rd June 1993, he answered questions, he
14 made no admissions and the interviewing technique and
15 preparation is similarly criticised by the Kent
16 investigators. You will need to decide whether those
17 criticisms are justified, if not understated.
18   I have mentioned a number of identification
19 parades which were carried out. The first parade is
20 on 7th May involved Mr Brooks and Mr Shepherd being
21 invited to attend. Why no-one else? We need an
22 answer to that from the other eyewitnesses. The
23 other candidates included Westbrook -- if I drop the
24 Mr from time to time I mean no disrespect, as I hope
25 everyone appreciated -- Mr Westbrook, who the police

Page 94

1 said they could not contact, although why not, it is
2 not readily apparent and a number of others who come
3 into the category of eyewitnesses or those who were
4 nearby and whose details were set out in the note.
5   The parades on the first occasion were not, as
6 you have heard, productive. As is customary an
7 inspector not associated with the case was charged
8 with conducting the parades. You will need to ask
9 whether he was given any or sufficient information to
10 enable him to run them properly and if not why not.
11 In the result that day only Jamie Acourt was put on a
12 parade and was not, in fact, identified by anybody.
13 Those parades planned for Neil Acourt and Dobson had
14 to be postponed.
15   Bullock later asserted that the solicitor acting
16 for the suspects was deliberately obstructive and did
17 his best to discredit the parade by whatever means
18 possible. We need to look into that to see if it is
19 justified and we have asked the solicitor as well for
20 assistance.
21   Mr Shepherd after his experience on 7th May
22 discontented with a number of aspects of the way he
23 had been treated refused to participate in any
24 further parades. The question is to be asked: how
25 could this have been avoided?

Page 95

1   The parades that were arranged after Norris's

2 arrest therefore did not have the benefit of

3 Mr Shepherd appearing to see if he could identify

4 anybody. Only Mr Brooks and Mr Westbrook on this

5 occasion were called along. Why not others?

6   Westbrook did not, in fact, identify either Neil

7 Acourt or Dobson on the parade. He did not see

8 parades of Norris or Jamie Acourt. He had been told,

9 had Westbrook, that he would probably be required for

10 an hour or so at the police station, he was after all

11 a volunteer. Having been kept waiting for some six

12 hours he got fed up and he left. How could that have

13 been avoided?

14   It is right to record that subsequently he did

15 attend further parades on 24th May and did not

16 identify anybody present.

17   I have already mentioned Mr Brooks did identify

18 both Neil Acourt and Knight on different parades.

19 The conduct of those parades, the integrity of them,

20 the circumstances surrounding them, will, for the

21 reasons I have already given, require to be

22 considered in some detail.

23   Now, an issue amongst those that we will be

24 considering is the forensic scientific evidence and

25 the handling of it. For the moment, let me just

Page 96

1 headline what we have in mind there. There are

2 questions arising as to why some tissues found near

3 the scene were not submitted for forensic scientific

4 examination, albeit they appeared to be a

5 bloodstained, why one of those was lost. Why no

6 examination was made of the fibres in the bags that

7 were covering by then, sadly, dead Stephen's hands to

8 compare with any clothing recovered from the

9 suspects. Why, as I have already foreshadowed, there

10 was no more thorough testing examination of the

11 HOLMES of the suspects.

12   The fourteenth of the issues on your statement

13 of issues relates to the management of the first

14 investigation. I am not going to deal with that in

15 any detail by way of opening. Obviously, to the

16 extent, if at all, subject to your findings, that it

17 is established that the investigation did go wrong

18 the ultimate responsibility for that must rest with

19 the managers of that investigation, that is the

20 senior officer's involved.

21   A sub issue, as you have seen, concerns the

22 continuity of the senior investigating officer.

23 There was first a change over after the first

24 weekend. Initially, Crampton, Superintendent as he

25 then was, was in charge. He was taken over by Weeden

Page 97

1 on 26th April. Mr Weeden was unavoidably, and let me

2 say for good and obvious reasons, personal reasons

3 that were compelling, had to be absent from 9th to

4 15th May, during which period there appears amongst

5 others to be some confusion as to who was supposed to

6 be in charge of the operation. So what effect did

7 those changes have on the efficiency and the

8 direction of the investigation? We will be inviting

9 consideration too to the so-called policy file

10 maintained by the senior officer and the adequacy of

11 the record that there appears.

12   One of the sub issues identified there refers to

13 the use of the HOLMES computer. That computer system

14 is reasonably well-known and was used for the

15 purposes of this Inquiry. We on behalf of the

16 Inquiry, in particular I am indebted again, and I am

17 happy to acknowledge it to Miss Weekes for the work

18 she has done on this, we have liaised with

19 independent experts properly called that, an

20 independent expert report we have commissioned from a

21 Detective Chief Superintendent Burdis from the South

22 Yorkshire Police. That force and he have been

23 assisting us in a number of respects. They, of

24 course, are wholly independent of the Metropolitan

25 Police and wholly independent of the Kent Police for

Page 98

1 that matter. His report will, I hope, very shortly

2 be with all of the parties. It refers to many

3 messages and actions recorded on the computer which

4 could identify witnesses and therefore require some

5 editing or redaction, as I have called it.

6   He can exhibit and will comment upon the use

7 that was made of the HOLMES system. He can explain

8 the significance of the record maintained upon it.

9 Interestingly, he indicates that amongst the purposes

10 that can be served by the computer are these: "the

11 system", he says, "should assist investigators to

12 make inquiries to establish whether any person has

13 previously come to the notice of the investigation."

14 If we pause there and we think of that plethora of

15 information from different people about the same

16 names and put it into that context:

17   "It can also provide investigating officers with

18 a ready means of acquiring all the knowledge which

19 the system contains about the Inquiry subjects.

20 Again, the variety of information received by the

21 police as to some or all of the five suspects in the

22 days immediately following the murder ought,

23 therefore, to have readily been capable of being

24 identified and considered."

25   I mention that redactions will be required to be

Page 99

1 made to some of the information referred to and
2 annexed to his, Mr Burdis's report. What will not be
3 redacted but will be put before you in full view for
4 your consideration will be his criticisms that he
5 makes of the investigation team. He will make severe
6 criticisms of the adequacy of the numbers of police
7 allocated to the investigation. He has commented
8 that the staff allocation was, to use his word
9 "inadequate". That the allocation of officers to
10 the major incident room was derisory and that the
11 reduction in already inadequate staffing levels for
12 the weekend of 1st to 3rd May, a bank holiday
13 weekend, was at least surprising.
14   Inadequacy of numbers of staff, police officers,
15 is a recurrent theme throughout his report and will
16 be the subject of his detailed evidence. As an
17 example only he suggests that the first witness
18 statement made by Duwayne Brooks would and should
19 have kept all of the investigating officers available
20 for outside duties busy for the first four days of
21 the Inquiry. If that is right it does indicate that
22 there was woeful, to adopt his adjective "derisory"
23 and obviously very serious questions thus thrown up.
24 Such shortages of manpower if you find that his
25 criticisms are right will in part explain but of

Page 100

1 course not excuse some of the apparently inexplicable
2 reaction. This is an important and in fact new area
3 for this investigation to consider.
4   I refer, if I may, wholly separately to the
5 issue which is described as issues of race. This was
6 a racist murder, there is no doubt about that. It
7 was recognised as such by the police. The attackers
8 were violent thugs, apparently, who did not limit
9 their gratuitously violent attacks to black victims
10 but were nonetheless plainly racist. I am bound to
11 say, it does not require me to say, but I am bound to
12 say that it is repellant that anybody who commits a
13 murder should get away with it and anyone who does so
14 and murders for racist motives and should escape is
15 doubly repellant.
16   It is, of course, a fact that the police
17 investigations have not produced a successful
18 prosecution of anybody for Stephen's murder. So the
19 overall question that I identified earlier does
20 require to be answered: whether the failure in that
21 sense -- the failure to produce a successful
22 prosecution was affected by racism on the part of any
23 or all of the police officers concerned?
24   Those police officers who had the allegation put
25 to them directly, in particular by the Kent

Page 101

1 investigators, have all to a man, woman vehemently
2 denied that they had any racist attitudes or that any
3 racism affected in any way their part in the
4 investigation. Those denials must be tested by
5 examining the conduct of the investigation, finding
6 out then in detail what did go wrong and enabling
7 you, Sir, to assess with the assistance and advice of
8 your colleagues, to assess whether any short comings
9 in the overall failure of the investigation are or
10 may be attributable to police racism.
11   We want no-one to be under any misapprehension
12 that my dealing with this issue at this stage of my
13 opening in any way demotes it in the order of
14 priorities, it does not. We need first to look at
15 the events immediately concerning the investigation
16 of Stephen's death, and that I have done in outline,
17 and now I wish to return to the topic I mentioned at
18 the outset as being important, the relevance of race
19 to all aspects of this Inquiry.
20   We must surely first seek to ascertain what
21 happened when we, more particularly when you, can see
22 what happened and what went wrong and then you will
23 want to know why things happened or did not happen.
24 The issue of race has been at the forefront of our
25 minds in preparation for this case and will be known

Page 102

1 to remain at the forefront of the minds of this
2 Inquiry throughout. It is to be noted that contained
3 within the issues is a specific reminder to us all,
4 not that reminder is necessary, that the Inquiry will
5 consider whether issues of race affected any or all
6 of all of the other issues to be considered.
7   The issues document sets out a number of
8 sub-issues, I am not going to refer to them in
9 detail, they will be considered, of course. We will,
10 of course, be asking whether any officers were less
11 enthusiastic in their investigation because Stephen
12 and his family were black. Were any problems that
13 occurred in family liaison affected by racism.
14 Similarly, was the handling or treatment of any
15 witness affected by racism.
16   It will be necessary and appropriate to look at
17 the experience of the local police officers of racist
18 crimes of violence, what lessons they have learnt and
19 however at all those lessons were used in the
20 investigation. You have seen already that there was
21 information available about other racist attacks in
22 the area, what use was made of that and what training
23 was given to these officers and what training was
24 given generally to race issues and racist crime.
25 Were there any, and if so what, policy decisions or

Page 103

1 guidance or direction given to the police as to how
2 they should deal with racist attacks.
3   There was, as you know, a unit at Plumstead
4 Police called the Plumstead Racial Incident Unit, set
5 up apparently by reason of police and local concern
6 as to racial tension and in relation to racial
7 attacks. Were the investigators themselves
8 sufficiently aware of those sensitivities and what
9 use was made of or what further use could have been
10 made by the appointed racial incident officer. Those
11 are amongst the questions to be posed and sought to
12 be answered during this Inquiry.
13   We expect to be assisted in finding answers to
14 those and the other questions relating to race from
15 the other represented parties, in particular, if I
16 may say so, from the Commission of Racial Equality,
17 from the London Borough of Greenwich, those who are
18 committed to combatting racism and their specialist
19 knowledge will therefore will invaluable to us and I
20 anticipate to you.
21   If I may then continue and complete this opening
22 in a few more minutes. There are some other issues
23 that require to be considered after the first
24 investigation. The questions arise as to the conduct
25 of the Crown Prosecution Service. The original

Page 104

1 prosecution of Neil Acourt and Knight charged, as you
2 remember, following Duwayne Brooks's identification
3 was formally discontinued on 29th July, 1993
4 following on discussions internally and advice given
5 by counsel. That decision has met with some
6 criticism and so we will ask, was the CPS justified
7 in concluding that the evidence was insufficient?
8 Did it have all of the information it ought to have
9 had from the police to enable it to reach an informed
10 decision? Could or might it, if it was aware of
11 them, and if it had been told of them, have sought to
12 rely upon other attacks apparently by some or all of
13 the same suspects to corroborate the murder
14 allegation.
15   We, hopefully, will be assisted by resolving
16 those issues by evidence which is to be given by
17 representatives, senior and otherwise, from the Crown
18 Prosecution Service.
19   An issue arises in this sense in that we would
20 like to know, you will want to know, how the decision
21 was made to communicate the discontinuance in July
22 1993 to the Lawrences. As I understand it, they
23 heard through the media, which was the least
24 satisfactory way in which they should have been
25 told.

Page 105

1   I have mentioned already the questions arising
2 in relation to the Crown Prosecution Service's
3 decisions concerning Mr Brooks and the Welling
4 prosecution. I will not revisit that.
5   In the course of the Inquiry we will also look
6 at what, in shorthand, is referred to as the Barker
7 Review. Superintendent Barker, as he then was, in
8 the autumn of 1993, was commissioned by Mr Osland,
9 Deputy Assistant Commissioner of the Metropolitan
10 Police to carry out a full review of the
11 investigation to date. We need first to ascertain
12 what the purpose of that review was. Mr Osland
13 himself has candidly said that his hope was that the
14 Review "would show that what we had done was right".
15 Mr Ilsley said that he understood the idea was to
16 bring in a fresh pair of eyes to see if anything had
17 been missed the first time around.
18   Barker was new to the case. He was appointed to
19 conduct the Review, as I say, in the autumn. His
20 terms of reference were finalised in August 1993, you
21 will need to consider how adequate they were, and his
22 report was finally produced on 1st November. He,
23 Barker, was alone amongst the senior officers
24 interviewed or contacted by Kent, who declined to
25 assist in respect of his dealings with the Review.

Page 106

1 Everybody else cooperated fully and it seems
2 Mr Barker was advised to maintain silence. If that
3 is so, he cannot be criticised for what might be
4 thought to be misguided advice. Be that as it may,
5 he has now provided to us answers to the questions
6 that were unanswered in some detail and has provided
7 a substantial and detailed statement describing what
8 he did and did not do.
9   His report in 1993 concluded that the
10 investigation had "progressed satisfactorily and that
11 all lines of inquiry have been correctly pursued"."
12   One is bound to say in the light of what I have
13 described just briefly in the course of this opening,
14 that appears on its face to be a most astonishing
15 conclusion.
16   There are a variety of inaccuracies in that
17 review report set out in the Kent report itself but
18 we might use that as a check list -- it is not
19 exhaustive -- in due course and consider whether
20 those criticisms are justified. Particular attention
21 is obviously going to be required as to the Barker
22 review failing to deal with the follow up, or lack of
23 it, to information received from informants, in
24 particular the Grant and the DD issue.
25   It seems, sadly, but I am afraid consistently,

Page 107

1 that that report too was incompetent. Criticism of
2 the report by itself perhaps would not have been
3 especially relevant to this Inquiry, except of course
4 that the Review presumably gave comfort to the most
5 senior officers in the Metropolitan Police that the
6 original investigation had been properly carried out
7 and that, therefore, nothing else could essentially
8 be done. A properly and constructively critical
9 review ought, surely, to have encouraged there to
10 have been a more thorough and further
11 reinvestigation.
12   It seems the report, the Barker report, in its
13 draft or at least interim state, was discussed by him
14 with, in particular, Weeden and Ilsley, neither of
15 whom, according to the information recently given to
16 us by Barker, expressed any reservation whatsoever
17 about its content. So the Barker review will be
18 looked at.
19   We will also consider with the witnesses in due
20 course, if I can describe this briefly, events after
21 the Barker review. Perhaps it is not appreciated:
22 the Kent Report investigation did not go beyond that
23 at in time. Your terms of reference, sir, require
24 you to consider matters arising to date. You have
25 ruled, as the parties, I hope, remember, but let me

Page 108

1 remind them, that "to date" is not to be given a
2 legalistic interpretation restricting it to say the
3 date of the Home Secretary's announcement of this
4 Inquiry, but is to include anything coming to light
5 since; and indeed anything, as you have said pursuant
6 to your invitation, which anyone who comes forward at
7 this Inquiry while it is running may have to
8 contribute should be considered. So we will look at
9 the ongoing investigation of the murder. The murder
10 investigation did not end in 1993; it continued.
11 There may be some criticism from some as to the
12 adequacy of its continuation but we must wait and
13 see.
14   In July 1994 Weeden retired to be replaced as
15 the senior investigating officer by Superintendent
16 Mellish, who has also now retired.
17   In May 1994 the commander in charge, Commander
18 Nove, had concluded that it was time for "a new
19 investigation" to take a fresh look at the
20 investigation. This was led by Mellish and became
21 known as the second investigation. The extent to
22 which there are complaints about that remains to be
23 seen. We will look at it.
24   We also will have to take into consideration, of
25 course, because it is part of the history of this

Page 109

1 very unhappy saga, is the private prosecution that
2 was brought by the family's representatives in April
3 1995.
4   The Acourts, Knight and Norris were all arrested
5 after informations had been laid at a Magistrates'
6 Court on behalf of the family, alleging their
7 participation in Stephen's murder. Dobson's arrest
8 on the same allegation came a little later.
9   There were contested committal proceedings in
10 the Autumn and in December 1995, separate hearings
11 because of Dobsons' later arrest, the upshot of which
12 is that Jamie Acourt and Norris were discharged by
13 the Stipendiary Magistrate -- that is that he took
14 the view that there was not sufficient evidence for
15 them to be permitted to stand their trial.
16   The other three, that is Neil Acourt, Knight and
17 Dobson were committed to stand their trial at the
18 Central Criminal Court.
19   It is now well-known that that prosecution did
20 not result in a conviction. The case was tried
21 finally in April 1996 at the Central Criminal Court.
22 There was prolonged argument relating to the vital
23 identification evidence by Duwayne Brooks at the end
24 of which the trial judge excluded his evidence. In
25 those circumstances, although he had some other

Page 110

1 evidence at his disposal, it is right, I hope, to say
2 that Mr Mansfield, who was prosecuting that case,
3 had, in effect, little option but to offer no further
4 evidence. The prosecution's case was emasculated by
5 the exclusion of Duwayne Brooks's evidence. Thus,
6 those three defendants: Acourt, Knight and Dobson
7 had to be acquitted. It is not for me to make any
8 assumption as to who was responsible or not for the
9 murder, but it does mean that they having been
10 acquitted, Acourt, Knight and Dobson can never again
11 be charged whatever evidence is forthcoming about the
12 murder of Stephen Lawrence.
13   We cannot ignore the private prosecution, and we
14 do not intend to ignore it. It is one of the matters
15 arising and it should be the subject of proper
16 analysis. We set out some of issues arising,
17 including the roles of the police, the Crown
18 Prosecution Service and the legal advisers in Issue
19 20 of the issue document. We are awaiting further
20 evidence and information from some of those who are
21 involved. There will be time for that to be
22 considered and adjudicated upon by this Inquiry.
23   I think I should add to that, with, I know, your
24 approval, that it does not lie within the remit of
25 this Inquiry to second guess the judicial decision it

Page 111

1 is that have been made during the course of the
2 private prosecution indeed the inquest. So the
3 rights and wrongs of the committal for trial do not
4 fall to be questioned, or the non-committal; and the
5 rights and wrongs of the decision of the trial judge
6 in April 1996 cannot sensibly be the subject of
7 review by this Inquiry, we respectfully suggest.
8 They are part of the history of the case and no more.
9   The inquest, similarly, is not to be questioned
10 -- that is the outcome of it. The much adjourned
11 inquest was finally held in February 1997, after
12 hearing evidence not from the main suspects, who I
13 think it is well-known refused to cooperate. After
14 hearing evidence, the Coroner's jury recorded that
15 Stephen Lawrence was unlawfully killed by five white
16 youths. That is a fact and part of the history of
17 this case.
18   Can I mention, please, briefly, because it is
19 going to arise in due course, that, as everybody here
20 knows, the Kent investigators identified a number
21 (some 11) further lines of inquiry which they
22 suggested ought to be pursued by the Metropolitan
23 Police investigators of the murder. Many of those
24 concerned further pursuit of those who had given
25 information to the police at the time. It has been

Page 112

1 very recent that there has been a report made to us,
2 and to the Lawrence's advisers, about the outcome of
3 those inquiries. It is right to say that no
4 significant progress has been made. Mr Mansfield has
5 been kind enough to indicate to me that there are a
6 number of areas of real dissatisfaction felt on
7 behalf of the family with those further inquiries and
8 the conduct of them, and that is a matter at which we
9 will have to look in some further detail in due
10 course. It has arisen, however, very recently, and
11 rather than my saying anything more about it prior to
12 it being properly researched, for the moment I simply
13 bring it up.
14   I am going to say no more by way of opening in
15 this case. You might have thought I have said quite
16 enough, if not too much, already.
17   As I understand it, after opening addresses,
18 later today, on behalf of the family, Mr and
19 Mrs Lawrence, and on behalf of the Commissioner,
20 brief opening addresses by each, we will begin the
21 evidence tomorrow. We are, and I know you are, very
22 pleased that Mr and Mrs Lawrence are able to assist
23 us and, as I understand it, they will be able to give
24 their evidence tomorrow, starting it tomorrow
25 morning, and that will be evidence, I think wholly

Page 113

1 appropriate, if I may suggest this, which might be
2 led from them by Mr Mansfield. Most witnesses, I
3 think, you will expect me to lead the evidence from
4 the witnesses, but I think in this case it is only
5 appropriate that Mr Mansfield does that.
6   Thereafter, we will embark upon the evidence
7 relating to the issues, as I said, I hope in roughly
8 the order that is set out in the issues document.
9   That is all I say at this time.
10 THE CHAIRMAN: Thank you very much, Mr Lawson. I
11 should indicate that as much prior information as is
12 possible will be given to the press and the public of
13 when witnesses will be called. It may not be
14 possible to stick to what I might call a strict
15 batting order of witnesses, but we will do our best
16 to keep the public informed as to when a particular
17 witness may give evidence.
18   We will shortly adjourn and at 2 o'clock I will
19 ask Mr Mansfield to indicate by his preliminary
20 remarks the position of the family and himself, not
21 in detail of course, but to give him an opportunity
22 to say what he wishes on their behalf; and then
23 Mr Gompertz will do the same, if he so wishes, on
24 behalf of the Commissioner of the Metropolitan
25 Police.

Page 114

1   I am not going to invite any other opening
2 statements. I have indicated that already. That is
3 not, of course, to exclude the point of view of
4 individual officers or Commission for Racial
5 Equality. Everybody will have their full opportunity
6 both to ask questions if necessary when the evidence
7 is given and also to address me at the end. It is
8 much more appropriate that some of those who are
9 represented should summarise the matter to assist us
10 at the end rather than anticipate matters at this
11 stage.
12   May I finally say this. I, too, am very happy
13 that Mr and Mrs Lawrence are here and have indicated
14 that they do wish to give evidence before the
15 Inquiry. I understand, of course, that that may be
16 something of an ordeal for them; and I leave it
17 entirely to Mr and Mrs Lawrence and their advisers to
18 decide how and, indeed, when they give their
19 evidence. If they change their minds and do not wish
20 to give it tomorrow, as the first witnesses, then of
21 course I would understand the position. If they wish
22 to be first to give their evidence tomorrow, that is
23 a matter entirely for them to decide with their
24 advisers. At the moment we will assume that Mr and
25 Mrs Lawrence will wish to do that. Furthermore, if

Page 115

1 they wish part of the statements which they have made
2 to be read by counsel on their behalf to avoid them
3 having to go on for too long in the witness box, I am
4 perfectly happy that that should be done, provided
5 that Mr and Mrs Lawrence wish it. The way in which
6 they give their evidence and the length of their
7 evidence is entirely and wholly a matter for them and
8 their advisers. There may be some questions asked of
9 them, but I am quite sure that the questions asked of
10 Mr and Mrs Lawrence will be both restrained and
11 restricted.
12 　　We will start again at 2 o'clock.
13 　　　　<(Luncheon Adjournment)
14 THE CHAIRMAN: Yes, Mr Mansfield, are you ready?
15 MR MANSFIELD: Yes, I am. I was going to just have a
16 test run by using -- is this working?
17 THE CHAIRMAN: Yes, it is certainly working for us.
18 Can you hear, Mr Mansfield at the back?
19 MR MANSFIELD: If I speak like this does it carry?
20 THE CHAIRMAN: The press are indicating that they can
21 hear too. I think you will find it works pretty well
22
23 MR MANSFIELD: We have had a discussion that some of
24 us feel it is a little bit easier to stand rather
25 than sit because these machines are in the way. May

Page 116

1 I just, before I begin, indicate that there is a
2 fourth member of the team who has not been mentioned
3 yet, she sits to my left, Margot Boye-Anawoma
4 representing the Lawrences.
5 THE CHAIRMAN: Yes, thank you.
6 MR MANSFIELD: May I also indicate that in the light
7 of your very proper suggestions that we keep to
8 certain time limits, I think in the cases of those
9 who follow the Inquiry team, there are two of us, we
10 should approximate to 30 minutes and I will endeavour
11 to do that.
12 THE CHAIRMAN: There will not actually be a red light
13 like there is in the Supreme Court in the States but
14 I think it is sensible to try and limit.
15 MR MANSFIELD: I think so.
16 MR MANSFIELD: Nearly 50 years ago from now, namely
17 in 1948, in the Southern States of America there was
18 a black Baptist minister by the name of Dr Vernon
19 Johns and his parish was a Baptist church in Dexter
20 Avenue, Alabama. Following a series of murders of
21 young black men in that town in 1948 and just before
22 by gangs of white men those murders having gone
23 unchecked, no sanction and in the face of enormous
24 public disapproval and the risk of violent
25 retribution to him he entitled his last sermon, "It

Page 117

1 is safe to murder Negros". He was detained by the
2 police and forced to leave. He did. His successor
3 was Dr Martin Luther King and hence the birth of the
4 Civil Rights movement in the United States of
5 America.
6 　　Dr John's point then and our point on behalf of
7 the Lawrences now is this: Stephen's teenage killers
8 and their close friends and relatives all felt safe
9 in what they did and in the knowledge of what they
10 did. We suggest that the Inquiry needs to examine
11 closely how a climate has been created in which such
12 obvious and overt racism can breed and wreak such
13 appalling habit with impunity.
14 　　In part there are three answers to this: the
15 first is that it lies with those in our community who
16 continue to applaud and support these attitudes and
17 activities. It also lies with those who remain
18 silent or indifferent and who are not prepared to
19 confront such attitudes at source;
20 　　There has already been appropriate reference
21 made to Dantes Divine Comedy and the hottest places
22 in Hell being for those who remain neutral;
23 　　Thirdly, and perhaps most pertinently for this
24 Inquiry, the climate is created by law enforcement
25 agencies which fail to take speedy and effective and

Page 118

1 committed action to pursue such illegality.
2 　　The magnitude of the failure in this case, we
3 say, cannot be explained by mere incompetence or a
4 lack of direction by senior officers or a lack of
5 execution and application by junior officers, nor by
6 woeful under resourcing. So much was missed by so
7 many that deeper causes and forces must be
8 considered.
9 　　We suggest these forces relate to two main
10 propositions. The first is, dealing with the facts
11 themselves, that the victim was black and there was
12 as a result a racism, both conscious and unconscious,
13 that permeated the investigation;
14 　　Secondly, the fact that the perpetrators were
15 white and were expecting some form of provocation and
16 protection. More particularly, obviously,
17 protection.
18 　　Some mention has already been made in opening on
19 behalf of the Inquiry that one of the principal
20 figures and principal suspects in this case had been
21 leading what might be described as a charmed life at
22 the hands of the law. Either, and it is Mr Norris,
23 he was not arrested or if he was arrested and charged
24 it was not proceeded with or if it was proceeded with
25 the trial was aborted.

Page 119

1 The inordinate and extensive delays and
2 inactions, some of which to use the phrase already
3 applied were "crass", give rise to one plain
4 inference and one plain question which we suggest has
5 to be boldly addressed: was the initial investigation
6 ever intended to result in a successful prosecution?
7 The process being undertaken by all of us must
8 begin from a clear and unequivocal premise that this
9 was a racist killing. It may be said that that is
10 rather obvious now, but we remark, hopefully for the
11 last time, that there has been a reluctance in some
12 quarters to recognise this, we say, obvious fact. It
13 was not until the verdict of a jury in Southwark in
14 February of last year could any hesitation about the
15 description of this murder in those terms that could
16 be finally laid to rest, an unprecedented verdict by
17 a jury which said very clearly it was an unprovoked
18 racist attack.
19 The fact that the same teenagers are equally
20 capable of killing or maiming anyone in their way
21 does not preclude them from being racist; racists
22 rarely concentrate their venom on the black
23 population or the Jewish population or whoever
24 happens to be the ethnic group of which they regard
25 as barely worth living.

Page 120

1 The forces that applaud and support and continue
2 to support go unabated up to the doors of this
3 Inquiry, those forces of racism. As you will hear
4 tomorrow when the Lawrences give their evidence that
5 when Doreen Lawrence first left home after this
6 appalling crime, merely to go shopping locally, in a
7 car park she was confronted by a woman who indicated
8 that her son would not have got killed if he had not
9 have been here. This is redolent of certain
10 politicians and speeches in the past about the fact
11 that they should not be here in the first place.
12 It went on, this racist force. Their tyres have
13 been slashed, their home has been watched by white
14 youths and barely two weeks ago the memorial plaque
15 was desecrated, painted daubed and smashed with a
16 hammer. These are activities that the Jewish
17 population are only too familiar with it. It was on
18 the spot where Stephen died.
19 In 1981 on 30th October Lord Scarman in the
20 previous Inquiry to this one which looked copiously
21 at the problem then facing Londoners said this in his
22 conclusions:
23 "The evidence which I have received, the effect
24 of which I have outlined, leaves no doubt in my mind
25 that racial disadvantage is a fact of current British

Page 121

1 life. Urgent action is needed if it is not to become
2 an endemic, irradical disease threatening the very
3 survival of our society. The role of the police is
4 critical. A new approach is required. Determination
5 and persistence in the formulation and application of
6 the necessary polices will be required." That was,
7 we say, prophetic and unfortunately has not yet borne
8 fruit.
9 In 1994, more recently, the Home Affairs
10 Committee, in other words a year after Stephen's
11 death had this to say:
12 "Racism in whatever form is an evil and
13 destructive force in our undeniably multi-racial
14 society. We are in no doubt that racial attacks and
15 racial harassment and the spread of literature which
16 preaches racial hatred are increasing and must be
17 stopped. Racial attacks and harassment now are as
18 bad and probably worse than the last report of this
19 committee in 1989."
20 It is against that background that Mr and
21 Mrs Lawrence, who both arrived in 1960, and will give
22 more detail, where it is necessary, of their
23 individual backgrounds. They have been here,
24 therefore, for 38 years. They have been, both of
25 them, hard working, committed citizens who by

Page 122

1 everyone have been described as a respectable and a
2 law-abiding and themselves both regular church
3 attenders.
4 Nevertheless, it is that family who were driven
5 at the Inquest where the jury came to the very clear
6 conclusion about it being a racist murder began their
7 evidence in this way, and it has to be remembered
8 that this is the strength of the feeling that has led
9 to this Inquiry. Doreen said this:
10 "My son was murdered nearly four years ago. His
11 killers are still walking the streets. When my son
12 was murdered the police saw my son as a criminal
13 belonging to a gang. My son was stereotyped by the
14 police. He was black and he must be a criminal and
15 they set about investigating him and us. The
16 investigation lasted two weeks. That allowed vital
17 evidence to be lost. My son's crime is that he was
18 walking down the road looking for a bus that would
19 take him home. Our crime is living in a country
20 where the justice system supports racist murders
21 against innocent people."
22 It was that force that led them to bury
23 Stephen not in London, not in the United Kingdom but
24 in Jamaica.
25 It has to be said clearly now that had both the

Page 123

1　Lawrences not at the end of that inquest last year
2　registered a complaint about what had happened the
3　official position about this investigation would have
4　been maintained and that position has been very clear
5　up until very recently. The official position of the
6　Metropolitan Police, for whom the prime
7　responsibility for investigation rests, was:
8　　(1). There was nothing wrong with the
9　investigation. Everything that could be done had
10　been done;
11　　Secondly, if there was a problem it lay with the
12　community because there was a wall of silence within
13　that community. Those were the reasons regularly
14　promoted.
15　　However, as a result of the complaint, as you
16　know, an investigation was established, as was this
17　Inquiry. The Kent Investigation, if I may call it
18　that, exploded both what I would call those myths
19　that everything had been done and there was a wall of
20　silence.
21　　In short form, in the first place, the
22　Kent Investigation discovered and identified 28
23　shortcomings and on page 158 of their report they
24　said this:
25　　"These failures are either missed opportunities,

Page 124

1　potential lines of enquiry not pursued or poor
2　judgment by the senior investigating officer, and in
3　some cases all three."
4　　As a result of this they suggested eleven lines
5　of further inquiry. We say in passing that it was
6　another serious misjudgment not to allow Kent to
7　finish the job rather than passing it back to the
8　Metropolitan Police, who then reported that all those
9　lines of enquiry had come to nought.
10　　On behalf of the family we have not accepted
11　that and in one particular case it is being
12　resurrected and pursued at this moment.
13　　Secondly, in relation to the wall of silence,
14　there is now overwhelming evidence that the initial
15　squad, and this is page 236 of the report, were
16　provided with a wealth of specific information about
17　the main potential suspects. Much of it was not
18　anonymous and the majority of it did, in fact, come
19　from the local community. It was, therefore, only on
20　the 15th December, 1997 following the publication of
21　the initial Kent Report through the PCA did the
22　official position shift, although in a very guarded
23　way, but the Commissioner of Metropolitan Police on
24　15th December 1997 said this:
25　　"They did accept that there were significant

Page 125

1　weaknesses, omissions and lost opportunities during
2　the first murder inquiry and that these were not
3　identified by an internal review of the Stephen
4　Lawrence case carried out by the Metropolitan Police
5　in 1993, the Barker review."
6　　Of course, now we have a statement, not on
7　behalf of the police but on behalf of the Inquiry,
8　which we welcome, a recognition that something has
9　gone badly wrong. This is one year later and we say:
10　why was this not recognised before the Lawrences had
11　to go to the length of registering a complaint and a
12　police inquiry and also, of course, a Public
13　Inquiry?
14　　We say that these significant weaknesses run as
15　a theme and a scene throughout the whole
16　investigation, and in particular the first two weeks,
17　because once the dye was cast in those first two
18　weeks it has proved virtually impossible to undo.
19　　May I, therefore, turn to the kernel of the
20　case. I have asked, and very kindly it has been put
21　on screen, that you have a map of the area. What I
22　intend to do is to condense and summarise, rather
23　than repeat and obviously there are some matters
24　which go beyond what has already been said. I want
25　to make it clear that there are some very important

Page 126

1　omissions which we say are not the benefit of
2　hindsight. We say very clearly that in any
3　investigation, particularly one of this kind, time is
4　of the essence and any police officer of whatever
5　rank would recognise that unless you act, obviously
6　judiciously, but quickly, it is going to be too late.
7　　I am going to propose that we start with this
8　proposition, which must have been how they started,
9　if you look at Dickson Road there, what they knew on
10　the day, and I am going to take it chronologically,
11　and there are twelve areas of immediate concern to
12　this Inquiry which need to be examined, what they
13　knew was that five or six young white man had
14　decamped from the scene down Dickson Road. What that
15　obviously means is that the likelihood is they were
16　local. They were not in a car. They were white and
17　they were in a group.
18　　This is of extreme importance because if you
19　look at the map, only and barely a year before in
20　July 1992 just the other side of the roundabout where
21　it says "Tudor Barn" on the map, you will see was the
22　scene of a murder that has already been referred to,
23　Rohit Duggal. He was fatally stabbed outside a kebab
24　bar. That kebab bar has been the scene of yet
25　another incident, it is the Tudor Parade. In that

1 case the culprits were local.

2   So it is, we say, very clear that had the police

3 started to think in a logical and in an obviously

4 investigative sense from the beginning the first

5 thing, and this is the first area we ask for close

6 examination, we say there was a failure on the night

7 to pursue obvious lines of enquiry and the most

8 particular of these lines of enquiry was an

9 effective, coordinated and systematic search for

10 offenders.

11   This is not a murder in a room where it is

12 necessary to seal the room off so nobody tramples all

13 over it, this is a much bigger scene in which the

14 need, of course, to preserve the immediate murder

15 scene for forensic purposes should not have precluded

16 what should have been an obvious house to house,

17 garden to garden, road to road search, because, as we

18 say, the potential suspects did all live in the

19 adjoining roads to Dickson Road. One of them lived

20 in a road that leads into it, Phineas Pett Road, just

21 above Dickson Road; two of them lived in Bournbrook

22 Road, which is just above that and a fourth one lived

23 in Well Hall Road. The fifth lived elsewhere.

24   As became clear had the police once they got

25 information they could have recognised within days,

1 what I am saying is precisely right, namely these

2 suspects did live locally and did gather in one set

3 of premises that night within half a mile of this bus

4 stop.

5   What is extraordinary is that there is not just

6 no scene log, we are not complaining about the lack

7 of administrative documentation, we say the omissions

8 here indicate that there was not essentially a

9 coordinated and effective house to house search

10 within hours.

11   There is not only no scene log, there is no tag

12 sheets, those are the TSG deployment sheets, there is

13 no audio tape for the night with police

14 transmissions, there are no personal records or notes

15 and despite attempts by some officers to claim there

16 was one kept it has never been found, we say, because

17 it was never done.

18   Secondly, and this is dealing with on the night,

19 the second area is a failure of information and the

20 provision of information to the officers doing the

21 work on the ground, because they should have had

22 access to, and it should have been available,

23 certainly with the technology that is now available

24 and has been available over the last few years,

25 information about local individuals and groups. In

1 the old days, obviously, the Bobby would have done it

2 or the collators card might have done it but there

3 are much more efficient ways now of collating

4 information.

5   I mention two features here about information on

6 the night that would have led them to the relevant

7 houses and how much would have been discovered. The

8 Brook Estate, as this area is known as, which I have

9 ringed in orange on this map, was known locally and

10 there was a gang on that estate known as, and it came

11 up in the Grant information barely within 24 hours,

12 they were known as The Krays. It is most unlikely

13 that no police officer in that area did not know, had

14 never heard of The Krays, as they were called. There

15 was good reason for why they were called The Krays

16 and you may have to look at that connection.

17   However, that is what they were called and that

18 overall term included four or five of the named

19 suspects. In addition to that, one of those named

20 Norris, his family, as the Kent aptly described, were

21 a well-known criminal family to the police. I

22 appreciate one single officer may not have it, but

23 the access to that information could have been,

24 indeed, speedy. Norris himself had been and was on a

25 charge relating to 1992, the Witham case, the Witham

1 brothers, a serious stabbing. So, again, he was not

2 unknown himself, never mind the family's name.

3   So we say, on the night there should have been

4 information to help with the process of concentrating

5 on particular areas and particular premises and

6 particular individuals.

7   Thirdly, we say, and it applies to the night,

8 but it applies later as well, there was a failure to

9 deal comprehensively, sensitively and swiftly with

10 all eyewitnesses. By that we mean witnesses who

11 obviously saw the actual incident, may I call them

12 the "bus stop witnesses", one of whom clearly is

13 Duwayne Brooks himself. He is not just a witness; he

14 is a victim; and it is quite clear from the

15 beginning, we say, not only were the witnesses at the

16 bus stop not properly debriefed and handled, Duwayne

17 Brooks himself was not properly debriefed and

18 handled. Those are matters which you will have to,

19 as it were, examine, because, if this does not

20 happen, if witnesses are not debriefed, if witnesses

21 are not handled sensibly, then the ability to

22 identify evaporates, as we say happened in the course

23 of time.

24   Of course, in this particular instance, three of

25 the witnesses -- they have already been mentioned, I

Page 131

1 do not repeat all of them, but there is Brooks,
2 Shepherd and Westbrook -- all mentioned this blond
3 offender. There seems to have been virtually no
4 investigation of that avenue of thought at all; and
5 there are people who match that description in this
6 locality associated with this gang.
7 　　May I pause. Those are three deficiencies in
8 the first very short space of time. It cannot be
9 said that during the first 24 hours that there was a
10 shortage of personnel or experience. On the night,
11 there were 44 police constables, five sergeants, one
12 inspector, one detective inspector, one detective
13 constable, one chief inspector, two detective
14 superintendents and two chief superintendents. That
15 is roughly speaking -- this is a minimum figure -- 56
16 officers. If you put their combined experience
17 together, it is 200 years of experience. That 200
18 years of combined experience was quite unable, as it
19 were, to cover the first three areas that we have
20 already mentioned. It is beyond explanation other
21 than of the forces that I have already indicated that
22 we say must have been at work in this case; and Kent
23 themselves -- that report suggests that it was unique
24 to have two chief superintendents at the scene within
25 the first two hours of a major crime.

Page 132

1 　　Thereafter, the police were amplified in terms
2 of the people available with senior officers who had
3 in some cases up to 30 years, the senior officers, of
4 experience: Ilsley, Weeden and Bullock; all of them
5 very experienced officers.
6 　　The fourth area which we say is of concern in
7 the first 24 hours is the failure to administer
8 first-aid. I do not develop it; it will be
9 developed.
10 　　The fifth is a failure to liaise adequately with
11 the family; and the details of that will be given by
12 the Lawrences themselves in the sense that they were
13 under the very clear impression that the police, as I
14 have already read out, were more interested in them,
15 their son and the visitors to the house than, in
16 fact, what had happened on the night.
17 　　I pass chronologically now, to item number 6
18 which is really flowing into the subsequent two
19 weeks. We say the single most disastrous failure in
20 this case, which points very clearly to those two
21 forces of racism and protection being expected by the
22 white boys, is clearly indicated by what happened
23 over the man called Grant.
24 　　Here there was a failure to take immediate,
25 effective action on very detailed and very specific

Page 133

1 information. It has been made clear: he was not
2 anonymous within one hour of a public appeal; and one
3 has to remember this must have taken considerable
4 courage to come into the police in the first place.
5 He came in and he gave three specific names, adding a
6 fourth later. He gave the descriptions. I do not
7 ask for it all to be called on screen again. He gave
8 descriptions of two of them, namely the Acourts. He
9 gave an address of the Acourts. He indicated it was
10 a group of five. He indicated they were known as the
11 Krays. He indicated how they linked, all of them, to
12 the Stacey Benefield case, to the Lee Pearson case
13 and to the Duggal case that I have already
14 mentioned. None of this was properly actioned, and
15 again, given the experience of these police officers,
16 there can be no sensible explanation other than the
17 ones we have sought to provide.
18 　　There was a delay and the big question that he
19 was never asked, and it has not been mentioned yet,
20 is how was it that somebody such as this, within such
21 a short space of time, unless he was, to use the
22 vernacular, close to the action, how was he able to
23 provide this information? We have not found a single
24 document that indicates that he was ever asked that
25 rather simple, straightforward question; and you do

Page 134

1 not have to be Maigret to concede. And of course
2 surprise will not be forthcoming on this occasion
3 because, we say, on sensitive areas the records are
4 just not available. There are no adequate records of
5 the contact with this man. On several occasions
6 there were at least seven meetings that we found
7 records of in the sense of being able to identify the
8 dates, but the contents of those meetings are only
9 set out in three messages and, of course, it has been
10 maintained until recently that he was anonymous.
11 　　This is of a level, we would say, of criminal
12 negligence for this material. And is worse than
13 that, because the names that he gave, and that of
14 Dobson, were repeated to the team many times. You
15 have had them gone through, but the total is that
16 between 23rd, the day when it occurred or just after,
17 and the 6th May, which is the day before the arrests
18 of the suspects, there were 26 different sources
19 giving the same names: 26. 14 of the 26 were known
20 to the police, so they were not, the majority, barely
21 half were known to the police. Of those 14, three
22 were police officers giving information not on the
23 murder squad. So this was reliable, named and
24 specific information that was not acted upon at all.
25 They had plenty of powers to do so, and it may be

Page 135

1 that the senior officers will now say that they do
2 recognise that they did have powers to do so, but
3 have other reasons for not. It will be interesting
4 to see what conceivable reasons there could be. The
5 powers that they had on the information alone,
6 although they had other evidence as well, other
7 information, that would certainly provide a basis for
8 an arrest and a search are under section 17, 18, 19,
9 24 and 32 of PACE. So that by the end of the very
10 first weekend, namely Sunday the 25th April,
11 particularly because in that weekend Stacey Benefield
12 had provided a statement, had agreed to support a
13 prosecution, those named suspects could and should
14 have been arrested.
15   The seventh area of concern: a failure to
16 collate and analyse information from witnesses who
17 not necessarily saw something, but heard something.
18   In this category, I am going to stick to letters
19 unfortunately. K is one of them. K relates to
20 Grant, in the sense that there is a connection
21 between the two. There are certain girlfriends that
22 fall into this category, and a particular officer
23 needs to be named in this category. The failure to
24 collate this information essentially is to sit down
25 and see what all these different people are saying

Page 136

1 they overheard others saying, to build up a picture
2 of the movements on the night, which could have been
3 done with some kind of flow chart, whatever you want
4 to call it. None of this was done, so the one
5 witness could be confronted with what another is
6 saying. Not only was it not properly actioned and
7 not properly developed, today, this day, we have,
8 this morning, been provided with a five page
9 statement from yet another witness that falls into
10 this category, only it is extremely significant
11 material by this witness. I am not going to name him
12 -- in fact, I do not know his name -- but he can
13 speak and could speak about conversations, and could
14 have spoken about conversations with the identified
15 suspects that took place both before and after this
16 incident which make it perfectly clear that the group
17 of people he is describing are the group of suspects
18 in this case.
19   He went to the police in the first place. No
20 statement was taken. We are yet to discover how it
21 is that there is yet another significant omission,
22 because there is no question but that, had this
23 material been available at any earlier stage than
24 today, a very different position might have pertained
25 in relation to prosecution. We did not ask for an

Page 137

1 adjournment this morning in order to have it
2 investigated: it is being investigated; but we
3 merely indicate that right up to the doors of
4 this court, this Inquiry essentially, there is
5 material coming to light which should have been
6 properly processed in the first place and which would
7 have made a difference.
8   The officer concerned, not with this witness,
9 but the officer, as far as we know -- we do not know
10 whether he did or not -- certainly the officer who
11 was concerned with Grant and the officer who was
12 concerned with K, and certain other of these
13 witnesses in the key area, was a DS Davidson. He has
14 subsequently been suspended. We are concerned that a
15 witness such as this, an officer such as this, played
16 such a crucial role in this investigation; and it
17 will be of some concern, no doubt, to the Inquiry to
18 discover what explanations this officer has for the
19 way in which Grant was handled.
20   Area number 8: instead of developing
21 eyewitnesses, key witnesses and arresting, what did
22 the police squad do in this case? They mounted a
23 completely pointless and ineffective surveillance
24 operation for the week of the 26th to the 30th to
25 prove, they claimed, an association between these

Page 138

1 people which, once they had achieved, they never put,
2 as has already been indicated in interview, upon
3 arrest. Of course, without repeating all of the
4 detail, they missed at least two opportunities, `two
5 opportunities', when one or more of these men were
6 removing material in plastic bin bags from that
7 property.
8   So when we say: "Was it ever intended to be a
9 successful prosecution?" One has to pause for a
10 moment at the point at which there had been no
11 arrests and they mount, as we say, a vacuous
12 surveillance operation.
13   We move to area number 9. That is the arrests
14 themselves made on 7th May, two weeks later. It has
15 already been made clear, the criteria for the arrests
16 were no different than they would have been in that
17 weekend I have already mentioned. These could have
18 been done well before. But, having, as it were, gone
19 to some of the relevant addresses on that day, the
20 searches of those addresses were quite inadequate,
21 particularly for scientific purposes and forensic
22 material in relation to blood, knives and clothing;
23 there were on the premises other people who occupied
24 the premises, particularly at Bournebrook Road, who
25 do not appear to have been pursued vigorously, and in

Page 139

1 that context I mean Bradley Lamb and Scott Lamb.

2   10th: Interviews that were conducted, I am going

3 to deal with briefly indeed. They were, we say,

4 again like the searches, totally inadequate; in some

5 cases they were little more than formalities and they

6 were perfunctory.

7   The next area of concern, area number 11, is of

8 course the Barker review, as I have called it. Again

9 comments have been made about that area, and I do not

10 intend to develop it other than that is all part of

11 what was the Metropolitan Police position; namely,

12 there was nothing wrong with the original inquiry.

13 How they could have not discerned that something had

14 gone badly wrong when they looked into it in the

15 autumn of 1993 beggars belief.

16   The final area of which we have concern is, in

17 fact, the role of the Crown Prosecution Service. We

18 say there are questions to be asked about their

19 approach and their criteria. When 102

20 Bournebrook Road was searched in relation to this

21 case, this is what was found at just that address:

22 five knives, one of which was a Gurkha, the second

23 one was a tiger lock knife; a sword in a scabbard; a

24 revolver and a shoulder holster, all from the one

25 address. How had that been allowed to develop? How

Page 140

1 did these people feel safe that they could not only

2 commit the assaults outside, but that they could

3 generate that kind of armoury within their premises?

4   How does this relate to the Crown Prosecution

5 Service? It relates in this way because, again, we

6 go back to the Witham case: two brothers attacked

7 for no obvious reason, another unprovoked attack,

8 which we say lies at the door of Jamie Acourt,

9 Mr Norris, yet again, and Luke Knight. Norris

10 stabbed one of the brothers with a knife; Jamie

11 Acourt had the use of a truncheon on the other

12 brother.

13   In this particular case, Norris was charged with

14 wounding and Jamie Acourt with possession of an

15 offensive weapon; but for reasons that we find

16 entirely unacceptable, both cases were withdrawn by

17 the Crown Prosecution Service, one in January 1994,

18 just before this attack -- that is the one against

19 Jamie Acourt -- and another in May 1993 against

20 Norris just after this attack. So there are

21 questions to be asked about how the Crown Prosecution

22 Service arrive at decisions in relation in particular

23 to these individuals.

24   May I finish, and I apologise; I have overrun.

25 THE CHAIRMAN: Do not hurry, Mr Mansfield, please.

Page 141

1 MR MANSFIELD: I want to, because I appreciate part 2

2 embraces to some extent part 1, and there may be

3 elements on the back of all of this which are

4 important to establish for the future.

5   What we would say is the catalogue and the

6 chapter that I have just gone through rather quickly,

7 the 12 areas of real and deep concern which we say

8 underlay these forces of both racism and

9 protectionism for the white perpetrators, has to be

10 addressed directly; and these are some of the factors

11 which we say should be involved in the process of the

12 future.

13   Firstly, there has to be a recognition, both of

14 racism, racist attitudes and racist attacks.

15   Secondly, there has to be collated and

16 accessible information in this field which relates

17 not only to investigation but also training, and it

18 may be that specialist squads of officers have to be

19 available in the areas where this kind of attack has

20 been prevalent; and no-one could say this part of

21 London has not suffered more than most.

22   There needs to be an element of independent

23 supervision, by which I indicate a non-police

24 supervision of inquiries of this kind in order to

25 ensure as far as possible that racist attitudes,

Page 142

1 racist information is made available and acted upon

2 quickly. The problem so far has been that it is, in

3 fact, because senior officers, and others below them,

4 have not acted on this kind of information, for

5 reasons we have explained, that an independent

6 element is required. We also suggest there should be

7 an element of public accountability, which would help

8 and concentrate the mind wonderfully of those who

9 have to carry out these investigations; and there

10 should be within that broad ambit a regular and close

11 scrutiny of how the system which is allied to those

12 principles is operating, because no system is any

13 better than the people or the personnel within it.

14 It is in that light that, clearly, if there were to

15 be, as it were, checks and balances in which there is

16 close scrutiny of how people are operating, not of

17 the level of the Barker review again, we say it would

18 have to be independent of the police.

19   I would seek to end, with those factors being

20 taken into account for the future, with one quotation

21 from Doreen Lawrence's statement which will be heard

22 tomorrow. She says this:

23   "I want Stephen Lawrence to be remembered as a

24 young man who had a future. He was well loved and

25 had he been given the chance to survive maybe he

1　would have been the one to bridge the gap between
2　black and white because he did not distinguish
3　between black and white; he saw people as people and
4　once, we say, those who people the investigation do
5　the same, then there might be a safer future for
6　all."
7　THE CHAIRMAN: Thank you. Yes, Mr Gompertz?
8　MR GOMPERTZ: Sir, it is a matter of the greatest
9　regret to the Commissioner and to the Metropolitan
10　Police Service that no-one has been successfully
11　prosecuted for the callous murder of Stephen
12　Lawrence. No words can express the horror of the
13　unprovoked attack upon him and its devastating effect
14　upon his family and friends. It is, therefore, only
15　right that at the start of this Inquiry I should
16　emphatically restate the sympathy and understanding
17　which all police officers who have been involved in
18　this tragic case feel towards the Lawrence family.
19　　　With hindsight, the Metropolitan Police Service
20　acknowledges that it should have done better. The
21　Metropolitan Police are determined to learn every
22　possible lesson from any constructive criticism which
23　emerges from this Inquiry. May, I on behalf of the
24　Metropolitan Police, once again reassure Mr and
25　Mrs Lawrence and the general public that errors made

1　during the investigation will not be overlooked.
2　　　The Commissioner, therefore, welcomes this
3　Inquiry. Where mistakes were made then they should
4　be exposed so that improvements can be made. The
5　Commissioner shares the Lawrence family's desire for
6　truth and justice. Every support will be given to
7　the Inquiry to ensure that it can make a thorough
8　investigation of all relevant matters. Unlike my
9　learned friends, Mr Lawson and Mr Mansfield, I do not
10　propose to comment on the facts. I prefer to wait to
11　hear the evidence and to comment later.
12　　　The Commissioner has no doubt that the Inquiry
13　will undertake its task with an open mind in fairness
14　to the many serving and retired police officers who
15　will be giving evidence and require that such an
16　approach be taken. The positive and the negative
17　aspects of the Metropolitan Police investigation must
18　be examined in equal measure. Mr Lawson's opening
19　may have given the impression that counsel to the
20　Inquiry will be seeking to establish a case. That
21　would be wrong. The Commissioner sincerely hopes
22　that the Inquiry will look at all the evidence and
23　not merely at that which supports police
24　shortcomings.
25　　　During the course of the next few weeks the

1　Inquiry will learn of the effort and dedication which
2　was given to the attempted solution of this terrible
3　crime. On the night itself it was an off-duty police
4　officer who stopped his car and provided assistance.
5　Within a very short space of time many officers were
6　involved in trying to identify and arrest those
7　responsible. They did so with great vigour. Many
8　lines of inquiry were pursued and many hours were
9　spent trying to obtain evidence from witnesses.
10　　　The second investigation was pursued with energy
11　and innovation. Later when the family decided to
12　bring a private prosecution every assistance was
13　given to their legal team. The outstanding lines of
14　inquiry suggested by the Kent police have been
15　rigorously pursued. Indeed, the investigation has
16　never been closed, as you have just heard from
17　Mr Mansfield; it remains open and is continuing at
18　this very moment.
19　　　The pressure upon the investigating officers,
20　together with the complexity and sheer weight of
21　information which had to be assessed, must also be
22　taken into account. Their judgments and decisions
23　will come under close scrutiny and in some cases will
24　undoubtedly be criticised. The investigating
25　officers, however, did not have the benefit of the

1　eight months of hindsight which were available to the
2　Kent police during the PCA investigation. The
3　answers which may seem obvious now may not have been
4　so apparent at the time. Once the crossword is
5　completed the clues often appear easy.
6　　　There remains today the same problem of turning
7　information into evidence; the same problem as was
8　encountered at the time. There is a huge difference
9　between direct evidence of what actually took place,
10　which is capable of withstanding robust testing in a
11　Court of law, and the supply of information as to the
12　identities of those who may have been involved in the
13　murder. Unprovoked attacks on strangers are always
14　the most difficult to solve, particularly when there
15　is in the locality an all persuasive fear of
16　retribution.
17　　　Many witnesses were repeatedly visited and
18　questioned during the course of this investigation
19　and although many people provided information, very
20　little direct evidence has been forthcoming. Such
21　was the case during the investigation. It remained
22　so at the time of the private prosecution and it is
23　still so today. It would be a source of great
24　satisfaction to the Commissioner if this Inquiry
25　could provide the key with which to unlock the

Page 147

1 reluctance of witnesses to assist. The Metropolitan
2 Police Service urges anybody who can help to come
3 forward and do so.
4   It is also important in this short opening
5 address to cover the issue of race. The racial
6 dimension to this Inquiry will no doubt extend
7 throughout its deliberations. It is vitally
8 important to people living in and working in areas
9 where racial tension, harassment and violence blight
10 their lives, so that they should see that the racial
11 dimension is thoroughly investigated.
12   Why does racism exist? What is it that creates
13 such wickedness? What can be done to stop it
14 happening and, of course, what steps should the
15 police be taking with the assistance of others to
16 remove the blight of racism from our community?
17   The Police Service wants to protect people in
18 ways which have hitherto perhaps been considered
19 unattainable; namely, in partnership with other
20 bodies. These are not simply empty words, for there
21 are very encouraging signs that such partnerships can
22 be developed. The knowledge of how to reduce crime
23 and disorder effectively and the willingness of local
24 authorities and others to assist is far greater now
25 than in the past. Indeed, within the London Borough

Page 149

1 justification.
2   Moreover, the evidence will show that the family
3 liaison officers took steps to help the family which
4 were in some cases well outside the normal call of
5 their duty. Whatever the reasons, why communications
6 broke down, it is important that misconceptions and
7 misunderstandings be put aside and that all parties
8 demonstrate a willingness to listen. The
9 Metropolitan Police certainly hope that renewed
10 understanding and reconciliation will become an
11 enduring feature of the future.
12   The main cause of distrust seems to have been
13 the belief that from the very start of this
14 investigation police officers involved did not do
15 their jobs properly because they were racist.
16 Although critical of many areas of the Metropolitan
17 Police's investigation, the very full and thorough
18 Kent investigation concluded that there was no
19 evidence of racism. As I have said, shortcomings in
20 the investigation are accepted, however, it is quite
21 possible to be highly motivated and to try hard but
22 to get things wrong. That is human nature. It is
23 also quite possible to get things wrong, perhaps even
24 very wrong, without being racist and without being in
25 any way influenced by conscious or subconscious

Page 148

1 of Greenwich itself the Joint Police Local Authority
2 Racial Incidents Unit is an excellent example of the
3 determination that practical steps can be taken to
4 combat racism and racial crime. The Greenwich Unit
5 was a pioneer in this field.
6   Partnerships, however, require mutual confidence
7 in the other partner's motivation and integrity.
8 These qualities can easily be undermined in such a
9 sensitive area. If lessons are to be learned and
10 progress continued then sensationalism and unfounded
11 allegations of racism are extremely detrimental.
12 Distrust and suspicion are destructive whatever their
13 source and their target. It is a matter of real
14 regret that communications between the Lawrence
15 family and the police have not been anywhere near as
16 close and trusting as they should have been.
17   Once again, however, it is not a simple
18 picture. There are very good reasons, for example,
19 why certain information cannot be passed to the
20 relatives and their legal representatives in advance
21 of a prosecution in spite of their desire to be fully
22 briefed and kept up-to-date. Sometimes such
23 dissemination of information might jeopardise future
24 arrests or the success of a future prosecution.
25 · Events have shown that these fears were not without

Page 150

1 feelings of antipathy towards certain individuals or
2 groups.
3   The police officers involved in this case are
4 all different personalities. They have different
5 backgrounds and live in different circumstances.
6 Some have children of their own; some hold deeply
7 religious and personal beliefs. In short, they are
8 individuals capable of feeling grief and being upset
9 like anybody else. They are not robots. They have
10 been angered and upset that Stephen's killers have
11 not been brought to justice. They are also deeply
12 concerned that they have been portrayed as callous
13 racists. Those allegations have affected not only
14 the officers but also their families who have been
15 upset by this unfair labelling of their loved ones.
16   This Inquiry provides an opportunity for them to
17 put the record straight and to give explanations for
18 their actions. It has been suggested that they might
19 have done this at the inquest, but an inquest is not
20 designed, nor intended, to accommodate such evidence.
21   They cooperated fully and openly with the
22 investigation by the Kent police. This is a real
23 indication of the desire to resolve the concerns of
24 Mr and Mrs Lawrence, albeit at the expense of
25 personal criticism. The unprecedented effort and

Page 151

1 assistance given to the private prosecution was
2 likewise an indication of the genuine desire and
3 commitment to bring Stephen's killers to justice.
4 　　Every day in London there are countless examples
5 of selfless bravery, commitment and immense hard work
6 by police officers. That will not be any consolation
7 to the Lawrence family but their commitment and hard
8 work should not be underestimated or taken for
9 granted. Although it is right and proper that their
10 actions and attitudes should be closely scrutinized,
11 the broad allegations of racism are unfair to all of
12 those officers to whom many people owe a great debt
13 of gratitude.
14 　　It is also particularly disappointing to read in
15 draft statements made by Mr and Mrs Lawrence, which
16 were supplied to us this morning, suggestions of
17 corruption and conspiracy by police officers to
18 conceal the identities of Stephen's killers. There
19 is not a shred of evidence to support these
20 allegations. They were rejected by the Kent
21 investigation.
22 　　On behalf of the Metropolitan Police Service I
23 utterly refute the allegation that there was any form
24 of cover up or corruption.
25 　　Nearly five years have passed since 22nd April

Page 152

1 1993. Since that date many lessons have already been
2 learnt. The way in which murders are investigated
3 has been subject to constant review. Indeed,
4 approaching 90 per cent of murders in the
5 metropolitan area are solved with the colour of the
6 victim making no difference to the success rate.
7 　　The Commissioner accepts, however, that there is
8 more to be done and the Metropolitan Police are
9 committed to learning the lessons of this Inquiry.
10 It is the hope of the entire Police Service that some
11 good will come out of the tragedy of Stephen's
12 death.
13 　　Stephen's murder was a callous, evil act
14 committed by callous, evil people. It is they and
15 they alone who should bear the guilt for ending such
16 a promising and optimistic young life. It is they
17 and they alone who should feel the contempt of all
18 civilised people. We now have the opportunity to
19 build a future where such evil is constrained and its
20 impact ever diminishing. An atmosphere of openness,
21 fairness and reconciliation to all of us here will do
22 much towards the achievement of that ambition.
23 THE CHAIRMAN: Thank you, Mr Gompertz.
24 　　Ladies and gentlemen, the scene is set, in one
25 sense, and there is much evidence for all of us to

Page 153

1 listen to. I simply repeat Bishop John's words:
2 　　"Listen, wait and see must be the best
3 articulation."
4 　　We will do our utmost when we have heard all of
5 the evidence to reach a fair and a just conclusion in
6 connection with all of the matters which have been
7 and will be raised in this Inquiry.
8 　　We will adjourn now and we will start again
9 tomorrow at 10.
10 　　There is one matter I think I should mention. I
11 think a number of people have regarded my requirement
12 that we should sit from 10.00 until 1.00 without a
13 break as imposing undue hard labour upon all of us
14 and, in particular, the shorthand writers have asked
15 that there should be a short break. So at a
16 convenient moment in the morning's hearings we will
17 have a quarter of an hour break from now on. So my
18 first decision is already altered in that way and I
19 hope that is to everyone's satisfaction. Thank you
20 very much. We will meet again tomorrow at 10.00.
21 　　(The Inquiry adjourned at 3.00 p.m.)
22
23
24
25

STATEMENT OF DOREEN LAWRENCE - 8th March 1998

[As provided to the Inquiry; read to the Inquiry on 25th March 1998].

My name is Doreen Lawrence. I was born on 24th October 1952 in Clarendon, Jamaica. I have two brothers and a sister. I am the eldest of the four of us. We were all born in the UK.

I lived with my mother in Jamaica and in 1954 she came to England leaving me with my grandmother until her death. I came to the United Kingdom in 1962 at the age of 9 years old on my own because my mother had sent for me. I lived then with my mother and stepfather in Brockley, South-East London. My mother had remarried before I arrived in England. My father had also remarried and now lived in North London. When I arrived in London I found it very frightening. The houses were close together and smoke would come out of the chimneys and all was generally dark and gloomy. I attended the John Stainer Primary School and then the Christopher Marlowe Secondary School in New Cross.

I obtained CSEs and when I left school I got a job as a bank clerk for NatWest Bank. I worked there for 4 years and left when I had Stephen. At that time I only had CSE qualifications but in the last five years I have gained a BA in Humanities and I am now doing an MSC in therapeutic counselling.

I met my husband Neville in early 1970, I was living in Greenwich with my other at the time. Neville and myself got married in 1972 in Lewisham Registry Office and went to live in Brockley. Later we moved to a flat in Plumstead and that is where Stephen was born on 13th September 1974.

I personally have never had any racism directed at me. There was always something I felt on the outskirts but nobody ever directly approached me and was racist towards me. I went to a racially mixed all girls school and I do not remember any. I don't have any close white friends from my school days, but I do have five black school friends who I am still very close to.

I didn't go into further education because in those days where black children were concerned you weren't really encouraged at school. I remember clearly when it was time to leave school - I can't remember exactly what I said I wanted, but I think I told them I wanted to go into banking or something like that and the teacher said, no, you must go and do that and the teacher said, like working in a factory. Being the eldest of four from a West Indian background I was given much more responsibilities than other children. I looked after my younger brothers and sisters and that prevented me from studying in a way I wanted to. I did know, however, that doing something with my hands was clearly not something that I wanted to do.

I went on then and looked for my own job, I just applied for things through the papers. I had quite a few interviews, all in banking, and I went to NatWest Bank. About three of us from school went and worked at the same bank. I did the normal entrance tests and I passed that and worked there for four years.

I remained in contact with my brothers and sisters throughout this period, we were all relatively close. We did have problems as youngsters, of course, as teenagers growing up, rows with your mother and that sort of thing, that went on for a while. At times there was the odd major thing and we lost touch but we all got back together again afterwards.

When Stephen was born there were no major problems with him as a child. He was a good child and he was very happy. His early years were not problematic. He always knew, though, when things weren't right with him. You always felt that. Right up to primary school I can. You always felt that. Right up to primary school I can recall that Stephen was very bright. He knew what he wanted from a young age. He learned very quickly before he started school. He could write his name and he always picked up things quickly. He knew his alphabet as well. He could count and he recognised a few words. He was the type of child that whatever you taught him he always wanted to go one further but colouring and drawing was his special thing.

Stephen went to Cyril Henry Nursery in Woolwich on part-time basis and then later on to Eglington Primary School. I didn't work until Stephen was 18 months old. I didn't have a full-time job even then. Neville at that stage was learning his trade as a plasterer but by the time Stephen was born he was into retail, selling leather and things and after that he moved into the building trade.

At Stephen's primary school he was very happy, he got on well and he was well liked by the teachers. Every day each child would have a set of things they would do when they first came in. She would write letters and he had to go over them with a paintbrush and I think that helped him to develop his handwriting. He left primary school to go to Blackheath Bluecoat. We wanted him to go to Thomas Moore Catholic School but because we weren't practising Catholics we couldn't get him into there. I felt that this was a good school on academic achievements but because he wasn't accepted on religious grounds we had to start looking at other schools. I was impressed with Blackheath Bluecoat because I saw how the children were actually working. When you turned up at the school it looked very hard working and I was impressed, so we decided to send him there.

Stephen coped well at school. He had no problems academically at all. He did his GCEs but Stephen didn't really work as well as he could. I think because he was very bright it went a bit to his head and had he studied harder I think he would have got a much higher grade. However, having said that he did pass all of his GCEs. I certainly don't remember Stephen ever complaining about Blackheath Bluecoat. I know that sometimes he had felt that the Head Teacher was unjust in some of his ways. For example, quite a lot of black children were excluded from the school, but he personally never really encountered anything. His only brush with racism was back in primary school when he was quite young. There was a boy who lived up the road from us. They used to be friends. So I can't remember what started this off, but I do remember being called into school because apparently he had been getting into fights with this boy and, when I asked him about it, he told me that the boy had called him racist names. I'm not sure what the exact names were, but he would here it and so would his friends. I think at the time he was one of the few black children in the class, so the majority of his friends were white, and they would tell him what this boy had been saying about him. So he had the support of his white friends against this boy and they used to get into fights. When I went into the school, I told the Head that if the child was being racist to him, then Stephen was justified in sticking up for himself. That was the end of it and it didn't go any further because I think the Head recognised that Stephen was not the kind of child to be in fights and that it was only because of this incident. I would say that Stephen was aware of the racism however.

Stephen was also into sport. During Sports Days he always came top. He got a certificate, which is a Five Star, the highest award Blackheath Bluecoat awarded to anybody, he had a couple of those. He also ran for Cambridge Harriers. Initially he used to go to Sutcliffe Park, which is another athletics club, but there he was always experiencing some difficulty with the trainers. It was as if they had a sort of favouritism within that club and they saw him as being very young and, even though Stephen wanted to get on, I felt they were holding him back a bit.

Stephen's main interests were sport and education. He saw himself going into architecture as a profession, however. When he was about 7, or even before, he would set himself goals. I remember before his 6th birthday he said he wanted a watch for his sixth birthday and I said: "Only if you can tell the time", and he said: "When I am six, I will be able to tell the time", and of course he got his watch because he could tell the time by then. When it came to drawing and things, he was always doing that, he would do birthday cards, Christmas cards, and he would always make his own cards as a child and Mother's Day cards for me, and he was always into the Arts.

Racism isn't something that we dwelled on, I think and, looking back at things, Stephen actually protected me from a lot of things that were happening to him. He never told me everything. Occasionally he would mention the same boy that he had the original incident with, even though, when they left primary school and were on secondary school, this boy used to go to Eaglesfield, which is at the top of the road from where we lived. They were at different schools, but when they were coming home, because of the bus stop that the child would take home, they would meet each other, and I think that the child thought that maybe, as Stephen didn't have anybody around him on the way home, he could start on him; but no matter where he was, Stephen would never tolerate anything like that from him.

In secondary school Stephen didn't go around in a group. He had a close circle of friends. I remember by the time he was a sixth former though, you would only see him with one person, who was Elvin. Elvin was his best friend. Elvin was an arty person and, because he did a lot of work in art and they both had a flair for it, they would spend a lot of their time together. Elvin wasn't interested in sports however, so they never went training together but Elvin would come to our house. They went to Woolwich College together and spent time together, as they had done at school: they had been to the same secondary school.

Stephen also started Cubs at the age of eight. The church that we belonged to had their own little group and, because we were members of the child Stephen got involved in that. So he started off as a Cub and moved up to be a Scout. He was in the Scouts until he was in secondary school at about 13 or 14. In terms of activity, they had the Sports Day and, of course, Stephen loved to run. We have lots of his certificates at home. He had won all sorts of things. They would also put on shows and Christmas plays. It was a big thing for him being in the Scouts. I remember in one particular play in which he played Rupert the Bear, and dressed up in a costume with a white face and stripy trousers, he really enjoyed that. It was something that he enjoyed initially but, obviously, began to outgrow. They used to meet once a week, all the Scouts, and play games together and things; and because it was something to do with the church, they would have a parade one Sunday in the month as well. Stephen used to ask if he could carry the flag, which he really enjoyed. There was the Union Jack, St George's and other Guides and Scouts and Brownies and the different organisations would meet together on this day, so you had all the different flags.

Stephen had his black identity, and I would say he called himself a Jamaican. He went to Jamaica when he was four. He spent his first birthday out there, but he would never remember that. When he was four we went again and he was old enough to remember. He enjoyed his time out there, and it was something that he always said that he would like to do again.

He met Duwayne at secondary school because when he started they were in the same class. His relationship with Stephen only developed, I think, because Duwayne knew my brother and Duwayne's mother and my brother were friends; and I think that that is the way that Duwayne fits in. I felt that Duwayne - I'm not sure if it was about his own insecurity, but it often came across to me that Duwayne needed Stephen more than Stephen needed him. Stephen was an outgoing person: he would make friends easily and he had a lot of friends; he was extremely popular.

Stephen did work experience from school with an architect's firm for two weeks. He did this in November when he was doing his final year of GCEs. I am not sure what year it was, but I think it was 1991 and then the final year of GCEs. This placement we sought ourselves for him because what the school do is that they send a letter home telling you that the time is coming up, and that the school can provide something, but if you know anybody, you can accept that place.

Neville worked with someone who was a surveyor, or an engineer, and he introduced us to Arthur Timothy. Neville took Stephen along to meet him, this Arthur Timothy, and I think that, once he and Stephen met, they liked each other. They got on well and he was offered a place. It was at Tower Bridge, and Stephen went there for two weeks. It wasn't a big office. It was quite a small place, so Stephen was left on his own for quite a while, especially when Mr Timothy had to go out to meet clients, Stephen was left in charge to answer the phones and take messages and all sorts of things. I presume that in that space of time it was shown that he could have the responsibility of doing that sort of thing and he was given the chance. When Stephen came home he would talk about it a lot and show us the work that he had produced. I was very impressed with it, I remember, because I used to talk to my colleagues about it and I thought it looked very professional. One of the designs he did was used on a building in Deptford. It is easily recognisable from his drawings, the shape of the windows and everything Stephen did. This building is on Deptford Broadway. The architect who did the design for this, that Stephen was working for, copied Stephen's drawing; and you can see that. Stephen was very proud of this.

In 1993 Stephen was doing his A-levels in English Language and Literature at Woolwich College. That took up two days of his week; and he was at Blackheath Bluecoat doing A-level Designer Technology and re-sitting his GCE Physics, so he was studying, effectively, full-time. Stephen also worked at the Fun Junction which is a play centre where you take kids for an hour or so. He did that for a while on a part-time basis just at the weekends. The money he earned helped to support him for school, or whatever outside activities he wanted to do. When that closed down he went to work at the McDonald's in Old Kent Road; and he was doing that right up until he died, really.

Stephen always wanted to be an architect, as I have said. He had set this for his goat, and, hence, the A-level subjects that he chose reflected what he felt were necessary to do architecture. He was to go to college and then to university, but we hadn't got to the start of looking at what university he was going to.

Stephen was a healthy boy: he never had anything wrong with him. He had a slight touch of asthma when he was running, but nothing really major.

Stuart, Stephen's brother and Stephen got on well. Well, usually well until they fell out from time to time, as children do, especially when Georgina was little: having a baby sister was really something. When you look at the pictures of them when they were small, Stephen used to push Stuart out; Georgina was his baby sister. Stuart and Stephen got on because they shared a room. Parents really don't know half of what goes on between youngsters when they fall out. I am not sure exactly why they would fall out, but it wouldn't be for a long time. They had one fairly really long period, but that had started building up again just before Stephen had died.

As to music, Stephen mainly liked women singers, but he was also into Pop and Reggae and Hip-Hop.

From the time that I left school and I went to the NatWest Bank and worked there and had Stephen, I was doing temporary, part-time jobs. So I was working temporarily, or not for very long periods, while Stephen was growing up. I worked at Goldsmith's Bookshop; I was a care assistant; I did office cleaning and, up until 1981, those were the sort of jobs I did. I then started working in schools, because they fitted in well with the children's holidays. I was a Guide, where you take children from one school to another if they have special needs; and I did that up until 1982 when I had Georgina and stopped when she was about three. That would take me to 1985, because she was born in 1982.

I was then working at the school where Stuart and Stephen attended, Eglington Primary School as a lunchtime supervisor. I did that for about six months, and by 1986, I started working full-time as a "special needs helper" with the school, and stayed there for a couple of years. After that I went back into education.

I did an Access course because I didn't have any A-levels to go to university. I went back to university because, when I was working at the schools, I was doing a lot of work with the teachers. They encouraged me, told me that I was wasted there and that I had the ability to do a lot more, and asked me why I didn't. One of the teachers got the prospectus for me and told me what courses to attend. At this point we were living at Llanover Road, and that's where we were living when Stephen was killed.

The area we were living in was quite tense, but I think, because of the person I am, I didn't really take any notice. As long as it wasn't interfering with me or my children, there was nothing major happening.

I know that Stephen had incidents with other children around the area when playing. I can remember one time that a boy spat in his face, and how angry I was, and I challenged the mother over it. He was about nine and he used to ride his bike around the back of our house; and it was in this play area that the incident happened.

When we moved to Llanover Road we started going to the Methodist Church where Stephen was baptised and most of his childhood was spent. Stephen went to church regularly. He was part of the junior church and, in those days, there was a lot of activities for youngsters within the church which he took part in. He took his religion quite seriously. At one point he said that he wanted to be confirmed, but it is quite a big step and, at the time, I felt that he was too young and that he should wait a bit because it wasn't something that you should go into lightly. I wanted him to think about it.

As teenagers do, however, they grow out of the church because the church doesn't really have that much to offer them; and a lot of people who used to be youth leaders had left Trinity Church, so they lost that leadership that the church used to have. We used to go to church in Burrage Road on a weekly basis. Stuart and Georgina went as well. Children tend to go and continue up to about their early teens, but then by the time they are 14 or 15, that is when they start to trail off.

By 1993 I was at college doing my first degree in Humanities. In April 1993 I went on a field trip. I was a first year then, and that is something that you do on our course in the university. We had gone to Birmingham for two days. I left on the Tuesday morning and we travelled down and came back for the Thursday night. The last time I saw Stephen alive was on the Tuesday morning. I was leaving early because I had to be at Woolwich by 8.30am and he came down for breakfast. You just don't think about it at the time. If you knew that it was the last time you were going to see somebody, the things that you would say to them and all that. I told him I was going to be away for a couple of days, that I would ring him that night to tell him if there was a telephone number of anyway that he could get in contact with me and that was it. I just said that I would see him when I got back. I did the things that you usually do when you go out. You say where you are going, how long you are going to be away for and I will ring you. When I rang on the Tuesday night Stephen wasn't home yet, so I didn't speak to him. I arrived back in London on the Thursday night at about 9 o'clock. Neville picked me up and we went back to the house. Stuart was awake and Neville said that Stephen wasn't home yet and Georgina was asleep. It wasn't unusual that Stephen wasn't home. He had to be home between 10.00 and 10.30. I said that because I felt that, being at school and studying, it is quite a reasonable time; but then again, Stephen was 18, so even though we said that, if he didn't get home by then, there is not a lot you can do because of his age.

We had set that time a long time ago and it hadn't really changed over the years. We had been quite strict on being home on time in the beginning, but after the influence of Duwayne, it was different. Duwayne was allowed to come and go as he pleased, and it didn't really matter what time he got home.

I remember, Stephen was 14 when we first had this argument. It was 10.30 and then it was 10.00, because at times he wasn't coming in for 10.30, and the argument to me always was: "Duwayne doesn't have to be home", until whatever time it was, "so why do I have to be home, because it isn't really that late?" And I told him straight: "What Duwayne and his parents do is up to them, but you are our child, and I expect you to be in because you have school the next day." He found that Duwayne had the freedom to come and go as he wanted and, I suppose, that he wanted the same.

On the Thursday, I arrived home at about 9 o'clock. I got indoors and Stuart was awake, so I went up to see him. I talked to him about what he had been doing while I had been away. I went in to see Georgina who was asleep. I had a bath and we had something to eat. We sat and watched ITV news, because it was 10 o'clock, followed by the local news. At that time I was thinking: "I wish that Stephen would hurry up and come home, because I was really tired and I wanted to go to bed, and I didn't want to go to bed until I knew that he was home. I watched the news, and then the local news and, just as that finished, I remember getting up to go to the bathroom and the door knocked, and I thought: "Okay, Stephen is home." I could hear voices downstairs and I heard Stephen's name mentioned, so I went down.

As I got to the front door I couldn't see who was at the door, because I couldn't see past Neville who was in the way. I moved Neville aside and I saw the family from around the back, Joey Shepherd and his father and brother. He had come to tell us how Stephen had been attacked. He didn't know how seriously Stephen had been hurt. All he said was it was at the bus stop and the Welcome Inn pub. That is all he said. Then the father said to get some information perhaps it would be best to phone the police and see what they could tell us. They were at the door for just a short time. So I went inside and dialled 999, because I didn't know the local police station number. What they told me over the phone was, "It is news to us, we don't know of any sort of incident." I said to the operator that I had just been told that my son had been involved in an accident down the road and I wanted to know if they could tell me anything about it. I gave them the name of the road and the pub and all of that and they said it was news to them. They hadn't heard of any incident and they couldn't give me any information.

We decided to leave. I wasn't dressed, but I suppose just the thought of something having happened to Stephen, I just put on my overcoat and I went out. I remember Stuart coming downstairs. He brought my trainers and things for me and he had his coat on and he said he was coming too and I said he couldn't because Georgina would be in the house by herself so he had to stay and we left straight away. We stopped by the traffic lights at the top of Shooters Hill Road. Neville was driving and at that time of night there is hardly any traffic. We went over the lights, past the pub and the bus stop. The bus stop is further down there on the left hand side. We passed there. There is a road, I'm not sure of its name, but I think it is the first turning on the left after the bus stop. We got as far as there but we still couldn't see anything.

At that time we looked down the road and on Friday night just gone when I was driving down, I noticed that you can see all the way down to Well Hall roundabout. You can't see the roundabout itself but if there were blue lights flashing or anything happening you would be able to see it. We didn't notice anything. We couldn't see anything on the Thursday night. We went right as far as that road but we couldn't see anything. We turned around and I said to Neville, "They must have gone to the hospital" because Brook Hospital is not far away. I thought, "Well, that is where they will have gone". I don't remember if we physically looked down the road, but I think we probably would have done because it is straight in front of you and you would be able to see it. We saw no lights or anything.

We turned around and we just thought. "Well, probably they had gone to the hospital under their own steam. We didn't think anything serious had happened because we couldn't see any evidence of it. I thought that Stephen was hurt but I didn't think anything as serious as it was.

I know that for a long time beforehand I used to talk to Stephen about the dangers of being out and the dangers of the police as well because of stories that you hear that used to frighten me. The stories that you would hear would be about walking on the street on your own with your friends or whatever and the police would stop you and bundle you into the back of the van and beat up the kids. That is the story that would be going around, especially with black children.

I would tell Stephen that when he was walking down the road he should do so with the traffic going into the opposite direction so he could see when cars were coming and if there was any traffic and then there was more chance of getting away. That is the sort of thing I would tell him. I would also tell him if he was travelling on a train never ever sit in the carriage by himself and to sit in an open carriage. Stephen's attitude towards the police was always: "Well, if I'm not doing anything wrong how could they do that to me?" I used to say to him from what I am hearing you don't have to be doing anything. I didn't trust the police, I never have done and I certainly don't now. Stephen didn't have that mistrust, however, because as far as he was concerned if he wasn't doing anything wrong he had nothing to worry about. That was his attitude. He had never been in any sort of trouble. He had never been in any sort of trouble with the police. He had never been arrested or even spoken to the police. He never had any dealings with then at all. I don't think that Stephen would know what to do if he had because he had never had anything to do with them.

Because of how we lived as a family we got on with people. Our immediate next door neighbour were a white family and we got on with them very well. The children were the same age as my children. We lived in each other's houses and we had no problems.

By 1993 there had been three murders in our area. I wasn't aware of them all. I was aware, of course, of the Roland Adams one because Stephen knew Roland and that was a big thing for him. They were having a march or something and he wanted to be there. I was very worried for him because Thamesmead is an area you always hear about with racism connected to it, it is always happening down there. I remember saying to him: "I don't want you to go" because he would be a stranger to the area and a strange face and if anything happened they would pick him up quite easily. He had a strong conviction where that was concerned because it was his friend and he told me "no" and in fact he actually went. I felt really frightened that Roland had been killed for no reason but I presume at the same time you hear it, and until it happens to you it doesn't really sink in. The fear has always been there.

I have always been worried for Stephen. Always him more so, because Stephen was a very independent person and he liked going out. He went out with his friends up Central London and he knew a lot of places. I wouldn't say that he was exactly inquisitive, but he wanted to know what his surroundings were like.

Going back to that night we turned to go to Brook Hospital. We drove to the hospital. When we got there I won't swear that I noticed the police car there, perhaps I did, but I can't really remember. All that was on my mind was Stephen. Neville dropped me outside the ambulance entrance, Accident & Emergency Department. I remember walking - because the hospital is somewhere that I have been several times, it is a hospital that I know - I walked through the doors and I turned right.

Because the ambulance entrance is much further than the Casualty Department it is that bit further to walk. I turned right and I walked down to the Casualty place and I think there were just one or two people sitting there, nobody that I knew, because all I was looking for was Stephen. When I first came through the door I could see a black boy standing in front of me and I saw a police officer next to them standing there. I didn't recognise the black boy, but now I know it was Duwayne. At the time all I was looking for was Stephen, so I wouldn't have noticed. I would have passed anybody by. I didn't have to pass them to go to the Casualty Department, though, because they were further down. I walked down and I looked in the waiting area but I couldn't see Stephen.

I was turning around to go back through the front door again when Neville came walking in. I was going to tell Neville that Stephen was not there, I had decided in my mind that he was not there. I didn't see any medical people about, or anyone. All I was looking for was Stephen. I didn't go to the enquiries counter, I didn't even notice whether there was one or not.

When Neville walked in he recognised Duwayne straight away. He walked up to Duwayne and said something to him and it was then that I recognised him. I went over to Duwayne and asked him what happened and where Stephen was. At that point some people from the medical team came out. There was a man, someone in green, I think. The medical team came out with him. I'm not really certain, I think they came out of the examining rooms opposite where Duwayne was standing and walked over to Duwayne and I think the man in green asked what they hit him with. I'm not certain if the iron bar was mentioned by Duwayne, but I can remember hearing about an iron bar. That was what they asked him about.

I started asking them questions like: "Where is Stephen? Can we see him?" They said they were working on him. I must have asked three or four times if we could see him and they kept saying they were working on him. We were shown into a room, a family waiting room or something and I remember not sitting down. I was quite anxious and that was when I went off to phone my sister. In the room at the time it was just me and Neville. I don't think Duwayne came into the room at the point. I know eventually he came in but not at first.

Neville and I didn't speak to each other much. I said to them that I couldn't just sit there so I went and got some change to phone my sister. That was the only phone call I made. I told her that we were at the hospital and that Stephen had been attacked. I couldn't tell her anything because I didn't know anything and she said that she would come down. By the time I put the phone down and went back to the room Neville had gone to phone his cousin so I stayed in the room on my own.

When Neville came back I think Duwayne was shown in then. I remember when he sat down. I asked him what was happening and what was going on. He was very confused and didn't make any sense. He said that they had been coming from my brother's place and that it was not long after that, but I couldn't make any sense of anything else. Half the time he wasn't talking anyway. He was just extremely anxious. He couldn't sit still. He wasn't with a police officer in the room. The police didn't come into the room. the police officer that was near Duwayne as we came in was standing outside. He was a uniformed man, but I'm not sure of any of his features. I couldn't tell you if he was dark or blonde or anything but he was about the same height as Duwayne and of medium build.

Neville, Duwayne and I stayed in the room but we weren't there for very long. I think it was about 5 or 10 minutes, it didn't seem that long. At that stage I thought Stephen was seriously hurt, but not fatally. When I spoke to my sister all I could tell her was that Stephen had been attacked and we were at the hospital. I didn't know anything more. I didn't know how serious hurt he was because I hadn't seen him and nobody had told us anything about him, nobody had said what had happened to him. As for being stabbed, that's the last thing I expected. I never expected that.

We were waiting still in the family room and two people came in, one was a ginger haired woman. She was a staff nurse and I presume the doctor, was also a woman. They said that Stephen was dead. I looked at them as if to say: "How do you mean he's dead? He can't be dead." I don't remember what I did then. I can't remember whether I cried out or anything. That was it.

I was sitting at the time when we were told and asked if we could see him. I didn't believe that he was dead and I was saying: "No, he is not dead. He is not dead. He can't be." I don't remember how Neville reacted. I remember Duwayne because he was sitting next to me. He let out a cry. While we were sitting there the wall was next to us. There were three seats and they were flush to the wall. Duwayne was on the end by the door. Neville was in the corner. Duwayne was by the entrance and he was literally climbing the walls when he heard that Stephen had died. Nobody did anything to comfort him and not long after that the police took him away. I don't remember him going to see Stephen with us at all. We were told Stephen was dead and we asked to see him. The doctor said we had to wait because they were preparing him or something. By that time my sister had arrived with her husband. We told them that Stephen had died while we were in the family room. We all sat there for a while. A few other members of the family arrived. At the time I didn't know, but my sister had phoned my brother and nephew. I remember my brother turning up so there was myself, Neville, my sister, her husband and my brother. They were the only ones that were there when we went to see Stephen. There were no police officers.

The next thing I remember was us seeing Stephen. We were shown into the room where he was, the examination room, Neville, myself, my sister and her husband. The nurse took us in and I'm sure she had her arms round me and my sister was on the other side. I don't remember anyone else being in the room. When we got in we saw Stephen lying there. He looked as though he was just sleeping. He was covered from his neck downwards and I didn't move the covers. I just kissed him and more or less cuddled him. I remember the cut on his chin but I didn't take the cover off him. We stood there for a while and then went back into the family room and that's when the other family members arrived. After we had seen Stephen, my nephew came and his sister and both my brothers arrived at the same time. We were in the family room but there was nobody from Neville's side of the family there.

Even at this point it hadn't hit me what had happened. I was completely numb. I don't remember thinking anything. I suppose eventually what came to me was the fact that Stuart and Georgina were at home. Neville drove us home, just the two of us in the car. My sister couldn't follow because they had left their children on their own. We got home by about midnight because I remember checking the time. It was either midnight or just before. Stuart was still awake and I told him. I told him that Stephen had died, what else can you say? Stuart just cried and cried. Georgina was asleep and I suppose it was at that stage that I took the decision not to wake her.

That night Neville's cousin arrived with her husband at the house. I'm not sure what time it was but Duwayne's mother also came to the house with a friend who I don't know but I had seen around. Neville opened the door because I was frightened of ever opening the door again. They came upstairs into the living room and she said that she had been to see Duwayne at the police station and the only thing that stuck in my mind was that she said she was glad it wasn't Duwayne and that was it.

The other person who was with her said that she had a son and that Stephen knew her son. She knew us but she wasn't someone I had much contact with. I don't know why Duwayne's mum came around. She would have had our address from a friend. I presume she came around in sympathy but at the time it didn't come across as that.

Eventually, I went to bed. I didn't sleep. I just lay there. I couldn't sleep. Nothing else happened that night.

The next morning when Georgina woke up Neville was on the phone. I'm not sure who he was talking to but various people, telling them what had happened to Stephen because I didn't want to speak to anyone. Georgina woke up as usual, I didn't want to wake her. She could hear voices talking and she came into the living room and looked at me and said: "Mum, what's wrong?" She could hear Neville downstairs talking and she went down. She probably heard the conversation over the phone, she just went mad. She started screaming and screaming and ran up the stairs to me. I held her and she kept repeating: "It is not true. It is not true. Where is Stephen?" So I told her. It was really strange behaviour. It was as if she had taken it in but not really taken it in. This was about 7 o'clock in the morning.

Georgina had an alarm in her room so she would wake up with the boys getting up in the morning. The routine was that Stephen would be up first: he went in the bathroom first, followed by Stuart and because she was the youngest and because her school was local and she didn't have to be up until much later, her routine was always that she was the last one in the bathroom. Georgina and Stuart then went off to School. I told them about staying at home but they said they weren't staying at home. I phoned a friend of mine to tell her what had happened and she phoned some friends and by 8 o'clock they came to the house. In fact three of them arrived. They arrived and Georgina and Stuart were saying they wanted to go to school and I was trying to persuade them not to go. They said they wanted to go so my friends said they would walk them to school and let the school know what had happened. One friend with Stuart and the other two went with Georgina. Georgina was due to go off on a school trip for a week on the Monday but, of course, I didn't want to let her out of my sight so I just said: "You are not going", and she said "I want to go". At this time we let the school know what was happening and they said they would keep an eye on her and if she wanted to come home at any point they would bring her home. She was only 10 at this time and Stuart had just had his 16th birthday.

"The rest of the Friday people started coming to the house. After 8 o'clock or 9 o'clock the police came. I don't know who from the police arrived but somebody did. We didn't inform anybody that we didn't want to be disturbed by the police on the Thursday night and no police officers spoke to us on the Thursday night. The first contact we had with the police or knew of the police officers' involvement was the Friday morning after about 9 am. I would never had said that I didn't want to be contacted by the police. Something like that of course you want to know what happened, and you want to know straight away what would happen. I wanted to know. If the police had arrived in the middle of the night to speak to us we would have been happy to speak to them. We would never have turned anybody away. No officer spoke to us at the hospital. I didn't see any as we left the hospital.

On the Friday whoever opened the door told us the police were there. I don't remember speaking to them on the Friday morning. I can't remember what was said. I know that they came in the morning because it sticks in my mind but I don't know any of the conversation.

I remember Palma Black from the ARA being at our place. She was introduced to us but how she got to our place I don't know. Nobody from our family would have contacted her. I understand that Ros Howells was contacted, I presume by the police or hospital because she is a member of the Greenwich Race Unit. She may have contacted ARA, although not directly. I think she would have spoken to Vicki Morse, who is a counsellor in Greenwich, and I understand now that Vicki Morse is an ARA member. I didn't speak to Palma Black directly when she was at our house. I was just aware she was there. I had no real feelings towards her being there or not.

On the Friday I was still not aware of how Stephen had been attacked and murdered. All I knew is that he had been stabbed. I would have thought I was informed by the hospital. I was not told that he was stabbed as far as I can recall but that was my understanding.

By the Friday I knew that the murder had been racist, I think that had come from Duwayne's mother but I am not sure how I knew that. At the time I didn't think about it. Neville was going to a press conference. I think when the officers came to the house in the morning, it was because they wanted a press conference to be held, and he was the one doing it because I didn't feel that I could do anything like that, so he was the one who went along. I saw the press conference on the television. I can't remember much more about the Friday except that there were a lot of people in the house. Most of them friends and relatives.

On the Saturday I remember we got up and we were going to see Stephen. I think that was arranged on the Friday, probably because we asked to see him when the police came. I don't remember being told that it wasn't possible. I don't remember being told that. On the Saturday I remember a woman officer, not in uniform, a Linda Holden came, she was one of the liaison officers. I remember her coming to the house and we travelled in the car with her, both Neville and myself and a friend. I remember that also part of the group were my sister and her husband and some other members of the family came along. We travelled with DC Holden and I found out that the driver was an off-duty policeman, the driver who had stopped Duwayne on the night of Stephen's death.

We drove down to Greenwich mortuary, which is off the Greenwich High Road. We were in a room with quite a few glass panels. We were on the opposite side of the glass panel and we could see through that as they brought his body in. They brought him to the window and I must have asked because I wanted to touch them. At first the Coroner's office or the police said no we couldn't. I think I wanted to see the wounds and everything because someone else had told us that they had arrived later at the hospital and they had been in to see them and that he had pin pricks on his arm. I didn't know what this was suggesting - all over his arm - but this concerned me because I wanted to know what had been done to him. I didn't tell them why I wanted to see them but eventually they allowed only Neville and myself in. Neville asked then if his friend could come in because we wanted things explained to us and his friend knew about medical things, he had worked in hospitals and we trusted him. We wanted them to tell us and hoped he could explain what these pin pricks were because we didn't trust anyone else to tell us the truth.

We were allowed to go behind the glass panel and saw Stephen who was on a trolley covered. I took the covers off to look at him. By then they had carried out a post-mortem on him because you would see the wounds going right down the middle of his chest. That's when I noticed the stab wounds. I checked for little pin pricks. There were loads of marks on his arm but Neville's friend wasn't sure what they were. It may have been treatment he had at the hospital and if it was maybe they did quite a few and they couldn't find a vein. We never really found out what it was. As well as that, we wanted to see the head wounds. He had a bruise on his face to one side of his cheek, probably from when he fell. I think we were there for about 40-45 minutes.

Then we went and drove via the spot where he died; not where he was stabbed but where he died. I don't remember if we asked for that, or if the police officers suggested it, but we went via that way. We were told that he died by a spot near the tree, and we were pointed up from there to where he was attacked at the junction of Dickson Road. At that point I couldn't believe that he had managed to run so far with the wounds that he had.

The Saturday is the first recollection that I have of DC Holden. I don't think it was every made clear what her role was. Later it became clear that she was supposed to be there in a supporting role. We saw her several times on the Saturday, but as far as I'm concerned, once they had left the house, they didn't come back. They dropped us off and I could swear they didn't come back to the house. I remember it wasn't long, and Palma was at the house. If she was there when we left, I'm not sure. She was just sitting there with, I think, a Carl Booth from the ARA, but I'm not certain if he had been there in the morning. Members of our family and friends were taking all the phone calls. I didn't take any calls. We had a book, but I cannot remember when that came in. It was my friend's idea to make a note of everybody who called, because she must have noticed how many calls we were getting, and inquiries. We just wanted to keep a record of people who were calling, as well as people knocking on the door; not members of the family, but people who we didn't know, who were coming.

On Saturday the Anti-Nazi League came to the house and the Black Panthers; the ANL arrived with some money that they had collected. I think I met them directly. I thought it was a surprise that they had gone out to collect money because they had heard that Stephen had died, and they were out there and, I presume, in the area of Eltham. I thought it was really strange that people that we didn't even know were giving us money. When the Black Panthers came I found it really frightening. They were dressed in hoods with dark glasses. I think I opened the door when they knocked and was shocked seeing these people from wherever and I think I went inside and sent Neville to the door to talk to them. While Neville was at the door talking to them Palma said to me that we did not want to get involved with them as they are dangerous. They had attacked her in the car park, which frightened me even more. I couldn't really understand why they had come. Palma Black was there every day.

On the Saturday my mother came down, which was also a traumatic thing, having to explain to her about her grandson.

On the Sunday we went to church in the morning. The people at the church knew what had happened because on Friday members of the church had come to see us. The news must have spread quite quickly and quite wide. I felt that I needed to go to church. They say that in times of trouble you turn to whatever you feel comfortable with, and I felt comfortable and I wanted to go, so we all as a family went. Neville, who doesn't often go to church, also came. My mother also came with Stuart and Georgina. When we came back from church, I remember a lot of people were around and hardly anywhere could I be on my own. There just wasn't any room. I remember David Cruise. He used to be the Minister of Trinity Church and he had known Stephen since he was six or seven. I spoke to him on the Sunday because somebody from the church would have contacted him. We went to the boys' bedroom to talk, because at the time every other room in the house was occupied. I remember the police being there, and I think we spoke to them in our bedroom. I remember a letter arrived and David read a letter from the Taffes, who were the couple who were at the scene when Stephen collapsed. He read the letter to us. It was really comforting, I felt, to know that somebody was with him because I think my question was, and still is: did he know that he was dying? And who did he ask for? And how was he? And was he frightened? Those are all the things that I want to know. In some ways the letter had said that he was calm and at peace, so it was reassuring to some degree to know that he hadn't been frightened.

Nothing else stands out in particular of that Sunday. I do remember a man, who was supposed to have been some security man, came. He was frightening as well. He was part of the ARA people with Palma and Marc Wadsworth.

My relationship with Palma and Marc was that I didn't know them or anything about them. They were trying to reassure me that they were there to support. I remember seeing Palma forever using the phone, and I pointed out to her it was our phone bill. She said not to worry about anything; that they would help us through everything.

On the Monday morning Georgina went off for a week, and I think my sister went with her to the school trip and Stuart went to school. From then on someone always went with them to school, even Stuart. Carl Booth would walk Stuart to school because it is walking distance. Practical support was being provided by the ARA. Nothing further stands out about the Monday.

On Tuesday, I can't remember anything specific. I remember that in between all the times, the police were there on a regular basis, more or less every day. They would have been Holden and Bevan. They never actually told us what their role was. We were never given any up-to-date stuff; we didn't know what was happening with the investigation or even if there was one. The only think I could gather from them being there was that they wanted information: they wanted information about Stephen. They used to ask us about his friends and whether he was in a gang. They asked us about gloves that they found and a cap that was in his bag or something. All that was coming across all the time was: "Who are the people in your house; and what are their names; and what are they to do with Stephen?" We were never given any information. We were never told that they were there and that we could go to them if we wanted to know about the investigation. Linda Holden left her mobile number with Neville.

I remember that Imran Khan was representing our interests. I was first aware of this on the Sunday. I didn't think it was unusual. Mind you, it is difficult to say what is unusual or usual; you don't really know what the norm is; you don't know what procedures are to follow. But I was just really glad that there was somebody there who could find out on our behalf what was going on. We were just not being given any information. The police did not come to us and say: "Your son has died. This is how he died. This is what happened. This is how it happened." We don't know the full story about how he died and we weren't being told that his death was being investigated. At least I was never told that.

The first time we started to get an idea that information was coming to the house, surrounding names and details of the murder, was during the first week. I can't remember the exact day. I haven't actually spoken to anyone directly regarding this. It was through somebody. I understood that people were saying that they knew who had committed the murder, and that they had information and that they felt that they needed to come and tell us. This information was all kept in the book. I don't know when the book started, but it was from the time when people started telephoning to give information; calls came in and we kept a note of the messages. As far as I can remember, information being passed to the house was passed to Imran Khan, who in turn passed it on to the police. As days went by we were never made aware of anything that was happening. That was the most frustrating thing. We asked the officers that come to the house, and we found that at one point, a week or so later, Bevan said to us, in a very sarcastic way, that we should go to the incident room and see how hard they were working on the case. I said I didn't want to hear that; I didn't want to see the Incident Room; that wasn't going to tell me anything: I just wanted to know exactly what was going on: who had been caught; had anybody been caught; had any suspects been arrested? They must have an idea of who they were, because I was getting all of this information that the boys were known to the police. This information was coming to my house that these boys were well known in the area; that the police knew they had knives; that they always clean the knives in the front room; and that police have seen them; and that this was something that the police were aware of. I felt that the police were not doing anything and they were too busy investigating Stephen.

Eventually, we heard a rumour that the police were at Duwayne's place all the time as well, questioning him and anybody who visited him because he was living on his own. They wanted to know who the visitors were, and all their names, and why they had come, and all of that sort of thing. During that week I didn't have any contact with Duwayne. I heard rumours that he was on his own and I was worried about him because of that. I remember somebody saying that they knew him or his mother well; and I suggested that that person talk to his mother to take him away. I felt that the police were having too much access to him and he had nobody to support him. They would must turn up at his place and I didn't think it was right. He had been through such a lot. He was on his own and he needed adult support. My concern was that he was really vulnerable.

I remember going to a press conference at Woolwich Town Hall, arranged by Marc Wadsworth from the ARA. I think this was before Georgina's birthday on the 30th April. Holden came to the house on the afternoon of that day, which was the time that she usually came. I can't remember what the discussion was about, but we were asked as parents to send a letter to Georgina to keep in contact while she was away. It suddenly dawned on me that it was her birthday. Usually presents and cards are bought in advance, so I must have bought her card but not a present when Stephen died; and I remember saying that I hadn't got to post her birthday card as I had wished and, even though she was returning on that day, I wanted to do that. Linda Holden offered to take it down for me and post it. That surprised me because that was the last thing I expected. I thought it was good of her. I read somewhere that I didn't thank her for that. To me this is out of character, and there is no way I would have been so rude and arrogant about the whole thing, and at this time I still trusted her.

The first time I went out after Stephen's death was on the 30th April. I went to the shops in Woolwich. There is a car park above the Sainsbury's and that was the first time I drove and went out. I went out with my sisters, my two sisters and my cousin. The four of us travelled in the car. We drove into Woolwich. I looked for somewhere to park, and I was going up to the next level and I could see a space but you needed to get round and round to get up to it. As I drove up and on to the next level, there was a woman and her daughter pushing a trolley, and I saw them and I stopped. They stopped. I thought they would move on. They started to move. We went back and forwards, and I suddenly said: "What are you doing?" I said: "What are you doing", in the car to myself so she wouldn't have heard it, but I think she saw my gesture which was. I remember she made a remark. I can't remember what it was, but it was definitely racist and everybody in the car just got angry because of what had happened to Stephen. They were saying: "Let us out", and was trying to park the car. All three of them were asking to be let out to challenge her. I went down to the parked car and they got out and they ran down to her. I was not in earshot of any of the stuff and I didn't see any of the things that went on, but I was told later that my sister had said to her: "It was one of you bastards that killed my nephew", and her reply was: "If he hadn't been here, he would still be alive", meaning if he wasn't in this country, he would still be alive. What do you say? What could you say? Before they approached her the white woman had got a brick. She had got a brick from the boot of her car. She was holding the brick and it was like: "If you come anywhere near me, this is what you will get." All they could do was take the woman's registration, which they did. They came back and told me about it, and they told Imran Khan the details and he reported it to the police. My sister and me and the others made statements on that night, or a few days later, but as far as I know nothing had happened with this incident. Weeks later we were told at Greenwich Race Office, where there was a meeting with the police, some sort of community meeting - I think it was Philpot who told us that no action would be taken, because we had to understand that at this time the white woman had had a bereavement. So that was the end of it.

By the end of the first week there was disappointment with the liaison officers. Their attitude when they came to the house was just checking up to see who was there, anyone who was of interest because they were more concerned with the people in the house than they were with us. They would see us and in fact I have read, that they claimed they could not get any access to us. It is complete rubbish. Whenever they came down they would see us. They were shown into the living room and it was just us in the living room with nobody else. There were no organisations. We would make room to see them. My sister may have been there, but certainly no organisations. Each time they came they were shown up to wherever we were and they would ask questions about Stephen. The problem with liaison officers is that they were only interested in the people who were in the house. The people in our house were all black. The people who killed my son were white. Why should they be interested in the people who were in the house? It has been suggested that they were looking to build up a picture of Stephen, but that is not what I would say. What I would say is they were gathering information of interest about the people in the house, and that as black people in the house, there must have been something criminal or whatever. If they were trying to build up a picture of Stephen, it was simply to see if he was in any sort of mischief. They never asked us any questions about Stephen, about him as a young child. There was nothing genuine that they asked. There was none of that.

Their attitude towards the family as a whole was patronising. Once incident sticks out in my mind, which was with Bevan. He was in the living room one day, and I think I must have been in my usual mode of asking: "What is happening? What is going on?", and how we have not been given any information and: "Has anybody been caught?" He started going on again about how hard they were working and he didn't know if we would understand, that the procedure is not what we think it is: they have to ask questions and do this and that. We said that we had been passing on information and we wanted to know what was being done about that information. We were told to speak to someone else as they couldn't give us that information. The whole thing, how they were talking: I don't know, I can't say that, if it was a black police officer, it would have been better. I mean, how many black police officers do you know anyway? How many black police officers do you see within the force? So I don't know who they would use for a family like ours. Perhaps it would have been different. That is something that we will never know. I do think, though, that the liaison officers did not understand us. I would say that they came with a preconceived idea of what black families are like, so they had that notion in their heads to start off with. They came with the idea that we wouldn't ask questions and that we would just accept what we were told; and the fact that we were asking questions and that we wanted to know everything, is something they didn't anticipate would happen.

We were only asking questions like: "From the information we had given them, was it useful? Were any of the names of any use? What happened? Where they able to go around to the houses? Are these people really known by the police?" I wanted to know, if the police officers knew these boys, were they actually capable of doing what was alleged they had done to Stephen? I had the feeling that, if people in the community knew what was going on and who was responsible and were trying to tell us, that the police should arrest them. What was said was that the police knew of them cleaning their knives and thing, and all the other attacks and all the intimidation in the area. I would have assumed that, during that first night, if they knew all that, they would have arrested somebody. In days that followed, information kept coming to us before, we had information, we knew no names; we knew nothing about the area, nothing about the boys, nothing at all. I knew nothing. Once the information started coming in through the questions, it was the question following: "Why has no one been arrested?" It started dawning on me that, if it had been the other way around that night, somebody would have been arrested, regardless of whether they had done it or not. We were never asked by any of the organisations supporting us to ask the police for information, or that they wanted to be present when the police spoke to me and, anyway, being the person that I am, I would never have allowed that to happen.

Within the first few weeks we then heard that the boys were now hanging around out house. I heard from a relative. She was one of the people last to have left the house on that particular night. It had gone midnight, and when she reached home, she rang me. She said that when she left the house she had seen some boys coming from different entrances to our road. There were several entrances to our road. She didn't say which entrance exactly but, as she came out of the door and walked to her car, she was aware of two boys turning the corner and coming towards her. She then saw another two boys from another corner walking towards her. She got frightened then and then she ran to her car and shut the door. She said she drove a little way and looked in the mirror and saw that the four boys were standing together across from our house just starting at our house. After that she stopped at Shooters Hill Police Station and she told them what she saw. They said that they were unaware of any murder having taken place in the area. She went home and she rang us. She spoke to Neville. We then spoke to Imran Khan to tell him. No police cars were sent that I was aware of. I was later told that a car was sent. Nobody knocked on our door or said anything to us. That incident really frightened me. How did they know where we lived? Then earlier on during the week I think our address was in the papers.

There was another incident where our tyres were slashed, that was done during the night. I know it was a Sunday but I am not sure of the date. We had started to go away at weekends because it was the only break we were getting from people being at the house. We would spend the weekend with Neville's cousin's. We came back on the Sunday night and they had slashed our car. That was reported to the police but they never took a statement about any of that stuff that has happened.

Our concerns were such that we then started making inquiries to move from that address. I made enquiries with Greenwich Council. I remember we were having weekly meetings with the police so this was after 6th May and I remember telling the Police about the boys watching our house and Illsley's remarks were: "What boys? What house?" as though we wanted to brush it aside. As far as he was concerned it was nothing serious and we were just being paranoid. It was as if to say we were being stupid, not paranoid, but stupid.

There was a press conference at Woolwich Town Hall which I think was being organised by Palma and Marc. I remember being asked to attend by them, so Neville and I attended. My sister may have been there and Roz, I think. I know that Imran was. This was done to highlight the fact that time was passing, nobody was arrested and nothing seemed to be taking place. It was just a request for information. We didn't ask for this to be arranged.

There was then an invitation to meet President Mandela. We went because we saw him as a way of highlighting the fact that the British government and the people in power here were not interested, and that nobody had come to visit us except for the local MP, Peter Bottomley. I remember saying to him during the week of the murder: "Does the Prime Minister know about my son?" He said, "Well, I don't think so." I said: "Why not?" and he couldn't answer. Nobody was showing an interest that a young man had been killed and that the papers, even though they ran the story, there was nothing on the Friday, but they ran the story on the Saturday. Then you had the London bombing and that was it, no more mention of Stephen.

When we went to meet Mr Mandela we talked about Stephen being killed and that the Government, the people, the police weren't doing anything, his killers weren't being brought to justice. We felt, perhaps, I suppose we were a bit naive at the time, thinking that perhaps this meeting with any official on our behalf we may be able to bring that up. He went on to say about black life being cheap in South Africa and that how he thought it was different in this country. He didn't realise it was still the same as what was happening there. He was quite concerned that this had happened. Nobody showed any interest in that.

As a result of that meeting the following day they arrested somebody. We weren't told who was arrested but we were informed that two boys had been arrested. I remember when the first arrest was made we weren't told as a family, we were told it by the media. When the second arrest was made because we complained that the last time we had been the last to hear and we had to hear about it just like everybody else on the news, on the next arrest Bevan phoned to tell us that two more boys would be arrested but to keep it quiet. Within half an hour of being told that it was on the news.

Another incident a week after the incident the GACARA, Greenwich Action for Racial Equality organised the candlelit vigil. I heard about that from Palma, I think, probably. The information was coming through them that GACARA was doing something with the schools. I remember a big fuss was being made that the family had not been consulted and they had done this thing off their own back. At the time I wasn't concerned that we were not informed, I hadn't given it any thought. This was before things like this started to happen regularly. I was aware that Imran had been asked to write to organisations to say: "Please consult the family before they do anything."

I was never approached by any organisation directly to support but I was aware of GACARA and different groups. Because we were not personally taking calls we were told a lot of stuff that was happening. I knew from a lot of other people who were there. If anyone from GACARA came to the house - I couldn't say specifically who, I don't remember meeting anyone or any letter or any phone call from GACARA that I took - I never took any calls but I was always told or it would be in the message book.

There were then our regular meetings with Philpot. I went to those meetings with members of the family. Our first meeting with them, which I can recall was on 6th May, because it was after we met Mandela, so I remember it was the very first meeting. Before the meeting with the police I remember being concerned that although they had all the information that had been sent from us, from my own mind I decided to write down the names, so I got the book, I wrote all the names on a piece of paper and I took it with me. I remember walking into the room where Philpot and Illsley were. I handed the paper to Illsley. I don't know why I handed it to him. I sat on the chair. My sister was there, Imran Khan and Neville. I don't know if Ros was there but I remember sitting very quiet listening to what was happening around me and watching Illsley, having given him the paper, to see what he was doing. That's when I saw him fold the paper up so small and I think on that meeting - I don't think I said anything because it was too much of a shock. He rolled the piece of paper up in a ball in his hand. I was so shocked by what I saw.

He didn't tell us anything. He wasn't giving any information away. He wasn't telling us how far he had got with the investigation or what was happening or who they suspected of doing the murder. Meeting were taking place with him and not the liaison officers because we were getting fed up with them. They weren't telling us anything or giving us any information. They were not saying what was happening with the information we passed on. We told nothing about what was going on. The decision not to use the liaison officers came much later. When we had the first meeting they were still coming to the house. No one told us that we should not use them. Perhaps in the first week I wasn't being very coherent or taking an active part in what was happening. As the week progressed I was getting more and more angry because nothing was happening. We were not told anything. Nobody was being arrested and it just dawned on me at the time that they had no intention of doing anything about Stephen's murder and that's when I started taking an active role at the meetings with Philpot. Ros and Carl were there, I think because they were members of the community and because Ros is a worker from the Greenwich Racial Equality Unit. They would have come possibly on Neville's invitation but it would have been discussed beforehand. I don't remember saying I wanted them to be there or inviting them but Neville may have asked them to come.

When I eventually found out that someone had been charged with the murder it was like a relief. At long last something is going to happen, someone has been arrested in connection with the murder. What followed was "If any of the names had been given, was it one of those boys who was going to be charged?" I didn't attend the Magistrates' Court when they were being produced, either we didn't know about it or we weren't asked to go. Then there as the question of the release of Stephen's body. At one point they said that they didn't want to release his body until his killers had been caught. We were told in a police meeting that the suspects, all had rights to their own post-mortem being done. When the first lot was arrested, a post-mortem was done and when the second lot were arrested there was a rumour but nobody could decide whether it was going to happen. We were told after the second post-mortem that his body would be released so we could start making funeral arrangements.

These arrangements were that he would be buried in Jamaica because if he had been buried here it would have been on Cemetery Lane, Charlton where he used to walk. That was the route to Elvin's house. Even late at night I used to ask him if he was frightened but he would never let on that he was. It was discussed where we would bury him and Jamaica came up. I made enquiries and then it was, where in Jamaica? Some of the names I was not comfortable with and I think someone said that they bury people on top of each other and I didn't want that. There was a plot of land, though that belonged to myself and my aunt and I remember ringing my aunt in Florida and saying: "Could we bury him there?" My grandmother is already buried there so there was no objection to that. We said okay, so my sister made most of the arrangements for Jamaica.

Near to the time when his body should have been released there was a question mark that it might not because the second lot might want to do their own post-mortem. They couldn't decide whether they were going to or not. The date was drawing near, it was 12th or 18th June. A memorial service was held in the Trinity Church and I had a lot to do with that organisation. I decided what I wanted. This was held because he went to that church and to give the people the opportunity, members of the family and people who couldn't attend the funeral in Jamaica to attend some service.

I went to Jamaica in the knowledge that people had been charged with the murder. The British Embassy in Jamaica was very strange considering that nobody in this country was interested in Stephen's death but the High Commissioner, he attended Stephen's funeral. One of his officers met us on the plane, but they had (which was really funny) no jurisdiction so they had to queue with everybody else and it took forever to get out. We had to get through Customs and everything. They came around to the house where we were staying. I think Neville went on his own to the Embassy and when he asked if he could attend the funeral, which he did, he made several contacts while we were there and we were invited to their place for tea. At the time his wife was out of the country, but Derek Milton invited us to the house and even let the children go swimming. They had a pool. I understand that he had found out from Paul Boateng about Stephen. I remember him saying that he would contact them to make things easier for us. It didn't because they didn't have any jurisdiction but they did what they could for us. No government authority from this country contacted us as far as I know.

It was at some point towards the end of July, a Thursday, that we found out that charges had been dropped. I was shocked because this was a phone call. I don't know if Imran Khan or my sister made the call. I think it was Imran Khan and I spoke to him. I was angry and I was shocked and I wanted to know what the hell was going on. Why were the charges being dropped? We had no idea they were dropping charges or why. When we returned to the UK it was to the story of them releasing the boys.

Neville didn't want to stay at our house so we never went back to our house at Llanover Road. It was all to do with the fear of what had happened and all the stuff with the car, the boys and they knew where we lived and what we looked like. They could identify us but we couldn't identify them. So personally I always felt like a target. We stayed at Neville's cousins for several weeks and then we stayed with Ros.

Greenwich didn't do anything to help us by re-housing us. We went to meet with the Assistant Housing Director Cedric Boston. He came before we left for Jamaica in June and the proposal was that they could swap our house or because we had bought our house it was no longer a council house and he was going to look into whether the council could set up an exchange or something for the same value. We didn't find any alternative accommodation when we came back. There were rumours, apparently, that we were not coming back to this country, that we had heard on our return so there was no point in looking for anywhere for us to live. That thought hadn't crossed our minds. I was doing my degree and my children were at school. There was

(FROM 25 MARCH 1998)

[As provided to the Inquiry; read to the Inquiry on 11 June 1998].

Information had allegedly come to Greenwich about the murder, they and we thought the police would apply to get the Inquest adjourned to investigate further information. The police did nothing to assist us and they wanted it to go ahead. Mr Mansfield had to argue hard for it to be adjourned. I felt that the police deliberately did this to try and stop us proceeding with the private prosecution. At this stage we became extremely concerned and we asked for a meeting with Commissioner Condon.

The first time I met Weedon was after we had met the Commissioner. He said how sorry he was about what had happened and how hard they had been working. I pointed out to him that the newspapers said he had spoken to the family when I knew nothing about him or of his existence. I asked him why he spent most of his time doing newspaper interviews and not introducing himself to the family when he had the opportunity but he didn't. He said that it was because there was a lot of activity at the inquest and it was not the right time to introduce himself to us. I felt he should have introduced himself from the time he was put in charge of the case. That would have been the "right" time to have met with us.

The police were not interested in keeping us informed about the investigation. We were simply regarded as irritants. We were never formally told that Illsley had taken over liaison. We never knew who was in charge. As for Weedon we read in the papers that he had been congratulated by us on how well he was doing, before that we didn't know he existed. We didn't actually meet the man until a year later. DAC Osland, we also read about in the papers. He said that if we persisted in accusing the officers of being racist he would recommend that they could sue us. I now see in briefing notes that in July 1993 he said that he was "fed up to the back teeth with the Lawrence family."

When we started our series of meetings with senior officers things did not get much better. I have seen references to our "thirst" for information which I frankly find offensive. This was after all the murder of our son. It was also claimed that the police found dealing with our solicitor a hindrance. Basically we were seen as gullible simpletons. This is best shown by Illsley's comment that I had obviously been primed to ask question. Presumably there is no possibility of me being an intelligent black woman with thoughts of her own who is able to ask questions for herself. We were patronised and fobbed off. As the meetings went on I got more and more angry. I thought the purpose of the meetings was to give us progress reports. But what actually happened was they would effectively say, "Stop questioning us, we are doing everything. That simply wasn't true and it led me to believe then and now they were protecting the suspects. In September 1993 we hoped to get some feedback from the Barker review. We met with him too, he said he couldn't give us a copy of the report but he promised we'd meet again so that he could tell us what he had found out. That was the first and last time we ever saw him.

The second investigation started with meeting Commissioner Condon in April 1994. We discussed the Barker review and it was the first time we met Ian Johnstone. This led to another meeting with Nove and Weedon. I thought the second investigation would have highlighted what had gone on the first time around - what did and did not happen. I expected it to produce enough evidence to charge the boys.

Commander Nove, tried to come across as someone who cared. He gave his personal assurance that he would do everything he could in order to catch the people who were responsible for Stephen's murder, although a year had elapsed and there may be little in the way of evidence, he would do the best they could. I did not believe him 100% but I wanted something to happen. I was getting more information from those officers. Although they were still cautious about the information, they would give us. Eventually we were told about them "taking out a key player", but we were never informed who this was. We were given an idea of what was happening. I don't think we were told in detail about the surveillance that was happening. We did not want all the details, just were the names we gave useful? Yes or no. Even though I was uncertain I had very high hopes of a new squad. My question though was why were they suddenly running round being so helpful - who were they trying to protect and what lay behind it. My concern was the rumours that the first investigation had all gone bad because there was some link between the police and the Defendants. These rumours were everywhere. I therefore thought that a special squad set up from outside the area would be impartial and able to get to the truth. I now feel that I was deceived again. I felt that the second team wanted us to believe that they would get to the bottom of what went on and with their help we would get a conviction. When I think of the hours that our legal team spent down at Shooters Hill and for what? It bore no fruit. What concerns me is that the number of the officers - senior officers - who have been involved - years of experience and at the end of the day we never got further than square one.

There was also little regard for our safety. Even if you ignore all the information coming in, the history of stabbings in the area made these boys known to the police. If they were black, they would have been arrested straightaway just in case, especially if they were known to the police as local troublemakers.

For the majority of this case the boys knew our whereabouts and what we looked like and we didn't know them. I told the police on several occasions how frightened we were and about several incidents, it was not taken seriously. There was the incident with the brick I mentioned before. Our tyres were slashed twice. Some boys were hanging around our house as I mentioned before and we also got threatening letters. There was never any investigation.

When I mentioned these things to Illsley he said "What boys?", "What house?" and when I explained he made a brushing aside gesture with his hand and said, "Oh them, they're just thugs", as if we were over-dramatising things. On one occasion I was at a bus stop and two boys started spitting towards me. They looked at me hard. It was clear that they recognised me. They stared at me and I stared back. I got onto the bus and suddenly became very frightened. I thought they knew me, they would know where I got off the bus, where I lived and I was in danger. It was incidents like this that I kept relating to Illsley and all the time they were thinking the boys needed protecting from us.

When I look back now I feel we were misled in those meetings. We were told there was a wall of silence. We couldn't understand this because people were constantly visiting and phoning our own home giving names and information. All of this at least once, often twice a week was passed to the police. We now also know that the police received a vast amount of information, not only from the public but several police officers via their informants.

I can't believe that if these matters had been investigated properly they couldn't have helped the Inquiry. We asked Illsley whether there could be any connection between the other stabbings and Stephen's killing. He categorically stated no and that they had looked at that. Now we see about a red car that was travelling up and down the scene that had two known racists in it one of whom was connected to the murder of Rolan Adams. The plethora of information about these boys who was in the area, they were known to the police because of the other stabbings that they had committed.

We were still kept in the dark about some things in the second investigation. The police would not tell us exactly what was happening but we heard rumours that things had gone wrong during the first investigation. I think there was some cover up about what was going on.

It was then decided that the Crown Prosecution Service would not take matters further. I felt that we had no choice but take a private prosecution. I don't believe they would have been acquitted if we could have presented everything to the jury.

I believe that the decision we made at the time was the right one because if we had waited we would have had less chance, so the decision was right. The forensic that they should have found, we found. The forensic that matched the fibres from Dobson's jumper we found ourselves. It cost us £10,000 from the Campaign Fund to get an expert. Money that people had sent into us. I feel that we had to do most of the investigative work ourselves.

I think, looking back at the private prosecution, we were led to believe that we would get a just outcome. We had passed the hurdle of the committal and it was clear that these boys were the ones who had murdered Stephen - we weren't being vindictive. I believe after what we saw and heard that the Magistrates' decision was the right one. Had we been able to present the same facts to the jurors the outcome would have been different.

The committal was the first time I heard the evidence. It was difficult to hear everything, it was still too shocking and disturbing. At the time of committal however we felt extremely optimistic. I had a false sense of security about the private prosecution, looking back on it, because I felt that for the first time the police were working with us not against us. I felt the officers from the second team were really committed and had laid a foundation to show their commitment and that we could actually achieve something. At the committal the boys whole attitude was extremely arrogant. They felt really strong and secure about themselves. They never once looked worried. They had a sort of "come and get me if you dare" attitude. On one occasion two of them were seen to make cut throat gestures while looking in our direction. It also shocked me to see how much people were prepared to lie for them. Gary Dobson's girlfriend's mother was called and the Magistrate actually put her in the cells for contempt because she refused to say anything. She wouldn't confirm her earlier statements to the police and she almost ended up spending Christmas there.

After the committal my feelings were of hope. I felt that we were at long last getting somewhere. We were going to achieve what had been denied to us for so long. On the first day at the Old Bailey I was extremely optimistic but from the minute the Judge opened his mouth my hopes were dashed. It was clear from the outset that he had come the intention of not letting the matter proceed any further. We'd been warned that the State was against us and it wasn't in the interest of anybody to let private prosecutions by black families succeed because it would set a precedent. It was clear that this was not a man who would allow us to present to the Court the full story and let the jury decide. He made a ruling from the outset that the jury could not hear from Dwayne, the most important witness. The Defence with the Judge's resistance set about discrediting Dwayne completely. The whole mood was set for me by the almighty fuss that the Defence made out of people around the Court wearing Stephen Lawrence ribbons. They spent some time arguing for a ruling that people around the Court couldn't wear ribbons which of course the Judge acceded to. This was the sensitivity with which the private prosecution was received and these were the issues with which Judge Curtis chose to concern himself. In my opinion, however, it was clear from the expressions of the jury that they wanted to do their job and they obviously felt cheated when the Judge instructed them to return a verdict of not guilty. When he told them that there was no other alternative they actually went out to consider and then came back in. They didn't want to do it.

When it became clear that the Judge wouldn't let us go any further, I collapsed at Court. I just couldn't cope with anymore and I had to be carried out. I wasn't even there for the last day. I didn't want to hear one more word the man said. I just couldn't face it. I could not believe it. From the first day in Court I could sense that things were going wrong from the time the Judge sat down. It was as though we were just pawns, being played, we had no say. We had no part of it, we had nothing to do with what has being directed. We were just being swept along. It was like watching a play where someone is behind the screen being a puppet and someone pulling the strings. You think you are in charge yet you are not. You are led to believe that you have a say. I think after the committal I thought we were getting somewhere and we are going to prove that this is what the CPS should have done and achieve what they should. After the collapse at the Old Bailey I realised there was no way that the State would have allowed us to have done that, because that would have been a slap in the face for the Government and the Crown Prosecution Service. What was coming across for me at the time was - "Who do we think we are - some black family telling them that their justice system stinks."

Looking back I believe I was naive to hope that we would have got somewhere with the prosecution.

Then there was the inquest in February 1997. Again we heard more evidence we had not heard before. I stayed in Court and heard a lot more than I did at the committal. A lot more was brought to my attention than before. I was given a greater sense of what went on with the police and the information that was coming from them at the inquest. That was the first time I found out how Stephen really died. The coroner said he bled to death. He would have bled at the scene heavily and running made it worse. It was the first time that I knew there was an issue about First Aid and realised that nobody had put Stephen in the recovery position. No First Aid was given by any police officers present at the scene.

I realise that they did not touch him. My only thought was it must be because he was black. When someone is injured you expect the police to investigate where the injuries are. I did say at the inquest that they probably could not have saved his life. I am not saying that if they had done the first aid he would have lived. What I am saying is that they did not even look. They did not see his wounds, they had no idea how seriously injured he was - they knew nothing. I thought that the police had put Stephen in the recovery position but they did not even touch him. The off-duty policeman I understand used a blanket from his car to cover him. Police officers are aware of First Aid - it is basic training as they are sometimes the first on the scene of an accident.

When DCI John Carnt said there were no problems with the first investigation I was shocked. I felt it must be some sort of conspiracy happening. After so many years of listening to rumours that the first officers messed up. The fact that he stood there and blatantly lied, saying as far as he was concerned the investigation was fine and the only drawback was the relationship with the family. I could not believe it - then again he is a policeman. The discussions with and investigations of the second team showed that the first team missed so many things that they could have picked up on. They knew, we knew and now the Kent Report shows it. That is when I put in the complaint. Before that everything was kept closed and guarded and if they could have kept it that way they would have continued to do so. It's taken me 4 years to read in the PCA report that a man walked into the police station to try to give information within 24 hours of the murder and it's taken me 5 years to discover that James Grant's real name was known to senior investigating officers all along.

The Coroner was extremely supportive to us as bereaved parents from the start. It also came across that the jury were affected by what they were hearing. This of course was the first time that the story had been heard in open court. They wanted to make a statement of support to us but obviously they weren't allowed to. It was empowering however to see that members of the public hearing the evidence coming out for the first time were as shocked as we were. I was also extremely touched by the support of the Coroner. I collapsed at Court towards the end and he looked after me and took me into his room and gave me a cup of tea. Even in the public hearings he dealt with the whole procedure in an extremely sensitive way I felt. On the last day after John Carnt had given his evidence the day before Ian Johnson came down, I obviously didn't appreciate his presence at that stage. I was still feeling very let down and I felt that he'd just come to support his officers and pacify me. I was actually quite offended.

I believe the Kent (Police Complaints Authority) Report "has not got to the bottom of what went on. It's scratched the surface." At the beginning it was saying that the police officers were not racist in their attitude and behaviour towards the case, but clearly by the end of it their actions show there has to be some reason. If it was not racism what was it? Incompetence? Corruption? That only goes some way to explain. We are told that these officers have years of experience at investigating murder so this was not new to them. What when wrong? Something did. Their attitude tells me it was racism. Police have a pre-conceived idea of what black people are like, and their behaviour demonstrates this yet again. According to my understanding the only regular dealings police have with black families is when they are criminals. So, coming across a black family who have no criminal background is new to them - an alien concept. It was like you have to be a criminal if you are black. When the PCA asked the question to all officers "Are you racist?" did you really expect them to say yes? One white person cannot ask another white person if they are racist. How would they know? There is overt racism when people are blatantly racist in your face and then the other covert racism, and how do you prove it?

Racism is institutionalised. From what I have read in the PCA report it's like "How dare you think I am racist." Well I say - how dare I think you are not, because nothing in your actions has proven to me that you are not, and I see no other explanation for your attitude and behaviour.

I believe because the police spent so much time investigating my family and Stephen they came to the conclusion that we were not criminals and so they had no case. They were trying to prove that Stephen was involved in something and was not attacked just for being black. They spent their time asking people in our house who they were. There was a candlelit vigil - I was only there for half an hour and it was recorded. I am sure it was the police who recorded it and there was a young man there who knew of Stephen - his connection was that his parents were friends of my sister so he would have seen Stephen, but not visited our house or vice versa. He would meet Stephen occasionally. This black young man was very tall so he stood out from the crowd. He was tracked down because he was shouting "racist murderers". He was visited by the police to find out his relationship with Stephen and the family. If the police could do that by picking someone out of a crowd and tracing them to their address - they could have found Stephen's killers.

What I want from this Inquiry is to show the police's behaviour and their inaction. Through their negligence these people have been allowed to walk free, and through the legal system three of the boys can never be brought to justice. I believe the police had a hand in the whole thing.

If I could, I would change every single police officer in the country and get a black person in charge of investigations. I would like to get someone who is truly black and not token black. There is a difference. Somebody who knows and can relate to the issues. I do not expect an officer who is black to brush everything aside and not act in the proper way but to uphold law and order for everyone. I am asking for someone who is impartial and will treat people as individuals and equals.

With hindsight you need groups like ARA to point out issues to you because someone like myself was not aware that this sort of thing was happening on a daily basis. We did not continue with their support because we felt they had an agenda. They said they were there for the family but they were there to highlight ARA and they weren't taking the family's feelings into consideration. They saw this as something to push themselves forward and to make themselves better known.

One thing I resent very strongly is the constant allegation that our solicitor somehow stop them doing their job. How could he?

Weedon says that there were more solicitors for witnesses in this case than there were for defendants. It is not surprising; the police upset Dwayne, they upset us, they upset Jo Shepherd, they upset us all. We certainly felt that we needed a solicitor to support us.

They say they were unfamiliar with the solicitor representing a family. They are supposed to deal with solicitors on a daily basis, I don't understand the hostility. It was obviously necessary for us to have a solicitor, to act as a buffer between us and the people who were dealing with us so insensitively in our time of grief.

I believe it was right to have a solicitor representing us. In hindsight it was a good thing that we did it when we did. People need that, especially if you have never had dealings with the police before. You do not always understand how the law works. It was a great help because we had no idea. We needed some background knowledge on the sort of police procedure. We needed to know how the police investigation worked. We were not getting any of this information from the family liaison officers. No black person can ever trust the police. This idea is not pre-conceived. Its based on experience and people I know who have had bad experiences with the police.

They don't seem to understand, we are not accustomed to visiting police stations, we are not accustomed to dealing with the police and we have no reason to trust them. They say that we were their "first and prime consideration" but, for example, they wouldn't set out minds at ease by letting Imran Khan come to the Incident Room with us and then they complained that they invited us to the Incident Room and we declined. We didn't want to go into a police station on our own.

At the meetings I always felt that Philpott wanted to be helpful, it seemed as if he wanted to give us more information but that Illsley was preventing him. It was just a feeling but at the meetings he would often look over to Illsley before he answered and then sometimes stop saying something. Illsley believed that we were primed beforehand that we were told what sort of questions to ask and how to ask them. There was one incident that has stuck out in my mind when I was asking about the boys in prison. I was asking why couldn't they not put a bug in with them in the room to listen to what was being said, because if they would not talk to the police they would talk to individuals, and Illsley said "We do not do things like this - no way" and I could remember that he was very angry because he assumed I was told to ask that question. There were many incidents like this where they patronised me - as if I cannot think for myself. It was a constant argument with him. He would never give a straight answer to my questions. I was getting frustrated because I was asking simple questions and if they had ever said, "This is what's happening, we have arrested so and so, it was as a result of the names you gave us, this where we are at and we are moving from here to there." I would have been satisfied. That was all I was asking for. What I'd like to know is what were the police looking for? What else did they want before they could effect an arrest? The information that I was getting, instead of passing it on to the police I should have gone and made a citizen's arrest myself. Then there would have been no need to waste time and taxpayer's money now on an Inquiry because the guilty would be behind bars. My hope now is that people will come forward to the Inquiry and give evidence. When I hear now that there wasn't in fact a wall of silence as we were told by the police, I realise how brave the people of Eltham actually were. It seems that people who were themselves at risk in the early days had made themselves vulnerable by coming forward and giving information were not rewarded by the boys being captured. I am now not surprised that no more witnesses would come forward at that time. After all, the boys were still on the street. Witness K's father actually complained about Davidson "harassing" his son. This is what was happening. You raise people's profile in the community and you still leave the boys on the street. This is exactly what happened with Joey Shepherd. He really wanted to help but they shouted his name out at the identity parade, made him public property and left him vulnerable. Basically the people who did go and give information to the police at the beginning of this Inquiry were rewarded by the police's inaction. In practice we all make mistakes but we pick ourselves up and sort things out and try harder. In this case there's been nothing but mistakes. Every officer who has come in has made matters worse. When you list the catalogue of errors you have to ask yourselves whether there possibly can be so many mistakes or whether they must be deliberate acts. By keeping us occupied they kept the black community quiet, it gave us a false sense of security and it made black people feel that justice could be achieved. We now know after the Kent Inquiry just how much had gone wrong and how much should have been done that wasn't and we are discovering more everyday.

I would like Stephen Lawrence to be remembered as a young man who had a future. He was well loved and had he been given the chance to survive, maybe he would have been the one to bridge the gap between black and white because he didn't distinguish between black and white. He saw people as people.

Statement of Neville Lawrence
7 March 1998

[As provided to the Inquiry; and read to the Inquiry on 30 March 1998].

My name is Neville Lawrence. I am the father of Stephen Lawrence.

I was born on 13 March 1942 in Kingston, Jamaica and I came to England in August 1960 at the age of 18.

Most of my relatives are still in Jamaica. The relatives I have in this country are one sister and several cousins. My mother's name was Hilda Truwe, my father's name was Adrian Lawrence. We gave Stephen my father's middle name.

I have a sister, Jean Lawrence and one brother, Norman Rose who is now living in Atlanta. I am the eldest of the three children and am the one who would do everything regarding the looking after my mother. My brother and sister left everything to me to deal with.

My mother used to run a restaurant inside the Daily Gleaner, in the early days. My father was a leather turner. He worked in a factory down in Kingston, a place called Three Miles for quite a long time. My mother died in 1989 after losing one of her legs because she had diabetes. My father is still alive and living in Kingston, Jamaica.

When I came to the UK I stayed with my aunt and uncle in law, who emigrated to England in the early 50's. My aunt did not have any children and I was more or less looked upon as her son. My sister came over before me. My aunt was instrumental in raising me and my sister. It is something that is widely done in Jamaica where the old families are responsible for bringing up a child.

When I first came here I lived in Kentish Town which at the time was notorious for Teddy boys and things like that. I was available to work as an upholsterer because I had left school and done my apprenticeship and was therefore qualified. Unfortunately I was not able to get a job. I believe that this was because of racism. The racism that we experienced then was not as bad as that we now experience. In those days it was mostly verbal, not physical. The violence is much worse nowadays.

London was not what I expected it to be. From what I read and heard it was the mother country and the streets were paved with gold. It was completely different to what I expected. It was not as advanced as I thought it would be. Maybe some people won't agree with me but it was not as advanced as Jamaica.

In the early days we did not have much contact with the white population. Because there were not a lot of black people around we tended to stick to ourselves. We entertained ourselves and went to each others house for dinner. Generally the only contact we had with the white population was at work.

I experienced racism when I first arrived here but I did not recognise it as such at the time. People used to make jokes about us in a way that you did not realise it was actually being racist. They used to call us "coons" and the like but then you thought it was just like a nickname.

There is one incident in particular that sticks out in my mind. Just after I came here, I went to the job centre although I was a fully qualified upholsterer they classed me as an improver. The morning when I was supposed to start work the people who had offered this job then realised that I was black and then all of a sudden the job disappeared. I was aware of racism back then. But, I thought to myself that this was not my country so I had to put up with certain things.

Most of my friends I met in England just after I arrived. Thirty years on we are still friends and they are just like family. My best friend is a man called Winston Shaw who was also my best man. He moved to the United States in the mid seventies. Most of the time I have lived in London. I have friends who live in Birmingham, Manchester and places like that.

Because I could not get a job as an upholsterer I went to work for the Borough Council in a factory. While I was there I thought I should not be doing this kind of job so I started to go to Woodberry Down School in Manor House, North London during the evenings. I studied tool-making. We had to do a three year City & Guilds course in order to go on and do the actual job which I passed. When it came to getting a job all the other white students got places in factories but I did not. I had wasted three years studying. I then went into furniture making. I think I stayed there for about a year and then moved on to work with a friend who had a suede and leather factory. I spent nine years tailoring at the factory.

When the work got scarce we started looking for work in the newspaper. There were lots of jobs giving work out to people who sewed at home so I used to go and pick up the work from the factory and sew it at Aspinal Road, where I lived before I got married. I then got to know Doreen's mother who was also a machinist but she only did dresses and things. While I was looking for a job for myself I used to look for work for her as well and I used to collect her work and take it to her. By meeting Doreen's mother I eventually met Doreen.

I married Doreen on 4th November 1972 in Lewisham Registry Office. Just after we got married the employment situation changed. At that time the work was scarce so I started to do painting and decorating which I had learnt in Jamaica. I started to work with two plasterers. I got a job at a plastering firm and decided that I should learn to plaster. I have been doing plastering and decorating for the last twenty years.

When we first got married we lived in Aspinall Road, Brockley for about a year. We later moved to Lindus Road. We joined a company with about fifteen people. Each person would give £1,000.00 towards setting up the company. We purchased a house in Nunhead with a shop underneath and a flat above. We proceeded to do the place up and rented out the bottom which was an off-licence.

Eventually we bought our second house in Whitworth Road, Plumstead where we lived for a couple of years. Stephen was born on September 13th 1974 at Greenwich District Hospital. I was present for the birth. It was frightening I did not think I could manage to stay there while this was happening but I'm pleased I did.

There were no problems with Stephen as a child. He was a very good baby in the sense that he did not really sleep through the day. I think he woke up once at night. Stephen went to the nursery at Woolwich Common and from there he went to the primary school on Whitworth Road. He went to Blackheath Blue Coats Secondary School where he did his GCSE exams. On obtaining his GCSE's Stephen went on to do A levels at the sixth form college.

Stephen was very talented at school. I remember we went to see the Head of his House before he went to school and there were so many good reports about him. We used to go to all his open evenings to make sure that he did not fall behind. His favourite subject was art. One of the things we discovered was that he wanted to be an architect so he was very good at drawing.

Stephen also wanted to run. I used to take him to a group near Schofields Park. He joined a club and used to go twice a week. We used to go and take him to meetings all over the country. When the London Marathon started, there was a mini marathon which Stephen took part in and did very well. I think he came 16th out of several hundred.

Stephen did work experience with Arthur Timothy who is a well known black architect. We soon realised how gifted Stephen was because at the end of two weeks Arthur Timothy told us that Stephen was so good at his work and so punctual that he had been allowed to stay at his office in charge. Normally work experience students do not get paid and yet Arthur Timothy paid Stephen for the two weeks that he was there and asked him to return to work for him once he had finished his training.

We have two other children, Stuart and Georgina. Stuart is two years younger than Stephen and Georgina is about five years younger. Stuart was also born at Greenwich District Hospital. Again I was present.

When Georgina was born we were living at Llanover Road in Woolwich. Georgina was also born at Greenwich District Hospital. I was not present for her birth because Georgina was not born on the day we expected. Doreen had gone for a check up and then something happened and they had to rush her into emergency. I received the news work whilst I was still at work. By the time I got to the hospital, Doreen had already given birth to Georgina.

Stephen got on with Georgina and Stuart in the way I got on with my sister and brother. He was the eldest one and he saw himself as somebody who had to look after them. Stuart was sickly at the time, he had eczema and asthma and a lot of time was spent going backwards and forwards to the hospital. There were occasions when Stuart was so bad he had to stay in the hospital for about three or four days at a time. Stephen would always be there with us to make sure that Stuart was alright. He was really concerned about both the kids.

Stephen has never been in trouble. We brought our children up to respect the law. As far as I know Stephen had never even spoken to a policeman.

One of Stephen's best friends was Elvin Odoru. He and Stephen used to go everywhere together. When I did not see Stephen, as Elvin's stepfather once told me when he came to our house, Stephen would be at his house. There were other friends, as he was very popular, but the one I saw most of all was Elvin. Stephen had friends of all races. We brought Stephen up in the belief that you did not see colour as a problem. I do not see colour as a problem because that is the way we are brought up in Jamaica.

Another of Stephen's friends' was Duwayne. Doreen and I met Duwayne at a christening party just before Stephen started at Blackheath Blue Coats. In the early days I used to work 14 hours a day so I used to leave at 6.00 a.m. and never got back until 9.00 pm/10.00 pm so if Duwayne used to come to the house I never saw him.

My mother was a Seventh Day Adventist. I used to go to a Catholic School so from an early stage religion has been part of my life. The children attended Trinity Church in Woolwich from an early age. Stephen was christened there. He was also blessed at a Seventh Day Adventist Church. We would go to church every Sunday.

Stephen was in the cubs and later the scouts. He was involved in numerous activities. They would regularly put on shows in the evening and take part in other charitable events.

Stephen has never said anything to me about having problems concerning race so as far as I know he didn't have any.

In the early 1990's there were several murders of black people in our area. Although I heard about them I did not know the details. It had never occurred to me that the area was unsafe for black people to live in. I had not thought that racism was so bad in the area.

The week of Thursday April 22nd 1993 Stephen was at home because his mother had gone away on a field trip to Birmingham as she was studying to be a teacher. I was unemployed at the time so I was at home. I lost my job around 1989 when the building trade started to have problems. I was taking evening classes in glass staining and during the daytime I was home and was in charge of looking after the children on those occasions that Doreen was away. I made dinner and made sure that the children went to school on time, came back on time and didn't go to bed late.

On the morning of Thursday April 22 1993 I sent Georgina and Stuart to school. Stephen normally left a bit later. He came downstairs and had some tea. He went back to get his stuff, came into our bedroom overlooking the road and said "Seeya later". I said to him "Don't go anywhere because your mum's coming home later". He asked me if I was okay and I said yes. He went down and returned upstairs and said "Are you sure you're alright dad?" and I said "Yes". Because I was not working, I was not feeling all that good about myself.

I watched Stephen go down the road with his rucksack over his back. That is the last time I saw him alive. I made dinner in the afternoon for all of us. Stuart and I were waiting thinking that Stephen was coming home at about 3.30 pm/4.00 pm At 4.30 pm when he did not turn up we had dinner and I put his in the oven with his mother's. We waited for him thinking he was going to come. I did not worry though because I assumed he was at Elvin's house.

At about 9.30 pm I went to collect Doreen from Woolwich because the coach was dropping her off there. She had her dinner and sat down to watch the news with us. Stephen had still not returned. Just after 10.30 pm there was a ring at the doorbell I thought it was Stephen. I went downstairs and opened the door. It was Joey Shepherd, his father and brother. Joey told me that he had seen Stephen being attacked down the road at a bus stop by the Welcome Inn pub by about six white youths. When he said that Stephen had been attacked Doreen came downstairs. Joey's father said that we should ring the police and find out what was happening. Doreen called the police who told her that they knew nothing about the incident.

We decided to go down to the spot that Joey said he had seen Stephen. We got into the car and I drove. We could not see anything happening when we got there. We drove down as far as the Welcome Inn pub just beyond the bus stop to the next turning on the left and we looked straight down the road. We could see straight down the road to the roundabout at Wellhall Road because it is a wide long straight road. We couldn't see any flashing lights. We were looking to see if there were police or ambulance vehicles about. We saw no lights. We saw no indication that anything was happening there so we decided to go to the hospital just to make sure. I still did not believe it had anything to do with Stephen.

We drove to the Brook Hospital which was a few minutes away. When we got there we did not see any activity that indicated that something bad had happened. We went to the Accident and Emergency Department where there was a police car parked outside. There was a policeman sitting outside in the car with the door open and another officer standing at the hospital entrance. We walked towards the reception area to see if we could see Stephen. We did not see him sitting anywhere. We looked to the waiting area and there was no Stephen so we started to look in the cubicles but he was not there either. We turned round to go back out and on the way I saw Duwayne on his own on the right hand side standing against a wall. At this point I realised that Stephen was there. I went up to Duwayne and was about to say "What happened to Stephen?".

Before I could say anything to him a man dressed in a green overall came up to Duwayne and asked him something like "What did he hit him with?". Before we could talk to Duwayne the nurse and doctor came and we started to talk to them. We asked if Stephen was there they said yes. We then asked if we could see him but they said 'no'. We asked why and were told that he was being worked on. I do not recall if it was the doctor or the nurse that spoke to us but they were both women.

We were told to go and wait in a nearby room. Doreen and I sat down but Duwayne did not. He just stood next to the door. You could see that he was distressed. We thought maybe Stephen had been stabbed in his arm or he had cut his hand or something. I was just praying that he was not dead. I thought it was just a fight in which he got cut badly but at no time did I think he was dead.

I don't remember if we talked to each other, we just sat there. All sorts of thoughts were going through my mind. I don't remember how long we were sitting there but it could have been about half an hour. Both the doctor and the nurse came in together. As I watched them coming towards us it reminded me of the hospital TV programmes you watch. As they were walking I was thinking "Are they coming to tell me that Stephen is dead". That is what was running through my mind because it was taking so long for them to come back. I started to think all kinds of things.

They came in the door. I do not remember if I stood up. I don't even remember the exact words they used but I do remember they said that Stephen was dead and we could phone our relatives or something like that.

It still did not hit me. When they said Stephen was dead Duwayne went wild. I just sat there. I was numb. Duwayne was acting as though he wanted to climb the walls. I could not take it in.

We were told we could phone our relatives so Doreen phoned her sister. I went and rang my cousin Sonia in Marylebone. I told her that we were at the hospital and there had been an accident or something and that Stephen was dead. She went crazy on the phone and said she was coming down. Some time later Doreen's sister Cheryl and her husband came. We were asked to give the hospital staff some time to clean Stephen up before we could see him.

I cannot remember if Cheryl went in to see Stephen with us but I am sure she did not go in on her own. We may have already been in there, just me and Doreen alone at first. We went into a separate room not far from where we had been sitting to see Stephen. He was lying there as if he was sleeping. I cannot remember if he was covered.

I was just looking and thinking that he was not really dead and that he was lying there asleep. I know that I left the hospital that night and drove home but I cannot remember driving home.

Nobody actually told us what had happened to Stephen. Nobody. None of the policemen at the hospital spoke to us. When we got through that door, nobody stopped us to ask us who we were, if we were the parents of Stephen or what. No policeman stopped and said anything to us. I am sure I would have remembered if they did. We were at the hospital for just over an hour. Stuart and Georgina were at home asleep. I started to worry about them being there on their own because of what had just happened to Stephen so we did not stay very long.

I do not remember if Duwayne was there when we saw Stephen and I do not know if he saw Stephen. I did not speak to Duwayne. I drove back home. I can remember Cheryl, Michael and Millie being at the hospital. I do not remember anybody else being there. Doreen went to bed but I did not. Georgina and Stuart were still sleeping.

I do not remember telling Stuart and Georgina. I do not know who told them. The first person I rang the next morning was Elvin. There is no way would I have thought that Duwayne would have been with Stephen. I would have thought that it was Elvin. It then became clear to me later on that Elvin had to go somewhere that evening and that is why he was not with Stephen. Sometimes when I used to pick up Georgina from school it would be Stephen and Elvin I would see going off for the evening. If Elvin had been available that night Stephen would have been with him.

The next day is very cloudy. We still did not know how Stephen had been killed. All we knew was that he had been attacked as we had been informed by Joey Shepherd. After I had rung Elvyn I spoke to a councillor in Stoke Newington. I then spoke to Clara and asked her to phone Doreen's school friends and let them know what had happened. Clara arrived at the house and took charge of the day to day running of the house.

I was expecting to see something about Stephen's murder in the papers on Friday morning. When I looked in the papers there was nothing so I rang up a reporter friend whom I had done some work for earlier on and told him what had happened. I asked him questions about notices going up in a press room or somewhere where journalists go to look for a story. I asked him if he had seen anything about a young black boy being killed in Eltham the night before and he said 'no'. He said he had stopped writing but was still working for the paper and that he would come down and do my story which he did. The next reporter was a person from The Voice. My cousin rang The Voice and told them what was happening. The reporter came down and did an interview. The first news report about Stephen's death came out in the Independent on the Saturday morning.

At the Press Conference the police said that they were going to appeal for witnesses to come forward. They still had not told us what had happened to Stephen. I met with the person who was in charge of the investigation on the evening of the Press Conference, Mr Crampton. He said to me that he would not be on the case for very long because he was going to do another case on the Monday and that somebody else was going to take over from him. I was told to appeal for anybody who had seen or heard anything to come forward and give evidence so that they could catch the killers.

We were introduced to the two liaison officers DS Bevan and DC Holden on the Friday before the Press Conference. They informed me that they would be keeping us up to date about what was happening on a day to day basis. I had met PC Fisher earlier that day. I understood their role to be to let us know what was happening with the case everyday, what kind of leads they had or what was happening generally but without giving anything away. To let us know how many people they had questioned although not anything specific that would jeopardise the case. They said they would keep us informed by coming round or telephoning us. They asked us if we wanted counselling but we said 'no' because we had people from the church, like the Minister of the Church, so we were not on our own.

There were Social Services people around and anti-racist groups were there to support us, the Anti Racist Alliance (ARA), another guy, Karl Booth, and later on people from the Panther UK also came. I did not see them on the Friday but they came back on the Saturday after having done a collection. As far as I know the various groups at our house were there because news had spread about the incident and because there was another incident in our area before where a black boy had been murdered. I was in no position to ask these people to leave because if what I was hearing was true, we needed people to help us handle the situation. They said they would do various things for us and because of the state we were in we did not know what to do.

I was clear by Friday that Stephen was murdered because he was black. When we were at the Press Conference people were saying that it was a racist murder and one of the people from the TV station made a comment that Stephen had been in the wrong place at the wrong time. I do not know where the information came from. The media coverage gradually lessened. I was angry because I thought that for anyone to see that and to get sense of it, it had to run the whole length so I started to think that I should talk to one of my friends in the media who was a Director for a news company.

On the Saturday I do not recall speaking to a lawyer. I am told that I went to church that day but I do not recall. I remember meeting Imran Khan on the Sunday. Various people that were telling us we had to make a decision as to how to deal with the situation. Mark Wadsworth and Palma Black who were from ARA, and others were telling us that we needed a bodyguard in case our house was attacked and to make sure that the other two children were not attacked when they were going to school.

What these people were saying was making me even more frightened because I was not expecting anything like this. I was very worried. I accepted the invitation of support because I felt we needed the support. I could see that the police weren't being supportive in any real sense. When the liaison officers arrived that Sunday they started questioning us about the amount of people in the house and the purpose of them being there. Holden asked me why all these people were there so I told her that it was my house and I was entitled to invite anyone I wanted. She told Clara that I was mad.

Holden made a remark about woolen gloves and a hat being found. I do not remember if she said they found them in Stephen's bag but it was clear that she was implying that Stephen was a cat burglar. I said that lots of people carry woolen gloves and a hat. I was very upset that she was implying that Stephen was a criminal.

I lost sense of the days that followed on from the Sunday. I just kind of got up in the mornings not knowing what day it was. As the days went by I was just getting more worried seeing that nobody was being arrested. The liaison officers would come regularly. I don't remember if it was every day that they came. I did not look forward to their visits because as far as I was concerned they were not telling me anything. I remember at some stage they mentioned something about an identification parade. I think we had some kind of argument about going to see Stephen's body at Greenwich mortuary. The liaison officers were saying that we could not see Stephen's body. Rickie Morse a counsellor was at our house and was instrumental in setting up the viewing of seeing Stephen on the Saturday 24th April 1993.

As far as I can remember it was Doreen, myself, Cheryl and possibly Michael who went to see Stephen at the mortuary. The thing that sticks in my mind was that they were saying that only Doreen and myself were allowed behind the screen at the mortuary because it was a glass screen and that the rest of the family would have to stay outside the screen and look through the glass. We were all very distressed and crying. I turned round and saw PC Fisher standing right behind me. I told him that this was a private matter and that he should not be there and should be standing so close and that we wanted some privacy. After that they let us inside to where Stephen was. I cannot remember if he was fully covered to the neck or but they did show us where the wounds were, the one that was coming down from the top of his collar bone to just below his chin. I think they described that the knife had gone in straight through his lungs and it had gone through his muscle and through to the other side and touched his heart.

My feelings at that point were that I was looking at my son lying there and thinking what butchers could have done something like this to a human being. I could not believe what I was seeing. I was hoping that the police would catch Stephen's murderers quickly because one of the mortuary attendants said that they might not release Stephen's body for burial until somebody had been caught. I became concerned about Stephen lying in this place because I was told they had to freeze him and for them to do a post mortem they had to take him out and unfreeze him and then put him back. I had been told that any persons arrested for Stephen's murder would have the right to conduct their own examination of Stephen's body. I was thinking that if there were five or six people involved in this murder they would have to take him out five or six different times and I was not looking forward to that at all.

At some point during the week following the murder a woman came to our house with information. I was upstairs at the time and could not therefore see the woman. Someone in the house answered the door and spoke to her. She said that there had been people in her house on the night of the murder who had washed blood off themselves. She gave the names of the Acourts', Norris and Knight. We then passed these details on to Mr Khan because we felt it was better for him to deal with the police. We thought as Mr Khan was the solicitor representing us, he should be the one to contact the police.

After that we were given a mobile number of Linda Holden in case we needed to contact her if we felt threatened or had information. There was one occasion, late at night, where I was walking around the house looking out of the front and back windows. We didn't have a fence or gate. I could not see everything in the road. When Millie left our house that night she noticed that there were two boys coming towards her so she rushed to her car. She looked towards our house and saw a van with another two boys standing behind it. She went to the local police station to tell them what she had seen. She was told by the officer on the desk that they knew nothing about our family. When she got home Millie rang us to let is know what had happened. She said the we should call the liaison officers and let them know. It was around midnight. We then rang Linda Holden on her mobile phone. She said she would ring the station and tell them to send someone. I recall standing by the window for a while but no police officer arrived. I range the station and they said they did not know anything about the incident.

Later on a police officer arrived. I spoke to him. He said he would drive around and look for the boys. He also said he would be keeping an eye out and would make more frequent visits.

There were other incidents where our car tyres were slashed. On another occasion someone stabbed a screw driver in to our car tyre. That happened on a day we were doing a piece for they BBC. The BBC filmed this. Somebody called the police and as I recall two officers came. I said that it was clear we were being targeted but they said this was not so and that it was probably just a nail or something that we had driven over.

This latest incident made us feel even more threatened. We wanted to move away from the area as we were very concerned about our children's safety. It was clear that not only were police not going to protect us but they didn't believe that we were any danger. We approached the Council to see if they would re-house us, even temporarily but they said that they could not since we were not council tenants. Dorothy Thomas from the Housing section came to see us about alternative accommodation. Palma Black and her team from ARA were at our place more or less everyday from early in the morning till late at night. She treated our house as though it was her office.

Someone suggested that we might receive obscene phone calls so Clara and other family members screened our calls. Our post was vetted by our neighbours who were concerned for us. ARA were also taking calls. They were also meant to keep records of all the calls. I do not know if they did or not. It was because of that some people, like the workers at GACARA may not have been able to contact us.

At no stage were we advised by anyone not to trust the police. It was clear to me from the outset that the police had no real interest in catching Stephen's murderers and for this reason we did not have much confidence in them. In other murder cases you often see the police stopping traffic and asking drivers if they have seen anything. Usually just after a murder there are lots of police vehicles at the scene and lots of activity. We saw none when we first went to look for Stephen.

I remember there was a march organised by GACARA of local schoolchildren to the spot where Stephen was murdered. Nobody approached us before doing that, it was just done. Letters were sent to organisations by Mr Khan because they were speaking to the press without contacting us first and we did not want the situation to get out of hand. The letter said that no statements should be made nor should anything be done unless they have spoken to us. This was suggested by myself and Doreen and had nothing to do with the ARA. I wanted to meet with the organisations who were supporting us so we could talk to them and discuss how things could best proceed.

We began to experience difficulties in getting contact with Holden and Bevan. Both their mobile phones always seemed to be turned off. This coupled with the comment about Stephens hat and gloves caused me to feel that they were not sympathetic. They way they spoke to us made us feel as though they regarded us as nuisance. I felt as though they resented us wanting to know what was happening with the investigation. I decided that I no longer wanted either Holden or Bevan to come to our house. I rang up CSU Philpot and told him not to send them to my house because they were not doing what they were supposed to do. A suggestion was made that we should then come to the station at Plumstead on a weekly basis and they would give us any information or tell us what was happening there. We were told that we could not come if we were going to bring Mr Khan. I then said if Mr Khan was not coming then neither were we. We had no previous experience of dealing with the police. I think that they did not want someone to attend with us who would know whether or not they were really investigating Stephen's murder properly. I think that they wanted to try and pull the wool over our eyes. In the end even with a solicitor they still failed to properly investigate our sons murder.

Eventually it was agreed that we could take Mr Khan and any family member that wanted to come to the police station once a week. Karl from the ARA came to the meeting at one stage but not at our invitation.

The meetings with Philpot were not very constructive because the questions we were putting to them were not being answered. I kept asking about forensics. Millie had told us that when she had driven to the area where Stephen had been murdered was not cordoned off. One of the investigating officers attempted to reassure me that they were looking at the forensic angle. I kept asking about this every time we met and always given the same answer. The only time I was told that there was no forensic evidence was a week before the people who were arrested were to go to court. I believe that if the police had properly cordoned off the area they would have found some forensic evidence.

Whenever we had a meeting with the police I was anxious to know what progress they had made and if we had a good chance of winning this case. They hardly ever told us anything. On one occasion Doreen had written the names of Stephen's murderers on a piece of paper because we had been given information that they were responsible. She wrote the names down and gave them to a senior officer. He then proceeded to fold this paper up in his hand like a ball as if he were going to throw it away. All of the suggestions that we made about trying to get these people quickly were treated as if we were trying to interfere. I asked them that after Stephen's body was released to me and my family to bury him were they allowed to go back and dig it up if they felt like it. They said 'yes'.

We were beginning to feel that the killers of my sons had more rights than we had. We heard that killers were being protected and being moved and all these kind of things and that was worrying. At one stage I heard a rumour that the police had moved the families of the boys responsible for Stephen's murder. We were thinking that those families were not under any kind of threat from us yet they were being protected and moved whilst we were in a house where we felt threatened and not moved to anywhere.

The first time that we became aware that someone had been arrested for the murder was when we heard it on the TV or radio. We did not hear it from the police. We heard it from the media and it was a surprise. We thought, that because we were going to the police station, we would have been the first to hear and then maybe after you would have seen it on the news.

We were approached by a member of one of the organisations to see if we would be interested in meeting President Mandela while he was in the UK. We said yes but never thought we would ever meet anybody like him because seeing that he had nothing to do with the government in this country we did not think he would be interested in meeting us. This was something to do with Britain and not South Africa. When it was finalised that we were going to meet this man we were pleased because at least somebody was going to listen to what we had to say. I was surprised to see that he was really interested and wanted to spend twenty minutes with us listening to our grievances about the way in which we were being treated by the police. The government did not make a statement about the death of our son. We did not get a message from the Queen or anything like that. President Mandela made a statement about the lives of black people in South Africa being cheap. The media and everyone was there the morning that we met him and straight after that, the following morning all of a sudden these guys were arrested.

That suggested to me that the government of this country did not care about me and my family unless the media was present or our outcry came from certain sections of the community or someone as powerful as Mandela. That was a bad thing. It showed me that all along the police knew who the people were but were not prepared to take any action unless somebody of some kind of substance said something in public that would be noticed by the world. That was our feelings. This meeting took place with Mandela in Central London in a hotel. I will always remember it. Not long before Mandela was released I had listened to a friend of his, a lawyer or someone who explained what kind of person he was and seeing that this man was inside prison for twenty odd years. I just wanted to see what kind of a person he was, if there was any kind of bitterness after being locked up for twenty odd years. All that I heard and all that this woman described about this man was true because he sat there and he listened to us talk and didn't interrupt us at any stage. He let us explain to him our feelings of losing our son and he sympathised in such a way that I felt really good after leaving.

I don't remember if our weekly meetings with the police continued after people had been arrested and charged. I felt that we would get to the bottom of this quickly after the arrest. I was hoping that the first two people who were arrested would then talk and name the other three, four or five or how many there were and then they would be arrested. But, not long after they were arrested they were released.

I remember the relief we felt when the first two were arrested. When the second post mortem took place I said to myself that we might get Stephen's body so then we could bury him. A few weeks later they said to us we could take his body but then said no so we had to get in touch with Sir Montague Levine, the coroner, and explain to him what was happening. I don't remember if a third person was arrested but a third post mortem was carried out and then Sir Montague Levine said to release the body to the family, which they did.

We had fears about burying Stephen here because of the situation surrounding his death and also the fact that it was explained to us that they were going to be able to go and dig his body after he was buried. I did not fancy the idea of my son's body being dug up after he was buried. I remember watching films where after a long period of time when somebody was dead and buried they would go and dig them up. I did not wish that to happen to my son so the family sat down just before we knew we were going to have his body and came to the conclusion that the best thing to do was to take him home to Jamaica. We had a memorial service in June 1993 and after that, towards the end of the month we flew out to Jamaica with the body. We buried Stephen a week or so later. We wanted to bury him on 4th July 1993 so we could remember American Independence but I think we had to bury him on

3rd July 1993. He is buried on a piece of land which belongs to Doreen and her cousin. Stephen's grandmother is also buried on that piece of land so he is lying beside his grandmother in Clarendon in Jamaica.

Most of my family are still in Jamaica. When they heard what was happening they felt a bit cut off because it is nearly 5000 miles away. I think they were pleased in a way that we had brought his body over so that they could take part in at least the burial. I feel that he is home, and I can be assured that nobody is going to violate his grave.

After we were in Jamaica for a while, two or three days before we left to come back, we heard that the charges against these people had been dropped. Also, in the same week we heard that somebody else had been killed. Joy Gardiner had been killed by the police. We were in constant touch with the UK Embassy in Jamaica. When we got to Jamaica with Stephen's body one of the people from the Embassy came to meet the plane and to explain to us that they were not involved, that they had no power in Jamaica but for phone calls and things relating to the UK that we needed to do we could go to the Embassy and do it from there which I used to do.

We arrived back to the news that the charges have been dropped. I felt, at least when these people had been arrested, that we were getting somewhere. To be told that the charges had been dropped and this had been decided whilst we were out of the country was a devastating blow to us. At least they could have waited until we had come back and try to explain to us the situation before they did it.

I think we stopped going to see the police then. Since the charges had been dropped I doubted that the investigation was on full scale and I think the police were saying that they would have a few people working on the case to see if anything came up. I think we stopped seeing them on a weekly basis to try and come to terms with the fact that these people had killed our son and were going to get away with it.

The inquest was in December 1993. By this time we had discussed the case with our solicitors had decided we would consider taking out a private prosecution ourselves. Later on down the road, just before the inquest there was a witness who had come forward who the police had been informed of. On the morning of the inquest the police were asked if they had investigated this new evidence. I am almost certain that they said yes but it then turned out that they had not. Because of this the inquest was adjourned. We decided that we would make sure that if they tried to do an inquest we would stop it and we would serve papers to ensure that we could bring our own private prosecution.

By this time we had moved from Llanover Road to 15 Rayton Road, Charlton. On Stephen's birthday we held a candle lit vigil at the spot where the incident happened and then marched from the spot to the estate and back round to the spot in a 3_ mile circle. After that we did a linking of hands on a Sunday linking from the spot where Stephen fell to the spot where Rohit Duggal died. That was well organised.

After we left the house where we used to live a meeting was set up with Barker. He had been chosen to look at the way the case was done and what was happening to see if he could come up with a different angle that might lead to the case being reopened. We met with him for about 4_ hours or so at the house and we went through the whole case, our fears and everything. We asked him if we would see his report. He said no we could not but he would let us know what happened. We never heard from him again. We never met him again so we do not know what he reported.

After the inquest we were coming up to the first anniversary of Stephen's death. There was a meeting with Mr Etherington of the Crown Prosecution Service. I remember he said that there was not enough evidence to take the case any further. Following that there was a meeting with Sir Paul Condon. I do not remember what was said at the meeting.

CONTINUATION STATEMENT OF NEVILLE LAWRENCE
FROM 30 March 1998

After that Commander Nove came onto the scene. He said he would be doing things differently. We used to meet with him at Plumstead police station. It seemed to me that Commander Nove was a little bit ashamed of what had happened during the initial investigation. I felt more comfortable with Commander Nove than I had with Weedon.

At the time I felt that the second investigation was conducted in a way that increased the chances of there being a prosecution. Commander Nove did not tell us exactly what he was doing but he used to tell us some things. We now know that surveillance was being used on the suspects and police were trying to see if they could get an informant to provide information. I had more confidence in Commander Nove because he treated us differently from Weedon who was hostile to us. Weedon treated us as though we were trying to get information and give it to somebody else.

It was clear to me that the police saw us as a threat. I do not know why. I have seen documentation where the police accused the family of Roland Adams of being "hostile and unco-operative". It is clear to me that the police come in with the idea that the family of black victims are violent criminals who are not to be trusted. I feel as though Bevan and Holden came in with the same attitude.

The police were saying that it was not normal for a family to be kept informed. In my view the family should be kept informed throughout. The family has just lost somebody. They want to be reassured that the job that the police are supposed to be doing is being done the right way. Given that the police failed to properly investigate my son's murder I am not surprised that they did not want us kept informed. It is clear to me that only now is the truth beginning to come out.

We had already decided that if the police and the Crown Prosecution Service were not going to do anything we would consider bringing a private prosecution. Commander Nove introduced a new Commander who was going to take over, Commander Griffiths, and the same policeman that is still here now, John Carnt.

I felt that the Private Prosecution was the only way left open to us to put Stephen's killers behind bards. I hoped that Stephen's killers would be exposed by bringing them into the public eye, even if we failed to get a conviction against them.

When the decision was made to privately prosecute I was frightened. I knew that we were entering into something that was going to be difficult. There would be lots of people who wanted the prosecution to fail. I had confidence in everybody who was on board that they would do their best. When the summonses were issued I realised that I was going to see my son's murderers for the first time. When I saw these people I knew that it was them. I just knew it was them.

The committal proceedings were one of the most frightening periods of my life. I had been advised that if we did not get past committal then that was it. So that was the most crucial stage for me. When the committal took place it was the first time that I heard the details of what happened on the night. This was three years later. I had always thought that this incident happened at the bus stop until we saw the photographs showing that it happened in the middle of Dixon Road. At Court a description was given of how these people surrounded Stephen. The part that got to me was the way that Stephen shouted out. I could just feel a pain. I felt the pain myself and I could not stand it. I collapsed at court and was rushed to hospital.

Once the committal proceedings were over I felt relieved and relaxed because I thought we had gone through the hardest part of this thing. At the Old Bailey we were going to have twelve people who were going to decide whether or not these people were guilty. We had a good chance.

Before the beginning of the Old Bailey trial, I was worried because we had heard a rumour about the judge who would be in charge of this case. We had heard bad things but I was hoping that because of the publicity around the case he would not do anything to jeopardise the trial. The morning of the trial, as usual before we went in to the court, Michael and myself had a run through of certain things.

On the final day we were breaking for lunch when Michael said to me that we were in trouble. From then on we knew that we were not going to get what we wanted. After the trial collapsed I felt that I did not want to be anywhere around this part of the world. I could not believe what I had just heard and seen. I had initially been concerned that we had got an all white jury. When the jury were told to bring in a not guilty verdict I saw the look on their faces of disbelief. It seemed to me that they could not believe that the judge was actually telling them to do this. I could not believe what I was hearing. I just sat there and I froze. I would describe that day as one of the worst of my life when I saw those guys get up and walk out of there. You could see disappointment, the anguish on everyone's face. There was no doubt in my mind that it was these people and I still do not doubt it. If I had to make this decision again, I would do the same again because we had no alternative. I could not live with myself if I had not done anything and sat back. At least I can say to myself that we have exposed these people to the public.

After the trial collapsed I felt that I could not remain in this part of the world. While I was in Jamaica trying to recover from the collapse of the case I felt that there was no way we were going to get any kind of justice. I was able to look back on all that had gone on over the past three years. I knew that the inquest would be coming up soon and I could not stand the thought of sitting in court and seeing these people who were accused of the murder of my son walk away a second time. I decided that there was no way I could face the inquest. It was not until after I heard that the government had changed that I thought there might be a chance of getting something more positive from the new government. I came back just in time to meet with the new Home Secretary and later on he agreed to set up the public inquiry after listening to some of our concerns. I have been shocked at some of the things we have heard during the progress of the inquiry. We suspected that much had gone wrong but it is clear that it is much worse than we could ever have imagined.

We have exposed some of the things that the police get up to behind the scenes. They make it clear that the investigation of racist murders or attacks are not important and often treat the victims or relatives worse than the suspects. I don't know - it's frightening.

I feel that the Metropolitan Police should be ashamed that they allow members of their force to behave in such a way which. They should find ways of stopping this from happening. If there had been a black policeman in charge of the investigation with powers to do what he wanted, I feel the outcome may have been different. However, if there is a black policeman in charge of the investigation with no power to do what he wants then it will make no difference. If there are black liaison officers, maybe they would see the family in a different light.

I would say that both racism and corruption played a part in this investigation. Racism I think, because the police always see a black person as a criminal - even when they have not committed a crime and are victims. As to corruption, I think that some of the police officers investigating my son's death were connected to the murderers in some way or the other. We kept hearing all sorts of rumours. Nobody can tell me different because I have always had the feeling that this case has not been dealt with in the right and proper way despite all the publicity. The PCA report confirms much of what I was thinking. One example concerns the delay that occurred in arresting the suspects. They could have been arrested in three days and if they had been we would have had a better result because they would not have had enough time to get rid of certain items of evidence. Fifteen days gave them ample time to get rid of. Why give them so much time?

I really believed in the officers who reinvestigated Stephen's murder because I thought that we were working closely with them and we were told that they were doing only our case and they were answerable to us in a way.

I feel that because they are all policemen, once they realised that the first lot of officers had screwed up, they decided not to let us know. That is wrong because we had put our confidence in them. In one sense I feel even more let down by the second team of police officers than the initial investigation team.

At the Inquest John Carnt suggested that there were no problems with the first investigation apart from communication with the family. He reached this view having read all the documentation in the case. Does he mean that he would have investigated in the same way? Police officers are meant to be protecting the community from things like this happening. It is their job and they take money for it. They did not do it properly. They were covering up for the failings of their colleagues.

One of the things that I hope will come out of the Inquiry is for everyone to see that the things we have been saying the past five years are true. I hope that this can be a step towards ensuring that when another tragedy is suffered by the black community, the police act responsibly and investigate the crime properly. When a policeman puts his uniform on he should forget all his prejudices. If he cannot do that then he should not be doing the job because that means that one part of the population is not protected from the likes of those who murdered Stephen.

Statement of Duwayne Brooks

[Given to DC David Cooper at Eltham Police Station on 23rd April 1993; as provided to the Inquiry, and read to the Inquiry on 15 May 1998]

have lived at the address supplied to police since 001192. I live there alone. Prior to this I have lived mainly in the LEWISHAM area in bedsits and hostels in LEWISHAM, DEPTFORD and CATFORD, after having left home when I was sixteen.

When I was about nine years of age, my parents separated and I lived with my mother, Shirley and my younger brother, Daniel, and my younger sister, Sian, initially in DEPTFORD. At this time I attended GRINLING GIBBONS PRIMARY SCHOOL in CLYDE STREET DEPTFORD. We stayed in DEPTFORD and when I was 11 years of age I moved onto Secondary School and attended BLACKHEATH BLUECOAT CHURCH OF ENGLAND SCHOOL in OLD DOVER ROAD BLACKHEATH.

I recall that on my first day at this new school I met Stephen LAWRENCE, he was in the same class as me at the school. We got on very well and became good friends. Stephen has always lived with his parents in LLANOVER ROAD WOOLWICH COMMON SE18 and has also got a younger brother and sister. His brother is called Stewart and is now about 15 years of age. I don't know his sisters name.

Over the years since I've known Stephen, we became what I would say as best friends. We always went around with each other at school and spent a lot of time together out of school hours during the weekday evenings and at weekends. We were both interested in sport and music and more recently computers and computer games. Stephen would often come over to my house and sometimes spend the night, he was a well liked person by everyone at school and by my family.

I left BLUECOAT SCHOOL when I was sixteen, after taking my GCSE exams. Stephen stayed on at the school in the Sixth Form and was studying to take 'A' level exams this summer. I moved onto the WOOLWICH COLLEGE WOOLWICH ROAD CHARLTON where I started a BTEC course in Electrical Engineering. However, I couldn't attend some of the classes because I have moved about so much recently and I gave the course up after a year.

I have settled now and have recently started another course in Electronic Servicing at LEWISHAM COLLEGE LEWISHAM WAY LEWISHAM. During the time since I left BLUECOAT SCHOOL up until now, I have kept in regular touch with Stephen and we still see each other most days. I often meet him after he finishes school or at lunch time depending whether or not I'm at college.

For me Thursday is my day off as I have no lectures or classes to attend. Yesterday, Thursday, 220493 was no exception and as is my normal practice I went down to see Stephen during his lunch break at BLUECOAT SCHOOL. I met him at the school gates at about 1240, this was by prior arrangement made when I saw Stephen the previous day.

The two of us then walked down from OLD DOVER ROAD to the BLACKHEATH STANDARD where we went to the Chip Shop at the top of WESTCOMBE HILL near to the Post Office. We didn't buy any food there, but we played on the video game, we didn't see anyone else there that we recognised. We had arranged to meet some girls from JOAN ROAN SCHOOL in BLACKHEATH so after finishing the video game we walked towards the school. I don't know the name of the road we walked in to see if we could see the girls who were meant to be meeting us at the chip shop.

It got to about 1300 and we didn't see the girls at all, so we decided that they mustn't be coming and to go back to BLUECOAT SCHOOL. Stephen and I talked at the school gates for five minutes or so and he went back into the school at about 1320 to go back to his class. I had arranged with Stephen to meet him at the school gates at 1510, when he finished school for the day. We had decided that we were going to go down to LEWISHAM, to the RIVERDALE CENTRE to see who was around.

As arranged I met Stephen at BLUECOAT SCHOOL and we caught a bus to LEWISHAM. Stephen's cousin, Karina and her friend Zerin came with us together with another boy who is a relation of my friend Leon. The bus we caught didn't go all the way to LEWISHAM and we had to change at BLACKHEATH VILLAGE and got another bus, a route 54, to complete the journey.

We must have arrived at LEWISHAM at around 1600 and we went direct into the RIVERDALE CENTRE. Zerin had stayed on the bus from the school and Karina stayed on the second bus, so Stephen, myself and Leon's relation went to the centre. We walked around for sometime and spoke to a few people that we knew, we met up with Leon and his relation, whose name I don't know, went off with him when Stephen and I decided that we were going to catch a bus to GROVE PARK. We had also met a girl called Anne, who lives in GROVE PARK and I haven't seen her for sometime so the three of us travelled together.

We caught the bus and got off it at GROVE PARK train station, it would have been around 1745. Stephen and I had discussed visiting his uncle who lives on the CHINBROOK ESTATE. I don't know the exact address, his Uncle is called Martin LINDO and he lives with his girlfriend Millie. At this point Stephen and I split and he went directly to his Uncle's house. I walked with Anne part of the way to her house which is somewhere off DOWNHAM WAY. I had arranged with Stephen that I was going to meet him later at his Uncle's, I told him that I wasn't going to be long.

After leaving Anne I actually caught a bus to CHINBROOK and walked alone to Stephen's Uncle's house, I would have arrived there at roughly 1830.

Martin, Stephen and I chatted and played some computer games, we stayed at the address until about 2200 when Stephen and I left and walked to the bus stop in DUNKERY ROAD close by to catch a bus home. Nobody else was with us and we caught a route 126 bus at about 2205 from the bus stop which is the first stop after the junction of DUNKERY ROAD with MARVELS LANE. The bus was a single decker and I think there were only five other people on it. We travelled to ELTHAM HIGH STREET on this bus and got off it outside MCDONALDS or just a bit further up the road than it. I remember looking at my watch and it was 2215.

We walked round the corner, past MCDONALDS and into WELL HALL ROAD where we waited at the bus stop, opposite ELTHAM POLICE STATION for a route 161 bus that would have taken us to WOOLWICH. I don't recall that there were any other persons at this bus stop, but I remember there was a man standing a little bit further up the road.

We had only been waiting at the stop for a couple of minutes when we decided to walk down to WELL HALL ROUNDABOUT where there would be a better selection of buses to catch, we began walking down WELL HALL ROAD we were about half way to the ELTHAM BRITISH RAIL STATION when I saw a bus coming behind us, it was a route 286 that would have taken us to BLACKHEATH STANDARD where we could both have got on a route 53 to take me to CHARLTON and Stephen on to WOOLWICH. I told Stephen about the bus and we ran to the next stop opposite ELTHAM STATION. The bus actually overtook us as we ran but there was a woman at the bus stop who flagged the bus down and as we got there she was talking to the driver. I remember her asking the driver how she could get to SHOOTERS HILL POLICE STATION by bus. The woman was speaking with a foreign accent, possibly French or Spanish, eventually the bus driver told her to get on his bus and that he would show here where to get off to continue her journey to SHOOTERS HILL POLICE STATION.

I would describe the woman as being white european, she was short and had long dark hair that was wavy, I got the impression she might have been a student and aged about 20 years. She was slim and dressed in a white shirt, dark jacket and dark coloured skirt or trousers. I'm not too sure which. She was carrying a shoulder bag. I don't think she was having any difficulty understanding the driver. She was the only person at the bus stop. The route 286 was a single decked bus and there were about five other people on it. Stephen and I sat close to the back on the left hand side of the bus.

During the journey down WELL HALL ROAD Stephen told me that he wanted to go home more directly than going to the STANDARD and we decided to get off the bus at the WELL HALL ROUNDABOUT outside the cinema.

I forgot to mention that the woman stood up on the bus close to the driver.

From the roundabout we could catch a 161 or a 122 that would go directly to WOOLWICH.

We got off the bus at the cinema, a male passenger also got off. The bus pulled away and stopped right at the junction with the roundabout about 25-30 yards from where it had stopped for us and I saw the woman get off the bus.

Stephen and I walked up to the roundabout and directly across the middle of it and into the continuation of WELL HALL ROAD. We walked on the left hand side of the road as you face towards WOOLWICH.

We walked passed the junction with the first road on the left which I now know to be called DICKSON ROAD and onto the first bus stop you come to on the left which is about halfway from DICKSON ROAD to the next road on the left.

Already at this bus stop was the foreign sounding woman and the man who'd got off the bus at the same stop as us.

I would not really be able to describe the man very well but he was white, in his thirties, about my height or a bit shorter. He was slim and had short dark brown hair. He was wearing a black jacket and dark coloured trousers and shoes. The jacket he was wearing was a thin cotton type which had a zip up front, it was waist length.

Stephen and I waited at the bus stop and we chatted between ourselves. We had got to the bus stop at 2225. I remember this because I had looked at my watch again.

At about 2230 I remember somebody else stopping at the bus stop. He was white, about 18 years of age, 5'10 tall, slim built. He had blond hair which was short and over his ears, it was spiky on top and wavy at the sides. He seemed to have acne or shaving bumps on his face, but he seemed to be clean shaven. I didn't really take any notice of what he was wearing.

The bus seemed to be taking a long time and I remember looking at my watch again, it was 2237 or may be 2238. I discussed with Stephen whether it would be better to stick to our original plan and go back to the roundabout and get a 286 to the STANDARD. We decided to walk back towards the roundabout to see if any buses were coming. The man, woman and youth stayed at the bus stop.

We walked down towards the roundabout, Stephen was some distance behind me as I went ahead alone to look, as I crossed back over DICKSON ROAD I saw a 286 stopped in the distance at the bus stop by KIDBROOKE LANE, at the same time I noticed a group of youths crossing over the road to my left and actually crossing the ROCHESTER WAY. I remember that at this point I'd made a mental note of how many of them there were, six, this was because I wondered what they were doing.

I looked back and Stephen was about 8-10 yards behind me, I shouted, "Can you see the bus." He didn't reply, I turned round to see if the bus was any closer to the cinema stop and noticed the group of six youths were on the opposite side of the road (WELL HALL ROAD) by the zebra crossing.

By this time Stephen had joined me and began to walk closer to the roundabout to see if he could see the bus. I said to Stephen, "Can you see it." Stephen didn't reply as immediately I heard a voice from my left hand side shout, "What, what nigger." I turned to my left and saw the group of youths were crossing the road. The one that was in front was staring at me, I got the impression that he was the one that had shouted. Stephen was about 8 yards in front of me and I shouted to him, "Run, run." because I felt threatened by the menacing comment and the presence of the group of youths. I started running back towards SHOOTERS HILL, I'd only taken four or five paces when I turned back to see if Stephen was with me. Stephen hadn't moved from where he was originally standing and the group of six youths were next to him. I would describe them as having converged on him. The one who was at the front initially, reached into his jacket and took an object out, I was about 12 yards away from them and had a clear view of the group and Stephen. I saw the youth raise his arm, his right arm, in the air and could see on the object in his hand, it was of a similar size to a rounders bat and could have been made of wood or steel. I seemed to focus on this man alone and can't remember what the rest of his group were doing at this point. He raised his hand over his own head and I saw him strike a blow towards Stephen's head, I'm not sure where the blow landed but I heard Stephen scream as though he was in pain. I saw Stephen fall to the ground and I started to run back towards him. As I did this the group of youths started running down DICKSON ROAD away from WELL HALL ROAD, I don't remember seeing anyone else in the area.

As I ran towards Stephen and towards where he was on the floor in the middle of DICKSON ROAD and close to the junction with WELL HALL ROAD, Stephen jumped up and began to run across the road. I followed him across the road and onto the opposite pavement of WELL HALL ROAD, Stephen said "Duwayne" and I said, "Just run." We began running up WELL HALL ROAD towards SHOOTERS HILL on the right hand pavement. I sensed that Stephen wasn't keeping up with me and heard him call again. "Duwayne, look at me, tell me what's wrong." I looked back and saw blood on his jacket, it seemed to be pumping out from somewhere and absorbing into his jacket. I said to him, "Just keep running," and he said, "I can't, I can't." Stephen collapsed on the floor. We were opposite a junction on the other side of the road with a road that I now know as ARBROATH ROAD. We had run passed the bus stop we were originally standing at albeit on the opposite side of the road. I didn't notice if the three people were still there. I ran across the road where there was a telephone box, a phonecard box, I dialled 999 and put the phone down on the shelf in the kiosk and opened the door and looked out to see if the group were coming back. It was clear and I couldn't see the group of youths. I did see a man and a woman walk passed towards WELL HALL, I asked them if they could help as my friend had been injured or he'd collapsed. They just looked at me and didn't say a word and then carried on walking. I went back into the phone box, picked the handset up and spoke to the operator. I asked for ambulance and I was put through. I told the person what had happened and was asked for the location of the incident. I tried to give the person the address that was printed on a card in the phonebox but I think it was wrong and seem to remember the postcode saying SE26. I got frustrated with the woman as she kept asking me where I was and I eventually slammed the phone down on the shelf. I ran out of the kiosk and tried to stop some passing cars. I remember standing in the road and waving at the cars to stop. I recall trying to stop a Peugeot 205 which was white and being driven by a white man with no passengers in the car. He stopped in front of me, stared at me, then drove round and away.

After this car had driven away I saw a car had pulled up across the road next to where Stephen was lying. I went over to where they were and spoke to the male who was driving. He asked me if I'd phoned for an ambulance and I told him I'd tried. The woman who was with the man was crouching on the floor next to Stephen and I said, "Is he still breathing." Stephen was lying flat out on his front and the woman had her hand on his back. She said that he was still breathing. The man then went over to the telephone box and the man and woman who I asked for help when I was on the phone earlier walked up to where we were, I didn't speak to them and the man came back from the phone box and said the ambulance was on its way. I remember that I was angry and pacing up and down the pavement. Stephen hadn't said anything at all. I kept asking if he was still breathing, the woman said that he was. I remember another man joining us and he had some blankets that he put on Stephen. The police then arrived about ten minutes after and I told them what had happened. Other police officers came and spoke to all the people who had come to help Stephen. Ten minutes or so later an ambulance arrived and took Stephen away. I was taken to the BROOK HOSPITAL by a police officer and waited in a room. I was later told that Stephen had died and went to see him in the room where he was.

Of the group of six youths I can only really describe one of them. The one who had struck Stephen was white, about 5'8 tall, medium build and about 18-22 years of age. I would describe his hair as being long, over his ears and it was frizzy and stuck out at the sides. Most of his hair was down at the sides and I could clearly see his forehead. He had an oval face, I can't really describe his facial features, but I think I could recognise him again from his hair and general look. He spoke with a local accent. He was wearing a grey coloured bomber jacket with a zip up front, the lining of it was white and I recall that the front may have had a white strip at either side of the zip. I can't remember what he was wearing under the jacket, but I think he was wearing blue jeans.

Of the others, I can only say that they were all white, about the same age and that they were all wearing jeans.

Stephen is 18 years of age, he is black, about 5'10 tall, with a medium build. He is normally clean shaven and was tonight. He was wearing his black waist length jacket and I think a pair of corduroy trousers. Hew was wearing a green / yellow hat.

I am 18 years of age, 5'11 tall and slim with a medium build. Last night I was wearing a black string woolly hat with the words 'Stay Black' on the front. I had a grey, red, black and white patchwork jacket with a hood and zip up front on with a green shirt underneath. I was wearing a pair of green jeans with 'BOLL' and same embroidered on the left leg with 'Bullet Holes' embroidered on the right leg in yellow cotton. I was wearing a pair of white and blue Nike Air trainers, size 9_. I am black with West Indian features.

I am willing to give evidence at court. I have been given a form marked witness information - A.

Statement of Duwayne Brooks

[As provided to the Inquiry; read to the Inquiry on 15 May 1998]

1.   Stephen Lawrence was one of my best friends. We met on our first day at secondary school - the Blackheath Bluecoats Church of England School. We were both about 11 years old.

2.   Both Steve and I were 18 in 1993 when Steve was murdered.

3.   In 1993 Steve was at school and I was at college. We saw each other regularly. We usually met either at my house or his uncle, Martin and wife Millie's house. On April 22 1993 we were together at Martin and Millie's house.

4.   In the evening we were hurrying to get back, as Steve wanted to get home as soon as possible. We were just looking for a bus on Well Hall Road. We were attacked by a group of white boys, one of whom shouted "what what nigger".

5.   I can't bear to go into the details of it at this stage. So I will recount what happened after the murder.

The scene of the murder

6.   As we were running from the attack, Steve fell to the floor opposite the junction to Downham Road. I stopped on the pavement. I went back and I bent down and looked at him. He was lying by a tree. He was still breathing. I saw his blood running down the floor. He could not speak. I saw his blood running away.

7.   I ran across the road to the phone box and dialled 999. I asked for an ambulance. I left the phone hanging to run round the corner to see if the boys were coming back up the road.

8.   I saw a white couple. I have since been told they are called Taaffes. They were walking down the road towards the phone box from Shooters Hill. So I ran and asked for their help. They just ignored me. They looked at me and sort of shimmied away, and walked on.

9.   I have recently been shown Connor Taaffe's statement. I see he thought that we might be going to rob them. This fits with my recollection of how they behaved towards me when I first approached them.

10. I ran back to the phone box and picked up the receiver and spoke. I told the lady, who said something like I am still here what happened? We had an exchange about where I was. I knew where I was but I looked at a printed card in the phone box. It was wrong, I think it said the post code was SE26. I got confused and frustrated, I don't know whether she could hear me properly. I was shouting.

11. I can't remember if she asked me for a phone number. I cannot remember exactly what I told her about what happened.

12. I slammed the phone down on the shelf and left.

13. I am told it is said that I kicked the box. I don't recall this but it is possible given how frustrated I was. I was frustrated then because there was no help.

14. I ran out into the road and tried to stop some cars. I was waving my arms around. Cars passed me by. No-one stopped. A white Peugeot 205 slowed down, nearly skidded and nearly knocked me over. It was a white man who was in it. He stopped, looked at me and drove around me.

15. I am now not sure the order in which my trying to stop cars, phoning the ambulance and trying to get the Taaffes to help took place in.

16. A car stopped by Steve. I know now the driver was an off-duty police officer, Mr Geddis, who was with his wife Angela Geddis. He asked what happened and if I had called an ambulance and I told him we had been attacked. I said I tried to call the ambulance.

17. I said we had been attacked, and that an iron bar was used and that it was by white boys.

18. I was using the f-word, but not at him, in my speech. I don't use other kinds of swear words and didn't on that night.

19. He went into the phone box.

20. I waited with Steve and the Taaffes and Angela Geddis by the side of the road. At first one of them knelt by him, not holding him.

21. I was pacing up and down, up and down. I was crying. I was desperate for the ambulance. It was taking too long. I was frightened by the amount of blood Steve was losing. I saw his life fading away. I didn't know what to do to help him, I was frightened I would do something wrong.

22. Angela Geddis went and crouched down by Steve. I asked if Steve was breathing, she said yes. I kept asking.

23. The Taaffes may have prayed. Mr Taaffe may have told me that Steve was lying in the right position. It is possible that I told one of them that my name was Duwayne and that Steve was my friend. I can't remember.

24. Mr Geddis came back to us.

25. At some point either a woman or a man came and put a blanket on Steve.

26. Uniformed officers arrived later. They arrived before the ambulance.

27. A uniformed officer who I have since been told is called WPC Bethel came up and asked me who has done this. I said a group of six white boys. I then said where is the f-ing ambulance I didn't call the police. She said they were on their way. I said I'd called them about 15 minutes ago.

28. She said "what has happened?" I was saying where is the ambulance. That's what I wanted to know.

29. I told her we were attacked, but I had got away. She asked me where the boys went and I pointed out the road that they had gone down.

30. When I pointed to her where they had run, she did nothing. She did not make any use of the information. She did not do anything about it like tell the other officer there or anyone on her radio. She didn't ask what the name of the road was.

31. She asked me more than once where they had gone. The second time she asked I said something like "I f-ing told you where they went, are you deaf? Why don't you go and look for them". It was like she didn't believe me. She just kept saying calm down, which made me more frustrated her saying that and doing nothing for Steve.

32. She asked what they looked like and I said they were a group of white boys.

33. She asked how did we get here? I didn't answer that question.

34. She asked me our names and addresses and I gave them to her.

35. A male uniformed officer came up at one point.

36. She asked questions like who are they to you, what are their names, where do they live? I said I didn't know the boys. She said your friend is lying there and you say you don't know who those boys are!

37. She said, so how did it start, did they chase you for nothing? I said one of them shouted "what what nigger". She and other officers kept asking me what happened and if I was sure of what I was saying.

38. She asked if I had any weapons on me.

39. She was treating me like she was suspicious of me, not like she wanted to help.

40. When she asked me stupid questions I kept saying where is the ambulance, I didn't call for you. I wanted them to get him to hospital, and there they were talking rubbish in my ears and walking up and down doing nothing. I knew the hospital was only two minutes up the road. I became increasingly frustrated and loud and agitated.

41. I asked her and other officers more than once why couldn't they put Steve in the car and drive him to hospital. They said that they couldn't do that. They never gave a reason they just said I should calm down and "be sensible about it for your friend's sake". How could they say to me "calm down!" when they weren't doing anything about the situation?.

42. I got the impression that the police were repulsed by the blood that was there or on the whole they just didn't want to help. They should have known what to do. However horrible they found the blood it was their job to do something to help him. They did not do anything useful.

43. While I was talking to WPC Bethel I was walking up and down, pacing out of frustration and helplessness, and looking for the ambulance. She kept saying stand still, but I didn't.

44. I didn't answer those of her questions which I thought were stupid. I only answered her sensible questions. A sensible question she didn't ask would have been: "shall I drive you in the direction where they ran?"

45. If she had asked for more detail of the boys' descriptions or what they were wearing I would have told her. Those would have been sensible questions.

46. I have been told that she said that I said I did not witness the assault. This is not true.

47. She did not ask if I was all right or if I had been attacked.

48. She did not take notes.

49. Those by Steve were near enough so they would have heard me when I was shouting, I shouted when I was saying why can't you put him in the car, but they wouldn't have heard her questions.

50. She wandered off at some stage and came back. I didn't see her go to Steve at all but she could have done and I didn't notice. Another uniformed woman police officer came up at one point and joined in the questioning. I have been told she is called WPC Smith.

51. I heard something come over the radio saying the ambulance is at Well Hall roundabout - can't you see it? It wasn't her radio. I couldn't see the ambulance.

52. I started going frantic saying where is the ambulance? As the ambulance didn't come and she was asking stupid questions I got more and more wound up. I could feel the ambulance was going to be too late.

53. Various officers came and told me to calm down for my friend's sake. I again asked some of them to take Steve to the hospital but they wouldn't.

54. I overheard on the radio that the ambulance was coming from Shooter's Hill. Then a male police officer went off to go and get it. This may have been PC Gleason.

55. One uniformed officer went up to Steve and shined a torch in his face, "I said why are you doing that?" He said "It is supposed to be good for you". He carried on doing it. He was kneeling down. I walked off. I didn't know whether to believe him or not.

56. One male uniformed officer was different from the others. He asked me if I was injured in any way and if I needed to sit down. I said no I was fine. I cannot describe what he looked like. I have been asked if he had grey hair or a grey moustache. He didn't.

57. Apart from this one officer no-one asked me if I was injured. No-one asked me if I had been attacked. No-one asked me if I was all right.

58. None of the uniformed officers were doing anything for Steve. They should have known what to do. They should have done something for Steve. No-one appeared to be doing anything with the information I gave them about the attackers. They just stood there doing nothing. No-one went down Dickson Road after the boys.

59. None of the officers asked me if I would recognise any of the boys again. I obviously would have said yes if they had asked. I note PC Gleason says that I didn't give enough information to make a street id. This is unfair. I gave them the information that they asked for and I could have recognised the boys if they took me around.

60. I note PC Gleason says I was "virtually uncontrollable." What did they need to control me for? They should have taken control of the situation and organised help for Steve and chasing the boys. I have been told that other officers said I was "hysterical". I was very upset and frustrated

but I was not out of control or hysterical. I was perfectly capable of answering sensible questions and giving information as I did do.

61. The first time anyone made any use of that information that I gave them was when different police arrived - a police carrier came down the hill and parked near us. An officer went to the passenger side and pointed in the direction of Dickson Road. It left in that direction almost straight away. I saw no-one get out. I didn't see where it actually went to.

62. This was sometime after the first uniformed police arrived. It seemed like ages - it may have been about 10 minutes - but I don't know how long exactly.

63. Then another police carrier came the other way, turned round, stopped and went off.

64. I was very upset. I was wound up by the officers. I was very angry at the boys and increasingly at the officers and because the ambulance was not coming.

65. The ambulance arrived. Mr Salih says it takes 6 minutes to get there from Greenwich District Hospital and I think that is just about right.

66. Mr Mann, the other ambulance man, put a plastic thing in Steve's mouth - the thing you are meant to carry to save people's lives.

67. They carried Steve to the ambulance on a stretcher. His unopened ginger beer can fell from him onto the floor. I picked it up. I took it home and kept it in my room, until one day it exploded.

68. I tried to get into the ambulance with Steve but police officers would not let me. They said there was no space. I really wanted to be in the ambulance with Steve. I wanted to be with him. I wanted to see what was happening.

69. When they wouldn't let me I thought, well the hospital is only two minutes up the road, and agreed to go in a police car.

70. I don't remember much about the journey except that I told the driver to hurry up. I am told that WPC Joanne Smith says she drove me to the hospital. I am told she said I called the police "pigs" and used the word "c—t". I did not. I don't use those words.

The hospital

71. When I got to the hospital I walked behind the stretcher. Steve went into a different room. One of the nurses asked me to go with her, but I said it's ok and walked off. I went into a waiting room. I sat, and then I walked around.

72. A policeman came up, and said that he wanted to talk to me, to help my friend.

73. I was most probably shouting and walking off. He told me his name. I now know it's PC Gleason. He said he needed to take a statement of what happened. I don't know what I said. I lent on the reception counter. I kept walking off. It took a long time. I kept stopping. He kept saying I need a statement, I need a statement.

74. He kept asking me whether it was true that the boys said "what what nigger".

75. He took notes in his book. I didn't read the notebook. I don't remember signing it, but that is my signature on his notebook.

76. Some of Steve's family arrived.

77. I was told that Steve was dead when I was in an office. I don't want to talk about it.

78. I was taken to see his body. I don't want to talk about it.

79. At the hospital nobody enquired if I was all right or if I had been attacked. I was offered no comfort.

80. A policeman said that I couldn't leave. He said I had to go to the police station to make a statement. He said you can either wait here or go and sit in the police car until you are taken to the station so that "we won't lose you".

81. I didn't want to be in the hospital so I chose the police car option.

82. I wanted to leave and go home. I felt I couldn't. I felt if I left the police would have stopped me and arrested me.

83. The police man walked me to the car. It was parked in front of the hospital where the ambulances were. He asked me to wait until I was taken to the police station. I said OK and sat in the car on my own.

84. It felt like I was in the police car in the car park for half an hour or an hour.

Plumstead Police Station

85. I was then driven to Plumstead Police Station. I can't remember who took me or what was said on the way.

86. When we got to the police station the car went round the back and parked in the car park. I was taken in the back entrance of the station.

87. As far as I can remember I was taken up some stairs and into a room.

88. I remember sitting in a room and being calm.

89. I now know that in their statements the police said I broke a window in the front office. I didn't, I wasn't even in the front office. It just shows that they were treating me like a criminal and not like a victim.

90. I was waiting in a room opposite a big room. I can remember being in the room for what felt like ages.

91. Most of the time I was sat there on my own. An officer was in there standing up. He told me he had to stay in the room to look after me. I took it he meant to stop me wandering off or doing wrong.

92. He chatted with me. He was waiting for a senior officer to come. I think it may have been for an area commander but that may be wrong. He was filling in time.

93. He asked me if I wanted tea. I don't drink tea so I said no thank you. He asked me if I was all right. I said yeah.

94. Nobody asked me whether I wanted to be at the station or whether I would prefer to go home. Nobody asked me where I would like to have my statement taken.

95. Before my statement was taken a senior officer talked to me briefly about what had happened. The senior officer I saw was a small man. I can't remember much of the conversation except I told him that we had been attacked by a group of white boys one of whom said "what what nigger".

96. The officer who took the statement from me was DC Cooper.

97. Before and perhaps during the statement taking, someone came in and asked me to go with them to see how the investigation was taking place, and took me into the big room. This happened about twice. A number of officers said that I was important to this investigation and that was why I had to tell the truth.

98. They kept saying are you sure they said "what what nigger?". I remember someone, maybe the same senior officer, saying you know what this means if you are telling the truth, are you sure they said "what what nigger?" I said I am telling the truth. He said "you mean you have done nothing to provoke this in any way?" I said "no, we were just waiting for a bus".

99. I thought either they thought I was lying or they wanted to do a Jedi mind trick on me so that I would lie and say that it didn't happen. I thought that because they keep on at me. It was mainly the senior officer. I wanted to start shouting and calling them idiots but I couldn't, I was just too tired. It was this senior officer that they were waiting for before DC Cooper took my statement.

100. Both DC Cooper and the senior officer were suspicious of my account of how we were attacked.

101. I can't remember the names of the officers who I met in the big room.

102. I was keen to make a statement. I was keen to get it over and done with. I don't know what time we started doing the statement but I do remember getting home about 7 am.

103. DC Cooper asked me whether I wanted anyone with me. He was the only police officer to ask that. As it would have delayed everything to fetch someone I said I didn't, I just wanted to get it over and done with.

104. I wished I'd gone home from the hospital and slept and come back the next day. DC Cooper said if you want to go you can go, but I said no now I am here I want to get it over with. When he said that it was the first time I realise that I had had a choice about going home.

105. DC Cooper did not give me an idea of how long it would take to give the statement.

106. DC Cooper said ok lets start from the beginning. He asked me questions and I answered them. He was writing down my answers.

107. While I was answering the questions and giving my statement an officer told me that my mum was at the police station. I thought giving the statement would be over soon so at first I said I would finish it and then see her. But it took so long I asked to see her. They took me to a different room and she was brought in with Everton. I told my mum what had happened. What I said upset her. She said: "it's a racist murder". An officer told her to calm down. He said we don't know that yet, we are trying to establish the facts. I knew I knew the facts and that I had told them to the officers. I wanted to say something. I couldn't because I would have started crying.

108. I went back to making my statement.

109. While he was taking my statement DC Cooper asked the size of my foot and then said we need to take your trainers from you to take a foot print. I gave him my trainers. I was thinking what do you want them for? I haven't committed any burglaries, but I didn't say anything because I didn't want to make the suspicions of me worse.

110. There is nothing in my statement about the colour of the attacker's hair. I was telling DC Cooper everything I could. If he had asked me the colour I would have told him, just as I told PC Gleason.

111. At the end DC Cooper asked me to read my statement and sign it. I was so tired. I just scanned it and signed it.

112. At no stage did any officer ask me whether any of the white boys attacked me or touched me, or did they ask me for any of my clothes except to take the print off my trainers as I have mentioned. No one asked me more than is set out in the Section 9 statement that DC Cooper took that night.

113. I remember an officer driving me home. I got there about 7 am.

114. I spent the days after playing my Nintendo at home. This was a hostel. It was a half way house to getting a flat from a housing association. There were about six of us each with our own room kitchen and bathroom.

115. I note that the AMIP meeting of 25 4 93 says that I was not in the hostel. I was. The police came round and asked if I was ok after a couple of days. The police offered me protection. I think that it may have been DS Bevan who asked me. He did not tell me why I might need it, so I said no.

116. DS Bevan told me that he was my liaison officer. He said he was on the investigation. He said I should ask him for things I needed.

117. At no stage did he or any other officer ask me if I had been attacked nor did he refer me to victim support or offer me counselling nor did he advise me about the CICB.

118. At no stage did he or any officer consult me about whether I wished to press charges for the attack on me. They didn't treat me as a victim of crime.

119. At no stage did he or any officer advise me who to speak to or who not to speak to about what I had experienced and seen.

120. They didn't say keep it quiet or tell the world, to see if anyone recognised my description of the attackers.

121. Eventually they themselves advertised part of my description of one of the attackers.

122. At the time DS Bevan seemed to treat me more seriously than the other officers did, so I trusted him a bit more than I did the other police.

123. I saw DS Bevan on a number of occasions. I am concerned that they have become a jumble in my mind, so I would like to see his records of them before I make a detailed statement about them.

124. Some time soon after the murder I heard that fascists had been looking for me at the school that Steve and I went to. I had heard that headmaster told the school assembly that I had been with Steve that night. I heard the fascists had looked for other black students at other schools. That made me frightened.

125. I told the police and they did nothing. I became frightened that the murderers would come and find me. John Bevan told me that some of the other witnesses were under protection. I wanted the police to find the people who were looking for me and to find the murderers.

126. I can't remember if I asked then for protection then. I was confused and frightened. I was frightened that the murderers would get me but I was frightened of the police. It was unbelievable that they had not arrested anyone. I didn't trust their investigation.

127. I cannot recall the detail or order of all the meetings with the officers. They told me that there were other witnesses, I asked them questions about them but they didn't tell me anything.

128. I remember that they had not located the woman getting on the bus and I told one of the officers that I thought she was French as I heard her speak when she got on the bus.

129. Arrangements were made by police for me to do an artist's sketch at my home. I did it on 6 May 1993. I thought it was a good likeness but I couldn't fix the eyes.

130. I was not referred to my earlier statement on this day, I just had to think back and answer the questions. Nor was I referred to PC Gleason's notebook when I was giving my section 9 statement to DC Cooper.

131. I later did a computer sketch at Peckham Police Station. That was accurate too. I am told DS Bevan says that I played pool with him afterwards, this is correct. He also said I had tea, this isn't right. I don't drink tea.

132. I had a lot more contact with the police, including three identification parades that I would like to deal with in the second part of my statement.

Demonstration, 8 May 1993 and Croydon Prosecution

133. On 8 May I went to a large anti - racist demonstration outside the British National Party headquarters in Welling. I went to protest against Steve's murder and the way the police were handling it.

134. In October 1993 I was arrested and charged with offenses arising out of the demonstration of the previous May. They waited 5 months to prosecute me. They waited until after the Crown Prosecution Service had decided to drop the prosecution against the killers. It was devastating. I had no convictions at the time of the murder. It felt like the police and prosecutors decided to get at me to ruin my reputation - and the chance of any future prosecution of the murderers.

135. But the Judge at Croydon Crown Court wasn't having any of it. In December 1994 he stopped the prosecution saying that it was an abuse of the process of the Court.

136. In April 1994 I had been diagnosed as suffering from Post Traumatic Stress Disorder.

137. I'd like to pause this part of my evidence now with something about police protection.

Police Protection

138. I was frightened for my life, I had heard that other witnesses had been given protection. I was most scared when the case came into the media and there were Court hearings. I would like to say how unsafe I felt, and sometimes still feel. For now I can just recount the protection during the hearings.

139. I was not given any police protection during the Magistrates Court hearing, but I was during the Old Bailey hearing.

140. During that hearing I stayed at 4 different hotels. They were not very nice. It was with different officers each time, except one set of officers may have stayed two nights. On one occasion one of the officers who had arrested me for the demonstration, I think it was DC Dougall, was there.

141. On another night I was taken to an Eltham hotel. The police didn't explain why they chose Eltham. It was the worst area of London they could have chosen. It felt like they took me to Eltham to break my spirit. I didn't sleep that night, because I was frightened to be in my room. I spent the night downstairs watching television, scared. The next day, weak and tired, I had to give my evidence in Court.

142. I think of Steve every day. I am sad for his other friends and his family. I'm sad confused and pissed about this system where racists attack and go free, but innocent victims like Steve and I are treated as criminals, and at the outset ignored me when I pointed out where the killers had run to and refused to believe me that it was a racist attack.

143. Steve and I were young black men. Racist thugs killed Steve and shattered my life.

Signed: D A Brooks

Dated 6 April 1998

Supplementary Statement of Duwayne Brooks

[As provided to the Inquiry; read to the Inquiry on 15 May 1998]

<u>The murder</u>

1. I refer to the statements I gave to the police about the murder. They are accurate.

2. What I said on the night of the murder to DC Cooper was correct, save that I thought Steve had been hit not stabbed.

3. It was not until later that I remembered one of the boys chasing me. I gave DS Bevan a statement about on the 23 September 1993.

4. I had gaps in my memory. I wanted remember everything. I couldn't. I didn't know how to.

5. I have been asked if anyone from the police tried to help me understand what was going on or reassure me or suggested that I saw someone to help me. They didn't.

6. I know some witnesses say I was actually touched by the attackers. I wasn't.

7. I am told that a police man has given his view that Steve was goaded into "standing his ground when he heard the boys shout "What? What, nigger?". He is wrong. I never knew Steve to fight no-one. Steve wasn't used to the outside world. He wasn't street aware of the dangers of being in a racist area at night-time. I shouted to run. He had ample time to run as the boys were on the other side of the road. For the time it took the boys to run across the road he hadn't moved. Steve didn't understand that the group of white boys was dangerous or that anything would have happened.

<u>Helping the police</u>

8. I wanted to try and remember everything for the police and help them in their inquiries and do everything they wanted to help their case.

9. It was hard remembering everything and talking about the murder whenever they wanted me to. I dreaded it everyday when I woke up that I would have to be talking to the police again.

10. I made 9 statements, went on 3 identification parades, went to the Magistrates Court, Crown Court and the Inquest on several occasions and I kept meeting the police when they asked me to.

11. It was hard when they treated me like they didn't believe me and when they treated me with attitude and they didn't seem to care for my safety.

12. I remember DS Bevan asking me for a photograph of myself. It made me anxious. He didn't explain why he needed it. He said it was for "police purposes". I said no. I didn't see the point of having a picture of me and I was frightened it would be misused by police even though I trusted Bevan more than the others.

13. DS Bevan got upset about this. He got upset a lot if I couldn't remember something or if I didn't want to talk about something. DS Bevan kept saying to me what are you hiding? I told him "I'm not hiding nothing".

14. The main police man I saw was DS Bevan, he sometimes had a woman with him. The other policemen I saw were DC Tomlin and his partners, one I think was called Bull or Bullock.

15. DS Bevan contacted me through my mother. She arranged this. I remember my mum complaining to him that I shouldn't be harassed by the police.

16. DC Tomlin treated me in a funny way. He was awkward with me.

17. He had an attitude problem which came over when he spoke to me.

18. I felt he was trying to trick me at first. Later I just did't know. I didn't like him. I didn't really trust him.

My address

19. The police knew my address and the address and phone number of my mother. They had taken me to my address and been there themselves.

20. I moved from the address I had been in February 1993 to another address, and the police knew that address too.

21. The only address I did not want them to have was my girlfriend's address. I spent quite a lot of time with her. I was frightened for her and for my safety.

22. But I eventually showed DC Tomlin where she lived. He told me it would be kept a secret.

23. But he broke that promise. It was him or other officers who came to my girlfriend's address at 6 am one morning to arrest me for the Croydon incident. Luckily I wasn't there. But I was fuming that he had broken that promise and frightened because I didn't know who else he had told.

The identification parades:

First identification parade, May 7 1993

24. I was picked up from college at about 5 pm in an unmarked police car by an officer who was in plain clothes. It took about 20 minutes to get to the police station. We drove round the back and were taken upstairs into a room with chairs going round the side and a window onto the side where the van drives in. Noone else was in the room with me except the officer. I was there for about 4 hours. Even the officer kept leaving after a while.

25. We were told to help ourselves from the fridge which had canned drinks in it. We were not offered tea or coffee.

26. I was nervous, it was the first time I had done anything like this. I started getting pissed off ie angry after about an hour of waiting. I was fed up. The officer that brought me kept coming in and out, he was getting fed up at the length of time he had to wait as well.

27. I don't recall trying to identify anyone on the first occasion. I believed that the parade was cancelled until I was told that the records showed otherwise.

28. I note that the records state that I went round the parade and did not pick out the suspect Jamie Acourt. I note that this was at 9.24 pm. I see that Jo Shepherd is said not to have picked him out as well.

29. I remember calling Imran on the police's phone. I wanted him there. I just wanted someone there with me because I was nervous. I wanted someone to explain to me the procedure. All I was told by officers was that I would be taken downstairs and I had to make sure I walked down the aisle twice and pick out a person who fitted the question they put to me.

30. On none of the parades was it made clear to me that I could take my time or ask for people on the parade to speak or move about.

31. The officer took me home. I wasn't told the outcome of the parade.

Second day of identification parades, 13 May 1993

32. I was taken to this parade from the hostel in a police minibus. I got in the bus and I saw a "skinhead" there and a number of white boys. I was frightened until we started talking and then it became clear they were other witnesses. One of the officers said you shouldn't be discussing anything in the van. The "skinhead" turned out to be Stacey Benefield. It was the first time I had met him.

33. I waited for this parade with other witnesses. This was arranged by the police. Roy Westbrook was also there, and a woman who saw a stabbing at a Wimpey bar. As far as I can remember police officers came in and out of the room. We chatted about what had happened to each of us.

34. I was nervous and pacing. I might have been asking lots of questions. I didn't go through any papers. I can't remember speaking to anyone on the phone, but it's possible that I did.

35. Stacey Benefield said that the boys who stabbed him were known to stab people and not to get done for it, he said they knew people in the police.

36. I recall picking out one person on that parade. I remember very little of that day.

37. I know now that the person I picked out was Neil Acourt and I did not pick out Gary Dobson or Dave Norris.

38. As far as I can remember everyone was getting nervous and pissed that it was taking so long.

39. I see from the records that I looked at the parade with Gary Dobson in at about 2.25, the one with Neil Acourt in at about 3.56 and the one with Dave Norris in at about 5.27.

40. I then had to wait for Stacey Benefield to finish and we were taken back in the van together.

41. Stacey Benefield said something like he knew the people who attacked him. The one he just picked out was obvious anyhow becuase he looked like he had spent the night in a cell and he was wearing something like track suit bottoms. I don't recall seeing anyone myself in track suit bottoms.

42.   I was collected and taken to one police station and then, after not too long, to this parade at Southwark by Sgt Crowley, and taken back again afterwards. I did not have to wait at Southwark. I made a statement to Sgt Crowley about the identification. The conversation as set out in my statement to DC Doyle as far as Sgt Crowley talking about them next door took place at that time. I know now I identified Luke Knight on the parade.

43.   That evening two police officers came round to my home and told me that Sgt Crowley had made serious allegations against me and that I needed to make a statement. They didn't give me much detail but they said Sgt Crowley had said certain things to do with what happened today. I was wondering what now? I knew I hadn't done anything wrong and as the police said the allegations wre serious I wanted to have someone there when I spoke to the police again so they wouldn't make anything up. They wouldn't leave and in the end I had to shut the door in their faces. The last thing one of them said was make sure your solicitor is here tomorrow because if you don't make a statement we are going to have to arrest you.

44.   I rang Imran who said he would send someone but he didn't, so I agreed to make a statement in front of the supervisor of the hostel when they came back the next day.

45.   I see that there are two statements from me both dated the 4 June 1993. I don't remember signing two separate statements on the same day but I did make both of those statements. The statements are accurate in so far as they go but bits are left out.

46.   The police man told me what Sgt Crowley had said about me - basically that I was guessing. I was pissed off and said that he was a liar. The police man told me that he was a respected officer and I should have more respect for him, and say that Sgt Crowley had misunderstood what I had said. I wanted to put down he was a liar but the officer would not write that down, so I agreed that Sgt Crowley had misunderstood me.

47.   On one stretch of road Greenwich Park about 4 minutes from home Sgt Crowley said something to the effect that I was guessing. I got angry. We had an argument along the lines of the rest of my statement to DC Doyle. I got out of the car at home and told him to fuck off. I don't remember whether I told the officer this bit as he wouldn't let me say Sgt Crowley was lying.

48.   The policeman went through Sgt Crowley's statement and I told them my version.

49.   I want to know why Sgt Crowley said those things about me.

50.   The statements I made about both identifications made at the identification parades are correct. I remain sure that the people I picked out took part in the attack. I recognised the attackers from the attack and not from any outside information. The men on the parades looked quite similar to each other.

51.   Nobody described the Acourt brothers to me. There was a rumour that they had black hair but someone else said they didn't, so I didn't pay any attention. I never heard anyone say anything else about what they looked like.

52.   I made my identifications on what I remembered. It's not true that I relied on any descriptions given to me by my friends or anyone else. None were.

53.   I was never shown any statements by the police.

Other things that came up with the police

54.   The police kept asking me whether I recognised any of the boys from football, the officers included DC Tomlin and I think his friend Bullock. They drove me around Samuel Montague ground to see if it jogged my memory. There wasn't a match playing. They then drove me around the streets to see if I could spot anyone. I didn't.

55.   Sgt Bevan asked me if Steve and I went into a kebab shop on the night of the murder. He told me they had found half a kebab at the scene. I didn't see any kebab.

56.   At the same time he asked me whether we had harassed any white girls at MacDonalds as they had had reports of black boys doing that. I said no because we hadn't done. Sgt Bevan said that "we" couldn't believe that we had got attacked just like that for nothing and that they were looking for motives. He said that officers above him didn't believe me that it was purely a racist attack. There is a MacDonalds that we went past in Eltham but we didn't go into it

57.   It was about this time I started getting pissed with DS Bevan. It was like they were looking for excuses.

58.   Later DC Tomlin and his partner asked me about Peter Musoke. DC Tomlin alleged Peter had something to do with it. I can't remember when or where they told me that. I told them that Peter had nothing to do with it. I thought they were trying to make out it was black on black attack. I said why are you bringing him up, he wasn't there? All they said was that they had heard rumours he was involved but wouldn't say any more. I thought the officers just didn't want to believe me.

59.   I was frightened of the boys and didn't trust most of the police. I didn't feel safe on a daily basis.

The Crown Prosecution discontinue the case

60.   I did not know how important Sgt Crowley's lies were until I heard it on the news that the two men who had been arrested had been released and it was to do with my evidence not being good enough.

61.   I was upsetted. The police didn't explain it to me until after I had heard it on the news.

62.   I felt that the boys had only been arrested to make the police look good, because people were making their voices heard putting pressure on the police.

Noel Penstone

63.   In about August 1993 I met Noel Penstone from the Council. He tried to help me. He arranged for me to see someone called Eric who was a social or a youth worker to give me support and I saw him quite a bit. The police had nothing to do with that.

Ongoing Fear

64.   I saw men I recognised as the murderers once when I was going to visit my cousin and once when I was going to play pool with Heenan Bhatti. I was frightened.

65. I did not call the police at the time about the Greenwich incident because I was frightened my identity would be revealed. DS Bevan going into one about how I didn't tell the police earlier about this. I gave him a statement on 9 December about it. I have no changes to make to the statement he took.

Appearances at the Magistrates and Crown Court

66. I remember I felt that I had not prepared and I was unsupported. I was frightened of the atmosphere.

67. I was frightened for me. Another witness was allowed to be anonymous sand I wasn't. I wanted to know why. They feared for him or her and not for me.

68. I remember at the Magistrates Court going straight into the Court and Mr Lawrence had a nose bleed and there was a break and I had to come out and I was told that the parents of the boys who were defendants were in the room where I should have waited, so I had to wait on the landing.

69. I remember some of the questions jarring on me - like what clothes did Stephen wear? Everyone knew the answer to those questions. I remember thinking I got on the Magistrate's nerves.

70. I remember at the Crown Court wanting to see my statement and one of the boy's barristers laughing and saying hasn't he seen his statement?

71. I remember going out of the Court so I could read my statements and saying I wasn't going back in that day.

72. I felt everything was depending on me and I was going in blindfold.

73. I was alone on a big ship full of pirates. The pirates had me trapped.

74. Mr Kamlish told me that the case was going to be dropped. I said why? He said because the judge wouldn't allow my evidence to go to the jury.

75. I felt upset. I felt guilty that I wasn't able to give my evidence properly.

Signed: D A Brooks

Dated: 5.5.98

Sitting at:
　　　　　　　　　　　　Hannibal House
　　　　　　　　　　　　Elephant & Castle
　　　　　　　　　　　　London SE1 6TE

　　　　　　　　　　　　Wednesday, 17th June 1998

Before:

(THE CHAIRMAN)
SIR WILLIAM MACPHERSON OF CLUNY
(ADVISERS)
MR TOM COOK
THE RIGHT REVEREND DR JOHN SENTAMU
DR RICHARD STONE

**THE INQUIRY INTO THE MATTERS ARISING FROM THE
DEATH OF STEPHEN LAWRENCE**

MR E LAWSON QC, MISS A WEEKES and **MR J GIBSON** appeared
　　on behalf of the **INQUIRY**
MR M MANSFIELD QC, MR STEPHEN KAMLISH, MR M SOORJOO and
　　MS MARGOT BOYE-ANAWOMA appeared on behalf of the
　　LAWRENCE FAMILY
MR J GOMPERTZ QC and **MR J BEER** appeared on behalf of
　　THE METROPOLITAN POLICE
MS S WOODLEY QC and **MR P DOYLE** appeared on behalf of
　　three superintendents
MR ME EGAN and **MR R JORY** appeared on behalf of **officers
　　of federated rank**
MR J YEARWOOD and **MS M SIKAND** appeared on behalf of the
　　CRE
MR W PANTON appeared on behalf of the **LONDON BOROUGH OF
　　GREENWICH**
MR I MACDONALD QC and **MR R MENON** appeared on behalf of
　　DUWAYNE BROOKS
MR M CHAWLA appeared on behalf of **DCS BARKER**
MR B BARKER QC and **MS J SPARKS** appeared on behalf of
　　the **CPS**

**ALL PROCEEDINGS
DAY 45**

Transcript of the Stenographic notes of
Sellers Imago,
Suite 1-2, Ludgate House, 107 Fleet Street,
London, EC4A 2AB
TEL: 0171 427 0089

Page 8567

1   Wednesday, 17th June 1998.

2 MR LAWSON: We would like to call, please, this

3 morning, Mr Johnston.

4   <ASSISTANT COMMISSIONER IAN JOHNSTON, sworn

5   <Examined by MR LAWSON

6 THE WITNESS: Ian Johnston, Assistant Commissioner,

7 Metropolitan Police, sir.

8 MR LAWSON: Mr Johnston, you are, are you not,

9 Assistant Commissioner of the southeast of London,

10 and have been so since August 1994?

11 A. Yes, sir. I took over the running of 3 and 4

12 Areas, the old 3 and 4 Areas, at the end of March

13 1994, but when the new area structure began in August

14 1994, I became the Assistant Commissioner for one of

15 the new five areas.

16 THE CHAIRMAN: That is South London?

17 A. That is South East London, sir.

18 MR LAWSON: I am going to ask you about your

19 involvement with Mr and Mrs Lawrence and the ongoing

20 investigation from the Spring of 1994 onward, but

21 Mr Gompertz informs me that you wish, on behalf of

22 the Metropolitan Police, to make a statement before

23 we ask you to give your evidence. Is that right?

24 A. Sir, if that is at all possible, I would welcome

25 the opportunity.

Page 8568

1 THE CHAIRMAN: Mr Mansfield, you know about this, do

2 you not?

3 MR MANSFIELD: Sir, I was informed a few minutes ago

4 that something might be said.

5 THE CHAIRMAN: Are Mr and Mrs Lawrence here?

6 MR MANSFIELD: Mrs Lawrence, I think, is not.

7 Mr Lawrence is here.

8 THE CHAIRMAN: I think it would be desirable if he

9 was present. (Pause) Thank you, Mr Lawrence.

10 MR LAWSON: Mr Lawrence may have heard it outside;

11 I did mention it to him beforehand that Mr Johnston

12 does want to make a statement before his evidence

13 formally begins.

14 THE CHAIRMAN: Yes. Very well, Mr Johnston.

15 THE WITNESS: Sir, I wonder if I might stand and

16 address my remarks to Mr Lawrence?

17 THE CHAIRMAN: No, I think you can remain seated, but

18 of course you can certainly address them to him. I

19 am sure that will be regarded as no discourtesy.

20 THE WITNESS: Thank you, sir.

21   Mr Lawrence, I wanted to say to you that I am

22 truly sorry that we have let you down. It has been a

23 tragedy for you: you have lost a son, and not seen

24 his killers brought to justice. It has been a

25 tragedy for the Metropolitan Police, who have lost

Page 85

1 the confidence of a significant section of the

2 community for the way we have handled the case.

3   I can understand and explain some of what went

4 wrong. I cannot and do not seek to justify it. We

5 are determined to learn lessons from this. A great

6 deal has changed and yet will change. We have trie

7 over the last four years since the first

8 investigation, to show imagination and determinatio

9 to prosecute Stephen's killers.

10   I am very, very sorry and very, very sad that we

11 have let you down. Looking back now, I can see

12 clearly that we could have and we should have done

13 better. I deeply regret that we have not put his

14 killers away.

15   On behalf of myself, the Commissioner -- who

16 specifically asked me to associate himself with thes

17 words -- and the whole of the Metropolitan Police,

18 I again offer my sincere and deep apologies to you.

19 I do hope that one day you will be able to forgive

20 us.

21   Finally, I would like to add my own personal

22 apologies for supporting the earlier investigation in

23 ways in which it has now been shown that I was

24 wrong. I hope the reasons for my support will be

25 understood, and I hope that, eventually, you will

Page 85

1 forgive me for that, as well, Mr Lawrence.

EXHIBIT BRP/3

TRANSCRIPT OF COMPILATION VIDEO IC/3

NEIL ACOURT (NA)   CHARLIE MARTIN (CM) (TAFF)

GARY DOBSON (GD) (GAL)   DAVID NORRIS (DN)

LUKE KNIGHT (LK)   DANNY CAETANO (DC)

----ooooOoooo---

N.B. A.   (TEXT WITHIN ROUNDED BRACKETS DENOTES SPEECH
              WHICH IS OPEN TO THE INDIVIDUALS
              INTERPRETATION)

      B.   ---------- DENOTES UNINTELLIGIBLE SPEECH

      C.   [TEXT WITHIN SQUARE BRACKETS CLARIFIES
              SEQUENCE]

(GD)   NO -----------

(GD)   IS THAT WHERE IT WAS

(NA)   WHY, WHAT

(GD)   (LANDLORDS BEEN ROUND AND DONE THE FUCKING THINGS TODAY)

(NA)   WHO

(GD)   PAUL

(NA)   SHUT UP

(GD)   I DIDN'T EVEN KNOW HE WAS COMING ROUND MATE I CAME IN AND I SEEN
        ALL THE PLUGS AN THAT FITTED ON.

(NA)   -------------

(GD)   I DIDN'T EVEN KNOW

(NA)   WAS CHARLIE HERE

(GD)   NO NOT THAT I KNOW OF I COME IN AND

(NA)   WHAT HE COME IN YOUR HOUSE

(GD)   HE COMES IN HE COMES IN TO FIX THINGS, HE COME IN TO FIX THE
        CUPBOARDS BUT WE KNEW ABOUT THE CUPBOARDS

(NA)   YOU'RE JOKING

(GD)   NO I DIDN'T EVEN KNOW NEIL, I DIDN'T EVEN KNOW MYSELF, HE SAID TO
        CHARLIE I'LL BE COMING ROUND MONDAY TO DO THE DOOR IN YOUR
        BEDROOM.

(NA)   WHO PUT ALL THEM CASSETTES THINGS IN THERE

(GD)   (HE MUST HAVE) I DIDN'T EVEN FUCKING REALISE

(NA)   I DON'T BELIEVE YOUR LETTING THE GEEZER IN YOUR HOUSE, SO WHAT
        IF HE'S THE LANDLORD   I BET THAT CUNTS PRESSED IT IN ALL.

(NA)   I DON'T BELIEVE IT I DON'T FUCKING BELIEVE IT MATE

(GD)   I DIDN'T EVEN (REALISE)

(NA)   PHONE HIM UP

(GD)   I CAN'T SAY ----------- HE'S GONNA TURN ROUND AND SAY WELL GET OUT OF
        MY FLAT THEN

(NA)   YOU SAY BRING THE DEPOSIT DOWN AND POKE IT UP YOUR ARSE IT'S MY
        FUCKING HOUSE, WHAT'S HE DOING COMING IN

(GD)   I KNOW THAT NEIL

(NA)   GAL IT DON'T MATTER WHO HE IS HE CAN'T JUST WALK IN HERE LIKE THAT

(GD)   HE CAN NEIL ----------

(NA)	NO HE CAN'T I'M TELLING YA. HE CANNOT IT'S YOURS, YOU'RE PAYING FOR IT.
(GD)	I KNOW THAT, I KNOW THAT
(NA)	HE CAN'T WALK IN WHEN HE WANTS
(GD)	BUT BY LAW IT'S HIS PROPERTY
(NA)	IT AIN'T HE'S LEASING IT TO YOU HE AIN'T GOT NO RIGHT TO COME IN HERE. IT'S YOUR PRIVACY.
(NA)	I DON'T BELIEVE IT THE CUNTS BEEN IN HERE AND HE'S SEEN THE STUN GUN. HE'S DEFINITELY SEEN IT. IT WAS UP THERE.
(GD)	(IT WAS UP BY THE SIDE THERE).
(NA)	I BET HE'S BEEN PRESSING IT AFTER ALL THIS FUCKING TIME, FUCKING IDIOT HE IS GAL YOU'VE GOT TO GET ON TO HIM, HE'S SEEN THAT IMAGINE WHAT HE'S THINKING HE'S THINKING WHY HAVE THEY GOT ONE OF THEM.
(NA)	I DON'T BELIEVE IT, HE'S HE JUST COMES IN WHEN HE WANTS
(GD)	FIRST TIME HE'S DONE THAT
(NA)	WHAT, WHAT HAPPENED ABOUT THE WARDROBE THEN?
(GD)	--------------
(NA)	--------------
(GD)	--------------
(NA)	--------------
(GD)	THAT'S WHY THAT'S WHY I LIKE TO LOCK THE DOOR BUT I CAN'T LOCK THE DOOR CAN I
(NA)	--------------. WHO'S GONNA STOP YOU
(GD)	NO ONE'S GONNA STOP ME
(NA)	THAT'S WHAT I'M SAYING
(GD)	I COULDN'T IMAGINE HIM COMING IN SPINNING THE GAFF
(NA)	WELL HE'S MOVED THAT FOR A START
(GD)	YEAH HE'S TIDIED UP AROUND HERE ALL THE TAPES WAS ON THE FLOOR
(NA)	WHAT WAS
(GD)	ALL THE TAPES WAS ON THE FLOOR
(NA)	ALL THE WHAT
(GD)	THE TAPES
(NA)	WHO'S CLEANED UP THE TABLE
(GD)	ME -------
(NA)	WHAT BEFORE HE GOT HERE
(NA)	I DON'T FUCKING BELIEVE THAT, THAT CUNTS BEEN IN HERE
(GD)	THAT'S THE FIRST TIME I'VE KNOWN OF HIM COMING ROUND
(NA)	THAT, THAT THAT MEANS IT AIN'T THE FIRST TIME HE'S BEEN HERE THIS

3

GAFF COULD BE BUGGED TO THE EYES MATE.

(GD) THAT'S WHY I WANT TO LOCK THE DOOR WHEN I GO OUT BUT I CAN'T CAN I

(NA) I BET THIS GAFF'S BUGGED UP TO THE EYEBROWS MATE

(GD) I'M GONNA HAVE TO LOCK THE DOOR UP FROM NOW ON, EVERYONE ELSE
WILL HAVE TO WAIT TILL I GET HOME TILL WE CAN GET IN. THAT'S GONNA
HAVE TO HAPPEN FROM NOW ON INNIT?

(NA) --------------------

END OF SEQUENCE NUMBER ONE

SEQUENCE 2   DATE: 02.12.94.

                    START: 19:17:53

                    STOP: 19:18:51

(GD) THAT'S WHAT IT MADE ME LAUGH WHEN WAS, FUCKING I PUNCHED THAT
--------- I HAD TO DO IT MATE.

[OVERHAND BOWLING GD, STABBING ACTION BY NA]

(GD) FUCKING CRICKET INNIT. YEAH BUT HE KNEW YOU SEE HOW DID HE
KNOW THAT I WAS DOING THAT ABOUT THAT CAUSE HE TURNED ROUND
AND WENT, NO WHAT IT WAS, NO HE TURNED ROUND AND SAID THAT DIDN'T
HE BUT WHAT IT WAS IS AH I DUNNO I HAD ME HANDS IN ME POCKETS OR
SOMETHING HE RECKONS HE WENT LIKE THAT

(NA) AND THEN HE COMES OUT WITH HE THOUGHT I HAD A TOOL ---------

(GD) YES LOOK

(NA) LOOK YOU'VE BEEN ALRIGHT LATELY BUT

(GD) (E) AIN'T, (E) AIN'T BEEN TOO BAD LATELY

(NA) BUT THAT'S A PORKY

(GD) YEAH

(GD) OH DID DANNY GO AND GET A VERSACE, WHERE DID DANNY GET MONEY
FOR, FOR A FUCKING VERSACE JUMPER.

(NA) THINGYBOB

(GD) CHRISTMAS
[MUFFLED]

END OF SEQUENCE TWO

4

SEQUENCE 3   DATE: 02.12.94
                    START: 20:09:25
                    STOP: 20:12:10

(GD)   SOME OF THEM ARE ALRIGHT .... SOME, SOME, SOME OF THEM GET ON MY
        FUCKING NERVES.

(GD)   THERE'S A NIGGER THERE LIKE ME BROTHER USED TO KNOW YEARS AGO,
        HE AIN'T A NIGGER LIKE BUT HE IS BLACK

(NA)   HE'S A BLACK CUNT

(GD)   HE'S A BLACK CUNT BUT HE AIN'T LIKE

(NA)   ------------

(GD)   YEAH HE AIN'T A RUDE BOY OR NOTHING HE LIKE TALKS LIKE A FUCKING
        NORMAL WHITE GEEZER ...., DOES NORMAL WHITE GEEZER THINGS NOT
        MUG OLD GRANNIES AND THINGS LIKE THAT BUT LIKE HE'S JUST ONE OF
        THEM TYPE OF PEOPLE WHO NOT ON PURPOSE BUT LIKE JUST DRIVE YOU
        MAD GET ON YOUR NERVES LIKE THE OTHER DAY I NICKED HIS HAT LIKE HE
        WAS GETTING ON ME NERVES THE OTHER DAY LIKE HE'S FOREVER GOT HIS
        HAT ON HE'S LIKE ONE OF THEM NIGGERS WHO DON'T NEVER TAKES HIS
        BASEBALL CAP OFF SO I NICKED HIS BASEBALL CAP AND (HE TOE'D) RIGHT
        DOWN THE SCAFFOLDING HE DIDN'T CATCH ME I GOT AWAY AND HE SEEN
        ME LATER ON AND LIKE HE GOT ME ARM AND TWISTED IT BEHIND ME BACK
        AND STARTED MUCKING ABOUT TAPPING ME ON THE BACK OF ME ON THE
        BACK OF ME (LEGS) IT WEREN'T HURTING BUT I DIDN'T LIKE IT I JUST DIDN'T
        LIKE, LIKE HIM DOING THAT AND I HAD THE STANLEY KNIFE IN ME POCKET,
        PULLED IT OUT AND I BIT THE THING OFF AND I WENT THAT'LL DO THERE
        MICK BEFORE I END UP FUCKING CUTTING YA ..... ALL FUCKING DAY HE WAS
        GETTING ON ME NERVES LIKE, BUT IT WAS GETTING ON ME NERVES AND
        LIKE. I SAID TO HIM YOU TAP ME ONCE MORE YOU SILLY CUNT I'M GOING
        TO JUST FUCKING SLICE THIS DOWN YOU (ABOUT SEVEN TIMES) AND HE LET
        GO ME ARM AND SAID AH SERIOUSLY GARY WHERE'S ME BASEBALL CAP HE'S
        PUT LIKE THE BROOM HANDLE DOWN, COS HE'S PICKED A BROOM HANDLE
        UP, HE'S GONE SERIOUSLY GARY WHERE'S ME BASEBALL CAP. I WENT
        ALRIGHT SINCE YOU'VE ASKED NICELY I'LL GIVE IT TO YA, SO I GO
        DOWNSTAIRS AN SAY LIKE HERE IT IS HE WENT AH CHEERS.
        AND HE GOT UP AND WENT TO GET IN THE LIFT AND JUST TURNED ROUND
        AND HE'S GONE AH YOUR JUST A WANKER LIKE FOR NICKING THIS BASEBALL
        CAP HE DIDN'T MEAN IT FUNNILY BUT I TOOK IT THE WRONG WAY I WENT

5

ALRIGHT YEAH THAT'LL DO, LIKE AS IF TO SAY AH LEAVE OFF AND HE WENT YOUR JUST A WANKER BUT HE WAS LAUGHING AND JOKING ABOUT IT BUT I DIDN'T LIKE IT AND I SAID ALRIGHT MICK THAT'LL DO THERE, THAT'S ENOUGH AND HE TURNED ROUND, I THINK HE TURNED ROUND, AND SAID SOMETHING ALONG THE SAME LINES AGAIN AND I SAID ALRIGHT MICK DON'T SAY IT AGAIN THAT'S YOUR FUCKING LAST WARNING I AIN'T MUCKING ABOUT I'M BEING SERIOUS THAT'LL DO AND HE SHUT UP THAT'S WHAT I MEAN THEY'RE ALL WIND UP MERCHANTS IN WORK.

(NA)   THEY'RE ALL COCKS

(GD)   YEAH I AIN'T GOT NOTHING TO PROVE TO THEM SO I JUST IGNORE THEM IT'S LIKE SOMETIMES I DO FUCKING HAVE TO BITE MATE, LIKE JUST TO LET THEM KNOW THAT I AIN'T GONNA BE THERE JUST TO TAKE THE PISS OUT OF.

(NA)   TELL THEM TO FUCK OFF ANYWAY DON'T EVEN LET THEM FUCK ABOUT WITH YOU.

(GD)   MOST OF THEM DON'T NEIL BUT THAT MICK I'VE KNOWN FOR ABOUT FUCKING SEVEN YEARS THAT'S PROBABLY WHY HE'S GETTING LIKE THAT THAT'S WHY I SAID TO HIM LIKE THAT'LL DO FUCKING LAST TIME I WON'T SAY IT AGAIN.

END OF SEQUENCE THREE

SEQUENCE 4   DATE: 02.12.94.

                        START: 20:23:06

                        STOP: 20:23:41

[NA VIOLENTLY ATTACKS OBJECT, THROWING IT AND KICKING IT]

(NA)   DO HIM [STAMPS ON OBJECT]

(LK)   WHOSE ARE THEY, TAFFY'S OR SOMETHING

(NA)   THAT'D HURT 'EM MATE

(LK)   IT WOULD HURT EM IT'D KILL EM

(NA)   TAFFY DON'T WANT EM.

END OF SEQUENCE FOUR

SEQUENCE 5 DATE: 02.12.94.

START: 20:43:45

STOP: 20:45:08

(NA) WHAT'S HAPPENING MUSH

(GD) ITS AS SIMPLE AS THAT

(CM) WHAT'S THAT

(NA) YEAH HOW ARE YOU ALRIGHT

(NA) YOU GONNA BE IN TONIGHT, YEAH, WHAT TIME YOU GOING DOWN THERE, FUCK ME ARE YEAH, WHO'S IN, ER

[OVERSPEAK]

(NA) EVERYTHING. WHERE'S HE GOING, WHAT TIMES HE GOING HOME. CUSHTIE. WHAT SO HE'S GONNA BE IN, WELL I'LL POP DOWN TO HIS FLAT, I'LL GO DOWN HIS FLAT, LATER ON THEN, ALRIGHT. DON'T FORGET THOUGH WILL YA, ALRIGHT THEN MATE, CUSHTIE.   SEE YOU LATER ON, SEE YOU LATER.

[MOCK ATTACK BY NA ON CM]

(NA) ALRIGHT YOU CAN HAVE THAT, SORTED AS THAT.

(CM) DON'T HURT ANYWAY

(NA) COME ON LETS HIT FOXES, ALL GET CHIVED UP.

(CM) ---

END OF SEQUENCE FIVE

SEQUENCE 6 DATE: 02.12.94.

START: 20:55:28

STOP: 20:55:51

(NA) [YELLS] I'M BORED

(GD) I'VE BEEN DONE THE MOST WITH THAT THING MATE [STUN GUN]

(NA) RAISE YOUR HANDS, HANDS UP STRAIGHT

(LK) YOU'RE ACTING LIKE FUCKING NIGGERS

(NA) I'M GONNA GIVE YOU (TILL) 3

(NA) 3

(NA) UP IN THE AIR ABOVE YOUR HEAD 3, 2, 1.

END OF SEQUENCE SIX

SEQUENCE 7   DATE: 03.12.94.
                    START: 19:50:03
                    STOP: 19:50:30

[NA, DN AND LK DISCUSSING LOTTERY WINNERS, PRESENTER REFERS TO
SYNDICATES FROM OLD PEOPLE ESTATES WINNING]

(DN)   ------------------------

(NA)   FIFTEEN MINUTES

(DN)   WHY ON EARTH DO OLD GRANNIES (WANT TO PLAY) THEY'LL ALL DIE
        (TOMORROW)

(NA)   GOOD LUCK TO THEM, FUCK IT.

(LK)   AT LEAST THEY ARE WHITE.
                    END OF SEQUENCE SEVEN

SEQUENCE 8   DATE: 03.12.94.
                    START: 21:44:58
                    STOP: 21:45:33

(NA)   BLACK CUNT, GET OFF OUR FUCKING ROYAL PERFORMANCES YOU.
                    END OF SEQUENCE EIGHT

SEQUENCE 9   DATE: 03.12.94.
                    START: 22:34:39
                    STOP: 22:35:03

                    [NA TOYING WITH KNIFE]
                    END OF SEQUENCE NINE

SEQUENCE 10   DATE: 03.12.94.

START: 22:53:54

STOP: 22:54:27

(NA)   LOOK THAT'S A CUSHTIE LITTLE CHIP THAT, SEE THAT BIT THERE
                    [NA SHOWS SECTION OF HIS KNIFE TO LK]

(LK)   YEAH

(NA)   PUT IT ON SOMETHING ----- RIGHT, AND JUST GO DIG STRAIGHT IN DEEP,
          WATCH
              [NA DEMONSTRATES CUTTING ACTION OF KNIFE ON ARM OF LK'S CHAIR].

(LK)   ---------------- -----------------------------

(NA)   JUST GO [NOISE] ---------- DUG IT RIGHT IN

(LK)   ------------------------------

(NA)   SO ALL YOU GOT TO DO IS GO LIKE THAT
                            END OF SEQUENCE TEN

SEQUENCE 11   DATE: 03.12.94.

START: 23:25:28

STOP: 23:28:00

(LK)   WIN AND ALL THAT I THINK IT WAS CAMEROON, A FUCKING NIGGER
          COUNTRY

(NA)   WHO WAS SAYING THAT

(LK)   FUCKING OUR PRESENTER ENGLISH PRESENTERS SAYING OH YEAH WE WANT
          CAMEROON TO WIN THIS, WHY THE FUCK SHOULD HE WANT NIGGERS TO WIN
          IT WHEN THEY'RE PLAYING SOMETHING FUCKING LIKE ITALY OR SOMETHING
          LIKE A EUROPEAN FUCKING TEAM -------------

(NA)   IT MAKES YOU SICK DUNNIT

(LK)   GETS ON YA NERVES ----------

(NA)   YOU RUBBER LIPPED CUNT [LAUGHS]
    [NA PICKS UP KNIFE FROM WINDOW LEDGE SITS DOWN, STICKS KNIFE INTO ARM OF CHAIR]

(NA)   I RECKON THAT EVERY NIGGER SHOULD BE CHOPPED UP MATE AND
          THEY SHOULD BE LEFT WITH (NOTHING BUT) FUCKING STUMPS.

(LK)   D'YA REMEMBER THAT ENOOCH POWELL ------- THAT GEEZER HE KNEW

9

STRAIGHT AWAY HE WENT OVER TO AFRICA AND ALL THAT RIGHT -------

(NA)   IS THAT WHAT HAPPENED.

(LK)   YEAH HE, HE KNEW IT WAS A SLUM, HE KNEW IT WAS A SHIT HOLE AND HE CAME BACK HERE SAYING THEY'RE UNCIVILISED AND ALL THAT AND THEN THEY STARTED COMING OVER HERE AND HE KNEW, HE KNEW STRAIGHT AWAY HE WAS SAYING NO I DON'T WANT THEM HERE NO FUCKING NIGGERS THEY'LL RUIN THE GAFF AND HE WAS RIGHT THEY FUCKING HAVE RUINED IT.

(NA)   IS HE STILL ALIVE

(LK)   I SEEN HIM ON A PROGRAMME THE OTHER DAY -------- ---------

(NA)   WHAT WAS HE SAYING

(LK)   HE WASN'T SAYING NOTHING ABOUT NIGGERS AND ALL THAT HE WAS JUST SAYING ABOUT ------- SOMETHING ELSE.

(NA)   I WANNA WRITE HIM A LETTER ENOCH POWELL MATE YOU ARE THE GREATEST, YOU ARE THE DON OF DONS GET BACK INTO PARLIAMENT MATE AND SHOW THESE COCK SUCKERS WHAT IT'S ALL ABOUT, ALL THESE FLASH, ARROGANT, BIG MOUTHED, SHOUTING THEIR MOUTHS OFF, FLASH, DIRTY, RAPISTS, GRASS CUNTS

(LK)   YEAH FUCKING RAPISTS AND EVERYTHING

(NA)   SUPERGRASS THING MATE ONLY TOOK OFF SINCE NIGGERS COME INTO THE COUNTRY IT'S NIGGERS THAT'S ALL IT IS

(LK)   ------------------------------- -------------------- -----------------------

(NA)   FUCKING COREY SUCKERS THEY ARE

(NA)   BLACK COREY SUCKING CUNTS

END OF SEQUENCE ELEVEN

SEQUENCE 12   **DATE: 03.12.94.**

                                    START: 23:28:06

                                    STOP: 23:30:35

[NA TOYING WITH KNIFE STABBING / CHOPPING AT CHAIR ARM]

(LK)   --------------------- ---------------------- -----------------------

(NA)   --------------------- WHAT AND HIS MOUTH -------------

[NA STROKING BLADE OF KNIFE / GOES TO FRONT DOOR CARRYING KNIFE – SWITCHES OF PORCH LIGHT – STANDS IN DARKNESS IN PORCH WITH KNIFE]]

[NA RETURNS – STABS AT WINDOW AREA WITH KNIFE, JUGGLES KNIFE – RETURNS TO SEAT]

END OF SEQUENCE TWELVE

SEQUENCE 13 **DATE: 03.12.94.**

  START: 23:46:17

  STOP: 23:47:33

(NA) THAT (WENT LIKE) A ROCKET

(LK) --------------- I THINK (IT) WENT IN HIT THE BAR ----------

[LK AND NA DISCUSSING SPORTS PERSONALITY OF THE YEAR]

(LK) I GUARANTEE I KNOW WHO WINS IT LINFORD FUCKING CHRISTIE

(NA) GO ON --------------

(NA) FUCK OFF. AH DAMON HILL

(LK) HE'S GOOD

(NA) BOLLOCKS YOU NIGGER

(LK) I ------ LINFORD CHRISTIE

(NA) I WANT MONGOMMERY TO WIN IT

(NA) OR SALLY GUNNELL

(LK) AH SHE MIGHT WIN IT AS IT GOES

(NA) A MACROON BETTER NOT WIN IT MATE.

(LK) I GUARANTEE IT'S A MACAROON. EITHER COLIN JACKSON OR LINFORD CHRISTIE.

END OF SEQUENCE THIRTEEN

SEQUENCE 14 **DATE: 04.12.94.**

  START: 18:13:58

  STOP: 18:14:34

(CM) -------------- PUNCHING HIM, D'YOU KNOW WHAT I MEAN

(NA) OH, FUCK OFF WATSON, YOU'RE A BLACK CUNT.

11

( )   IS THAT WATSON
(NA)   YEAH   A CABBAGE, TURNED OUT

END OF SEQUENCE FOURTEEN

SEQUENCE 15   **DATE: 04.12.94.**

                       START: 18:43:05

                       STOP: 18:45:07

(NA)   I DON'T LIKE EVEN MIXING WITH THEM TAFF DO YOU

(CM)   I WENT IN THERE, THE DAY BEFORE AND I WALKED IN THERE AND D'YA
        KNOW THAT FAT CUNT, HE WAS IN THERE WITH A MATE AND A NIGGER AND
        THEY WAS ALL IN THERE AND WHEN I WENT IN IT WENT ALL SILENT. D'YA
        KNOW WHAT I MEAN CAUSE LIKE I COULD HEAR THEY WAS ALL WISPERING
        TO EACH OTHER

(NA)   WHERE WAS YOU

(CM)   IN THERE

(NA)   WHAT IN THE SAME ROOM

(CM)   YEAH I WAS WITH DANNY

(NA)   WHAT DO YOU MEAN WHISPERING WEREN'T THEY JUST GOING AH, LIKE
        TALKING QUITELY.

(CM)   I WAS JUST LOOKING AROUND

(NA)   WHAT AND DANNY WAS STANDING THERE

(CM)   NO DANNY WAS OUT IN THE KITCHEN WHEN I LOOKED AROUND AND I
        COULDN'T HEAR ..... IF IT WAS DANNY SO I WALKED OUT INTO THE KTICHEN
        AND I WAS IN THERE BUT (WHEN IT WENT SILENT STRAIGHT AWAY).

(NA)   WHO WAS THE NIGGER?

(CM)   FUCK KNOWS

(NA)   HOW OLD

(LK)   WHERE'S THAT

(CM)   ABOUT 25

(CM)   IN FOXES

(LK)   ----------------

(NA)   WAS HE A BIG CUNT

(CM)   YEAH A BIG NIGGER

(NA)   WHAT A BIG CUNT

(CM)   YEAH A BIG NIGGER

(NA)	YEAH I KNOW THE ONE YOUR TALKING ABOUT
(CM)	LIKE WHEN YOU SEE HIM STRAIGHT AWAY YOU DON'T LIKE THE LOOK OF HIM
(NA)	HE'S A BOUNCER
(LK)	OH YEAH I THINK I'VE SEEN HIM A COUPLE OF TIMES
(LK)	I THINK HE WAS A BOUNCER AT THE YORKSHIRE GREY AS WELL OR SOMETHING
(NA)	WAS HE LUKE
(LK)	I THINK SO
(LK)	LIKE GOT DREADLOCKS
(CM)	NO DIDN'T HAVE DREADLOCKS, WELL HE DIDN'T HAVE DREADLOCKS THEN
(LK)	COS ------------ DREADLOCK ROUND THERE
(CM)	WHAT SITTING IN THERE
(LK)	NO THIS IS, I'M ON ABOUT A GOOD COUPLE OF YEARS AGO OR SOMETHING AND JUST AS YOU MENTIONED IT I REMEMBERED HIM.
(CM)	NO THIS ONE HE WAS A BIG CUNT HE'D ALL GOLD ON HIM AND EVERYTHING AND I'VE SEEN HIM LOOK ROUND AND I LOOKED AT HIM AND I LOOKED OVER AND THERE WAS THAT FAT CUNT IN THE GREY T-SHIRT AND BLACK JEANS THAT HE'S ALWAYS WEARING AND THERE WAS ANOTHER ONE OF THEM. ------------------ STRAIGHT AWAY ------------------ GONNA TRY.

END OF SEQUENCE FIFTEEN

SEQUENCE 16   **DATE: 04.12.94.**

                     START: 19:04:43

                     STOP: 19:05:31

[CM (BACK TO CAMERA) REMOVES KNIFE FROM HIS TROUSER WAISTBAND, HANDS KNIFE TO NA WHO PLACES IT DOWN THE REAR OF HIS OWN TROUSERS – WALKS AROUND ROOM – RETURNS SECRETED KNIFE TO CM WHO PUTS IT BACK DOWN HIS TROUSERS WAISTBAND AND TOGETHER LEAVE THE FLAT]

(CM)	------------ GONNA CARVE EM UP IF THEY SAY ANYTHING THEN.
(NA)	--.
(NA)	--.
(CM)	--.

(NA)   HERE YOU ARE

(NA)   WHAT ----------------- WHAT THE FUCKS MARK EVER DONE TO ANYBODY ----------
----

(NA)   COME ON THEN LUKE

END OF SEQUENCE SIXTEEN

SEQUENCE 17   **DATE: 04.12.94.**

                        START: 19:31:22

                        STOP: 19:31:47

(NA)   START TALKING LITTLE MAN

[NA IS WALKING AROUND HOLDING A KNIFE]

(NA)   WHAT DO YOU RECKON ON THESE SHOES, DO YOU LIKE EM, OR NOT

(LK)   YEAH THEY SEEM (FAIR ENOUGH)

(NA)   I RECKON THEY'RE ALRIGHT, FUCK ALL THE MATTER WITH THEM. [NOISE]

[NA CARRIES OUT MOCK STABBING ATTACK WITH THE KNIFE ON LK WHO IS SEATED]

END OF SEQUENCE SEVENTEEN

SEQUENCE 18   **DATE: 05.12.94.**

                        START: 20:17:24

                        STOP: 20:21:32

[OVERSPEAK]

[CM IS HOLDING A KNIFE AND SEEMS TO CHOP AT THE TABLE]

(DC)   LET ME SEE YOUR JEANS

(NA)   THIS IS A DOSS HOLE MATE THIS GAFF THAT'S WHAT IT IS A FUCKING DOSS
        HOLE.

(CM)   THIS IS A CRACK DEN.

(NA)   WE'RE CRACK DEN HEADS.

(CM?)   THAT'S THE BIT THAT FUCKS YOU ON THIS.

[NA TAKES THE KNIFE]

14

(NA)   I KNOW TAFF, LOOK I WAS SHOWING LUKE THE OTHER DAY YOU KNOW
         THESE THINGS, LOOK IF YOU WANT YOU JUST PUSH IT IN, LOOK IT GOES
         STRAIGHT IN.

         [NA DEMONSTRATES THE CUTTING ABILITY OF THE KNIFE ON A CHAIR]

(CM)   NEIL, AH, AH, IT REALLY HURT YESTERDAY.

(NA)   IT GOES RIGHT IN LIKE, IF YOU WANT TO CUT SOMEBODY YOU JUST PUT THAT
         BIT ON THEIR FACE AND GO [NOISE] FEEL IT ON YOUR HAND

(DC)   LINFORD CHRISTIE DRIVING IN A LIMOSINE, WELL GETTING CHAUFFER
         DRIVEN IN A LIMOSINE, LATE O'CLOCK, IT'S LATE O'CLOCK [LAUGHS] IT'S
         LATE, HE'S TIRED AND HE WANTS TO GO TO BED. SEES THIS BIG HOTEL, HE
         GOES RIGHT DRIVER PULL UP THERE I'LL GET YOU A ROOM RIGHT WE'LL
         STAY HERE. AND HE GOES IN THERE HE GOES CAN I HAVE TWO ROOMS
         PLEASE. THE GEEZER'S GONE NO SORRY MATE YOUR BLACK YOU'VE GOT TO
         GO ROUND THE BACK. WHAT, WHAT, YOU'VE GOT TO GO ROUND THE BACK
         SORRY MATE LIKE THAT'S THE RULES YOUR BLACK YOU'VE GOT TO GO
         ROUND THE BACK. HE GOES, HE GOES WHA, WHAT. LOOK, LOOK GO OUT
         THEM DOORS WALK ROUND GO ROUND THE BACK IT DON'T TAKE 2 SECONDS
         AND HE GOES NAH DO YOU, DO YOU KNOW WHO I AM. HE SAYS LINFORD
         CHRISTIE. WELL IT WON'T TAKE YOU TOO LONG TO GET ROUND THE BACK
         THEN.

(NA)   [LAUGHS] WHO TOLD YOU IT DAN.
         [OVERSPEAKING]

(   )   WHAT DO YOU CALL A BLACK GEEZER (HITCH-HIKING)

(   )   A THIEF

(CM)   FUCKING BLACK

(   )   -------------

(DC?)   WHAT DO YOU CALL A HUNGRY NIGGER
         [OVERSPEAK]

(DC?)   WHAT DO YOU CALL A HUNGRY NIGGER

(NA?)   AN ETHIOPIAN

(CM)   RIGHT THERE WAS THIS GEEZER RIGHT,

(NA)   BLACK CUNT

(   )   HE HAD, HE HAD ENOUGH MONEY TO BUY A NICE PAIR OF BOOTS

(   )   SO HE BOUGHT

(NA)   A PAIR OF SANDALS AND BOUGHT A LUMP OF PUFF WITH THE REST.

(   )   NO SO HE WENT INTO REVELS AND BOUGHT A PAIR OF (JESUS CREEPERS)

(   )   I TOLD YOU [OVERSPEAK] HE BOUGHT A PAIR [OVERSPEAK]

(CM)   HE GOES I WANT TO BUY A PAIR OF BOOTS, HE GOES I'VE GOT TEN QUID

AND I WANT SOMETHING SPECIAL YOU KNOW ---------- WHAT HAVE YOU
GOT. HE GOES WELL WE HAVE GOT SOME NEW SHOES [OVERSPEAKING]

( ) SNAKES SKINS

(CM) WE'VE GOT SNAKES SKINS WHICH IS ONLY ONE HUNDRED AND FIFTY
QUID, HE GOES WE GOT RHINO SKINS WHICH IS ABOUT A (BOTTLE). HE
GOES AND WE GOT RACCOON YOU WONT HAVE A LOT OF PEOPLE WALKING
ABOUT IN THEM. ------------ (WHITE PEOPLE SKIN) HE SAID, HE SAID FUCK
OFF I JUST TOLD YA I ONLY HAD SEVENTY QUID THEY'LL BE FUCKING DEAR
HE SAID ABOUT AN HUNDRED POUNDS. HE SAID I'LL DO YOU A DEAL MATE
HE GOES WE GOT RACCOON FOR THREE BUCK.

(NA) ------------------ NIGGERS ON THE --------------

(LK / DC ?) WE'VE GOT A PAIR OF --------- BLACK MAN SKIN SHOES AND THERE (IN)
FOR 2 BOB.

(CM) WE'VE GOT BLACK MAN ONES AND WE CAN'T EVEN GIVE THEM AWAY.
[OVERSPEAKING]

(NA) NIGGERS .... GOT HARD SKIN IN'T THEY

END OF SEQUENCE EIGHTEEN

SEQUENCE 19   **DATE: 05.12.94.**

                                         START: 20:28:06

                                         STOP: 20:28:25

(NA) YEAH I SAID ARE YOU OUT OF THE BATH

(NA) [NOISE]

[NA CARRIES OUT MOCK STABBING WITH A KNIFE ON CM]

END OF SEQUENCE NINETEEN

SEQUENCE 20   **DATE: 05.12.94.**

                                         START: 20:29:15

                                         STOP: 20:32:01

(NA) YOU, ALRIGHT, YEAH HE'S HERE HOLD ON I'VE GOTTA GO ------------

[NA CHOPS AT CHAIR WITH A KNIFE – THEN WALKS AROUND ROOM CARRYING OUT OVERARM BOWLING STABBING ACTIONS WITH KNIFE]

(DC)   HELLO, ALRIGHT ----------------------- ---------------------------- DID YOU WATCH THAT (GOOD) MOVIE, NOT YET WHEN

(DC)   WHAT ON SKY, YEAH I'VE SEEN IT, WATCH IT, IT'S GOOD

(CM)   WHAT IS IT 'ALIVE'

(DC)   YEAH IT'S FUCKING FUNNY MATE

[OVERSPEAKING]

(CM)   LUKE, LUKE, LUKE

[OVERSPEAKING]

(NA)   CATCH

(CM)   ---------------------------------- NEIL

(NA)   WHAT

(LK)   THAT WAS MEANT TO GO BACK YESTERDAY

(NA)   I KNOW YOU GOT IT OUT MATE YOU GOT IT OUT

(LK)   (BUT I NEVER) WATCHED ALL OF IT

(CM)   ---------------------- ---------------------

(NA)   ------------------

(LK)   YEAH I KNOW, YEAH

(NA)   LUKE YOU'RE GOING RED MATE

(LK)   I'M TAKING THESE BACK

(CM)   IT DON'T SHUT TILL ELEVEN

(LK)   I CAN'T COME OVER TOMORROW

(NA)   YOU CAN'T

(LK)   NAH

(NA)   WHY WANTS HAPPENING

(LK)   I'M WORKING

(NA)   I'M WORKING, WHAT TIME DO YOU THINK ----------------

(LK)   I'M STARTING ABOUT ONE

(NA)   YOUR JOKING

(DC)   WHAT TIME ARE YOU GOING TO BED?

(NA)   I DON'T BELIEVE IT I WAS GOING TO ASK YOU TO DRIVE AND ALL

(LK)   I AIN'T JOKING

(NA)   THE FUCKING CARS GOT TO GO INTO WORK TOMORROW GET THE CLUTCH DONE.

[NA SLASHES AIR WITH KNIFE – GOES TO CHAIR PUSHES BLADE INTO CUSHION]

(DC)   WHAT TIME IS IT ON TEN

WATCH IT IT'S GOOD WHAT. YOU SHOULD WATCH IT THEY EAT EACH

17

OTHER'S FEET.

[NA IS SLASHING MOCKINGLY AT CM'S FACE]

(NA)   FUCK OFF YOU KNOW I DON'T LIKE YOU

(CM)   YOU KNOW THAT GIVES ME THE SHAKES

[NA DROPS KNIFE ONTO FLOOR CUSHION]

(CM)   WHAT DID HE SAY WHEN YOU DONE HIM IN THE LEG? I BET HE WAS WELL
         PARANOID.

END OF SEQUENCE TWENTY

SEQUENCE 21   **DATE: 07.12.94.**

                        START: 18:57:35

                        STOP: 18:58:12

(NA)   WHO'S THAT FROM

(DN)   I DUNNO ----

(NA)   WELL THAT BETTER NOT BE THE GEEZER

(DN)   WHAT

(NA)   YOU KNOW THE GEEZER COME IN HERE

(DN)   DID HE

(NA)   YEAH (GEEZER'S COME IN WHEN NO-ONE WAS IN) HE'S HAD SOMEONE ELSE
         WITH HIM AND I SAID FUCKING HELL (WHAT) IS THIS GAFF

(DN)   YEAH

(NA)   WHAT DO YOU RECKON ABOUT THAT DAVE

(DN)   OH

(NA)   I WAS GETTING [OVERSPEAK] I SAYS PHONE HIM UP MOOSH (GARY WON'T) I
         SAID PHONE HIM UP AND TELL HIM NEVER TO COME DOWN HERE AGAIN
         WITHOUT YOU BEING HERE IT'S YOUR FUCKING HOUSE.

(DN)   ---------------------- .

END OF SEQUENCE TWENTY-ONE

SEQUENCE 22   DATE: 07.12.94.

                     START: 19:02:28

                     STOP: 19:03:40

(DN)   I CAN'T BELIEVE IT

(NA)   WHAT

(DN)   (GEEZER'S) WALKED IN THE HOUSE

(NA)   OH THEY JUST WALKED STRAIGHT IN MATE. AND HE HAD A GEEZER WITH
       HIM. UNLESS HE'S A FUCKING ELECTRICIAN COS HE STUCK IN ANOTHER PLUG
       SOCKET AND ALL THAT, THAT'S WHAT I SAID THERE MUST HAVE BEEN TWO
       OF THEM AND GARY WAS GOING TO ME NAAH IT DON'T MATTER AND HE WAS
       GETTING ON MY NERVES. I WAS SAYING OF COURSE IT FUCKING MATTERS,
       YOU BROUGHT TWO PEOPLE INTO THE HOUSE AND HE'S GOING OH IT'S
       ALRIGHT.

(DN)   YOU DON'T ..... I KNOW IT DON'T MATTER BUT LIKE [OVERSPEAK]

(NA)   I KNOW BUT IT'S YOUR PRIVATE HOUSE INNIT.

(DN)   YEAH, IT'S A PRIVATE HOUSE.

(NA)   IT'S YOUR PRIVACY MATE AND THE GEEZER'S WALKING IN YOUR OWN
       FUCKING HOUSE.

(DN)   EXACTLY

(NA)   FUCKING CUNT

(DN)   WHOSE WRITING'S THAT

(NA)   I AIN'T GOT A CLUE WHOSE WRITING THAT IS MATE, NOT A FUCKING CLUE

(DN)   LOOKS A BIT LIKE A (WOMAN'S) WRITING

(DN)   ------------------ -------------------

(NA)   DOES, DUNNIT, UNLESS GAYNOR WAS HERE

(DN)   SHE MIGHT HAVE BEEN HAS SHE GOT A KEY

(NA)   NAH SHE MUST HAVE BEEN HERE WITH HIM.

END OF SEQUENCE TWENTY-TWO

SEQUENCE 23
DATE: 07.12.94.

START: 20:16:28

STOP: 20:16:42

[NA SLASHING THE AIR WITH KNIFE]

END OF SEQUENCE TWENTY-THREE

SEQUENCE 24
DATE: 07.12.94.

START: 20:30:59

STOP: 20:36:10

(DN)   --

(LK)   DID YOU HEAR WHAT HAPPENED TO DANNY HE HAD THE OLD BILL ROUND HIS
HOUSE

(NA)   WHEN

(LK)   THEN WENT ROUND 'IS HOUSE YESTERDAY BUT HE WEREN'T IN AND LIKE
THE OLD BILL ABOUT ----------- CANTERBURY AND ALL THAT ------- AND HE
WAS GOING TO TELL HIM TO GET IN TOUCH WITH ME CAUSE IT'LL BE
BENEFICIAL FOR HIM. IN OTHER WORDS THEY'VE NEVER -------

(DN)   -----------BY THE SOUNDS OF IT ------ HE KNOWS THIS, HE KNOWS THAT ----------

(NA)   ANYWAY LET, LET LET EM COME AND HELP HIM OUT HE AIN'T GOT NOTHING
TO HIDE.

(NA)   WHAT DO THEY WANT TO KNOW, WHATEVER THEY WANT TO KNOW MATE.
HE CAN TELL 'EM WHAT HE LIKES HE DON'T KNOW HE AIN'T INVOLVED IN
NOTHING, WE AIN'T INVOLVED IN THAT ------- LET HIM TALK TO THEM HE
AIN'T EVEN GUILTY SO HE DON'T NEED THEIR FUCKING HELP ABOUT IT'S
ALL BENEFICIAL FOR HIM.

(DN)   (BET THEY'VE ---------------) CAN THEY COME ROUND TO THE HOUSE. LET EM
IN ---------------- ABOUT IT AND IT WILL ------------------- ALRIGHT.

(NA)   RIGHT BOYS ----------------- THEY ALL SUCK COCKS, WE AIN'T DONE NOTHING,

         THEY PROBABLY USE IT ON THEMSELVES. THEY PROBABLY SHAG IT UP THE

         ARSE -----------

(DN)   ------------------------ [LAUGHS]

(NA)   ------------------- BUNCH OF SOCIAL WORKER BLACK CUNTS

(DN)   --------------------------- BETTER THAN ME ---------

(NA)   THE ONLY WAY THEY CAN GET IN THE POLICE FORCE IS IF THE FUCKING

         COMMISSIONER SUCKS IT FOR THEM.

(NA)   GAYLORDS BACK ON THE SCENE YEAH.

(DN)   ------------------

(NA)   GAYLORDS ARE BACK ON THE SCENE TRYING TO FIT PEOPLE UP AGAIN

         MATE THEY'RE PRESUMING WE'RE GUILTY SAYING AND SAYING LOOK WE'RE

         WE'RE GET YOU OUT OF THIS

(DN)   ------------ FOR SOME REASON NEIL THEY KEEP THEY KEEP DRIVING US MAD

         BECAUSE I TELL YOU WHAT --------- FOR SOME REASON THEY THINK

         THERE'S DEFINITELY A PROMOTION (IN THIS LOT MATE) .

(NA)   OI DAVE

(DN)   DON'T THEY

(DN)   FOR SOME REASON THEY WE KNOW SOMETHING, FUCKING DENSE MATE

(NA)   AND THEY AIN'T GOT NOTHING STILL

(DN)   ------------------

(NA)   THE THING THAT'S MAKING ME LAUGH

(NA)   (WE AIN'T DONE) NOTHING THAT'S WHAT I MEAN THERE'S NONE OF US DONE

         FUCK ALL. BUT THE THING THAT MAKES ME LAUGH DAVE THEY'RE GONNA

         BE DOING IT FOR THE REST OF OUR LIFES MATE AND I'M JUST GONNA BE

         LAUGHING ALL THE WAY TO THE LEEDS.

(DN)   DO YOU KNOW WHAT LISTEN NEXT TIME THEY TURN UP AT MY DOOR I AM

         GONNA ------------ -----------

(NA)   [LAUGHS]

(DN)   I AM GONNA MOON AT THEM YEE OH

(NA)   FUCK OFF YOU CUNTS

(DN)   [OVERSPEAKS]

(NA)   I'LL SAY YEAH I KNOW YOU FANCY ME BOYS BUT THERE'S NO NEED TO

        KEEP TO KEEP COMING BACK I AIN'T QUEER GO AWAY, I DON'T TAKE IT UP

        THE ARSE AND I DON'T GIVE IT SO FUCK OFF.

(DN)   (SOPPY) CUNTS --------

(LK)   --------------------- -----------------------

(NA)   (BRING YOUR WIFE ROUND)

(NA)   WHAT LIKE LUKE

(LK)   WHAT

(NA)   DANNY'S THING OR LIKE, THE OLD SHIT

(LK)   THE OLD SHIT

(NA)   FUCK EM THEY SUCK HAMPTONS MATE

(LK)   THEY'VE BEEN OVER SCALES'S AS WELL.

(NA)   SCALESY WHO'S THAT, STEVEN SCALES OVER THERE. LET THEM GO

        WHERE EVER THEY FUCKING WANT, FOR ALL WE KNOW IT WAS THAT MOB

        OVER THE EAST END DONE IT THEY'RE ALL THE FASCIST PEOPLE MATE, ALL

        THAT DEREK BEACKON AND THAT AIN'T THEY THAT'S WHERE ALL THAT

        RACIST ATTACKS HAPPEN.

(DN)   LOAD OF OLD BOLLOCKS ALL IT IS, IS FUCKING WHATEVER HAPPENS

        SOMEONE COME OVER FUCKING

(NA)   I FANCY THEY'VE HAD A CRACK DEAL ME SELF I FANCY [OVERSPEAK]

(DN)   YEAH THEY PROBABLY DID, THEY PROBABLY HAD

(NA)   [OVERSPEAK] CRACK

(DN)   PROBABLY HAD A BIT OF TOOT OR SOMETHING OR HAD A BIT

        OF CRACK IT'S ALL GONE WRONG, THE COON'S GOT KNACKERED UP AND

        ALL OF SUDDEN [OVERSPEAK] FOUR INNOCENT PEOPLE ARE GETTING DONE

        FOR IT.

22

(NA)   **YEAH THAT'S WHAT I FANCY** HAS HAPPENED.

(DN)   THAT'S DEFINITELY WHAT'S HAPPENED NEIL.

(DN)   EVERY TIME IT COMES ON THE NEWS ----- THE REAL PEOPLE ARE SITTING

          LAUGHING THEIR NUTS OFF.

(NA)   **WHAT THE REAL** PEOPLE

(DN)   YEAH THE REAL PEOPLE ARE SITTING LAUGHING THEIR NUTS OFF.

(LK)   THINKING THEY'VE GOT AWAY WITH IT MATE, FUCKING SCOTT FREE.

(NA)   **YEAH THEY'RE DEFINITELY DOING THAT.**

(DN)   -------------------- --------------------

(DN)   HERE NEIL

(NA)   WHAT

(LK)   YOU RECKON MAN U WILL GO O THROUGH

(NA)   YEAH

                  END OF SEQUENCE TWENTY-FOUR

SEQUENCE 25   **DATE: 07.12.94.**

                                START: 21:35:50

                                STOP: 21:38:36

[NA WITH COAT ON HAVING LOOKED OUT OF WINDOW RETURNS TO WINDOW LEDGE WHERE HE

PICKS KNIFE UP AND PLACES IT INSIDE HIS COAT – SUBSEQUENTLY LEAVES FLAT]

                  END OF SEQUENCE TWENTY-FIVE

SEQUENCE 26 DATE: 07.12.94.

START: 21:57:46

STOP: 21:58:01

(NA) IS CHARLIE IN

(LK) NO, HE'S JUST RUNG UP. HIS CAR BROKE DOWN ON THE FUCKING ISLE OF

DOGS.

[NA REMOVES KNIFE FROM INSIDE HIS COAT – REPLACES IT ON WINDOW LEDGE]

(NA) SO WHAT'S HAPPENING, HE AIN'T COMING OVER.

(LK) I DON'T THINK SO, HE SAID HE'LL RING BACK IN ABOUT TEN MINUTES.
                    END OF SEQUENCE TWENTY-SIX

SEQUENCE 27 DATE: 08.12.94.

START: 20:58:45

STOP: 21:01:31

N.B. [GARYNOR CULLEN (GC)]

(GD) HE SAID THE FUCKING BLACK BASTARD I AM GOING TO KILL HIM, I

CRACKED UP LAUGHING I WENT WHAT BLACK GEEZER. HE WENT THE WIMPY

ONE THE FUCKING BLACK NIGGER CUNT, FUCKING BLACK BASTARD. I WENT

WHAT THE PAKI AND HE WENT ------- THIRTY YEARS AGO I WOULD HAVE

FUCKING I WOULD HAVE TORN HIS HEAD OFF HE STARTED GOING ALL LIKE

THAT AND HE GOES WHEN I WAS YOUNGER I USED HAVE A FUCKING TEMPER

ON ME I DID. I SAID LEAVE OFF MATE WHAT YOU GOING ON ABOUT HE'S

GONE ER HE'S GONE WHEN I WAS FUCKING YOUNGER I DIDN'T TAKEN NO

SHIT OFF NO CUNTS, I USED TO JUST TEAR INTO THEM STRAIGHT AWAY.

OH I WAS A FUCKING NASTY BASTARD I WAS AND I WAS GOING WAS YA,

TRYING NOT TO FUCKING LAUGH MATE.

(GC)   WHERE'S ALL YOUR PALS

(NA)   CHARLIE'S JUST GONE WITH LUKE TO PICK UP A VIDEO AND TAKE IT TO

HIS MUM'S OR SOMETHING AND THEN HE'S COMING BACK, DANNY'S WITH

(GD)   THREE GUESSES WHERE

(NA)   CHERYL

(GC)   CHERYL

(NA)   -------------- THAT'S IT

(GC)   OH HERE YOU ARE THERE'S A LIGHT HERE.

(GD)   I'VE GOT A BIT OF PUFF FOR YOU TO SMOKE ALL TO YOURSELF.

(NA)   YOU DON'T PUFF DO YOU.

(GC)   NO I DON'T

(GD)   YOU FUCKING USED TO

(GC)   IS THAT A NEW PLUG

(GD)   WHAT

(GC)   IS THAT A NEW PLUG

(GD)   WHEN WAS THE LAST TIME YOU WAS DOWN HERE

(NA)   THE GEEZER LET HIMSELF IN THE OTHER DAY AND FITTED IT, LET HIMSELF IN

DID YOU TELL HER.

(GC)   YEAH HE SAID HE'D LET HIMSELF IN

(GD)   YEAH TO DO THE PLUG

(NA)   WITH SOMEONE ELSE

(GC)   CHEEK, THAT'S WRONG

(NA)   THAT'S WHAT I SAID I SAID PHONE HIM UP.

(GC)   YOU CAN GET HIM TO GET THE LOCKS CHANGED YOU REMEMBER WHEN WE

WENT DOWN CHRIS'S ------ YOU SAID YOU WAS GONNA MOVE IN SOMEWHERE

AND HE SAID FIRST THING YOU DO IS GET YOUR LOCKS CHANGED. I

(GD)   HE SAID FIRST THING YOU DO WHEN YOU MOVE IN WE'LL GET YOU A KEY

CUT

(GC)   BUT THAT'S RIGHT GAL

(GD)   I'M WORKING TOMORROW, I CAN'T BECAUSE THEY WON'T BE ABLE TO GET

        IN ------ TAKE IT TO WORK TOMORROW AND GET IT CUT

(GC)   IS THAT A NEW LAMP

(NA)   -------- KEYS A MASTER KEY ---------

(GD)   THAT IS A MASTER KEY THOUGH INNIT

(NA)   -----------------

(GD)   I'LL TRY IT ANYWAY.

(GC)   HAS HE SAID SOMETHING TO YOU 'CAUSE THAT'S WRONG

(GD)   I AIN'T SEEN OR HEARD FROM HIM SINCE, AND I OWE HIM A MONTHS RENT

        AND HE SAID IT'S NOT ALLOWED TO TAKE NO LONGER THAN THREE WEEKS.

        SO FUCK KNOWS (WHY HE'S GOT THE HUMP).

                    END OF SEQUENCE TWENTY-SEVEN

SEQUENCE 28   DATE: 08.12.94.

                        START: 21:09:59

                        STOP: 21:10:16

(GC)   GAL WHAT'S THAT LITTLE THING NEXT TO THE PLUG.

(GD)   MAINS SUPPLY. I'LL SOON BE ABLE TO TELL YOU WHAT IT PROPERLY IS

(GC)   IN YOUR DREAMS

(NA)   WHAT'S WHAT GAL, WHAT'S IT CALLED.

(GD)   WHAT'S THAT

(NA)   WHAT'S IT WHAT'S WHAT CALLED

(GD)   WHAT

(NA)   WHAT'S IT, MAINS SUPPLY OR SOMETHING

(GC)   NO HE SAID HE'LL KNOW SOON.

(GD)   I SAID, I SAID SOON I'LL BE ABLE TO TELL YOU PROPERLY WHAT IT IS

(GC)   WHEN HE (LEARNS HIS TRADE)

END OF SEQUENCE TWENTY-EIGHT

SEQUENCE 29   **DATE: 09.12.94.**

                        START: 20:30:57

                        STOP: 20:31:11

(NA)   OR D'YA WANNA GO A PUNCH BOWL

                    [NA IS BRANDISHING A KNIFE]

(LK)   DOESN'T BOTHER ME YOU KNOW

(NA)   I DON'T CARE MATE

(DC)   I'VE GOT TO GO I DON'T LIKE SITTING IN ALL THE FUCKING (TIME) IT

         DRIVES ME MAD

(NA)   THERE'S GOT TO BE SOMETHING BETTER TO DO THAN GOING TO THE PUNCH

         BOWL.

END OF SEQUENCE TWENTY-NINE

SEQUENCE 30   **DATE: 09.12.94.**

                        START: 20:36:34

                        STOP: 20:37:05

(DC)   THE VERSACE ONE FITS ME MUCH BETTER AND IT'S LIKE, IT'S A

         LIGHTER THINGY AS WELL.

(DC)   IT'S LIKE

(NA)   WHAT A ROLL NECK

(DC)   NOT A ROLL NECK BUT IT GOES LIKE THAT

(NA)   IT IS A ROLL NECK

        [OVERSPEAK]

(DC)   WHEN, WHEN JAMIE WAS -------- THE PRINGLE JUMPERS ROLL NECKS.

                    [NA PLACES A KNIFE INSIDE HIS COAT]

(NA)   I SEE YOU'RE IN THE CATALOGUE LIKE THAT [LAUGHS]

        [OVERSPEAK]

                    END OF SEQUENCE THIRTY

SEQUENCE 31   **DATE: 09.12.94.**

                        START: 20:48:43

                        STOP: 20:49:02

(NA)   WHY WHAT [OVERSPEAK]

(NA)   WHAT

(LK)   WHEN I REMEMBER I'LL TELL YA

                [NA IS CHOPPING AT THE FURNITURE WITH A KNIFE]

(NA)   WHEN I REMEMBER

(LK)   I CAN'T JUST (REMEMBER OF THE TOP OF ME HEAD)

(NA)   YES YOU CAN IF THERE'S LOADS OF THEM

(LK)   THERE IS

(LK)   SO WHEN 'AVE I BEEN ALL FOR MYSELF ANYWAY

        [OVERSPEAKING].

                    END OF SEQUENCE THIRTY-ONE

SEQUENCE 32   DATE: 10.12.94.

                     START: 00:02:27

                     STOP: 00:02:50

(NA)   YOU BLACK CUNT

END OF SEQUENCE THIRTY-TWO

SEQUENCE 33   DATE: 10.12.94.

                     START: 00:24:55

                     STOP: 00:31:10

(DC)   I LOOKED OUT THE WINDOW AND -----------
        (I LOOKED OUT) AND I SEE THE MOTOR AND I LOOKED --------- I KNEW IT
        WAS OLD BILL STRAIGHT AWAY.

(NA)   --

(DC)   ---------------- I LOOKED OUT THE WINDOW AND CHERYL ------------
        [MUMBLES]

(NA)   BAD NEWS DAN, BAD NEWS

( )   --

(NA)   SO WHAT YA GONNA SAY TO THEM

(DC)   IF THEY SAY UH;

(NA)   IT'S ALRIGHT I DON'T NEED TO KNOW

(DC)   I DON'T THINK THEY WILL NEIL I DON'T THINK THEY WILL GO BACK

(NA)   I RECKON THEY WILL
        [OVERSPEAK]

( )   I DON'T FANCY THEY WILL

(NA)   I THINK ---------------------------
        [OVERSPEAK]

(CM)   MY SOLICITOR ALREADY TOLD ME --------- ABOUT THE THING IN MAIDSTONE.

(DC)   WHAT I THINK CHARL, WHAT MY SOLICITOR SAID THE PROSECUTION LIKE
        THEY'VE PROBABLY GOT TO PROVE TO THE PROSECUTION THE OLD
        BILL (WAS COMING) FOR ME LIKE -------------------- AGAINST ME. THE
        PROSECUTION WILL PROBABLY THINK ------------------ LITTLE SCALESY

ALREADY KNEW ---------- (HE HAD A KNIFE) ---

(CM)   HE SAID, HE SAID TO MY SOLICITOR, SORRY HE SAID THEY'RE TALKING TO ME AGAIN HE SAYS I DON'T WANT TO GIVE HIM (THE) ADDRESS. HE SAYS ITS TOO LATE NOW WE'RE GONNA HAVE HIM AND THE SOLICITOR SAID HE GOES WHEN YOU GET HIM.
[OVERSPEAK]

(DC)   OLD BILL COME TO YOUR HOUSE

(CM)   IT'S BOLLOCKS AIN'T IT THE WAY THEY ALL TALK ABOUT YOU LIKE THAT.

(LK)   YEAH, THEY DON'T REALLY CARE ABOUT YOU THEY JUST CARE ABOUT WINNING THE CASE.
[OVERSPEAK]

(NA)   CHARLIE YOUR PIES OUT HERE.

(CM)   FUCK EM ANYWAY

(NA)   YOU'LL HAVE TO WASH YOURSELF UP A SPOON

(DC)   WANKERS AIN'T THEY NEIL

(NA)   COCK SUCKERS

(DC)   PRICKS MATE WHY CAN'T THEY DO THEIR JOB PROPERLY MATE.

(LK)   THEY AIN'T GOT BRAINS.

(NA)   THEY WON'T TURN UP ON MY DOOR MATE I KNOW THAT.

( )   ---

( )   THEY WON'T TURN UP AT OUR HOUSE
[OVERSPEAK]

( )   THAT'S WHAT I SAID TO NEIL EARLIER WEREN'T IT ------------------

(NA)   YEAH BUT IT AIN'T THE MAIDSTONE ONES THAT ARE GONNA TURN UP ON HIS DOOR STEP.

(CM)   YEAH I KNOW.

(DC)   YEAH I KNOW THAT, BUT WHAT IT IS WHERE CHARLIE IS THE MOST WANTED

(NA)   YEAH BUT THEY DON'T GIVE A FUCK

(DC)   YEAH I KNOW THEY DON'T BUT IT'S UP TO THE THINGY, IT'S UP TO THEY UH.

( )   ---

(DC)   YEAH, ITS UP TO THEM, THEY CAN SAY WELL YEAH WELL WE ACCEPT IF HE
[OVERSPEAK]

( )   THE OLD BILL, THE OLD BILL.

(CM)   LISTEN WHEN YOU THINK ABOUT IT THEY MUST NOW THAT GARY SCALES, THAT I SEE GARY SCALES AND THEY MUST THINK THAT EVEN IF THEY THINK THAT YOU'VE DONE IT FOR SOME REASON THEY MUST THINK THAT YOU'VE DONE IT RIGHT. THEY MUST THINK THAT WE GO ROUND OR THAT I GO

ROUND OVER THERE WITH GARY SCALES WHEN YOU'VE DONE IT. BUT
WHETHER YOU'VE DONE IT NO MATTER WHETHER YOU'RE GONNA SAY
ANYTHING ABOUT IT, NOTHING WILL EVER ---------- COULD HAVE DONE IT. DO
YA KNOW WHAT I MEAN. SO GARY SCALES WON'T KNOW NOTHING ------------.

(NA)   LET THEM GO ANYWHERE MATE.

         [OVERSPEAK]

(CM)   ---------- THERE'S NOTHING WE CAN REALLY --------------

(DC)   WHAT THEY SAID THIS TO GARY SCALES

(CM)   YEAH TO GARY SCALES NOT DARREN

(DC)   WHAT, NOT NOT DARREN

(CM)   AND DARERN'S SITTING IN THE CORNER AND HE WENT THAT'S A BIT HASTY.

(DC)   WHAT

         [OVERSPEAK]

(CM)   AND THEY BROUGHT UP ABOUT HIS ------------- CONVICTION

(DC)   WHAT THEY SAID IT TO GARY AS WELL.

(CM)   ------------------------

(DC)   THEY SAID TO GARY ------------------------

(CM)   GARY DIDN'T EVEN KNOW WHAT THEY WERE THERE FOR

(DC)   AH

(DC)   WELL MAYBE THEY WILL COME -------------

(CM)   THEY THINK THAT WE'VE DONE IT, THEY MUST DO THEY MUST THINK THAT
WE'VE DONE IT AND SOMEONE'S TOLD ME FOR SOME REASON AND THAT I'VE
GONE AROUND AND SAID YEAH, THAT'S WHAT THEY MUST BE THINKING.
THAT'S WHAT HE SAID AND GARY SAID NO I'VE NEVER HEARD HIM SAY
NOTHING. THAT'S THE TRUTH SO KNOW WHAT I MEAN. THEY CAN FUCKING,
IF THEY CAN'T EVEN FIGURE OUT WHO DONE THE FUCKING MURDER THAT'S
THEIR FUCKING PROBLEM. THEY CAN BLAME US BUT THEY AIN'T GONNA GET
NO JOY ARE THEY. NONE OF US HAVE DONE IT.

(NA)   PUCKER THESE LITTLE PIES AIN'T THEY.

(CM)   VERY NICE INDEED.

(CM)   ----------------- THEY MUST BE THINKING THAT I'VE GONE ROUND TO GARY AND
SAID YEAH ----------------------

(NA)   ALL THEY WANT IS A NAME, THAT'S WHAT THEY WANT. THEY DON'T CARE
WHO THE FUCK IT IS THEY WANT A NAME AND THAT'S ALL.

(DC)   THEY WANT A BODY.

(DC)   I KNOW THEY WANT SOMETHING

(NA)   ONE PERSON

(DC)   NO MATTER WHO IT IS, THEY DON'T MIND HOW INNOCENT THEY ARE, THEY

WANT EM MATE. THEY WANT TO PUT SOMEONE AWAY FOR IT.

(CM)   FUCK THEM ANYWAY IF THEY CAN'T DO (THEIR JOB IT'S NOTHING TO DO WITH US).

(DC)   IF THEY CAN'T DO YOU THE FIRST TIME THEY'LL TRY AND DO YOU THE SECOND TIME.

(CM)   I RECKON THEY PROBABLY EVEN KNOW IT AIN'T US BUT THEY THINK THEY'LL DO

        [OVERSPEAK]

(DC)   THEY KNOW IT AIN'T US

(LK)   OF COURSE THEY KNOW IT AIN'T US.

(LK)   IF IT WAS US SURELY THERE'D BE FORENSIC FUCKING EVIDENCE AND ALL THAT.

(CM)   COURSE THERE WOULD

(NA)   ANYWAY THEY TAKE IT UP THE ARSE.

END OF SEQUENCE THIRTY-THREE

SEQUENCE 34   **DATE: 10.12.94.**

                                     START: 00:59:28

                                     STOP: 01:01:10

        [OVERSPEAKING]

( )   --------------------------

(NA)   LET'S SPEAK SO WE CAN ONLY UNDERSTAND EACH OTHER, JUST TO BE SAFE, COS THE GEEZER COME IN THE OTHER DAY WITH SOMEONE AND DONE ALL THAT PLUG.

( )   WHAT, THERE WEREN'T TWO PLUGS THERE THOUGH BEFORE WAS THERE.

(NA)   NO THE GEEZER COME IN MATE AND I WON'T TRUST IT. I WOULDN'T TRUST IT AT ALL. WHAT DO YOU RECKON HE BROUGHT SOMEONE ELSE IN THE HOUSE.

( )   WALKED IN

(NA)   HE BROUGHT SOMEONE ELSE IN WITH HIM AND DONE ALL THAT ELECTRICAL ER ELECTRICIAN ---------- YOU DIDN'T KNOW DID YA ------------- WE GOTTA

32

ALL SIT QUIETLY WATCHING THE TELLY OR OVER HERE ....

(CM)   [OVERSPEAKING]

(LK)   WHY HE'S PUT TWO MORE PLUGS THERE THAT'S THE THING I DON'T
UNDERSTAND.

(NA)   AND THAT'S ON SO LIKE THAT'D BE WORKING LIKE THAT'D BE WORKING
AND SO WOULD THAT. THEY'D BOTH BE ON NOW. SO IF [OVERSPEAK]
ANYONE'S LISTENING THEY ALREADY KNOW THAT THEY SUCK HORSES
COCKS SO WE AIN'T GOT TO REALLY SAY NOTHING HAVE WE

( )   ----------- HE LET HIMSELF IN -------------

[INAUDIBLE]

(NA)   IT WAS ON TOP OF THE TELLY BUT WHEN HE CAME BACK IT WAS ON TOP OF
THE SPEAKER

END OF SEQUENCE THIRTY-FOUR

SEQUENCE 35   **DATE: 10.12.94.**

                              START: 19:25:39

                              STOP: 19:27:51

(GD)   LOOK, I THINK THIS IS RACIST THIS ADVERT.

(LK)   YEAH ALL WHITE PEOPLE SAD AND ALL THAT.

(GD)   AND YEAH LOOK ALL POWER STATION IN THE BACKGROUND AND THE
NIGGERS ALL GOT BEACHES, SUNSHINE, FUCKING

(LK)   YOU COULDN'T DO IT THE OTHER WAY ROUND

(GD)   I WANT TO MAKE A COMPLAINT ABOUT THAT ADVERT

(NA)   WELL MAKE ONE THEN

(GD)   I DON'T KNOW HOW TO DO IT.

(NA)   WELL PHONE UP THE FUCKING OPERATOR AND ASK TO MAKE A YOU WANNA,

YOU WANNA KNOW HOW TO MAKE A COMPLAINT ABOUT THE TELLY
ADVERT.

(CM)   THE MALIBU ONE.

(GD)   SOME GEEZER AT MY WORK (IS THE SPITTING IMAGE OF HIM MATE).

(NA)   WELL WHAT WOULD YOU DO IF, WHAT DO YOU RECKON WOULD HAPPEN IF
SOMEONE, OI YOU KNOW ALL THIS BNP BUSINESS RIGHT THIS DEREK
BEACKON AND THAT

(CM)   THEY'RE OVER THE THINGY NOW BY THE STREET MARKET.

(NA)   I KNOW BUT THEY'RE THICK AS SHIT TAFF COZ THEY'RE GETTING ALL THE
FUCKING SKIN HEADS AND ALL THAT TO STAND OUT AND BE ALL THEIR
ARMED GUARDS AND ALL THAT AND HOWS ANYONE GONNA WANNA VOTE
FOR THEM, PERHAPS LIKE YOU KNOW ALL THESE STRAIGHT BODS THEY
WANNA VOTE FOR THEM MATE BUT THEY SEE ALL THESE FUCKING YOBBO
FUCKING SKINHEADS AND THEY THINK WHO WANTS TO VOTE FOR THEM. IF
THEY WERE SENSIBLE AND WENT ABOUT IT PROPERLY AND GOT SOMEONE
STRAIGHT WHO PEOPLE WOULD LIKE AND ALL ALL THAT AND HE STOOD UP
AND WENT LISTEN WE DON'T WANT TO TAKE ALL THIS NIGGER BOLLOCKS
NO MORE, WE CAN'T EVEN SAY BLACK BALL, BLACK CAT, THIS, THAT

(LK)   [OVERSPEAKING]

(NA)   THEY COME OVER HERE CHANGE THE WAY OF RIGHTS ITS ABOUT TIME IT ALL
STOPPED PEOPLE WOULD STOP AND LISTEN

(LK)   SEE I RECKON I COULD DO IT BUT IT'S JUST THE POINT OF FUCKING GOING
OUT YOUR WAY TO FUCKING STAND UP

(NA)   IF SOMEONE WAS TO STAND UP WHO PEOPLE COULD TAKE A LIKING TO AN
ALL THAT THEY'D GO FAR.

(GD)   THIS IS THAT ----------

(LK)   WONDERBRA

(GD)   THINK SO

(LK)   THAT'S WHAT I THOUGHT EARLIER GARY .

(NA)   WHAT DO YOU RECKON TAFF

(CM)   ----------------------------

(NA)   WHY DON'T IT BE YOU. WHAT DO YOU THINK ABOUT DEREK BEACKON.

(CM)   WHO ME

( )   WHAT

(CM)   --------------------------------------

END OF SEQUENCE THIRTY-FIVE

SEQUENCE 36   DATE: 10.12.94.

                        START: 20:21:43

                        STOP: 20:23:36

[CM OPENS DOOR TO THE OTHERS HE DOES SO HOLDING A CARVING KNIFE WHICH HE

HOLDS AND GESTURES / TOYS WITH DURING CONVERSATION].

(NA)   ------------------------

(CM)   YOU DIDN'T SHUT THE DOOR DID YA, TWO MINUTES LATER, I HEARD THE

        DOOR GO SLAM I THOUGHT SOMEONE HAD RUN OUT

(CM)   DID YOU SHUT THE DOOR, YOU NEVER SHUT THE DOOR BEHIND YOU, DID YA.

(LK)   (HERE ABOUT THE TWO 'P') YESTERDAY

(LK)   A TWO P WAS CHUCKED AT CHARLIE'S HEAD NO ONE KNOWS WHO IT WAS.

(NA)   WHAT HAPPENED

        [OVERSPEAK]

(LK)   FUCK OFF TAFF.

(LK)   DID I CHUCK IT AT YOUR HEAD THEN OR DID IT GO TOWARDS YOUR HEAD

(NA?)   I WAS SITTING THERE (TAFFY) WAS THERE, LUKE WAS THERE, DANNY WAS

        OVER THERE WE WAS ALL WATCHING TELLY OR SOMETHING AND ALL OF A

SUDDEN WE HEARD THIS -------------- GOING ----------------

( )   YEAH

       [OVERSPEAK]

( )   GAL

(CM)   WHAT ARE WE GOING TO SAY TO HIM

       [MUFFLED - OVERSPEAKING]

(LK)   SO NO-ONE KNOWS WHAT HAPPENED.

       [OVERSPEAK]

(LK)   DON'T FUCK ABOUT TAFF

       [MUFFLED]

END OF SEQUENCE THIRTY-SIX

SEQUENCE 37   **DATE: 11.12.94.**

                           START: 17:59:50

                           STOP: 18:00:33

(NA)   [LOUD PIERCING SQUEALS]

       [HURLES SMALL OBJECT ACROSS ROOM]

(NA)   SMASH IT UP, (LETS) BEAT THE CUNT OFF THE GAFF MATE

[NA BANGS CHAIR ON FLOOR / PUSHES IT OVER BACKWARDS AND APPEARS TO KICK

SOMETHING ELSE]

(CM)   THE THING IS RIGHT IF WE DIDN'T HAVE THIS FLAT NOWADAYS, DANNY'S

       ALWAYS WITH CHERYL, WHERE WOULD WE GO

(LK)   I WAS THINKING THAT YESTERDAY.

(CM)   IN IT NEIL ONCE WE AIN'T GOT THIS FLAT, DANNY'S ALWAYS WITH

       CHERYL SO WE CAN'T GO TO DANNY'S.

END OF SEQUENCE THIRTY-SEVEN

SEQUENCE 38   DATE: 11.12.94.

                                    START: 19:40:39

                                    STOP: 19:41:13

[IN RELATION TO THE CARVING KNIFE CARRIED BY DOBSON FROM THE TABLE, IT

CAN BE STATED THAT AT NO TIME DURING THE OBSERVATION WAS IT NOTED THAT

FOOD WAS BROUGHT TO OR FROM THE KITCHEN TO THE TABLE FOR PREPARATION

(CHOPPING ETC)]

         [OVERSPEAKING - MUFFLED]

(NA)   I WOULD

[GD IS CARRYING A KNIFE AS HE WALKS AROUND ROOM HAVING BEEN SEATED BY TABLE]

(CM)   HOW COULD YOU HAVE SOMEONE'S FIST GO INTO YOUR

(NA)   [LAUGHS]

(GD)   I TELL YOU WHAT

(CM)   (INNIT NEIL) YOU'D BE SCREAMING ----------------

(GD)   THERE'S ONE WORD OR THERE IS TWO WORDS THAT MAKES ME ------------------

         WITH ANYTHING TO DO WITH SEX AND ------------- STRAP ON HAVING A

         FUCKING PLASTIC OLD DILDO ON, [OVERSPEAK] THE WORD FILTH DON'T

         EVEN COME INTO THAT, THAT'S JUST, THAT'S WHAT YOU CALL ROTTEN.

(NA)   AHH MATE.

                    END OF SEQUENCE THIRTY-EIGHT

SEQUENCE 39   DATE: 11.12.94.

                                    START: 19:47:23

                                    STOP: 19:49:01

(GD)   YEAH IT IS THREE

[GD IS HOLDING A KNIFE AS HE ADJUSTS THE STEREO]

(CM)   WHAT TIME IS IT

(GD)   THAT'S WHAT I JUST SAID WHAT IS THE TIME, I AIN'T GOT A WATCH ON.

(CM)   IT'S PROBABLY OVER LUKE

(LK)   NO IT AIN'T OVER

(CM)   I SAID IT COULD BE OVER LUKE.

(NA)   HE SAID.

(NA)   I SAID THAT WE SHOULD GO TO DANNY'S

(GD)   IT AIN'T ON TILL EIGHT THIRTY IS IT.

(NA)   NO

(GD)   IT'S FIVE TO EIGHT

[GD IS AGAIN HOLDING THE KNIFE AS HE ADJUSTS THE STEREO]

(NA)   I SAID I RECKON WE SHOULD GO TO DANNY'S PICK UP

( )   [MIMICS MUSIC]

(LK)   ----------- COME BACK

(CM)   ------------------ CAN'T YOU BORROW DESI'S ONE

(LK)   --------------------------

(NA)   I'VE GOT IT

(CM)   (HAVE YOU GOT THE CONTROLS)

(NA)   I'VE GOT THE CONTROLS AND THEY WORK

(CM)   YOU MIGHT AS WELL LEAVE THAT ON GAL.

(GD)   MM, I JUST WANT TO PUT THIS ON.

(CM)   --------------------

(GD)   WHAT THIS

(NA)   THERE'S NOTHING WRONG WITH THAT.

END OF SEQUENCE THIRTY-NINE

SEQUENCE 40

DATE: 11.12.94.

START: 19:53:00

STOP: 19:53:43

(NA)   ----------- GOAL MATE -------- THE WAY HE PUTS IT IN THAT TOP CORNER FROM

WHERE HE WAS

(NA)   [NOISE] [NOISE]

(CM)   WHY WON'T PAUL COME ROUND HERE ANYMORE, GAL WHY DOES HE WANT

US TO SEND IT WHY WON'T HE COME ROUND, WHAT'S THE MATTER WITH HIM

(GD)   HE'S PROBABLY TRASHED

(NA)   I RECKON HE IS GAL, I RECKON THE GEEZER'S BEEN BACK ROUND HERE,

BUGGED UP THE SOCKETS AND [OVERSPEAK]

(CM)   AND NOW HE WON'T COME NEAR US,

END OF SEQUENCE FORTY

SEQUENCE 41

DATE: 11.12.94.

START: 19:55:36

STOP: 19:56:06

(CM)   ------------------

(GD)   WHERE

(CM)   -----------------

(LK)   WHAT'S THE MARKS

( )   YEAH

( )   ---------------------

39

[GD IS HOLDING A KNIFE AS HE ADJUSTS THE STEREO]

(LK)   AND SPOTS

(CM)   IT'S GOT ALL RED MARKS ON THE BOTTOM

(GD)   WHAT THERE

( )   YEAH

(GD)   THEN WHEN ----------- GETS BACK -----------------

( )   MM

(NA)   HOW WAS YOUR NEW BIRD LAST NIGHT THEN GAL

END OF SEQUENCE FORTY-ONE

SEQUENCE 42   DATE: 11.12.94.

                          START: 20:02:41

                          STOP: 20:03:36

(NA)   AH LOOK WHAT YOU'VE DONE

(CM)   LET US HAVE A LOOK

[NA PASSES A KNIFE TO CM]

(NA)   IT CAN'T BE VERY STRONG THEN ------------ CAN IT (LAUGH) AIN'T IN IT,

FUCK IT ------------- LIKE THAT, IT AIN'T GONNA MAKE NO DIFFERENCE

MATE, AH IT CAN'T BE REALLY STRONG CAN IT ------------- PLASTIC

FUCKING THING MATE AND IT'S FUCKED IT

(NA)   THAT IS ----------------

[NA CHOPS AT A CHAIR WITH THE KNIFE]

(GD)   IT DON'T MATTER WE'LL WIN THE LOTTERY NEXT WEEK

(CM)   SOMEONE WON THE SEVENTEEN MILLION POUND A SINGLE WINNER

END OF SEQUENCE FORTY-TWO

SEQUENCE 43   DATE: 11.12.94.

                     START: 20:03:49

                     STOP: 20:05:02

(NA)   -------------- THE BIGGEST EVER LOTTERY PAYOUT IS (SEVENTY) MILLION

        POUNDS.

(LK)   WHAT IN AMERICA.

(NA)   YEAH LIKE IN OUR MONEY IT'S SEVENTY MILLION POUNDS.

(NA)   SO IN DOLLARS THAT'S LIKE

        [OVERSPEAK]

( )   I WOULDN'T EVEN (TRAVEL)

(GD)   THE SPANISH ONE'S GOOD, THE SPANISH ONE'S FUCKING GOOD IN ALL THE

        SPANISH LOTTERY

(NA)   WELL GAL TELL ME ONE THING WHAT'S THE MATTER WITH OURS SEVENTEEN

        AND A HALF MILLION

(GD)   I KNOW, THERE'S NOTHING THE MATTER WITH OURS I'M SAYING THE SPANISH

        LOTTERY'S A GOOD LOTTERY AS WELL.

(CM)   I RECKON IT'LL GET BIGGER THAN THAT [OVERSPEAK]

(NA)   SEVENTEEN AND A HALF MILLION POUNDS

(GD)   WHAT SOMEONE HONESTLY WON IT YESTERDAY

(NA)   YEAH SOMEONE TOOK IT, IT'S IN THE PAPER

        [OVERSPEAKING]

(NA)   ONE PERSON DID YOU SEE THE NUMBERS 26, 35, 38, 40 SOMETHING 40

        SOMETHING, 40 SOMETHING.

(LK)   FORTY FUCKING 3, 46 AND 48 I THINK IT WAS

( )   SOMETHING LIKE THAT [OVERSPEAKS]

(NA)   ONE GEEZER HAS WON SEVENTEEN AND A HALF MILLION POUNDS OR A

        WOMAN ORWHOEVER IT IS.

(CM)   SO IS IT A BLACK PERSON [OVERSPEAK] IF A BLACK OR PAKI'S WON THEN

THAT'S BOLLOCKS. IT'S GOT TO BE A WHITE.

(GD)   OR A REFUGEE OR SOMETHING FUCK THAT ----------

END OF SEQUENCE FORTY-THREE

SEQUENCE 44   **DATE: 11.12.94.**

START: 20:30:43

STOP: 20:31:02

(NA)   BLACK CUNT

(CM)   GET OFF

(CM)   SHE STARTED CRYING WHEN THE LITTLE BLACK KID KISSED HER.

END OF SEQUENCE FORTY-FOUR

SEQUENCE 45   **DATE: 11.12.94.**

START: 23:18:00

STOP: 23:18:36

(CM)   [MUFFLED] ----------

(GD)   I DON'T LIKE THE WARNING I DON'T LIKE THE LOOK OF THAT BOX WITH

WARNING ON IT.

(CM)   WHAT

(GD)   I DON'T LIKE THE LOOK OF THAT BOX WITH THE WARNING ON IT.

(CM)   YEAH

(GD)   NEXT TO THE PLUG SOCKET

[MUFFLED]

(CM)   NOSEY CUNTS THEY ARE I'M TELLING YOU, A WASTE OF TAX PAYERS MONEY.

(GD)   ---------------------------

(CM)   WHY THE FUCK DON'T THEY DO SOMETHING USEFUL LIKE

END OF SEQUENCE FORTY-FIVE

SEQUENCE 46   **DATE: 13.12.94.**

                                    START: 21:15:57

                                    STOP: 21:16:36

(CM)   YOU CAN'T EVEN HAVE A FUCKING CHAT IN HERE MATE I'M TELLING YOU

( )   YOU CAN'T CHAT, CAN'T CHAT WITH THIS SHIT

(CM)   THEY WENT AND FITTED ALL THEM IN DIDN'T THEY ----- WAS HERE ----- SO

WE COULD SAY THINGS AND THEY COULD STICK OUR VOICES ON A TAPE

RECORDER, TWIST IT ROUND AND TRY TO FIT US UP WITH SOMETHING ELSE

(NA)   FUCKING RIGHT AN ALL

(DC)   THEY COULD DO WHAT THEY DONE IN TANGO AND CASH

(CM)   [OVERSPEAK] YEAH THAT'S WHAT THEY DONE DAN

(CM)   NOSEY BASTARDS WON'T LEAVE US ALONE.

(CM)   GIVE US ANOTHER BIT OF THAT DAN.

END OF SEQUENCE FORTY-SIX

SEQUENCE 47   **DATE: 13.12.94.**

                                    START: 21:57:50

                                    STOP: 21:59:01

(NA)   ONE MINUTE

(GD)   COME ON JUNGALISTS, BLACK CUNTS

(NA)   WHAT IS THIS (ALBUM CALLED) THEN

(GD)   (I DON'T KNOW ABOUT THAT)

       [OVERSPEAKING]

(GD)   LISTEN TO THIS BIT

(DC)   A BLACK CHRISTMAS OR FUCKING

(GD)   YEAH BLACK CHRISTMAS, DICKHEADS

(NA)   WHY CAN'T WE HAVE SOMETHING CALLED WHITE CHRISTMAS THEN

(GD)   YOU WON'T GET THAT CAUSE THAT'S RACIST

(CM)   THAT WHAT HE WAS SAYING, I WAS WITH A PAKI

(CM)   HE GOES WHY DON'T YOU ARGUE WITH ME HE GOES

(CM)   HE'S A CUNT THOUGH WE WAS WINNING THOUGH WEREN'T WE

(LK)   (YEAH WE WAS WINNING)

(CM)   HE GOES, HE GOES, AH YOU ENGLISH PEOPLE ARE SCARED OF --------

(LK)   NO HE WAS SAYING IT THE OTHER WAY ROUND HE WAS SAYING

(CM)   [INAUDIBLE]

                    END OF SEQUENCE FORTY-SEVEN

SEQUENCE 48   **DATE: 14.12.94.**

                            START: 20:07:30

                            STOP: 20:09:27

(GD)   IT'S A PAKI

(NA)   FUCK YOU

(GD)   IT'S A PAKI MATE

(NA)   FUCK OFF

(GD)   A PAKI WHO WON, WHAT, LOOK THE LOTTERY JACKPOT IS A MARRIED ASIAN

       FACTORY WORKER WITH THREE SONS OR WHATEVER.

(NA)   YOUR JOKING

(GD)   FUCKING JOKING MATE

( )   [MIMICKING ASIAN LANGUAGE]

(CM)   WHO TURNED IT ON

(NA)   WHAT

(CM)   ----------- BIT OF

( )   NAH I DIDN'T EVEN TOUCH THAT

( )   YOUR JOKING

(CM)   OH, I SEE WHAT YOU MEAN.

( )   THAT'S BOLLOCKS INNIT.

(NA)   MR EIGHTEEN MILLION IS A CURRY MAD, WORKAHOLIC WHO PUTS HIS

        FAMILY AND MATES FIRST.

(CM)   ---------------- YEAH.

(NA)   WHAT ABOUT A PAKI WINNTNG MONEY

(CM)   YEAH

(GD)   THE PAKI LOST A HIGH COURT BATTLE TODAY WITH THE PRESS THEY'RE

        ALLOWED TO NAME HIM SO HE'LL BE IN THE PAPERS TOMORROW.

(CM)   (WHY ALL HE'S GOT TO DO IS TURN ROUND AND SAY BOLLOCKS I DON'T

        WANNA ANYONE KNOWING SIMPLE AS THAT).

(GD)   THE JUDGE RULED IT, RULED IT, RULED IT OUT HE SAID NO AND AH CAMELOT

        TOOK, TOOK THE, THE PAPERS TO COURT [MUMBLES] TO NOT GET HIM

        NAMED, LIKE THE LOTTERY ORGANISERS. THE JUDGE TURNED ROUND AND

        SAID NO HIS NAME CAN GO IN THE PAPERS AND I WANT CAMELOT TO PAY

        FOR ALL THE NEWSPAPERS LEGAL COSTS FOR TAKING THEM TO COURT AND

        ALL THAT.

(GD)   CAMELOT ARE BEING FUCKED MATE

(NA)   BOLLOCKS THOUGH INNIT.

(GD)   IT IS, NONE OF US, NO-ONE GIVES A FUCK IF IT'S A PAKI OR NOT.

                        END OF SEQUENCE FORTY-EIGHT

45

SEQUENCE 49   DATE: 14.12.94.

                     START: 21:14:24

                     STOP: 21:17:53

(DN)   I HAD A FIGHT WITH AN OLD MAN DIDN'T I ABOUT FUCKING FOUR MONTHS

       AGO. I WAS WALKING OVER THE PARK ANYWAY AN OLD GEEZER COMES UP

       AND (HE) WAS WITH WIFE AND KIDS AND THAT ANYWAY HE WAS MOANING

       ABOUT THE DOGS BEING OVER THE FIELD AND HE CAME UP TO ME AND HE

       WAS A BIG CUNT AND HE STARTED GOING, STARTED GOING LIKE THAT AND

       HE WAS GOING I'LL FUCKING TAKE YOU ON I SAID LEAVE IT OUT I AIN'T

       GONNA HIT YOU. ALL OF A SUDDEN HE WENT BOP ON ME JAW. SO I JUST

       STOOD THERE AND I WENT TO HIM SMACK UPPER-CUT AND HE WENT CRACK,

       ALL OF A SUDDEN I JUST FLIPPED. I WENT AND HE GOT ME SCREWDRIVER

       AND ALL THAT OLD LARK AND COME RUNNING OUT 'N' STARTED LIKE

       TRYING TO DO HIM AND I THREW IT AND ALL OF A SUDDEN THE GEEZER

       COME AND I WENT TO GET A CLUB AND HE GRABBED THE CLUB AND HE WAS

       LIKE HE'S DAUGHTER'S HUSBAND OR SOMETHING, SO IT WAS HIS SON-IN-LAW

(NA)   WHO WAS WITH HIM, WINNIT

(DN)   WENT DOWN THE GLOVE COMPARTMENT, GOT ME BROTHER BEN'S CLUB, SO I

       PICKED IT UP AND STARTED SMACKING HIM ROUND THE MOUTH AND ALL OF,

       THIS NIGGER COME ALONG AND (I JUST KNEED THE CUNT RIGHT IN THE

       BOLLOCKS).

(CM)   AND WHAT THEN THE NIGGER JOINED IN

(DN)   HE WAS A FUCKING GROWN MAN, HE WAS ABOUT 40 YEARS ODD AND HIS

       GRANDAD SMACKO AND I WAS KNOCKING THE GRANDDAD.

(CM)   AND THEN WHAT THE NIGGER COME ALONG

(DN)   YEAH, A BIG NIGGER COME ALONG AND SAID LEAVE THE FUCKING KID

       ALONE YOU SILLY CUNT.

46

(CM)   WHAT SAYING TO YOU.

(DN)   AND I WAS GOING WHAT YOU TALKING ABOUT, I START GOING ON AND

        CALLED HIM A BLACK CUNT AND ALL THAT SAYING HE WAS A FUCKING

        COON -------. HE WAS GOING 'LEAVE IT OUT MATE', AND ALL OF A SUDDEN I

        JUST FLIPPED AND HE WAS HOLDING THE GEEZER AND SO I WENT SMACK,

        PUNCHED THE NIGGER LIKE THAT AND HE WAS GOING FUCKING LIKE WHAT'S

        GOING ON. [LAUGHTER] ----------------

        HE WAS A MASSIVE BLOKE.

        DEFINITE FUCKING BODYBUILDER.

        DEFINITELY NEIL, HE WAS MASSIVE MATE AND THE WHITE BIRD

        BUT THE WHITE GIRL SHE WAS A BIT (CUNTLESS) SHE WAS LIKE OH WHAT'S

        HAPPENING.

        I SAID OH I TRIED TO TAKE THE DOGS FOR A WALK AND HE STARTED GIVING

        IT LARGE SO I'VE HAD TO DO HIM.

        AND SHE WENT BEST THING TO DO IS JUST GO BECAUSE THEY'RE GONNA

        CALL THE (POLICE) I SAID ALRIGHT ANYWAY RIGHT. FUCKING NIGGER'S

        ---------- AND HE WAS GOING I'M SORRY I HELPED, SORRY I HELPED YOU NOW.

        I SAID WELL DON'T BUTT YOUR NOSE IN THEN ANYWAY, WE STARTED

        HAVING AN. I WENT FAIR ENOUGH. JUST WALKED OFF.

(NA)   FUCKING HELL MATE.

(DN)   SHE WAS STANDING THERE THE DOG WAS GOING MAD THEN

( )   OH YEAH ROTTWEILLERS

(DN)   I SAID DON'T LET HIM GO MATE CAUSE HE WILL TEAR THE CUNT TO PIECES.

(CM)   WHAT WAS HE DOING WHILE YOU WAS HAVING

(DN)   HE WAS GOING MAD I SAID HOLD HIM CAUSE AS I'M FIGHTING HIM I'M GOING

        HOLD HIM, HOLD HIM LIKE THAT AND STILL FIGHTING HIM AND THEN HE

        WENT TO COME TO STEAM INTO ME BUT THE THING WAS HE KEPT MOVING

        AROUND ME AND I WAS STANDING THERE AND HE KEPT MOVING ROUND AND

        ALL HE'S DOING IS HE'S TRYING TO POSITION HIMSELF LIKE SO I KEPT

TURNING AROUND AND I PUSHED HIM AND I SAID DON'T FUCKING COME
NEAR ME CUNT COS I'M GONNA DO YOU ANYWAY HE CAME ROUND LIKE
THAT AND AS ----- I WENT SMACK ABOUT 50 TIMES IN HIS HEAD DUMB CUNT.
HE ------------ CUNT. HE WAS AND ALL ALL OF A SUDDEN HIS WIFE'S AND ALL
THAT STARTED COMING (ENCOURAGING HIM 'N' THAT)

(CM)   WHAT ABOUT THE NIGGER WE HAD ONE WITH THE NIGGER. HE TURNED
        ROUND TO ME AND HE GOES, HE GOES WHERE'S THE PRISON NEAR FELTHAM.
        [OVERSPEAK]

(NA)   IT WAS UP LONDON THE OTHER DAY IN THE CAR.

(CM)   WE WAS GOING ALONG I WAS LOOKING AT HIM AND I SEE HIM GO LIKE THAT
        YOU KNOW WHEN THEY GO LIKE THAT AND KEEP LOOKING AT ME AND SO I
        KEPT LOOKING AT HIM AND I'VE GONE LIKE THAT AND THEN HE STARTED
        GOING AND THAT YOU WANKER AND ALL THAT. TURNS OUT THE WINDOW,
        I WENT

(NA)   MILLIONS OF CARS, MILLIONS OF PEOPLE TRAFFIC TAIL TO TAIL WE
        COULDN'T MOVE

(CM)   WE WENT OI, OI MATE AND NEIL STARTED GOING YOU'RE A FUCKING LOLLY
        INNIT YOU GRASS, HE SAYS HOW AM I A GRASS I'VE JUST DONE A PRISON
        SENTENCE.

(NA)   [LAUGHS] WE LOOKED AT EACH OTHER AND HE WAS HERE AN [NOISE] TRY
        AGAIN

(DN)   PLASTIC MOOSH.

(NA)   YEAH YOU SOPPY BLACK CUNT.

(CM)   WHEN YOUR BLACK AND YOU'VE LOST

(DN)   JAILBIRD.

(NA)   LOOK YOU'RE BLACK YOU CAN'T WIN, SOPPY CUNT, I'VE JUST DONE A PRISON
        SENTENCE.

(CM)   WE WERE JUST LAUGHING AT HIM DRIVING OFF JUST PROPER
                        END OF SEQUENCE FORTY-NINE

(NA)   HE'S SITTING IN DOORS ON HIS OWN

(NA)   THAT'D MAKE ME DEPRESSED I'LL TELL YA THAT. THAT'D MAKE ME (FEEL

        BARMY) MATE I TELL YA.

(DN)   --------------------------

(NA)   I DON'T KNOW YOU WOULDN'T FEEL RIGHT WOULD YA

(DN)   TO TELL YOU THE TRUTH NEIL I WOULDN'T DO IT BUT IF I WAS LIKE TO

        ------------------ DO IT ------------

(NA)   [OVERSPEAKS]

(DN)   IF I NEVER ------------- I'D DEFINITELY

        [OVERSPEAKING]

(DN)   I'D JUST DO A BIG UN IN ME NUT

(NA)   RUNNING INTO THE WALL ------------------------------

(CM)   --

(DN)   IF YOU WERE GOING TO KILL YOURSELF WHAT WOULD YOU DO.

(CM)   [(NA) OVERSPEAKS] I'D GO INTO A POST OFFICE --------------- ROBBERIES -----

(DN)   -------------------- IF I WAS GOING TO KILL MYSELF DO YOU KNOW WHAT I'D DO.

        I'D GO AND KILL EVERY BLACK CUNT, EVERY PAKI, EVERY COPPER, EVERY

        MUG THAT I KNOW I'M TELLING YA.

        [OVERSPEAKING]

(DN)   I'M NOT TALKING ABOUT PEOPLE I LOVE AND CARE FOR I'M TALKING

        ABOUT PEOPLE I DON'T LIKE.

(DN)   I'M TELLING YA, I'M TELLING YA, THEN I'D JUST GO HOME AND GO BOOM

        STRAIGHT IN ME HEAD

(CM)   [OVERSPEAKS]

(DN)   THAT'S IF I WAS GOING TO DO IT BUT THAT'S MADNESS

(CM)   ----------- A SNIPER TAKES YOU OUT

(DN)   YEAH BUT RATHER THAN GET TAKING OUT BY SOMEONE OTHER I'D GO OUT

       (BY MY OWN SELF) RATHER THAN SOMEONE KILL ME I'D KILL MYSELF.

(DN)   WHAT WOULD YOU PREFER, SOMEONE KILLING YOU OR YOU KILLING,

       KILLING, KILLING YOURSELF.

(CM)   YEAH BUT

(DN)   ------------ PEOPLE WALKING AROUND AND SAYING I KILLED THAT CUNT I

       SHOT HIM RIGHT IN THE HEAD.

       [OVERSPEAK]

(DN)   IT SOUNDS SILLY MATE BUT I WOULD THAT'S TRUE NEIL I'M TELLING YOU. I

       WANT TO DIE (ON ME OWN) I JUST WANT TO DIE NATURALLY. I DON'T WANT

       TO GET KILLED, BUT IF I'D THE CHOICE OUT OF GETTING KILLED OR KILLING

       MESELF I'D KILL MESELF AND I'D TRY TO KILL THE CUNT THAT KILLED ME.

(NA)   HOW WOULD YOU GO ABOUT KILLING YOURSELF.

(DN)   OFF THE TOP OF, LIKE A MOUNTAIN.

(NA)   I FANCY I'D HAVE TO GO OUT ------------- I RECKON THE ONLY THING YOU

       COULD DO IS TO JUMP OFF THE HIGHEST BUILDING.

(DN)   NEIL, THAT'S THE WORST WAY TO GO MATE, KNOW WHAT I MEAN YOUR

       HEADS LIKE ...... POOOOF.

(NA)   DAVE YOU IMAGINE JUMPING OFF A BUILDING AND WATCHING IT COME,

       COME ON AT YA, YOU JUST, THINK YEAH, JUST WATCHING IT COME, JUST

       SPINNING YEAH ----

(DN)   (IMAGINE IF YOU NEVER DIED AND A TRAIN WAS COMING RIGHT AT YA ---------

       IT'D CHOP YOU IN HALF).

(CM)   ----------------- JUMPED OFF THE BUILDING AND IT'S HAPPENED BEFORE -------------

       BLOKES ------------------ PARADISE.

(NA)   NO I'M TALKING, I AIN'T TALKING A THIRTY FOOT JUMP, I'M TALKING

       CANARY WHARF MATE LIKE TO MAKE SURE YOU'RE FUCKING DEAD.

(CM)   --------------------

(DN)   --------------------

(NA)   I'D TRY AND JUMP ON SOME OF THEM

(DN)   I WOULD I'D GO DOWN CATFORD AND PLACES LIKE THAT I'M TELLING YOU

NOW WITH TWO SUB MACHINE GUNS AND I'M TELLING YA, I'D TAKE ONE OF

THEM SKIN THE BLACK CUNT ALIVE MATE, TORTURE HIM, SET HIM ALIGHT.

[OVERSPEAKING]

(CM)   I WOULD LOVE TO BUMP INTO ONE OF THEM ---------- JUST FUCKING SHOOT

THEM IN THE BOLLOCKS OR SOMETHING.

(DN)   I'D BLOW THEIR TWO LEGS AND ARMS OFF AND SAY AND SAY GO ON YOU

CAN SWIM HOME NOW

[LAUGHS]

(NA)   JUST LET THEM SQUIRM ------ (LIKE A TIT IN A BARREL)

(DN)   THEY'D BE BOBBING AROUND LIKE THAT.

[IMITATES WHAT HE HAS DESCRIBED]

END OF SEQUENCE FIFTY.

SEQUENCE 51   **DATE: 15.12.94.**

                         START: 20:09:23

                         STOP: 20:09:37

(NA)   BUG SOCKET ON.

END OF SEQUENCE FIFTY-ONE

SEQUENCE 52   DATE: 17.12.94.

                     START: 18:26:39

                     STOP: 18:28:39

(NA)   ----------------------------------

(GD)   I FOUND OUT WHAT THE UM THAT YELLOW BOX IS THERE IT'S A ----------------

         [OVERSPEAK]

(GD)   HE RECKONS THAT'S A CIRCUIT BREAKER AND SAID UH, IF ANYONE FROM

         THE LEB COME ROUND HERE THEY'D CONDEMN THAT ---------------- FUCKING

         AND, OR LIKE TELL HIM TO GET IT FIXED STRAIGHT AWAY THEY'LL TURN

         THE ELECTRICITY OFF IN THE HOUSE 'N' THAT ----------------- LIKE IT DON'T

         BOTHER. HE SAID IT DON'T BOTHER ME LIKE ---------------- PAID FOR NOT

         EVERYONE LIKES TO SEE THAT HE SAID, HE SAID SO WHAT ABOUT SO I GOES

         WHAT'S THAT WHAT'S THAT THING THERE --------------- WHAT'S THAT THERE,

         THERE. HE SAID IT'S ALRIGHT, UM, HE SAID ALRIGHT IF YOU -----------------

         YOUNG KIDS ABOUT THAT COME ROUND AND TRY AND (UNSCREW) THE

         PLUGS AND THEY MIGHT FUCKING KILL THEMSELVES SUPPOSED TO CUT IT

         OUT AND HE GOES BUT IT'S SO OLD I WOULDN'T TRUST IT, HE GOES SO

         THAT'S IN THERE IF YOU DO GET AN ELECTRIC SHOCK OFF THE PLUG THERE'S

         A CIRCUIT IN THERE IT'S A , I'LL OPEN IT UP IF YOU WANT AND SHOW YOU. I

         GOES NAH, IT'S ALRIGHT ---------------------------------- IT'S LIKE A CIRCUIT BOARD

         ------------------ HE SAYS YOU'LL SEE IT ---------------- WHEN THAT, WHEN THAT UH,

         STARTS WHEN THAT STARTS ELECTROCUTING IT CUTS OFF STRAIGHT AWAY

         SO YOU HARDLY REALLY GET A SHOCK.

(NA)   SO WHAT'S HAPPENED IS IF WE DECIDE TO OPEN THE BUGGED PLUG SOCKETS

         AND GET THE BUGS OUT, IF WE GET A SHOCK THEY'VE STUCK, THAT'S IN

         THERE SO THEY DON'T GET DONE FOR MURDER THAT'S HOW, I WORK IT OUT,

         OR MANSLAUGHTER, ANYBODY ELSE.

(LK)   IT'S THERE FOR SOME FUCKING REASON

        [OVERSPEAK]

(GD)   I TELL YOU WHAT, WE'LL GIVE IT, WE'LL GIVE IT A COUPLE OF MONTHS

        RIGHT, LIKE, OR WHATEVER AND I'LL OPEN UP ALL THESE BOXES WHEN I

        KNOW LIKE WHAT A, WHAT I'M DOING.

        [OVERSPEAK]

( )   THEY KNOW WE KNOW THEY'RE THERE ANYWAY.

(GD)   I COULD OPEN IT UP TOMORROW IF YOU THINK ABOUT IT.

(NA)   YOU COULD OPEN IT UP NOW

(GD)   IF WE OPEN IT UP NOW WE'LL -----------------

(NA)   I FANCY BEHIND THAT FIREPLACE

( )   BEHIND THERE

END OF SEQUENCE FIFTY-TWO

SEQUENCE 53   DATE: 17.12.94.

                     START: 18:28:40

                     STOP: 18:30:00

(NA)   I FANCY WE ONLY FUCKING, WATCH THIS [OVERSPEAK]

(LK)   IT'S A NIGGER AND THE OLD BILL GOT TO THE END

(GD)   I SEE, I DIDN'T NOTICE THEM WHITE LINES

(NA)   YEAH, NEITHER DID I

(NA)   SUPER ------------------------

(GD)   WHO ARE WE GONNA FUCK, WHO ARE WE FUCKING ROUTING FOR HERE A

        NIGGER OR A COPPER

(LK)   (NONE OF THEM)

(NA)   WE'RE JUST HERE TO SEE THEM GET BASHED BY THE FUCKING GLADIATORS

(GD)   --------------------- SERIOUS I'M TELLING YOU. I THOUGHT THAT WHEN I SEEN

THE CUNT DO IT, FIRST OF ALL

(NA)   THIS IS THE SEMI'S

( )   IS IT

(NA)   --

END OF SEQUENCE FIFTY-THREE

SEQUENCE 54   DATE: 18.12.94.

                            START: 19:42:25

                            STOP: 19:43:25

(GD)   (YOU KNOW SHELLEY)

(NA)   -------------------

(NA)   WHAT DO YOU SAY

(GD)   -------------------- SHE DON'T SAY ANYTHING

( )   WHAT'S THAT

(GD)   YOU KNOW MY MATES DAUGHTER MARRIED A PAKI FOR A GRAND TO STAY

          IN THE COUNTRY.

(NA)   FOR A GRAND

(GD)   FOR A GRAND

(NA)   SHE DESERVES TO BE KICKED UP THE CUNT MATE AND CHUCKED OUT OF

          A FIFTH FLOOR WINDOW

(GD)   (CHUCKED OUT OF) -----------------------

( )   FOR A FUCKING GRAND

(LK?)   SHE COULD EVEN SPEND THAT IN A COUPLE OF DAYS

          [OVERSPEAK] - [MUMBLES]

(NA)   THAT JUST SHOWS WHAT A FUCKING SUM BAG CUNT SHE MUST BE. WHAT'S

          HER MUM AND DAD SAY

(GD)   THEY CAN'T SAY NOTHING ABOUT IT

(NA)   THEY CAN ----------------- DIRTY PAKI, MATE, SAY GET OUT OF OUR COUNTRY

YOU PAKI CUNT.

(LK)   [OVERSPEAK]

(NA)   FUCKING HELL IF THAT WAS MY DAUGHTER MATE I'D (KILL) THE PAKI WELL

THEN THE GEEZER'S GOT TO BE FUCKING THICK. I AIN'T BEING FUNNY -------

(GD)   ------------------ THE GEEZER'S A (COP) I DON'T LIKE HIM.

END OF SEQUENCE FIFTY-FOUR

SEQUENCE 55   **DATE: 18.12.94.**

START: 19:46:59

STOP: 19:47:50

(GD)   IT WAS LIKE IN THIS FLAT I WENT ROUND. I WAS SITTING IN THIS FLAT WHEN

IN WALKED TWO NIGGERS WITH THE FUCKING JUNGALIST BLARING OUT.

(   )   OUT OF WHAT

(GD)   OUT OF A FUCKING STEREO LIKE FUCKING ALL GIVING IT NO HAD IT ON A

STEREO IN THERE. I WAS SITTING THERE REMEMBER ME TELLING YA, I WAS

THINKING FUCK THIS MATE I GOTTA GO. TWO WALKED IN AND ANOTHER

ONE WALKED IN SAT DOWN AND ANOTHER GEEZER WALKED IN. THERE WAS

A WHITE GEEZER SITTING IN THE CORNER AND HE WENT WELL I WAS MEANT

TO GO TO WORK TODAY WEREN'T I TALKING AWAY TO THE GIRLS AND HE 'S

GOING I DIDN'T GO LIKE I'VE BEEN ON JURY SERVICE AN I, I'M SITTING THERE

THINKING GET ME OUT OF FOR FUCKS SAKE AND IN WALKED ANOTHER

NIGGER, SO NOW THERE'S FIVE NIGGERS SITTING IN THERE WITH THE WHITE

KID ---------------- ALL STICKING THEIR JUNGALIST ON. THAT WAS IT I HAD TO

GO I WENT, I WENT, FU .... LIKE SEE YOU LATER.

END OF SEQUENCE FIFTY-FIVE

SEQUENCE 56   DATE: 18.12.94.

START: 20:41:58

STOP: 20:43:38

(GD)   THIS IS RACIST THIS ADVERT

(NA)   IS IT

(GD)   YEAH

(CM)   WHAT D'YOU MEAN

(GD)   NIGGERS HAVING A GOOD TIME IN THE SUN. ALL THE WHITE PEOPLE WAITING AT A BUS STOP. ALL THE NIGGERS ARE HAVING A GOOD TIME AT THE BAR DRINKING. THE WHITE FAT BOUNCER LOOKS A CUNT, NICE LOOKING BLACK CUNT SUPPOSED TO BE. GOOD LOOKING BLACK GEEZER IN THE CLUB ALL HAVING A GOOD TIME AND THE FUCKING WHITE GEEZER ARE ALL BORING.

(NA)   THAT'S RACIST THAT ADVERT.

(NA)   I KNOW HOW D'YOU COMPLAIN.

(GD)   YOU HAVE TO WRITE TO FUCKING TELEVISION COMPLAINTS DIVISION OR SOMETHING ---------- GIVE YOUR ADDRESS OR SOMETHING.

(NA)   IF HEINEKEN WAS TO DO SOMETHING LIKE THAT WITH ALL THE WHITE PEOPLE LIKE BEING HAVING A GOOD TIME WITH ALL THE NIGGERS ALL ALL THEM FUCKING PRATTING ABOUT ---------------

(GD)   YEAH IN THE (SLUMS) AND THE NIGGERS HAVING A RIGHT GOOD TIME WITH BEER AT A PARTY. THAT WOULDN'T EVEN MAKE IT ON THE AIR.

(NA)   YEAH BUT IT WOULD BE A RIGHT GOOD LAUGH FUCKING WITH ALL THE NIGGERS HATING IT.

(GD)   YEAH OR HAVE IT ALL IN THE SLUMS SHOOTING EACH OTHER.

(NA)   ---------------------

(LK)   JUST SHOW AFRICA HOW IT IS.

END OF SEQUENCE FIFTY-SIX

Calendar List | **4/22/93 - 4/25/93** | **LAWRENCE.OR2**

| March 1993 | April 1993 | May 1993 |

📖 Calendar

Start	End	Category	Description
22 Apr 1993 10:40 PM	10:40 PM	Information	◆ Stephen Lawrence stabbed
11:30 PM	11:30 PM	Eye witness	Witness Duwayne Brookes saw incident (S2)
11:30 PM	11:30 PM	Eye witness	Eye witness Barry Nugent who lives opposite Dickson Road in Well Hall Road saw white youths run off (S1)
23 Apr 1993 9:00 AM	9:00 AM	Information	◆ Post Mortem (S143)
9:30 AM	9:30 AM	Eye witness	Witness Joe Shepherd saw incident (S7) (D81)
1:50 PM	1:50 PM	Message	☎ Anon male telephones youths with knives on Kidbrook estate may have been involved in stabbing two of them are Neil Acourt and David Norris both of 102 Bournbrook (M4)
7:45 PM	7:45 PM	Information	◆ Anon male visits Eltham Police Station to say Jamie and Neil Acourt of 102 Bournbrook and David Norris plus two others are responsible. The Acourts are known as the Krays. Also stabbed Stacy Benefield. Peter Thompson was part of gang. Stabbed Lee in Woolwich. Gives desription of Acourts and states mum has left the home. (M40)
8:30 PM	8:30 PM	Letter	♠ Anon letter one left in telephone Kiosk and found by Sarah Callow (M48) (D7)
9:00 PM	9:00 PM	Message	☎ Anon female telephones to state Krays are responsible and also stabbed Stacey (M28)
9:35 PM	9:35 PM	Message	☎ Anon female telephones back to say full name Stacey Benefield and one of the offenders is possibly Andy Goodchild (M29)
24 Apr 1993 11:50 AM	11:50 AM	Message	☎ Anon male telephones to inform of letter placed in litter bin outside Welcome Inn Public House (M38) (D6)
12:15 PM	12:15 PM	Letter	♠ Kiosk letter taken to Shooters Hill Police Station by Mrs Martin (M48)
12:35 PM	12:35 PM	Message	☎ Anonymous male to Crimestoppers that Bradley Fox was responsible (M68)
1:40 PM	1:40 PM	Letter	♠ Kiosk note taken to MIR(S62D)
2:35 PM	2:35 PM	Message	☎ Mrs Wood employer of Emma Cook telephones to say that Emma saw 3/4 youths kicking fire door to cinema (M69) (S81)
3:00 PM	3:00 PM	Information	◆ Imran Khan now acts for family (M142)
3:10 PM	3:10 PM	Eye witness	Westbrook who saw incident comes forward as a result of appeal for witnesses (S11)
3:25 PM	3:25 PM	Message	☎ Anon female Alex of 87 Langbrook knows something (M56)
4:00 PM	4:00 PM	h2h	🏠 During house to house occupant of 100 Bournbrook Road states four male brothers in early twenties all live at 102 Bournbrook (H0031/16/01)
4:20 PM	4:20 PM	Message	☎ Anon female who telephoned twice yesterday states 5 not 6 gives Gary Dobson name and address and Jamie and Neil Acourt and their address. (M102)
5:30 PM	5:30 PM	Message	☎ Maureen Smith telephones to say persons to look at are Acourts and that her son Stuart saw them by the corner (M138)
6:00 PM	6:00 PM	Eye witness	Phillip Smith of Well Hall Road gives information about seeing 4 youths running across roundabout just before attack (M57) (S69)
6:05 PM	6:05 PM	Message	☎ Mrs Norsworthy contacts ref information coming from the Smiths. Micheal Norsworthy told by Lee Green that Acourt bros are responsible (A116)
6:55 PM	6:55 PM	Message	☎ Anon male telephones to suggest Acourts are the offenders (M89)
7:00 PM	7:00 PM	h2h	🏠 Donna Coller suggest Aycourts of 102 Bournbrook Road could be responsible (M67)
7:10 PM	7:10 PM	Information	◆ D.S Mackenzie has memory of the name David Norris believed to be from the LIO cards at Walworth or Peckham but cannot recall details (M76)
8:10 PM	8:10 PM	Message	☎ Anon male telephones to say its two brothers with elder twin brothers who killed him (M99)
8:15 PM	8:15 PM	Information	◆ D.S Kirkpatrick tells MIR of blue Datsun car outside 102 Bournbrook Road. Car belongs to John Burke (M105) (A156)
25 Apr 1993 9:00 AM	9:00 AM	Information	◆ No trace SO12 (M170)
5:45 PM	5:45 PM	h2h	🏠 From Mrs Abbot its common knowledge that one of the Acourt brothers carries a knife (M168)
6:00 PM	6:00 PM	h2h	🏠 From house to house at 13 Phineas Pett Road Gary Dobson says he was at home on the night of the murder (M79) (H0035/13/1)

🕐 Calendar

	Start	End	Category	Description
25 Apr 1993	6:10 PM	6:10 PM	h2h	♣ H2H enquiry made at 102 Bournbrook Road present were Patrica Acourt and boyfrien John Burke.Mrs Acourt gave names of Scott and Bradley Lamb, Neil and Jamie Acourt as her sons and reide there. None of them were present. (M183)(S24a)
	6:55 PM	6:55 PM	h2h	♣ H2H 13 Phineas Pett Road and Dobson plus girl followed to 102 Bournbrook Road. (S16)
	9:00 PM	9:00 PM	Information	◆ D.S Davidson takes statement from Stacey Benefield in which he states that David Norris and Niel Accourt were responsible for stabbing him (S46)
	9:05 PM	9:05 PM	Eye witness	Alex Marie who saw incident comes forward (D38) (M81)
26 Apr 1993	9:50 AM	9:50 AM	h2h	♣ Moody states offender from estate Phineas Pett (M198)
	11:15 AM	11:15 AM	Eye witness	Linda Williams gives information about seeing youths near roundabout just before attack and describes 'V' jacket (M98) (S57)
	11:30 AM	11:30 AM	Observations	🏃 D.Supt Crampton raises action for surveillance on suspects (A138)
	11:30 AM	11:30 AM	Observations	🏃 D.Supt Crampton raises action to establish O.P in Flintwell (A139)
	11:35 AM	11:35 AM	h2h	♣ From Linda Brace of 24 Crossbrook ' Acourts carry knives' and names Jamie (M85)
	1:30 PM	1:30 PM	Message	☎ From Sandra Smith ' David Norris' stabbed Benefield. names Acourts twins who live in Bournbrook thier house is full of knives and they are mad on the krays. (M219)
	2:00 PM	2:00 PM	Information	◆ D.C Sheridan puts message into MIR about youth seen to place letter on rear windowscreeen.(M88)
	2:30 PM	2:30 PM	Observations	🏃 Vic Smith meets with D.I Bullock to discuss targets subject of surveillance
	3:55 PM	3:55 PM	h2h	♣ Lovelle Asante ' says Angela Mould told her that offender lives on the Ferrier estate (M217)
	4:00 PM	4:00 PM	Message	☎ Jodi Dewhurst overhead in Castle Public House that Neil Acourt, his brother, Danny Catanio and 2 others (names forgotten) are responsible (M329)
	4:00 PM	4:00 PM	Observations	🏃 D.C Vic Smith and photographer Finch goes to 4 Crossbrook to commence observations on 102 Bournbrook
	4:30 PM	4:30 PM	Information	◆ Broughton called in at Eltham Police Station to say he saw youth with knife at 22.05 hrs on the Thursday (M195)
	6:00 PM	6:00 PM	Observations	🏃 Finch takes first photograph from Observation Post
	7:00 PM	7:00 PM	Observations	🏃 Surveillance team booked off duty. No log for any activity on 26.4.93
	8:00 PM	8:00 PM	Observations	🏃 D.C Smith and Finch stand down from Observation Point
	8:05 PM	8:05 PM	Message	☎ From anonymous female ' Gary Dobson is a member of a racist gang with Neil and Jamie Acourt. They carry knives and machetes. They hang around Well Hall Road' (D103)
27 Apr 1993	8:15 AM	8:15 AM	Observations	🏃 Finch commences observation from 4 Crossbrook Road
	8:55 AM	8:55 AM	Message	☎ Anonymous male caller states'You had better arrest the Acourt Brothers soon or else' (M227)
	10:40 AM	10:40 AM	Message	☎ From Fiona O'Shea ' She has been told by Tara and Michelle Casserley that five youths from the Brook estate are responsible two are brothers one named Jamie ' (M144)
	10:40 AM	10:40 AM	Message	☎ From Janice Casserley 'She has heard that Jamie, Neil Acourt and Gary Dobson has something to do with the murder. On the night of the murder an unknown youth went round to 102 Bournbrook and saw all three plus two other unknown males. All edgy and nervous' (M147)
	11:00 AM	11:00 AM	Observations	🏃 Finch stands down from Observation Point
	11:30 AM	11:30 AM	Information	◆ From Chief Superintendent Chapman ' my informant says Acourts are responsible' (M234)
	12:30 PM	12:30 PM	Information	◆ Boy of mixed race goes into Eltham Police Station and states Steve Hampton is responsible (M112)
	2:00 PM	2:00 PM	Information	◆ D.C Chase tells MIR Jamie Acourt no trace CRO but caution for drug offence and offensive weapon. Arrested 24.1.93 and 9.3.93 and David Norris is known (M117)
	2:00 PM	2:00 PM	Message	☎ From Frank Vinney states Jason Farmer or Fisher may be involved (M226)
	2:00 PM	2:00 PM	Observations	🏃 D.S Knight and surveillance team book on duty for surveillance
	3:15 PM	3:15 PM	Message	☎ From anonymous female ' Jamie Aycourt was concerned in the stabbing of Stephen Lawrence' (D105)
	3:50 PM	3:50 PM	Message	☎ From an anonymous female 'persons concern in murder are Jamie Almond and Gary Dobson' (M267)

Calendar

	Start	End	Category	Description
27 Apr 1993	6:00 PM	6:00 PM	Message	☎ From Ivalie Harris ' Stephanie Hylton has said that offenders are Neil and Jamie Almond and Gibson' (M135)
	7:45 PM	7:45 PM	Message	☎ From Smatha Purcell ' Acourts and their gang are responsible they also stabbed Lee Pearson. Saw Danny Caetano on 26/4 (M443)
	8:40 PM	8:40 PM	Information	◆ Jimmy Grant tells D.S Davidson that some blacks have been trying to find out the Acourt's address. He also gives information re Loius Catanio and an unknown witness on a bus who may have seen the murder.(M152)
	9:00 PM	9:00 PM	Message	☎ Stephanie Hylton gives information that offenders are Jamie and Niel Almond and Gary Gibson (A181)
	11:55 PM	11:55 PM	Observations	🏃 Finch and Surveillance team book off duty. Surveillance log completed. Movement and follow of Gary Dobson to local warehouse.
28 Apr 1993	6:00 AM	6:00 AM	Observations	🏃 Surveillance team on duty. Finch spends day producing albums
	11:30 AM	11:30 AM	Message	☎ Elvin Oduro suggests name of Danny Mutts (M127)
	12:00 PM	12:00 PM	Message	☎ Anon male via Crimestoppers gives names of Acorn brothers and address of 102 Bournebrook Road' (M317)
	2:00 PM	2:00 PM	Observations	🏃 Surveillance team book off duty. No log
	3:15 PM	3:15 PM	Message	☎ Micheal Mitchell gives names of Neil and Jamie Acourt, Gary Dobson, Alan Craig and Michael Bunn (M238)
	9:50 PM	9:50 PM	Message	☎ From Mick Garty ' The word on the street is Arcourts did the murder' (M122)
29 Apr 1993	7:00 AM	7:00 AM	Observations	🏃 Surveillance team book on duty. Seem to spend day at Berryfield.
	7:30 AM	7:30 AM	Observations	🏃 Finch books on duty but produces no photographs of this day
	9:30 AM	9:30 AM	Message	☎ Hazel Ward says rumours are Acourts are responsible (M357)
	11:20 AM	11:20 AM	Message	☎ Anon female telephones to state David Norris but not Acourts or Dobson (M244)
	12:00 PM	12:00 PM	Information	◆ D.C Chase informs MIR that David Norris is known (M121)
	1:10 PM	1:10 PM	Message	☎ Anon female telephones to suggest Dobson, Neil and Brian Acorn and Jamie Barrie (M270)
	5:00 PM	5:00 PM	Observations	🏃 Surveillance team books off duty
	5:30 PM	5:30 PM	Observations	🏃 Finch books off duty
	5:50 PM	5:50 PM	Message	☎ From Anonymous female ' twins are responsible the police must know who they are they act like the Krays and have been doing this for a while' (M377)
	8:00 PM	8:00 PM	Message	☎ Mrs Carty telephones to suggest Stuart Smith knows something (M160)
	9:00 PM	9:00 PM	Message	☎ Emma Cook telephones to suggest Acourts, Lukey Knight, David Norris and Danny Caetano (M131)
30 Apr 1993	7:00 AM	7:00 AM	Observations	🏃 Surveillance team books on duty. Observation at Berryfield.
	8:00 AM	8:00 AM	Observations	🏃 Finch books on duty processing film
	9:30 AM	9:30 AM	Message	☎ From Hazel Ward 28 Wendover Road ' General rumour suggest Acourt family did the murder' (M 357)
	10:30 AM	10:30 AM	Information	◆ Imram Khan suggest Zack Punt and Blue (M240)
	11:30 AM	11:30 AM	h2h	🎤 From Brett Green of 135 Well Hall Road 'suspects comes from Brook estate' (M319)
	2:30 PM	2:30 PM	Message	☎ From Luke Shepherd ' Rumours name Acourts and Dobson' (M305)
	2:30 PM	2:30 PM	h2h	🎤 From David Bowen of 19 Ross Way ' I have heard the name of Arbuthnot from Mick Carty at work' (M164)
	3:00 PM	3:00 PM	Observations	🏃 Surveillance team book off duty
	5:30 PM	5:30 PM	Calls	☎ From anonymous female 'heard yesterday in Bournebrook Road that Neil Acourt of 102 Bournebrook was a suspect for the murder' (M348)
	6:05 PM	6:05 PM	Message	☎ Anon male telephones to suggest David Norris and Danny Mutts (M262)
	10:50 PM	10:50 PM	Message	☎ Anon female telephones to suggest Krays and names Bradley and Jamie Allcott. (M283)

April 1993	May 1993	June 1993
S M T W T F S	S M T W T F S	S M T W T F S
1 2 3	1	1 2 3 4 5
4 5 6 7 8 9 10	2 3 4 5 6 7 8	6 7 8 9 10 11 12
11 12 13 14 15 16 17	9 10 11 12 13 14 15	13 14 15 16 17 18 19
18 19 20 21 22 23 24	16 17 18 19 20 21 22	20 21 22 23 24 25 26
25 26 27 28 29 30	23 24 25 26 27 28 29	27 28 29 30
	30 31	

🕐 Calendar

	Start	End	Category	Description
1 May 1993	12:15 AM	12:15 AM	Message	☎ From M/S Marrett of 87 Llandover Road (family member) 'We have been given the name Knox of Bayfield Road as being involved' (M166)
	10:05 AM	10:05 AM	Message	☎ From P.C Williams 'My baby sitter claims that two brothers called Acall or Acourt are responsible. A chech of LIO at RW shows James Acourt and two brothers have convictions for weapons' (M333)
	11:05 AM	11:05 AM	Message	☎ From anonymous female 'a boy named Nutty Turnover killed Stephen Lawrence his real name is Lee' (D106)
	1:00 PM	1:00 PM	h2h	♣ From Paul Onions of 30 Appleton Road rumours at Eaglefields school that Neil and Jamie Acourt are responsible for the murder (M389)
2 May 1993	9:00 AM	9:00 AM		No information
3 May 1993	9:00 AM	9:00 AM		Bank Holiday
4 May 1993	9:00 AM	9:00 AM	Letter	♠ Received 'Thursday letter' (M218)
	9:40 AM	9:40 AM	Information	◆ Khan gives name of Hobson (M263)
	11:05 AM	11:05 AM	Message	☎ D.S May says his informant has put up names of Blue and Zak Punt (M260)
	11:30 AM	11:30 AM	Message	☎ From an anonymous female 'Persons responsible are Acourt twins also known as Eltham Krays. They hang around with person call Nick. They also stabbed two white boys which was not reported to police' (M 345)
	1:45 PM	1:45 PM	Information	◆ From Maureen George she heard persons running from Dickson Road towards Wendover Road and one voice say 'hurry up 'J' or 'Jamie' (S76)
	2:30 PM	2:30 PM	Observations	📷 Finch on duty conducting observations and photographs of 564 Westhorne Avenue home of Tylers
	3:15 PM	3:15 PM	Message	☎ Anonymous caller gives names of Neil Acorn and Scott and Bradley (M269)
	3:45 PM	3:45 PM	Message	☎ Michelle Casserly tells of Matthew White visiting 102 Bournbrook and of the Benefield stabbing (M252)
	5:20 PM	5:20 PM	Eye witness	David Magee comes forward (M277) (S85)
	7:00 PM	7:00 PM	Observations	📷 Finch goes off duty
5 May 1993	8:00 AM	9:00 AM	Observations	📷 Finch on duty. Initially procesing film and then to Observation Point in Crossbrook Road.
	9:30 AM	9:30 AM	Message	☎ D.S Mick May gives names of Zak Punt and Blue (M239)
	11:50 AM	11:50 AM	Message	☎ Mary Wallace claims Leah Thomsett says Gary Dobson is involved (M255)
	4:00 PM	4:00 PM	E-Fit	🖼 Eye witness Linda Williams completes computer image of rear view of suspect wearing 'V' jacket (A578)
	4:00 PM	4:00 PM	E-Fit	🖼 Eye witness Dywayne Brooks creates computer image of offender (D184)
	7:30 PM	7:30 PM	Observations	📷 Finch goes off duty
6 May 1993	9:35 AM	9:35 AM	Information	◆ Knife found in front garden of 24 Wendover Road. (M281) (S155)
	12:00 PM	12:00 PM	Information	◆ From James Grant 'Acourts trying to purchase knives from Kebab shop - Lee Pearson was stabbed by Acourts and also Stacey stabbed by Neils friend - gives description of friend - Acourts have not been seen in area since murder - they usually hide knives under floor boards (M276)
	12:15 PM	12:15 PM	Information	◆ Chief Supt Chapman again gives names of Acourt (M275)
	1:45 PM	1:45 PM	Message	☎ From an anonymous female ' Norris, Acorn Neil and Jamie. Norris did the stabbing. (M284)
	4:00 PM	4:00 PM	E-Fit	🖼 Eye witness Joe Shepherd completes computer image of offender (M466) (D181)
	8:00 PM	8:00 PM	Information	◆ D.C.S Illsey is given six names by Mrs Lawrence namely;- Zak Punt, Blue, L. Catanio, Dobson, Knox and Arecourt. (M278)
7 May 1993	5:30 AM	5:30 AM	Message	☎ From Anon male IC3 'try 102 Bournbrook' (M397)
	7:00 AM	7:00 AM	Information	◆ Arrest of Acourt Dobson and Norris syncronised. Norris was not at home. (M393/5)
	10:00 AM	10:00 AM	Message	☎ Anonymous female ' Acourts changed their clothes (M285)

April 1993	May 1993	June 1993
S M T W T F S	S M T W T F S	S M T W T F S
1 2 3	1	1 2 3 4 5
4 5 6 7 8 9 10	2 3 4 5 6 7 8	6 7 8 9 10 11 12
11 12 13 14 15 16 17	9 10 11 12 13 14 15	13 14 15 16 17 18 19
18 19 20 21 22 23 24	16 17 18 19 20 21 22	20 21 22 23 24 25 26
25 26 27 28 29 30	23 24 25 26 27 28 29	27 28 29 30
	30 31	

🕐 Calendar

	Start	End	Category	Description
7 May 1993	11:45 AM	11:45 AM	Message	☎ From Ann Collier 14 Sedgebrook Road ' Scott Acourt and Chris Ellis were involved ' (M293)
	1:10 PM	1:10 PM	Information	◆ From YACS ' Dobson and Thompson are two names going around schoo as involved in murder'. (M289)
	2:00 PM	2:00 PM	Information	◆ D.C Wilcox ' Matthew Farnham is member of Haycourt gang and responsiblr for murder.' (M300)

POLICY FILE

Case of:—

Stephen LAWRENCE

REFERRED TO	DATE

STAFFING

INVESTIGATING OFFICER:— D/Supt Weeden

DEPUTY INVESTIGATING OFFICER:— DI Bullock

OFFICE MANAGER:— DS Flook

EXHIBITS OFFICER:— DC Crane

OTHER OFFICE STAFF:—
(SPECIFY)

INITIAL No. OF ENQUIRY OFFICERS:—

INDEXES (tick if used)

NOMINAL ✓

STREET

TELEPHONE

VEHICLE ✓

CATEGORY (SPECIFY)

SEQUENCE OF EVENTS (SPECIFY)

REASONS FOR NOT TAKING INTO USE ANY OF THE ABOVE INDEXES TO BE
DETAILED HEREIN

HOUSE TO HOUSE ENQUIRIES

YES/NO

OFFICER IN CHARGE:— DS McKenzie

AREA TO BE COVERED:— See initial foolio

M.I 84(E)

Form 5026

OFFENCE Murder

VICTIM/LOSER Lawrence

DECISION No. 25

OFFICER MAKING DECISION Det. Ch. Supt Ilsley
and Det. Supt Weeden

DATE OF DECISION 6.5.

DECISION Arrest, search for evidence and
interview the following suspects in
connection with the murder — this to be
done on 7-5-93.
    1) Jamie ACOURT
    2) Neil ACOURT
    3) David NORRIS
    4) Gary DOBSON

REASONS Sufficient ground exist for proposed
action based on
    1) All are known associates
    2) Artists impression similar to Acourts
    3) Information from numerous sources re their involvement
    4) Norris & possibly others thought to possess a knife/knives
    5) Strong possibility they were in the area around
       the time of the murder

Officer making entry

Signature

Date

POLICY FILE FORM 1

OFFENCE ...... Murder

VICTIM/LOSER ...... Lawrence .

DECISION No 2 4

OFFICER MAKING DECISION ...... Det. Ch. Supt

DATE OF DECISION 6/5

DECISION ...... All press enquiries in future to be dealt with by 3 APO, Co Press Bureau and Det. Ch. Supt ILSLEY and will not be handled by the Sio Det. Supt WEEDEN. (This relates to all aspects of the investigation - community issues will continue to be handled by Ch. Supt Phillpot) Det. Ch. Supt Ilsley will also attend all future public meetings / private meetings with solicitors/family, not Det Supt Weeden.

REASONS ...... The volume and intensity of press interest is seriously distracting the Sio from carrying out his main role in relation to the murder of Stephen Lawrence. The same reasons also apply to the heavy and continuing demands and arising from the family, relatives of the deceased and their various representatives.

Officer making entry ......

Signature ......

M.P.84(E)

Date ......

Form 50?.

OFFENCE ...... Murder

VICTIM/LOSER ...... Lawrence

DECISION No. 23

OFFICER MAKING DECISION S10

DATE OF DECISION ...... 5'

DECISION ...... Pending meeting between S10 and family on 6ᵗ do not visit the Lawrence family at present unless urgent or specifically requested. Refer to S10 before doing so.

REASONS ...... In view of the harsh and repeated remarks, reported by the media and attributed to the family, it appears to be inappropriate and perhaps counterproductive to continue daily personal visits until the wishes and needs of the Lawrence family have been clarified.

Officer making entry ......

Signature ...... V. Veeder.

POLICY FILE FORM 1

OFFENCE _Murder_

VICTIM/LOSER _Lawrence_

DECISION No. _22_

OFFICER MAKING DECISION _S10_

DATE OF DECISION _45_

DECISION _Suggest to d/Supt Phillpot that I attend the meeting he has arranged with the family - 5.3m 6.5.93_

REASONS _To resolve the apparent dissatisfaction the family may have regarding liason with police and to inform them in general terms about progress and difficulties in relation to the enquiry._

Officer making entry ....

Signature _Rweeder_

Date _45_

M P B4(E)

Form 3027

OFFENCE Murder

VICTIM/LOSER Lawrence.

DECISION No. 21

OFFICER MAKING DECISION Cdr Des Sio. AHo

DATE OF DECISION 4⁵

DECISION Do not attend press conference called by mrs Khan 2.30p today at New Town Hall

REASONS Organizers appear to have their own agenda

Officer making entry ....

Signature Meade

M P 84(E)

Date 4⁵ 93

Form 5027

OFFENCE Murder

VICTIM/LOSER Lawrence.

DECISION No. 20

OFFICER MAKING DECISION S10.

DATE OF DECISION 45.

DECISION Release PC Alan Fisher back to hannai incident office at RA - but ensure close liaison is maintained between him & the incident room eg attending briefings & updating as necessary.

REASONS Urgently req'd for community work at RA - demos planned etc

Officer making entry ....

Signature ....

Date 45

OFFENCE .... Murder ....

VICTIM/LOSER ...... Lawrence. ....

DECISION No. ...... 19 ....

OFFICER MAKING DECISION .... S.o ....

DATE OF DECISION ...... 15 ....

DECISION .... DC Wilkinson to return to Wembourne enq on ~~~~~ Tuesday 4. may 1993.

REASONS .... Was on temporary loan to this enq. Needed urgently on M_____ fields enq.

Officer making entry ....

Signature ...... K_____ ......

M P 84(E)

Date 15

Form 5027

POLICY FILE FORM 1

OFFENCE ..... Murder

VICTIM/LOSER ..... Lawrence.

DECISION No. 18

OFFICER MAKING DECISION ..... SIO

DATE OF DECISION ..... 15.

DECISION ..... Make arrangements for witnesses to murder to attempt body mapping / E-fit procedures

REASONS .....
1) as an aid to identification of offenders.
2) for elimination purposes
3) for evidential reasons
4) for possible publication

Officer making entry .....

Signature ..... Rweeden.

M P B4(E)

Date 15

Form 5027

OFFENCE Murder

VICTIM/LOSER Lawrence

DECISION No. 17

OFFICER MAKING DECISION Sro/Cdr Adams

DATE OF DECISION 30 4

DECISION Cdr to deal with future contact with solicitors representing the family. - phone call & letter from Cdr to family confirs this.

REASONS To enable Sro to concentrate on preparing the murder enq.

Officer making entry

Signature K... cccle.

M P 84(E)

Date 30 4

OFFENCE .... Murder

VICTIM/LOSER ..... Lawrence

DECISION No. 16

OFFICER MAKING DECISION S10

DATE OF DECISION 28.4

DECISION ..... Extend area of drain search to cover area where possible suspects seen.

REASONS ..... As above see attached map.

Officer making entry .....

Signature .....

Date 28.4

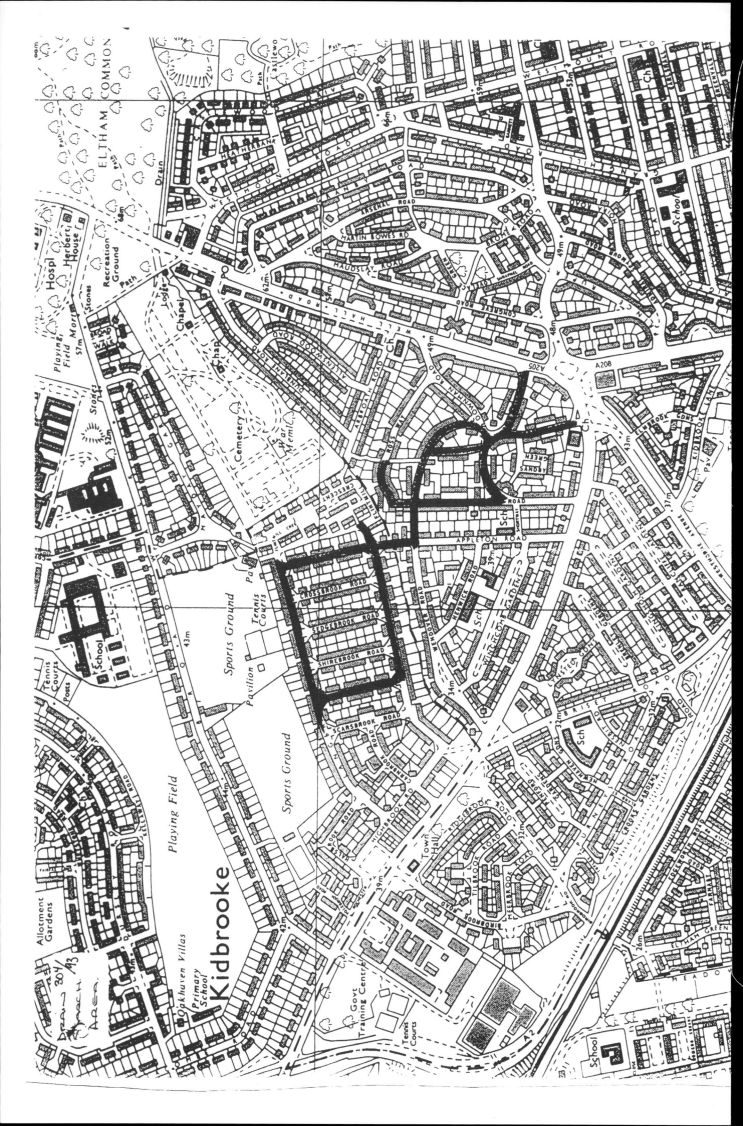

OFFENCE .... Murder ....

VICTIM/LOSER .... Lawrence ....

DECISION No. 15

OFFICER MAKING DECISION .... S10 ....

DATE OF DECISION 27.4.93

DECISION Arrange for adequate but not
excessive weekend cover for office
enqs. — voluntary basis.

    Sat   8 + 7
    Sun   2 + 4
    Mon   2 + 2 + by pm.

REASONS 1) Level of enqs to be done
   2) To receive further info. from public

Officer making entry ....

Signature ....

M P B4(E)

Date ....

form 5027

OFFENCE .... Murder ....

VICTIM/LOSER ...... Lawrence ....

DECISION No. ... 14 ....

OFFICER MAKING DECISION ..... 810 ....

DATE OF DECISION ... 284 ....

DECISION ...... Ensure that victim liaison is focussed firmly on the Lawrence and Brooks families and not diluted or deflected in effect by various intermediaries who have now claimed to represent the family. ....

REASONS ...... To ensure that proper information and support is direct to the family/families. To avoid confusion. ....

Officer making entry ....

Signature ....

N P B4(E)

Date ....

Form 5027

OFFENCE .... murder ....

VICTIM/LOSER .... Lawrence ....

DECISION No. .... 13 .

OFFICER MAKING DECISION .... Sro ....

DATE OF DECISION .... 27ᵗ ....

DECISION .... to not give detailed reply to solicitors
(J. R. Jones) as requested. Write a reply
explaining police position — write to Lawrence
family & Brooks family also.

REASONS .... See letters in old file — fully
explained

Officer making entry ....

Signature ....

Date ....

M P B4(E)

Form 5027

OFFENCE ....Murder...

VICTIM/LOSER ....Lawrence....................................

DECISION No. ......12.....

OFFICER MAKING DECISION ......SIO..............................

DATE OF DECISION ......26/4.....

DECISION ......All press enqs to SIO personally –
for comment/interviews etc or APPO if
SIO not available.

REASONS ......To ensure consistency of approach
on this sensitive case.

Officer making entry .... Signature ...... R Weeden

P 84(E)

Date...... 26/4/97

Form 5027

OFFENCE ..... *Murder* .....

VICTIM/LOSER ..... *Lawrence* .....

DECISION No. ..... *11* .....

OFFICER MAKING DECISION ..... *SIO* .....

DATE OF DECISION ..... *26ᵗʰ 93* .....

DECISION ..... *Obtain services of SIS analyst.* .....

REASONS ..... *To assist in collating, assessing & presenting material available or present* .....

Officer making entry .....

Signature ..... *[signature]* .....

Date ..... *44* .....

POLICY FILE FORM 1

OFFENCE Murder

VICTIM/LOSER Lawrence.

DECISION No. 10

OFFICER MAKING DECISION Ilo

DATE OF DECISION 26 4 93

DECISION As of now - redefine parameters of
H-H area as per decision sheet 6 as follows.
complete whole of Leadebrook / and Flintmill
(Nos _____ only) plus complete Bonnebrook
Suspend all other H-H enqs in area at
this stage.

REASONS) Sightings & information available
do not justify doing H-H in the whole
of the area shown at decision 6
2) Matching resources efficiently in line with
necessary tasks.

Officer making entry

Signature Kniedin.

M.P.5025

Date 26 4 95

Form 5027

OFFENCE .... Murder ....

VICTIM/LOSER ...... Stephen Lawrence. ....

DECISION No. ...... 9 ....

OFFICER MAKING DECISION .... DCS. ....

DATE OF DECISION ....

DECISION ...... Det Supt Weeden to be Sio ....

REASONS ...... Returned to duty & is available. ....

Officer making entry ....

Signature ...... Weeden ....

Date ...... 26ᵗʰ 93 ....

M P 84(E)

Form 5027

OFFENCE ....

VICTIM/LOSER ....

DECISION No. .... 8 ....

OFFICER MAKING DECISION ...... D/Supl. Crampton. ......

DATE OF DECISION .. 25/4/93 ..

DECISION ... To Seek Council Assistance To
Search Drains on Route Marked
In Green on Attached Map.

REASONS ... To Trace Any Potential Weapon.
Route Based Upon Information To Date

Officer making entry ...... D/Supl CRAMPTON ......

Signature ....

M P 84(E)

Date ..... 25/4/93.

Form 5027

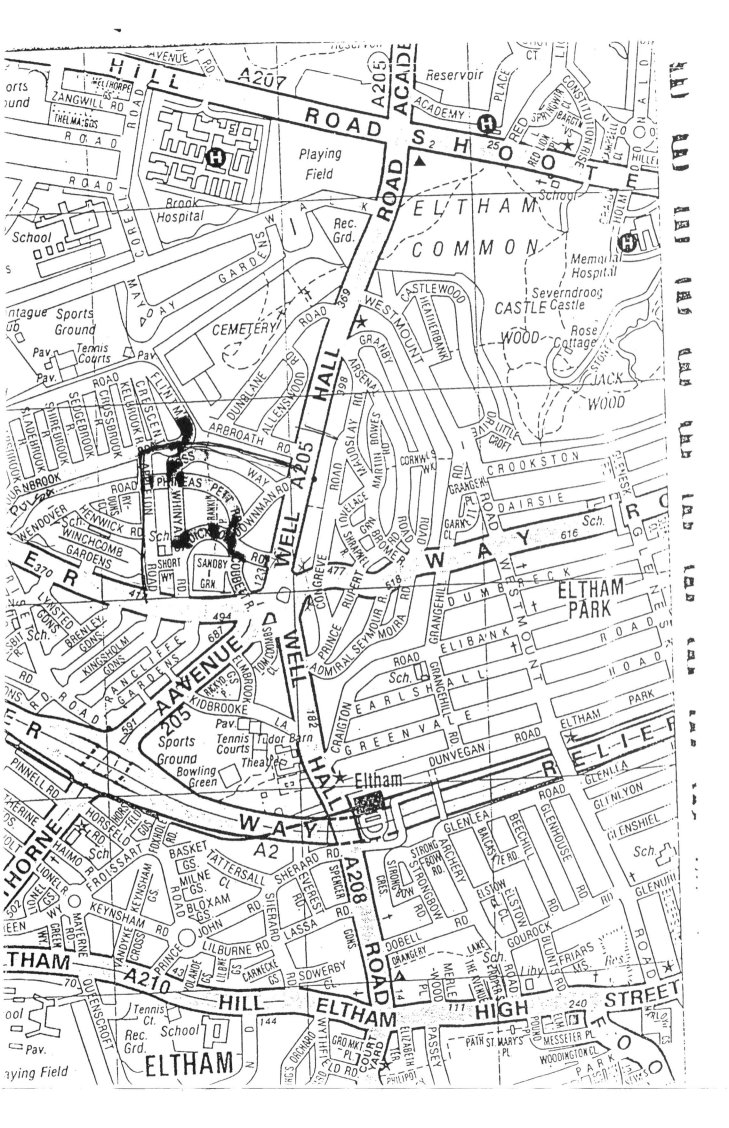

OFFENCE ....

VICTIM/LOSER ....

DECISION No. 7

OFFICER MAKING DECISION ...D/Supt Crampton...

DATE OF DECISION ...24 4 9...

DECISION ...To Inform Press That Witness from Bomb Stop Has Been Traced As Result of His Contacting Police...

REASONS ...Possible may encourage the 2 others to do same...

Officer making entry ...D/Supt Crampton...

Signature ...D/Supt...

Date ...24. 4. 93...

OFFENCE ....

VICTIM/LOSER ....

DECISION No. 6

....

OFFICER MAKING DECISION ...D/Supt. CRAWFORD...

DATE OF DECISION .24-4-93.

DECISION ....Extend House To House Enqs
.......As Shown On Green Area of
.......Attached Map.

....

REASONS ....Result of Information Recieved.

Officer making entry ...D/Supt. CRAWFORD...

Signature ....

Date ......24.4.93.

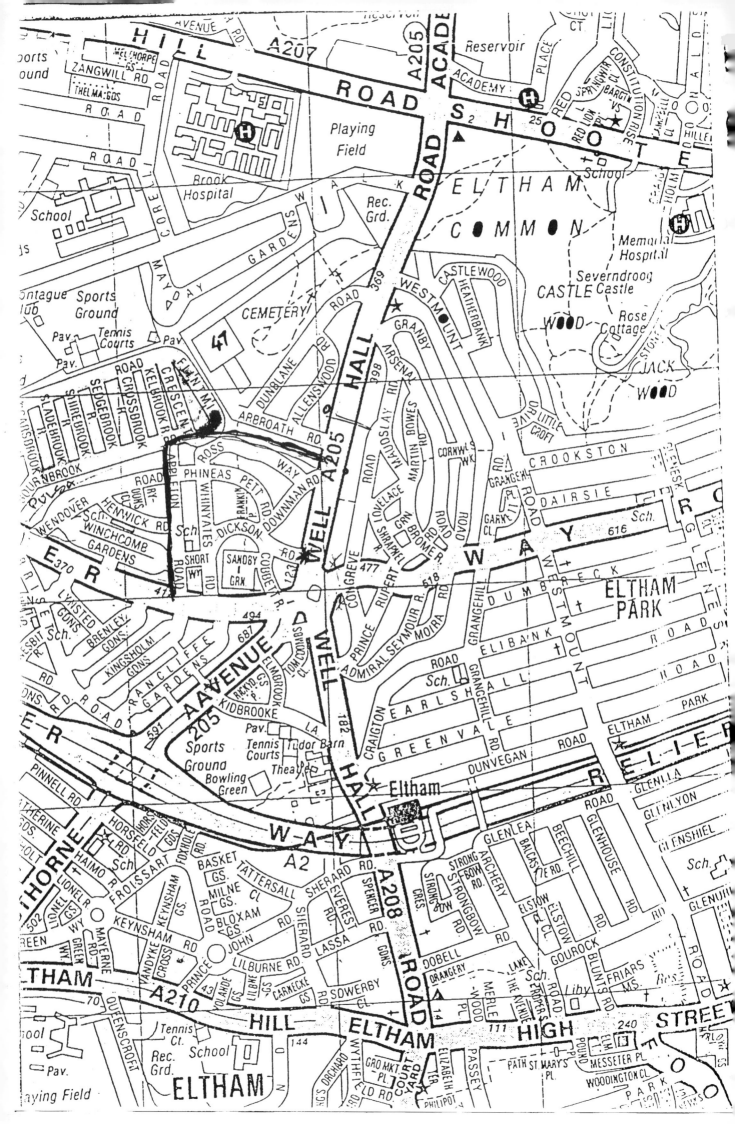

OFFENCE ....

VICTIM/LOSER ....   DECISION No. ....5....

....

OFFICER MAKING DECISION ....D/Supt. Crampton....   DATE OF DECISION ...23⁴/93..

....

DECISION ....To Conduct H/H Eqs of Area....
....With Orange Markings on Attached Map....

........Deploy TSG + 'A' Crime Squad.......
........Each Supervised By D/S.......

REASONS ....Witnesses Information As To Direction....
........Suspects Decamped.......

fficer making entry ...D/Supt. Crampton....   Signature ....

P.84(E)

Date ....24. 4. 93.....

Form 5027

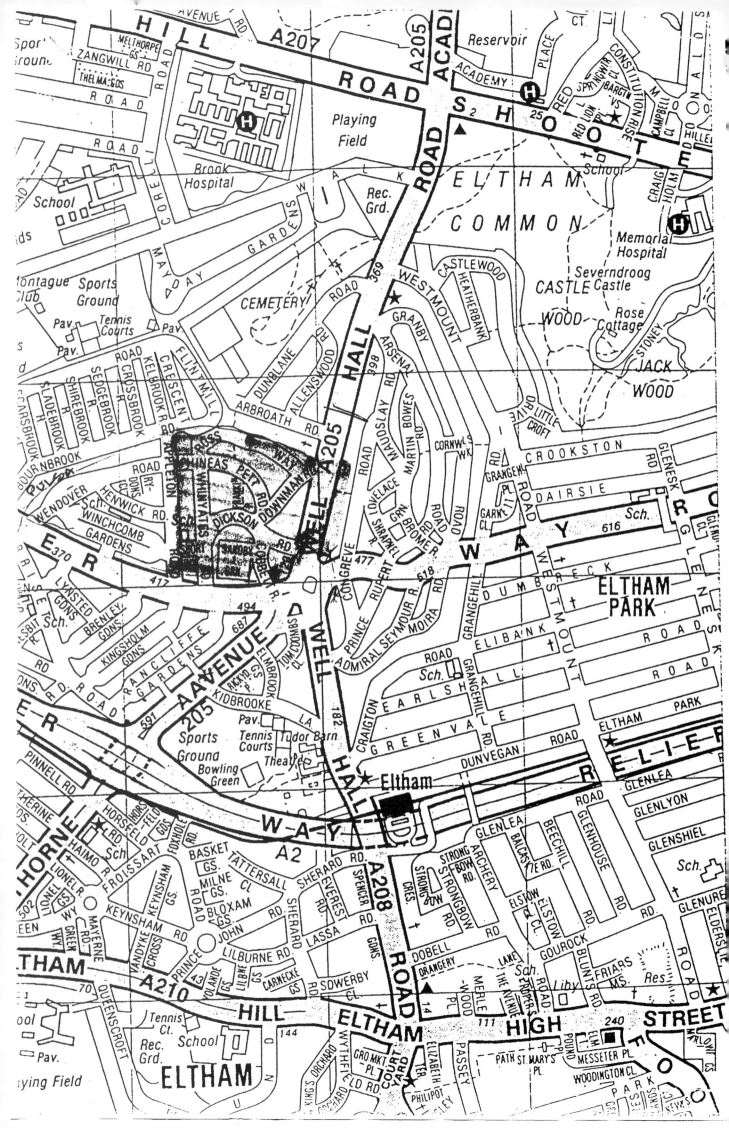

OFFENCE ....

VICTIM/LOSER .... DECISION No. 4
....

OFFICER MAKING DECISION *Des Insley* DATE OF DECISION 23 4/93

DECISION *To Hold Press Briefing / Conference At 'RA'*
....
....
....
....
....
....
....

REASONS *Witness Appeal + Media Attention.*
....
....
....
....
....
....
....
....
....

Officer making entry *A/Supt Cameron*   Signature

P.84(E)

Date 24.4.93

Form 5027

OFFENCE ....

VICTIM/LOSER ....

DECISION No. ....3.

....

OFFICER MAKING DECISION ...D. C. S. Ilsley...

DATE OF DECISION ...23$\frac{4}{9}$

DECISION ...Staffing Level of Incident Team.

3 x D.S + Further D.S. as from 24th

10 x DC. + 1 DC Exhibits Officer.

1 x DI.

3 x Indexers

Systems Manager

DS Office Manager.

1 PC (Alan Fisher) the Racial Incidents

Officer at RA to be Attached.

REASONS ...Nature of Enq.

....

....

....

....

....

....

....

....

....

Officer making entry ...D Supt. Crampton...

Signature ...

M.P.84(E)

Date ...24$\frac{4}{9}$3

Form 5027

OFFENCE ....

VICTIM/LOSER ....

DECISION No. .... 2 .

OFFICER MAKING DECISION ..... D.C.S. Ilsley .....

DATE OF DECISION ..... 23 $\frac{4}{93}$.

DECISION ..... Open. HOLMES Incident Suite
At Eltham Police Stn.

REASONS ..... Nature of Enq.

Officer making entry ..... D/Supt. Crampton .....

Signature .....

Date ..... 24 $\frac{4}{93}$.

P 84(E)

Form 5027

OFFENCE ....

VICTIM/LOSER ....
....

DECISION No. ...... 1 A.

OFFICER MAKING DECISION ...... D/Supt Crampton ......

DATE OF DECISION 23 4/93

DECISION ...... To Conduct Search with Search Team of Defined Area. (for Weapons.) (shown within Area of Blue Marking on Attached Map).

REASONS ...... Nature of Injuries to Victim

Officer making entry ...... D/Supt Crampton

Signature ......

Date 24.4.93

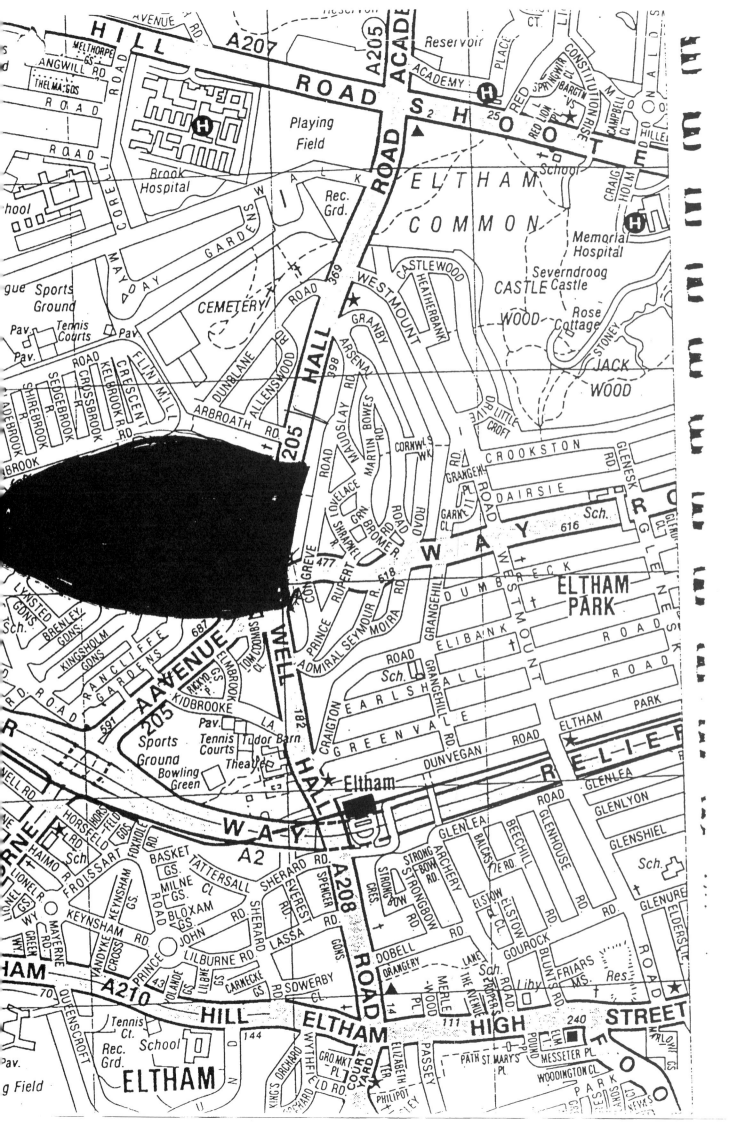

OFFENCE .... Murder.

VICTIM/LOSER ...... Stephen Lawrence.

DECISION No. 1

OFFICER MAKING DECISION ...... D/Supt Crampton

DATE OF DECISION 23/4/93

DECISION ...... Amip to Deal.

REASONS ...... Murder Identity of Suspects Unknown. Possible Racial Motive.

Officer making entry ..... D/Supt Crampton

Signature .....

M P 84(E)

Date 24/4/93.

METROPOLITAN POLICE

A REVIEW OF THE INVESTIGATION INTO THE MURDER OF STEPHEN LAWRENCE ON 22 APRIL 1993

R J BARKER
DETECTIVE CHIEF SUPERINTENDENT

NOVEMBER 1993

A REVIEW OF THE INVESTIGATION INTO THE MURDER OF STEPHEN LAWRENCE - 22 APRIL 1993

INDEX

A REVIEW OF THE INVESTIGATION INTO THE MURDER OF STEPHEN LAWRENCE - 22 APRIL 1993

Deputy Assistant Commissioner Osland - 3 Area,

1. Introduction

1.1   At your request, I have carried out a review of the investigation into the murder of Stephen Lawrence, which occurred at Plumstead (RA) Division on Thursday 22 April 1993. My terms of reference were agreed (Appendix A), and provided, on your behalf, by Commander Blenkin.

1.2   The terms of reference, together with the guidelines at section 4, paragraph 8.5 of the manual of AMIP Policy and Procedure (Appendix B), formed the basis of this review.

1.3   This report outlines the methodology used, the background and characteristics of the investigation, and key issues which feature by way of comment or recommendation for best practice.

2. Overview

2.1   This has been, and remains, an investigation undertaken with professionalism and dedication, by a team who have experienced pressures and outside influences on an unprecedented scale.   Issues which have been highlighted are intended to assist Senior Investigating Officer's (SIO's) and investigating teams in the future.   They should not be seen as criticism of individual officers' actions who were faced with complications and influences of politically active groups or individuals.

2.2   The investigating team remain frustrated, in that they have clear identification evidence, and a considerable amount of hearsay evidence relating to the Acourt brothers and their associates.   Public criticism of incompetencies, from family members, media and political groups has exacerbated that frustration.   Politicians, both from Local and Central government, have had meetings with the Commissioner and Area Senior Officers.   Each has been reassured of the dedication and commitment of the investigating team.   The Senior Investigating Officer has been well supported throughout the difficult task he faced.

2.3   My observations are:

* the investigation has been progressed satisfactorily and all lines of enquiry correctly pursued.

* liaison between the victims family and the investigation team deteriorated at an early stage.   This affected communication and confidence between the two parties.

* press and media relations were hampered by the involvement of active, politically motivated groups.

3.   **Methodology**

3.1   I have been assisted in this review by Detective Inspector Michael Rutter, Detective Sergeant David Miveld and Police Constable Jolyan van-Blankenstein (HOLMES indexer - 7 Area).

3.2   The review began with a briefing and scene visit with the SIO, Detective Superintendent Brian Weedon, and his deputy Detective Inspector Ben Bullock. My review team was based at New Scotland Yard, with access to the HOLMES database through MS22. Visits were made to the incident room at Eltham, for the purposes of clarification, research and to update the SIO or his deputy. There has been regular contact with Detective Chief Superintendent Ilsley.

3.3   The HOLMES database has been searched, the principal lines of enquiry examined to determine their appropriateness and extent, and personal interviews have been conducted with police personnel, CPS lawyers, Victim Support Scheme (VSS) staff and members of the victim's family. This information provides the basis of my observations and recommendations.

3.4   From the outset the investigation was recognised as one appropriate for the HOLMES Major Enquiry System, and categorised 'B' under the AMIP guidelines - "where the victim is/are known but the motive, scene and suspects is/are unknown". Detective Superintendent Ian Crampton was the SIO from the time of the incident until 26 April 1993 when Detective Superintendent Weedon assumed command.

4.   **Background Information**

4.1   On Thursday 22 April 1993 at about 10.00pm, Stephen Lawrence and Duwayne Brooks left the address of Stephen's uncle in Lewisham to return home, Stephen to his parent's home in Woolwich, Duwayne to his bedsit in Charlton. Having changed buses in Eltham High Street, they alighted at the junction of Well Hall Road and Rochester Way and walked north across the roundabout to the bus stop at the junction of Dickson Road. They intended to take a bus north to Woolwich, arriving at the bus stop at about 10.25pm. Shortly before 10.40pm they walked back towards the Well Hall roundabout to see if a bus was coming. Three other people were standing at the bus stop at that time. While crossing Dickson Road, Duwayne saw a bus in the distance and started to return to the bus stop. He shouted to Stephen 'Can you see the bus', and noticed a group of white youths crossing Rochester Way towards them. Stephen joined Duwayne at the junction of Dickson Road at about the same time that the group of youths reached them. One of the youths shouted 'What, what nigger', and Duwayne, fearing an attack, urged Stephen to run. The group attacked Stephen and he received two stab wounds. Duwayne, although running away, saw the assault on Stephen, with what appeared to him to be a length of wood or metal.

4.2   Stephen fell to the ground and his attackers went into Dickson Road. Duwayne urged Stephen to run from the scene. Stephen got to his feet, crossed the road, and ran with Duwayne about three hundred yards north in Well Hall Road, before he collapsed on the pavement.

4.3   Duwayne went to a nearby telephone kiosk where he dialled 999 and requested an ambulance, stating that his friend had been attacked. The operator sought clarification of the location, Duwayne who was distraught, became abusive and left the kiosk with the handset off the hook. The operator confirmed the location of the call with British Telecom and notified information room. CAD 8921 at 10.43pm refers.

4.4   P.C. Geddis, an off duty officer from Plumstead, and his wife, were driving home, saw Stephen on the pavement and stopped. Duwayne was close by, Stephen was apparently unconscious. P.C. Geddis went to the same telephone to call an ambulance and confirms the handset was off the hook. He requested the attendance of an ambulance and police. He then returned to Stephen, and attempted without success to obtain information from Duwayne. The night duty area car from Plumstead, Romeo 3, with P.C.'s Gleason and Bethel arrived at 10.50pm. It was apparent that Stephen had serious injuries from the amount of blood, but there was no visible wound. P.C. Bethel attempted to hurry the ambulance at 10.51pm, and it arrived at 10.53pm. At 11.05pm Stephen arrived at the Brook hospital. P.C. Gleason, accompanied by Duwayne who was in a highly emotional state and did not wish to leave Stephen, escorted the ambulance in the police car.

4.5   One of the witnesses at the bus stop at the time of the attack, Mr Joseph Shepherd, knew Stephen, and lives close to his home. He went home, told his father of what he had seen, and they personally informed Stephen's parents, after which Mrs Lawrence rang '999' at 10.56pm and gave information of the attack and the general area of its location. Mr and Mrs Lawrence then drove to the Well Hall Road area, saw nothing of particular note, and went to the Brook Hospital. When they arrived Stephen was receiving emergency treatment, P.C. Gleason and Duwayne were in the waiting area. Mr and Mrs Lawrence recognised Duwayne and spoke to him.

4.6   At Well Hall Road, P.C.'s Geddis and Bethel followed the trail of blood from Stephen to the scene of the assault at the entrance to Dickson Road, where they found a bag belonging to him. At 10.57pm TSG units, commanded by Inspector Groves arrived and assisted to place cordons around the two scenes, commenced a search of the immediate locality for a weapon, and began house to house enquiries, At 11.13pm the duty officer, A/Inspector Little and the night duty CID, D.C. Pye were called to the scene. At 11.25pm laboratory liaison and photographic staff were called, as well as D.I. Jeynes of Plumstead.

4.7   D.I. Jeynes arrived at the scene before midnight together with D.C. Cooper and a Trainee Investigator from Greenwich Division. At 11.26pm the area dog section were called, arriving at 11.30pm accompanied by Chief Superintendent Benn, 3 Area HQ. Chief Inspector McIvor, late duty senior officer at Plumstead, was informed shortly before midnight about the incident. He then attended the scene. Press bureau were informed at 11.45pm. Chief Superintendent Philpott, Plumstead Division, attended the scene sometime after midnight. The AMIP duty officer, Detective Superintendent Crampton, arrived at approximately 2.am. Having visited the scene, Mr Philpott and Mr McIvor returned to Plumstead Police Station to discuss strategy for possible public disorder, in view of the nature of the attack. Chief Inspector Whapham, Community Liaison officer was informed of the incident about 6.am and began liaison with community contacts/groups.

4.8   At the hospital, P.C. Gleason had been liaising with hospital staff as to Stephen's condition, at the same time trying to calm Duwayne, who remained in an agitated state, endeavouring to obtain further information from him. After Stephen's parents had arrived and spoken to Duwayne, P.C. Gleason spoke with Mr Lawrence, and subsequently other members of the family.   Unfortunately, Stephen Lawrence died from his injuries at 11.17pm, and at 12.02am on Friday 23 April 1993 P.C. Gleason was present when Mr Lawrence identified his son's body. Shortly before midnight A/Inspector Little attended the hospital, spoke to Mr Lawrence and then conveyed Duwayne to Plumstead Police Station for the purpose of obtaining a statement. Mr and Mrs Lawrence returned home and told P.C. Gleason that they did not wish to be disturbed that night. D.C. Pye attended the hospital after 2am to deal with the exhibits.

4.9   At about 3am Detective Superintendent Crampton went to Plumstead Police Station, where he spoke with Duwayne, who was by then making a statement.   Mr Crampton reviewed the information available with D.I. Jeynes, consulted Press Bureau, prepared a racial incident message and informed Detective Chief Superintendent Ilsley of the incident. Later that day, Mr Crampton attended the mortuary for the post-mortem, and arranged for the incident room to be set up at Eltham Police Station on the HOLMES computer system. He also directed D.I. Jeynes to attend the family address. At about 9am D.I. Jeynes, in company with P.C. Fisher, the divisional racial incident officer, attended the Lawrence address, spoke with Mr Lawrence and another family member before returning to Eltham. D.I. Jeynes was replaced as deputy investigating officer by D.I. Bullock during the morning of 23 April 1993.

4.10   Mr Crampton appointed Detective Sergeant John Bevan and Detective Constable Linda Holden as 'Family Liaison Officers' on 23 April. They attended the home address and made contact with the family. D.C. Holden is the owner of a mobile telephone and provided the number to the family as a means of contact. The family expressed their desire to view Stephen's body on the following morning, Saturday 24 April.   Although the officers attempted to make the necessary arrangements, their request for access to the mortuary on the Saturday was denied by Police Constable Bines, the Coroner's officer.

4.11   The family were unhappy at the refusal to view the body and contacted a Greenwich councillor, who in turn spoke to Chief Superintendent Philpott. Chief Inspector McIvor then made arrangements for the family to attend the mortuary on the Saturday morning. The incident room staff were unaware of the arrangements made by Plumstead officers. DS Bevan and DC Holden were told by the family of what was to take place and subsequently accompanied them to the mortuary.

4.12 During the afternoon of 23 April a press conference was arranged, at which Mr Crampton and Mr Ilsley met Mr Lawrence. The press conference was a crowded affair. It was confirmed by police to be a racially motivated murder, which heightened press interest.

5.   Arrests

5.1   On Saturday 24 April anonymous information directed police to a rubbish bin at the Welcome Inn Public House. While an officer searched the bin, an anonymous letter was placed on the rear of his car. The letter contained details of Neil Acourt, Jamie Acourt, David Norris and Gary Dobson, and alleged that they were responsible for the murder. Another anonymous letter, containing the same information, had been found in a telephone kiosk near to the incident during the evening of 23 April. This was handed in to Shooters Hill Police Station on 24 April. Observation of the suspects was commenced and the area for house to house enquiries was extended to include the home addresses of the Acourts and Dobson. Evidence of association was obtained.

5.2 On 07 May 1993, officers attended and searched the home addresses of all four suspects. The Acourt brothers and Dobson were arrested, Norris surrendered himself at Southwark Police Station on 10 May. No additional evidence was obtained from the suspect's interviews, three of whom chose to make no comment. Further information was obtained that Luke Knight was a known associate of the group. He was arrested and his premises searched on 03 June 1993. No further evidence was obtained during interview. A series of identification parades were held between 13.5.93 and 3.6.93. The only positive identification being made by Duwayne Brooks of Neil Acourt and Luke Knight. A conversation between Duwayne and his escorting officer after the identification of Knight, caused doubt as to whether or not Duwayne had been 'coached' by a non-police person. Neil Acourt and Knight were charged with the murder of Stephen Lawrence.

5.3 Acourt and Knight were remanded in custody, one to a detention centre and the other to local authority care. Subsequent meetings between the Crown Prosecution Service (CPS) and the SIO emphasised the need to corroborate Duwayne Brooks identification evidence. Forensic examination of some clothing taken from the Acourts home, and two knives found in Wendover Road and Pleasance Park remain outstanding. A further identification parade by the witness Royston Westbrook was scheduled for 29 July 1993.

5.4 The CPS had indicated at a meeting on 03 June 1993, that without this further evidence discontinuance was a possibility. In the event Westbrook failed to attend on 29 July and the charges were discontinued. This was six days before the committal proceedings.

5.5 A strategy had been agreed with the CPS and SIO that the police would be responsible for informing the family, formal notification to the two accused would be carried out by the CPS on 29 July if the identification was unsuccessful. In the event notification to Knight's solicitors arrived earlier than was anticipated and the news was released prior to others, including the Lawrence family, being informed. This created an impression of lack of co-ordination and last minute action, which was not the case.

6.   The Terms of Reference

6.1   I will now deal specifically with my terms of reference.

7.   **Progress the investigation by endeavouring to identify the persons responsible for the murder**

7.1   The investigating team have identified and interviewed those named at paragraph 5. Neil Acourt and Luke Knight were positively identified by Duwayne Brooks, following identification parades held at Southwark Identification Suite. The subsequent decision by the CPS to discontinue proceedings resulted from a conversation between DS Crowley, who was escorting Duwayne Brooks, after he had identified Knight. Duwayne indicated that he had identified Knight on the basis of what he had been told by friends, not what he saw following the attack.

7.2   The CPS were informed of Duwayne's comment and a statement was forwarded from DS Crowley. At meetings between Mr Medwynter, the Lawyer handling the case, Mr Grant-White (then Assistant Branch Crown Prosecutor) and Detective Superintendent Weedon, the possibility of discontinuance was discussed. The CPS view was that relying solely on Duwayne Brooks, without forensic, or other identification/admission evidence, discontinuance was a real possibility.

7.3   The only remaining evidence, beyond identification, is circumstantial and hearsay. It consists of:

7.3.1   a group of youths running from the scene into Dickson Road in the direction of the Acourt's address,

7.3.2   a witness overhearing youths running by at about the material time from Dickson Road, one using the name either "Jay" or "Jamie",

7.3.3   a knife found in Wendover Road at the rear of the Acourt's address,

7.3.4   a like attack by Neil Acourt and David Norris on Stacey Benefield, which is now the subject of an attempted murder charge.

7.3.5   an entry in a female associates diary that Acourt and Knight murdered Stephen Lawrence. She had been with them earlier on 22 April.

7.3.6   the anonymous letters left at the Welcome Inn Public House and a telephone kiosk in Well Hall Road, naming the Acourts.

7.4   With the exception of Dobson all suspects declined to answer questions during interview. At identification parades, the Solicitor Henry Milner of Milner and Co., employed tactics designed to frustrate the process of the parade by insisting on videoing and photographing volunteers. This also had an effect on the confidence of already reluctant witnesses. Fear and intimidation of witnesses underlines the overall lack of information and credible evidence in this case.

8.   Establish if the ACPO Guidelines and AMIP Manual in relation to murder investigations have been followed

8.1   Where practicable the ACPO guidelines and AMIP Manual of Guidance were followed by the investigation team, although the practicality of staffing the HOLMES incident room, in the context of demands placed on 3 Area at that particular time, was such that these levels could not be met. This will be particularly highlighted at paragraph 9.2. Actions were properly raised, allocated and dealt with by the enquiry team, although the absence of a full team of indexers, did slow down the process of statements being passed through the system. The fact that there were three changes of office managers affected consistency in some policy and practices.

9. Evaluate the appropriateness of the resources devoted to the investigation, i.e. the staffing, accommodation and finance

9.1   The staffing levels are shown at Appendix C with the recommendation of the AMIP guidelines shown in brackets. It will be seen that generally the investigation team has been staffed to a level appropriate to that recommended within the AMIP Manual. Insofar as the HOLMES team are concerned this is not the case. The changes of office manager throughout the enquiry, and the numbers of indexers fluctuated, as demands increased elsewhere.

9.2   The demand on 3 Area at the time of this enquiry was that ten AMIP enquiries were being undertaken, of these, two were HOLMES based. At the time the Area had only twelve trained, full time indexers out of an establishment of sixteen. This has now been increased to sixteen and twenty respectively. Trained indexers are available at divisional police stations, but are rarely used as their regular duties frequently take priority. This means that whilst the appropriate number of indexers are often shown as being available for a HOLMES based enquiry, the reality is that they are moving between incident rooms and not permanently employed in one location.

9.3   The AMIP Manual recommends three Detective Sergeants (DS's) and three indexers for a category 'B' enquiry. They are office manager, receiver and action allocator. With the emphasis on civilianisation of staff the only police officer will often be the office manager, fulfilling all functions. The AMIP Manual should be reviewed to take this into account.

9.4   The accommodation for the enquiry team is on the first floor at Eltham Police Station, occupying what is normally the Area Headquarters Conference Room. This is not a purpose built HOLMES Suite and therefore improvisation is necessary for the outside enquiry team (1 office) and the SIO/DIO (1 office).

9.5   It is 3 Area policy that the duty AMIP Superintendent commences an enquiry, in the first twenty four hours, handing over to the Superintendent scheduled for the next enquiry. In this case Detective Superintendent Weedon was on sick leave on Thursday 22 April, but returned on Monday 26 April, to assume command.

9.6   Mr Weedon's sergeant, DS Flook was involved from the outset until his retirement in July and therefore able to provide continuity, along with DI Bullock. There is however, an inherent danger in such complex, emotionally charged investigations that co-ordination and consistency of policy decisions will be affected through such changes.

9.7   The hand-over period for an SIO to read into the investigation after four days can be considerable, delaying some decisions which might progress the enquiry, particularly in building relations with the victim's family and pursuing new lines of enquiry.

9.8   In such complex, politically charged investigations, the original SIO should remain in command. In this instance the high level of competence of the SIO has not detracted from the overall effectiveness of the investigation, subject to my comments at paragraph 10.

9.9   The cost of the investigation to date is £85,362.73.

9.10   It is recommended that staffing levels for HOLMES Major Incident Rooms, should be reviewed against the categories shown in the AMIP Manual of Guidance, to reflect the availability of trained staff. (Recommendation 1).

9.11   It is recommended that wherever possible changes of SIO and key members of the investigating team should not occur. Especially in relation to racially motivated murders. (Recommendation 2).

10.   **Examine lines of enquiry to establish if they have been properly and appropriately pursued**

10.1   Each line of enquiry has been properly pursued and a total of 74 suspects identified. Of the suspects, 36 have been eliminated, 18 not pursued, 9 are no trace, 8 have not been eliminated and 3 remain outstanding. The focus of the investigating team's attention has, however, centred on those who are featured in the main part of the enquiry, albeit an 'open mind' prevails. Nine hundred and forty two actions have been raised and 443 statements taken from 326 witnesses.

10.2   A decision was taken to delay arresting the Acourt brothers and their associates by the original SIO, on the grounds that further background information was necessary. This was anonymous information and had to be treated accordingly.

10.3   This information emerged on 24 April 1993 and intensified over the weekend, becoming widely known throughout the community, in particular the victim's family, over the ensuing two weeks before their arrest.

10.4   Having assumed command on 26 April, Mr Weedon reviewed the decision not to search Acourts home or arrest them, deciding that any advantage to be gained had now passed, and to continue the surveillance for known associates.

10.5   These were not unreasonable decisions, given the available information, but I am bound to conclude that;

*   evidence **may** have been found connecting the Acourt brothers to the murder by an earlier search of their premises.

*   an earlier arrest **may** have diffused the victim's family frustration of perceived police inactivity, in not arresting people who were widely regarded as suspects from an early stage. The lack of a meaningful dialogue with the family compounded the issue, reinforcing the myths implanted in Mr and Mrs Lawrences minds by outside groups of police disinterest in the crime.

*   delaying the arrests **may** have enabled the suspects to establish alibis, albeit in the event they refused to answer questions during interview.

11. **Examine decisions to curtail lines of enquiry to establish if they were reasonable and justified**

11.1. All decisions to curtail lines of enquiry have been taken by the SIO or his deputy. I am satisfied that a consistent approach has been adopted in these decisions.

12. **Ensure that victim support and liaison arrangements for the deceased family were appropriate and sensitive**

12.1 Two victim liaison officers were appointed by Detective Superintendent Crampton on Friday 23 April 1993, as outlined at paragraph 4.10. Sergeant Bevan had not undertaken this role previously, but DC Holden had on one occasion. Both officers were briefed by Superintendent Crampton that they should support the family's needs as far as is practicable, acting as a communication channel, providing such information as appropriate, except that which is sensitive to operational needs.

12.2 The fact that the liaison officers were unable to arrange a viewing of Stephen's body on Saturday 24th, and also unaware of arrangements already made by officers at Plumstead Police Station, was the beginning of a breakdown in confidence, by Mr and Mrs Lawrence, in their relationship with the police.

12.3 The officers accompanied Mr and Mrs Lawrence and other family members at the mortuary on Saturday 24 April and the body was viewed. The difficulty over the viewing of the body arose as a result of two issues. Firstly, Mr Lawrence had formally identified his son's body at the hospital, and council policy is that the mortuary is not used for viewing purposes. There is some relaxation of this policy when the deceased is a child or murder victim, when 'viewing only' is arranged at weekends. Secondly, the coroner's officer, PC Bines, was of the opinion that arrangements to view the body had been made for the afternoon of Friday 23 April. As the family did not attend the mortuary on the Friday he felt they would have to wait until the Monday. In view of the fact that Mr Lawrence had been at the press conference during Friday afternoon, there was little chance of the family attending the mortuary. It does not appear that the investigation team had been requested to arrange facilities to view on the Friday.

12.4 The family were unhappy at the refusal to allow them to view the body and enlisted the assistance of a Greenwich councillor, who personally authorised the opening of the mortuary on the Saturday morning.

12.5 The councillor is not in an official position to give such 'authorisation', but his personal involvement, that of a senior police officer and increasing media interest, caused PC Bines to consult with the duty mortuary manager, Ms Ann Hopkins, who then made the necessary arrangements.

12.6 Over the ensuing weeks with the influence of outside pressure groups and the appointment of a family solicitor Imran Khan, the relationship with Mr and Mrs Lawrence deteriorated further. Mr Khan required all dealings with them to be through him. This requirement effectively cut police off from personal contact. It also allowed those with political objectives to use the Lawrence family to their own ends, including 'high profile'

9

criticism of police decisions and procedures. By May 1993, Mr Khan's demands on the investigation team were such that a decision was taken by Detective Chief Superintendent Ilsley and ex-Commander Adams that future liaison would be through Mr Ilsley and Chief Superintendent Philpott.

12.7 Mr Khan's role in advising Mr and Mrs Lawrence has, throughout, caused some concern to the investigating team. It is only now, following the channel four programme "Devils Advocate", screened after the disturbances at Welling on 16 October, 1993, that any public acknowledgement of a connection between Mr Khan and the Anti-Racist Alliance (ARA) has been made.

12.8 It was also apparent that the ARA deliberately isolated the Lawrence family from other Anti-racist organisations, by insisting that all contact with them should be through Mr Khan.

12.9 The local VSS appointed Mr Ahmed Pavangar, an Asian, as the Counsellor to work with the family. Mr Pavangar contacted the family by telephone and had a lengthy conversation with Mrs Lawrence's sister. During the conversation Mr Pavangar was at pains to explain the role of VSS.

12.10 At that time Mr Pavangar had only been with the VSS office for three to four weeks and had not received any training in dealing with the relatives of a murder victim. The local VSS management were aware of the difficulty facing Mr Pavangar, but took the decision that the point of contact should be a non-white volunteer. The role of Victim Support in supporting families of murder victims should be reviewed.

12.11 The offer of help by Mr Pavangar was not taken up by the family. It has been inferred that the family declined the offer because of Mr Pavangar's poor command of English. Whilst there may be some substance to this, no clear reasons for the refusal of help have been given by the family.

12.12 When I asked if they had a preference as to the colour or ethnic origin of the VSS counsellor or police officer assigned to them, Mrs Lawrence stated that their only requirement would be for a person who had the ability to empathise, and conduct themselves in a professional manner, above all else be in a position to give them information.

12.13 It is anticipated that the VSS will be contacting the Lawrence family again in the near future to renew their offer of help.

12.14 Victim support to bereaved families of murder victims is a delicate issue. The involvement of VSS volunteers is crucial, and amplified in a report dated April, 1990, by researchers from Liverpool University. This has recently been reinforced in research by Dr. Murray-Parkes of the Royal London Hospital. In both reports the common themes are that families of murder victims require:

    i)   **detailed** information on the means of death and injuries sustained,

    ii)   as **much** information as possible on the progress of the enquiry, and

    iii)   **full** details concerning persons arrested.

12.15 When I saw Mr and Mrs Lawrence they made allegations of insensitivity in the manner in which the liaison officers dealt with them, and their lack of understanding of the trauma resulting from their son's death. Mrs Lawrence is of the view that the police service is a racist organisation, which does not provide the same service to black and white people.

12.16 To understand why Mr and Mrs Lawrence became critical of police actions, it is appropriate to consider the events from their perspective. Their version is factually wrong on a number of important points, and other events have been blurred or misinterpreted. However, it remains their belief of what took place, and can be summarised:

* When Mr Shepherd and his son informed them of the attack on Stephen, Mrs Lawrence rang '999' to send police to the scene of the attack. The police operator stated that he had no knowledge of the incident. The location given by Mrs Lawrence was wrong, it was some three to four hundred yards north of where Stephen had fallen. They have had conflict with the Shepherd family in the past, on the issue of racial harassment, and resented being informed by them.

* Mr and Mrs Lawrence drove along Well Hall Road to look for Stephen before going to the hospital and did not see any police activity. Whilst it is not known if they drove as far as the incident, the only police vehicle which had attended at that time, had left the scene to accompany the ambulance to the hospital. Off duty PC Geddis was in his own vehicle. PC Bethel, the only officer in uniform, may have been somewhere between where Stephen collapsed and where the assault took place. No cordons or road closures had been commenced at that stage.

* Mr Lawrence does not remember formally identifying his son's body at the hospital. Clearly he did.

* They do not remember being spoken to by A/Inspector Little at the hospital, although the officer was present at the identification.

* They do not remember the visit to their home by Detective Inspector Jeynes and the Racial Incident Officer on the morning of Friday 23 April.

* It is believed by the Lawrence family that no house to house enquiries were commenced by police that night. This is wrong, the TSG unit covered all the houses with a view of the assault.

* They believed there was a delay in setting up the investigation team and a further delay in the decision to use the HOLMES system. Both these beliefs are wrong.

* The inability of police to arrange the viewing of their son's body at the mortuary without pressure being applied by a council member.

* The family liaison officers were concerned at the number of relatives and others in the family home. Mr and Mrs Lawrence took exception to being questioned about the identities of people visiting them and the purpose of their visit.

* Requests for information from the family liaison officers were frequently unanswered until the SIO had been consulted. Having been given a personal mobile telephone number by DC Holden and subsequently a further number by DS Bevan, the family were of the opinion that this offered a 24 hour response. They were disillusioned when inappropriate calls in the early hours were met with an unenthusiastic reply, or the telephone had been switched off.

* When a family member called at Shooters Hill Police Station to report suspects loitering near the family home, the person at the front counter had no knowledge of the murder, and proximity of the family home.

* Once the suspects became known they were concerned at what they saw as a delay in the arrests. Having had exposure by the media, Mrs Lawrence was intensely concerned that her son's killers knew all about her family, whilst she would not be able to recognise who they were. The family also feared further attacks on their children or their home.

* On a number of occasions information given to them by police as being confidential, later appeared on national or local news.

12.17 The enormity of the liaison officers task in attempting to satisfy the thirst for information by the family, often generated by their solicitor Imran Khan, which at times then became public knowledge, was beyond any previously experienced. This was a high profile police investigation, attracting wide media interest. Much speculation was being proffered as to who was responsible, the motive and in particular that there was a perceived lack of interest and energy in the police response.

12.18 Despite the experience of 3 Area in handling two previous racially motivated murders, this investigation broke new ground for all concerned. It is only now as time passes that a more meaningful and confidential relationship is being developed between Mr and Mrs Lawrence and the police. Attempts are being made to answer, as frankly as possible, questions raised by the family, in particular those which will be openly given at the forthcoming inquest. It is especially important that an action plan is available at the nearest police station to ensure a prompt police response to potential incidents. Liaison between the investigation team and divisional officers at all levels is vital.

12.19 Having considered police procedures in this and other enquiries with regard to the role of family liaison officers, I am of the view that careful consideration must be given when deciding who should liaise with the family. The possibility of the task being performed by the SIO should not be overlooked. The SIO should endeavour to personally oversee the family liaison officer's relationship with family members whenever possible. This reduces the opportunity for liaison officers to make subjective assessments of their own performance, allows the SIO to be more involved in assessing the level of information being supplied to the family, and early identification of attempts by outside pressure groups to subvert the

12

family for their political ends.

12.20 Where the liaison officer is the SIO, he/she can make instant decisions as to the level of information to be given, at times providing more than is, perhaps, desirable. This will gain their confidence and allay fears of police inactivity. Such a practice was recently employed in another high profile racial attack, and proved beneficial in establishing a closer relationship with the victim's family.

12.21 It is recommended that the role of the Victim Support Scheme in supporting families of murder victims should be reviewed in consultation with VSS organisers. (Recommendation 3).

12.22 It is recommended that a clear distinction should be drawn between, (a) the role of Divisional Senior Management in monitoring/responding to likely public disorder, and (b) the needs of the investigating team in solving the crime. At all times a clear communication channel should be established at operational and strategic level to ensure consistency and compatibility of purpose, in particular an action plan to deal with likely incidents at the family home. (Recommendation 4).

12.23 It is recommended that communication between the family and the liaison officers should be clearly determined from the outset and unrealistic offers of 24 hour mobile telephone cover avoided. Alternative means of contact should be provided. (Recommendation 5).

12.24 It is recommended that officers deputed to perform family liaison roles should be carefully selected in investigations of such potential sensitivity. The SIO should personally monitor the officers relationship with family members, and consider whether he/she undertakes the task. A briefing pack supplemented by a personal briefing, is essential for officers undertaking this role, and their parameters of responsibility and availability to the family clearly defined. (Recommendation 6).

12.25 It is recommended that the SIO or a nominated senior officer should visit the family at the earliest opportunity, to assess the liaison needs. Every effort should be made from intelligence or personal observation to recognise the potential influences of external political pressure groups, and a strategy to intervene with the family, either direct or through mediators, determined. (Recomendation 7).

12.26 It is recommended that the SIO or a nominated senior officer should routinely meet with the family with the liaison officers, to assess the relationship at first hand and deal direct with sensitive questions. (Recommendation 8).

13.   Examine practices employed and make recommendations for the conduct of future investigations

13.1   No scene log of events was kept in the early stages, despite the attendance of Senior officers and the presence of CID personnel. It is crucial that this need is reinforced to officers.

13.2 Activity at the scene was hectic and information scarce. Four detective officers were present before midnight but attended the hospital only after Detective Superintendent Crampton arrived.

13.3 P.C. Gleason was at the hospital, unsupported until about midnight, when A/Inspector Little attended. He was then left on his own for a further two hours or more when Mr Little took Duwayne to Plumstead police station. The officer had been attempting to de-brief a highly emotional witness, reassure and answer questions of the Lawrence family, in addition to liaising with hospital staff, particularly after Stephen had died.

13.4 This placed considerable pressure on the officer, who was acting also as the communication link with the scene. He responded well to the pressure. However, a CID officer and senior uniformed officer should have attended the hospital earlier to relieve this pressure, establish links with the family and attend to forensic evidence.

13.5 It is quite apparent that the two officers who first attended Well Hall Road later experienced post incident trauma, particularly when information about Stephen's background emerged, as being a well motivated and hard working person. They had seen the deceased apparently alive with no visible injury, not in any way expecting him to die.

13.6 The officers speak of guilt at having not done more to render first aid; frustration with an apparent delay in the ambulance arriving; and an overwhelming feeling of disgust at the futility of this savage attack. They recall being in a highly emotional state the following evening. The officers neither sought, nor were offered counselling. I am aware that the issue is now being addressed at Plumstead Division, but the problem should be addressed at service level. Your action as the Area DAC in personally thanking the three officers involved at the scene has been well received.

13.7 It is recommended that in scene management there is a need to keep accurate records of personnel attending and actions taken in the critical early hours of an incident. CID officers should attend the hospital, or location of the deceased's body, to oversee family liaison and exhibit handling at the earliest opportunity. (Recommendation 9).

13.8 It is recommended that post incident counselling should be offered to police officers/witnesses most directly involved with the care of the deceased and/or family as a matter of routine. (Recommendation 10).

14. **To determine the extent to which the investigation made the best use of community organisations and the media**

14.1 As a division which has one of the highest incidents of racial attacks in the Metropolitan Police Area, Plumstead has close contacts with community groups and considerable experience in this field. Chief Superintendent Philpott and Chief Inspector McIvor, having determined that this was a racially motivated murder, called out the Borough Community Liaison Officer (CLO) Chief Inspector Whapham, to make contact with community groups. A decision was then taken as to how tension would be monitored, reduced and potential disorder defused.

14.2 With the benefit of hindsight, had senior officers been able to establish a closer personal relationship with the family, the opportunity to utilise Mr and Mrs Lawrence's support in reducing tension within the community may have prevented disorder.

14.3 If such a relationship had been possible, it may have prevented the ability of external pressure groups to manipulate the family in their condemnation of police action. We may have missed the opportunity to build bridges, before others built barricades.

14.4 Media interest was instant and resulted in a press conference during the afternoon of Friday 23 April which was attended by Detective Chief Superintendent Ilsley, Chief Superintendent Philpott, Superintendent Crampton and Mr Lawrence. Mr Lawrence was appreciative of the police efforts in this regard and he made an emotional appeal for witnesses to his son's murder.

14.5 Media interest did not dissipate and was heightened by the torchlight vigil at the scene on 29 April 1993 by the family and attended by approximately 100 supporters. A march on 08 May 1993 at Belgrave Road and Upper Welling Road, Welling resulted in disturbances. Politically active groups sought to keep the murder high profile.

14.6 Local consultive groups were appraised of developments in this enquiry, through Chief Superintendent Philpott, and where necessary attendance at their meetings, by Detective Chief Superintendent Ilsley. It was, however, difficult to defuse the influence on the media by pressure groups, such as the Anti Nazi League and the Anti Racist Alliance, as well as locally active groups.

14.7 Media interest was used positively by the investigating team whenever possible, enabling appeals to be made for witnesses, nationally as well as locally. Media relations were through 3 Area Press Office, supplemented by Press Bureau. An appeal for witnesses is still being screened at the cinema in Well Hall Road, Eltham.

14.8 Various elements of the media and pressure groups inevitably used the family to highlight perceived weaknesses in police activity. Whenever this has happened the police have sought to respond, but not always obtaining the level of desired exposure. As the Area DAC, you were obliged to reply to family criticism in September on the 'Drive Time' radio programme.

14.9 Although the Deputy Area Press Officer, acting in the absence of her senior colleague, fielded most of the press interest, considerable pressure was placed on the investigation team. At one point the 4 Area Press Officer assisted, working from the incident room, taking calls and dealing direct with Press issues. Dedicated solely to that enquiry, the Press Officer removed considerable pressure from the SIO, and an expansion of this role should be considered for future enquiries.

14.10 During the period of this review enquiries have been made of other racially motivated attacks and close attention has been paid to the style of modern media coverage.

14.11 The perceived need for 24 hour news coverage and the 'race' to be there first has created a number of small, mobile, 'high tech', news gathering teams whose response times continue to improve. Their demands for hard information, video footage of the scene and/or persons involved, has increased the amount of media enquiries made at the scene, or of witnesses. The presentational style of a 'talking head', whether it be an officer, a witness or a local resident has led to media personnel doing their own house to house enquiries often before police. Where possible we should endeavour to be with, or ahead of their enquiries.

14.12 Investigating officers of all incidents likely to attract instant media coverage, should consider the traditional wisdom of delaying house to house enquiries until a suitable time of day. The possibility of witnesses being interviewed on the television before they have been seen by police, or a visible lack of police activity at the scene of a crime, at the time of a broadcast, should be avoided.

14.13 Consideration should also be given to the use of press conferences. The opportunity of the press 'pack' to intimidate a witness or family member may be considerable. The ability of SIO's to respond with a positive message may also be unduly tested in the face of a bank of cameras.

14.14 The alternative, although time consuming, is for the SIO to conduct individual interviews which will provide more detailed coverage; a positive police message and less opportunity for sensational journalism. It will also lessen the opportunity for external political groups to publicly decry police actions.

14.15 It is recommended that at times of intense media interest, a Press Officer should be available to take pressure from the investigating team. (Recommendation 11).

14.16 It is recommended that SIO's should carefully consider the policy of conducting press conferences en-masse, in favour of individual interviews. This will maximise the police response, and minimise opportunities for sensational journalism. (Recommendation 12).

R J Barker   1 November 1993
Detective Chief Superintendent

A REVIEW OF THE INVESTIGATION INTO THE MURDER OF STEPHEN LAWRENCE - 22 APRIL 1993

SUMMARY OF RECOMMENDATIONS

1. Staffing levels for HOLMES Major Incident Rooms, should be reviewed against the categories shown in the AMIP Manual of Guidance, to reflect the availability of trained staff. (Paragraph 9.10)

2. Wherever possible changes of SIO and key members of the investigating team should not occur. Especially in relation to racially motivated murders. (Paragraph 9.11)

3. The role of the Victim Support Scheme in supporting families of murder victims should be reviewed in consultation with VSS organisers. (Paragraph 12.21)

4. A clear distinction should be drawn between, (a) the role of Divisional Senior Management in monitoring/responding to likely public disorder, and (b) the needs of the investigating team in solving the crime. At all times a clear communication channel should be established at operational and strategic level to ensure consistency and compatibility of purpose, in particular an action plan to deal with likely incidents at the family home. (Paragraph 12.22)

5. Communication between the family and the liaison officers should be clearly determined from the outset and unrealistic offers of 24 hour mobile telephone cover avoided. Alternative means of contact should be provided. (Paragraph 12.23)

6. Officers deputed to perform family liaison roles should be carefully selected in investigations of such potential sensitivity. The SIO should personally monitor the officers relationship with family members, and consider whether he/she undertakes the task. A briefing pack supplemented by a personal briefing, is essential for officers undertaking this role, and their parameters of responsibility and availability to the family clearly defined. (Paragraph 12.24)

7. The SIO or a nominated senior officer should visit the family at the earliest opportunity, to assess the liaison needs. Every effort should be made from intelligence or personal observation to recognise the potential influences of external political pressure groups, and a strategy to intervene with the family, either direct or through mediators, determined. (Paragraph 12.25)

8. The SIO or a nominated senior officer should routinely meet with the family with the liaison officers, to assess the relationship at first hand and deal direct with sensitive questions. (Paragraph 12.26)

9. In scene management there is a need to keep accurate records of personnel attending and actions taken in the critical early hours of an incident. CID officers should attend the hospital, or location of the deceased's body, to oversee family liaison and exhibit handling at the earliest opportunity. (Paragraph 13.7)

10. Post incident counselling should be offered to police officers/ witnesses most directly involved with the care of the deceased and/or family as a matter of routine. (Paragraph 13.8)

11. At times of intense media interest, a Press Officer should be available to take pressure from the investigating team. (Paragraph 14.15)

12. SIO's should carefully consider the policy of conducting press conferences en-masse, in favour of individual interviews. This will maximise the police response, and minimise opportunities for sensational journalism. (Paragraph 14.16)

WITNESSES WHO APPEARED BEFORE PART 1 OF THE INQUIRY

Day 1	16 March 1998	Application by Michael Mansfield QC
Day 2	24 March 1998	Opening remarks by Chairman and Advisers followed by opening speeches from:

Edmund Lawson QC (for the Inquiry)
Michael Mansfield QC (for the Lawrence family)
Jeremy Gompertz QC (for the Metropolitan Police Service)

Day 3	25 March 1998	Part statement of Doreen Lawrence read

Police Constable Linda Bethel
Police Constable James Geddis

Day 4	26 March 1998	Conor Taaffe

Police Constable Anthony Gleason
Police Constable Joanne Smith
Police Sergeant Nigel Clement (part heard)

Day 5	27 March 1998	Police Sergeant Nigel Clement (part heard)

Geoffrey Mann
Michael Salih
Catherine Avery
Helen Avery
Graham Cook

Day 6	30 March 1998	David Sadler

Police Constable Stephen Hughes

Statements read:
Brian Wolfe
Denise Wolfe
Dr Priti Patel

Part statement of Neville Lawrence read

Superintendent Jonathan McIvor

Day 7	31 March 1998	Russell Mansford

Mandy Lavin
PC Michael Pinecoffin
Detective Sergeant Donald Mackenzie

Day 8	1 April 1998	Police Sergeant Nigel Clement

Police Sergeant Andrew Hodges
Inspector Steven Groves (part heard)

Day 9	2 April 1998	Inspector Steven Groves Police Constable Paul McGarry Police Constable Paul Robson Police Constable Samantha Tatton Police Constable Paul Smith
Day 10	6 April 1998	Detective Constable Steven Pye Chief Superintendent Christopher Benn
Day 11	7 April 1998	Inspector Ian Little Detective Constable Keith Hughes (part heard)
Day 12	8 April 1998	Detective Constable Keith Hughes Detective Inspector Philip Jeynes
Day 13	20 April 1998	Detective Sergeant David Cooper Detective Sergeant John Sparrowhawk Statements read: John Moroney Anthony Goodman Stephen Mendom Dev Barrah (part heard)
Day 14	21 April 1998	Detective Sergeant David Kirkpatrick Detective Constable Neil Stoddart Detective Sergeant Phillip Sheridan
Day 15	23 April 1998	Detective Inspector Clifford Davies Detective Sergeant Steven Knight Philip Pitham Detective Constable Peter Canavan
Day 16	24 April 1998	Detective Constable Michael Tomlin (part heard) Detective Constable Dennis Chase Detective Sergeant John Davidson (part heard)
Day 17	27 April 1998	Detective Constable Michael Tomlin Detective Sergeant John Davidson
Day 18	28 April 1998	Detective Constable Christopher Budgen Detective Constable Martin Hughes Detective Inspector John Bevan (part heard)
Day 19	29 April 1998	Detective Inspector John Bevan

Day 20	30 April 1998	Statements read: Detective Sergeant David Ashwell Chief Superintendent Kenneth Chapman Detective Inspector Michael Martin May
		Royston Westbrook Inspector Laurence Slone
		Statements read: Inspector John McIlgrew Inspector Barry Craig Sergeant Albert Russell
		William House
Day 21	5 May 1998	Detective Constable Linda Holden Police Constable David Pennington
Day 22	6 May 1998	Detective Sergeant Christopher Mould Stephen Christopher Fuller Detective Constable Robert Crane Adrian Wain (part heard)
Day 23	7 May 1998	Adrian Wain Dr Angela Gallop Detective Sergeant Christopher Crowley (part heard)
Day 24	8 May 1998	Detective Sergeant Christopher Crowley Inspector John McIlgrew
Day 25	13 May 1998	Detective Superintendent Ian Crampton (part heard)
Day 26	14 May 1998	Detective Superintendent Ian Crampton (part heard)
Day 27	15 May 1998	Statement of Duwayne Brooks read
		Detective Inspector Michael Barley
Day 28	18 May 1998	Detective Inspector Benjamin Bullock (part heard)
Day 29	19 May 1998	Detective Inspector Benjamin Bullock
Day 30	20 May 1998	Detective Superintendent Ian Crampton (part heard)
Day 31	26 May 1998	Detective Superintendent Ian Crampton Detective Superintendent Brian Weeden (part heard)
Day 32	27 May 1998	Detective Superintendent Brian Weeden (part heard)
Day 33	28 May 1998	Detective Superintendent Brian Weeden (part heard)

Day 34	29 May 1998	Detective Superintendent Brian Weeden
		Ahmet Ratip
		Detective Sergeant Peter Flook (part heard)
Day 35	1 June 1998	Detective Sergeant Peter Flook
		Detective Chief Superintendent Michael Burdis (part heard)
Day 36	2 June 1998	Detective Chief Superintendent William Ilsley (part heard)
		Detective Chief Superintendent Michael Burdis
Day 37	3 June 1998	Detective Chief Superintendent William Ilsley (part heard)
Day 38	4 June 1998	Detective Chief Superintendent William Ilsley
		Commander Raymond Adams (part heard)
		Detective Chief Superintendent John Barker (part heard)
Day 39	8 June 1998	Detective Chief Superintendent John Barker
		Deputy Assistant Commissioner David Osland (part heard)
Day 40	9 June 1998	Deputy Assistant Commissioner David Osland
Day 41	10 June 1998	Deputy Assistant Commissioner David Osland
		Commander Hugh Blenkin (part heard)
Day 42	11 June 1998	Commander Hugh Blenkin
		Doreen Lawrence
		Neville Lawrence
		Detective Superintendent William Mellish (part heard)
Day 43	15 June 1998	Detective Superintendent William Mellish (part heard)
Day 44	16 June 1998	Detective Superintendent William Mellish
		Acting Commissioner Perry Nove
Day 45	17 June 1998	Assistant Commissioner Ian Johnston
Day 46	22 June 1998	Chief Superintendent John Philpott (part heard)
Day 47	23 June 1998	Chief Superintendent John Philpott
		Police Sergeant Peter Solley (part heard)
Day 48	24 June 1998	Police Sergeant Peter Solley
		Police Constable Alan Fisher (part heard)
Day 49	25 June 1998	Police Constable Alan Fisher
		Harcourt Alleyne
		Dev Barrah

Statements read:
Richard Shepherd
Andrew Mitchell QC

Statement of Peter Finch summarised

Day 50	29 June 1998	Jamie Acourt Neil Acourt David Norris (part heard)
Day 51	30 June 1998	David Norris Luke Knight Gary Dobson Statements read: Phillip Medwynter Graham Grant-Whyte
Day 52	1 July 1998	Phillip Medwynter Howard Youngerwood
Day 53	2 July 1998	Superintendent Leslie Owen Detective Chief Inspector Alan Buttivant Statements summarised: Vivienne Pert Anthony Connell
Day 54	16 July 1998	Commander Raymond Adams Detective Sergeant John Davidson (recalled) Detective Constable Christopher Budgen (recalled)
Day 55	17 July 1998	Statement of Commander James Gibson summarised Imran Khan (part heard)
Day 56	20 July 1998	Imran Khan Statement read: Michael Mansfield QC
Day 57	17 Sept 1998	Closing submission, Michael Mansfield QC
Day 58	18 Sept 1998	Closing submission, Jeremy Gompertz QC Closing submission, Sonia Woodley QC Closing submission, Michael Egan
Day 59	19 Sept 1998	Closing submission, Ian Macdonald QC Closing submission, William Panton Closing submission, Jeffrey Yearwood Closing submission, Mukul Chawla Closing submission, Brian Barker QC

LEGAL REPRESENTATIVES
OF THE PARTIES TO THE
INQUIRY

Inquiry [*]

Counsel: Edmund Lawson QC
        Anesta Weekes
        John Gibson

Solicitors: Treasury Solicitors

Mr and Mrs Lawrence

Counsel: Michael Mansfield QC
        Stephen Kamlish
        Martin Soorjoo
        Margo Boye-Anawoma

Solicitors: J R Jones

Duwayne Brooks

Counsel: Ian Macdonald QC
        Rajiv Menon

Solicitors: Deighton Guedella

Detective Chief Superintendent Barker

Counsel: Mukul Chawla
        Gaby Bonham-Carter

Solicitors: Reynolds Dawson

Detective Chief Superintendent Ilsley, Detective Superintendent Crampton and Detective Superintendent Weeden

Counsel: Sonia Woodley QC
        Peter Doyle

Solicitors: Rowe & Cohen

---

[*] David Penry-Davey QC was originally appointed as Counsel to the Inquiry but in October 1997 he was appointed to the High Court Bench.

Police Constable Bethel, Detective Sergeant Bevan, Detective Inspector Bullock, Detective Sergeant Davidson, Police Constable Geddis, Police Constable Gleason, Inspector Groves, Detective Constable Holden, Detective Inspector Jeynes, Inspector Little and Detective Constable Pye

Counsel: Michael Egan
         Richard Jory

Solicitors: Russell Jones & Walker

Metropolitan Police Service and all MPS officers not otherwise represented

Counsel: Jeremy Gompertz QC
         Jason Beer

Solicitors: Metropolitan Police Solicitor's Department

Crown Prosecution Service

Counsel: Brian Barker QC
         Jocelyn Sparks

London Borough of Greenwich

Counsel: William Panton

Solicitors: Borough Solicitor's Department

Commission for Racial Equality **

Counsel: Jeffrey Yearwood
         Maya Sikand

Solicitors: CRE Law Enforcement Division

** Courtenay Griffiths was originally appointed to represent the CRE but in March 1998 he had to withdraw due to illness.

PERSONS WHO APPEARED BEFORE PART 2 OF THE INQUIRY

Those who gave evidence at Hannibal House

24 September 1998

Home Office
Paul Pugh

Her Majesty's Inspectorate of Constabulary
Dan Crompton
Michael Briggs

Association of Chief Officers of Police of England, Wales and Northern Ireland
David Blakey
Tony Burden
Lloyd Clarke

Police Superintendents' Association of England and Wales
Peter Gammon
Bill Patterson

25 September 1998

Metropolitan Police Service Black Police Association
Paul Wilson
Leroy Logan
Bevan Powell

Crown Prosecution Service
Peter Lewis
Alan Kirkwood

1 October 1998

Metropolitan Police Service
Sir Paul Condon
Denis O'Connor
John Grieve

Police Federation of England and Wales
Fred Broughton
Jeff Molesley

2 October 1998

National Association for the Care and Resettlement of Offenders
Beverley Thompson
Paul Cavadino
Anne Dunn
James Riches-Walker

Commission for Racial Equality
Sir Herman Ouseley
Christopher Boothman
Barbara Cohen

Criminal Bar Association and General Council of the Bar
Michael Grieve QC
Selva Ramasamy

7 October 1998

Society of Black Lawyers
Peter Herbert
Rosemary Emodi
Raj Joshi
Billy Enobakhare

Justices' Clerks' Society of England and Wales
David Chandler
Terry Moore

1990 Trust
Lee Jasper
Rita Patel
David Weaver

Those who appeared at the meetings held in public

EALING, 8 October 1998

Metropolitan Police, Southall Division
Michael Smythe
Angela List
Dilip Joshi

London Borough of Ealing
John Cudmore
Chris Dallison
Sumitra Gomer
Usha Choli

The Monitoring Group
Suresh Grover
Bali Gill
Sukhden Reel
Kwesi Menson

Greenford Baptist Church
Reverend David Wise

Asian Health Agency
Balraj Purewal

Africarib
Clarence Baker

Ealing Racial Equality Council
Bernice McNorton
Godfrey Cremer

Ealing Forum Against Racism
Helen Schofield

Ealing Police Community Consultative Group
Barbara Von Grundherr

MANCHESTER, 13 October 1998

Greater Manchester Federation of Victim Support Schemes
Glyn Morgan

Stockport Victim Support
Valerie Riley

Manchester Refugee Support Network
Liz Rutherford

Rochdale Race Equality Council
Mohammed Naeem
Sameah Khawaja

Greater Manchester Probation Service
Bob Mathers
Helen Allen
Elizabeth Wastell

Manchester City Council
Richard Leese
Steve Mycio
Geoff Little

Crown Prosecution Service
Clif Barker

North Manchester Crime Prevention Panel
Paul Henderson

Manchester Law Society
Nigel Day
John Potter

Manchester Council for Community Relations
Moghal Khan
Mahtarr Samba

Greater Manchester Police
David Wilmot
David McCrone
David Mellor
Harry Campbell

TOWER HAMLETS, 15 October 1998

London Borough of Tower Hamlets
Abdul Asad

Metropolitan Police, Whitechapel Division
Walter Poulter
Christine Jones

Senior Black Clergy Leaders Gathering
Reverend Abraham Lawrence
Reverend Joel Edwards
David Muir

Tower Hamlets Multi-Agency Action Against Racial Incidents
Reverend Christopher Chessun

Movement For Justice
Alex Owolade
Nick Di Marco
Shah Alam

Newham Monitoring Project
Barry Mussenden
Anita Kirpal
Ami Sey

Community Alliance for Police Accountability
Junaid Uddin
Arun Chattopadhyay

Tower Hamlets Race Equality Council
Dr Cyriac Maprayil
Taifur Rashid
Reverend Vaughan Jones

Tower Hamlets Anti-Racist Committee
Nasir Uddin
Kumar Murshid

Tower Hamlets Law Centre
Debashish Day
Lou Christfield

BRADFORD, 21 October 1998

West Yorkshire Police
Lloyd Clarke
David Richardson
Martin Baines
Stuart Brook

West Yorkshire Police Authority
Pat Sarathy

City of Bradford Metropolitan District Council
Mohammed Ajeeb
Diana Cavanagh
Frank Hanley
Sharmila Gandhi

West Yorkshire Probation Service
Randel Barrows
Nasim Akhter
Stuart Macpherson
Mohammed Aslem

Bradford Alliance Against Racial Harassment
Saleem Sharif
Ateeq Siddique

African Caribbean Economic Establishment
Karl Oxford
Doreen Thomas

University of Bradford University Students Union
Claudia Bradshaw

West Yorkshire National Union of Students
Alex Sobel

Bradford Trades Council
Mohammad Taj

Bradford Racial Equality Council
Lynne Kent
Ishtiaq Ahmed

Kirklees Racial Equality Council
Jamil Akhtar

Mohammed Amran

BRISTOL, 3 November 1998

Avon & Somerset Constabulary
David Warren
Nikki Watson
Alison Holver

Bristol City Council
Helen Ball
Stewart Smith
Manjeet Gill
Kulbir Shergill

Bristol Race Equality Council
Peter Courtier
Leotta Goodridge
Professor Rod Morgan

Support Against Racial Incidents
Batook Pandya

Avon & Somerset Police Authority
Ian Hoddell

Bath & North East Somerset Racial Equality Council
Merrick Johnson
Monira Ahmed Chowdhury

Bath & North East Somerset Partnership against Racial Harassment
Alan Bailey
Shamin Baloo
Susan Ramsden

Bristol West Indian Parents and Families Association
Paul Stephenson
Richard Stokes

Respect in Bristol
David John
Balraj Sandhu

Marge Harris

BIRMINGHAM, 13 November 1998

West Midlands Police
Edward Crew
Geoff Rees
Naheed Mushtaq
John Brown

Commission for Racial Equality, Birmingham regional office
Andrew Houseley
Peter Oteng

Birmingham City Council
Teresa Stewart
Michael Lyons
Dr Haroon Saad
Trish Torlan
Graham Farrant

Victim Support
Anne Viney
Deborah Singer
Jill Hogan
Jan Koster

Birmingham Racial Attacks Monitoring Unit
Maxie Hayles
Harjinda Singh

Society of Black Lawyers
John Robotham

Asian Resource Centre
Muhammad Idrish

Sikh Community Youth Service
Jatinder Singh

Sikh Welfare Centre
Aftar Jal Singh

Birmingham Assembly Against Racism
Roger Bethune
Martin Hoare

THOSE WHO PROVIDED WRITTEN SUBMISSIONS
TO PART 2 OF THE INQUIRY

Action Against Racism
Afro-Caribbean & Asian Forum
Association of Jewish Ex-Service Men & Women
Rev Roy C Allison
Anti Nazi League
Asian Resource Centre
Association of Black Probation Officers
Association of Chief Officers of Probation
The Association of Chief Police Officers of England, Wales & Northern Ireland
Association of London Government
Association of Police Authorities
Avon & Somerset Constabulary
Bath & North East Somerset Partnership Against Racial Harassment
Ranjana Bell
Gargi Bhattacharyya
Bindman & Partners, on behalf of the family of Michael Menson
Birmingham Assembly Against Racism
Birmingham City Council
Birmingham Law Society
Birmingham Racial Attacks Monitoring Unit
Black & Asian Studies Association
Black Police Association
Black Prisoner Support Scheme (on behalf of Satpal Ram)
Black Unity & Freedom Party
Black Women for Wages for Housework
The Board of Deputies of British Jews
Markus Boothe
Dr Benjamin Bowling
Bradford Metropolitan District Council
Bristol City Council
Bristol Racial Equality Council
Bristol Trades Union Council
Bristol West Indian Parents & Friends Association
Broad African Representative Council
Butetown Citizens Advice Bureau
Camden Racial Equality Council
The CAMILA Project
George Carter
Balvinder Kaur Chahal
Charnwood Racial Equality Council
Christian Fisher Solicitors, on behalf of Mr & Mrs Reel
John Christopher
Churches Commission for Racial Justice
Howard Cohen
Commission for Racial Equality
Criminal Bar Association
London Borough of Croydon

Crown Prosecution Service
Crown Prosecution Service North West Area
Ealing Community & Police Consultative Group
Department for Education & Employment
Clive Efford MP
Department for the Environment, Transport and the Regions
London Borough of Ealing
Early Years Trainers Anti Racist Network
Estate Management (UK) Ltd
Mr & Mrs Everitt
Fife Community Mediation Project
D Francis (and some members of the Public Gallery)
Friends of Mogous
Joy Gardner Memorial Campaign
Rev Cpt David Gray
Greater Manchester Police
Greater Manchester Probation Service
Greenwich Council
Greenwich Police/Community Consultative Group
Guru Granth Gurdwara
Hammersmith & Fulham Council for Racial Equality
The Hampden Trust
Keith Harris
London Borough of Havering
Department of Health
Her Majesty's Inspectorate of Constabulary
Dr Barnor Hesse
Home Office
Ros Howells
Basil Hylton
The Institute of Race Relations
INQUEST
Islington Council
Professor Gus John
Justices' Clerks' Society
Lambeth Community - Police Consultative Group
James Learmouth
Leeds Racial Equality Council
Leicester Racial Equality Council
Lewisham Council
Lewisham Racial Equality Council
Liberty
Local Government Information Unit
London Group of Labour MPs
Lord Chancellor's Department
Jerome Mack
The Magistrates' Association
Manchester Council for Community Relations
Ms Denese Mapp
Christopher McBride
Metropolitan Police Service
Mrs S E T Millins

Professor Rod Morgan
Movement for Justice
National Assembly Against Racism
National Association for the Care and Resettlement of Offenders
National Association of Probation Officers
National Association of Teachers in Further and Higher Education, Greenwich University Branch
National Union of Teachers
Newcastle City Council
Newham Monitoring Project
1990 Trust
Dr Robin Oakley
Gerald O'Connell
Olabisi Olaleye Foundation
Pan African Caribbean Community Organisation
Poale Zion - Labour Zionist Movement
Police Complaints Authority
The Police Federation of England & Wales
The Police Superintendents Association of England & Wales
Dr Jean Popeau
Prism Partnership Consultancy
Public & Commercial Services Union
Race Equality First
Redbridge Racial Equality Council
Rochdale Racial Equality Council
The Runnymede Trust
Sandwell Racial Harassment Unit
Searchlight Information Services
Sia
Slough Against Racial Attacks
The Society of Black Lawyers
The Society of Labour Lawyers
South East Wales Racial Equality Council
Southwark Council
Support Against Racist Incidents
London Borough of Tower Hamlets
Tower Hamlets Law Centre
Trades Union Congress
Union of Muslim Organisations of UK & Eire
Union of Shop, Distributive and Allied Workers
UNISON
Victim Support
Victim Support Southall
Gurpal S Virdi
West Indian Standing Conference
West Midlands Police
West Midlands Race Forum
West Yorkshire Police
West Yorkshire Probation Service
Dianna Yach

PUBLICATIONS SEEN BY THE INQUIRY

Black Power: The Politics of Liberation in America	S Carmichael and C V Hamilton Penguin Books 1967
Varieties of Police Behaviour	J Wilson Harvard University Press 1968
Police Power and Black People	D Humphry with a commentary by G John Panther 1972
Racial Disadvantage in Britain	D J Smith Penguin 1977
Racial Discrimination - A guide to the Race Relations Act 1976	Home Office 1977
Race, Crime and Arrests Home Office Research Study No. 58	P Stevens and C F Willis Home Office 1979
Ethnic Minorities and Complaints Against the Police. Research and Planning Unit Paper 5	P Stevens and C F Willis Home Office 1981
Ethnic Minorities, Crime and Policing. Home Office Research Study No. 70	M Tuck and P Southgate Home Office 1981
The Brixton Disorders 10-12 April 1981 Cmnd 8427 (The Scarman Report)	Lord Scarman HMSO 1981
Community and Race Relations Training for the Police. Report of Police Training Council Working Party	Home Office February 1983
Policing by Coercion	L Christian Greater London Council 1983

Police and People in London
Volume 1: A Survey of Londoners

D Smith
Policy Studies Institute
1983

Police and People in London
Volume 2: A Group of Young Black
People

S Small
Policy Studies Institute
1983

Police and People in London
Volume 3: A Survey of Police Officers

D Smith
Policy Studies Institute
1983

Police and People in London
Volume 4: The Police in Action

D Smith and J Gray
Policy Studies Institute
1983

Racism Awareness Training for the Police.
Research and Planning
Unit Paper 29

P Southgate
Home Office
1984

Controlling the Constable

R Grimshaw and T Jefferson
Frederick Muller Limited
1984

Victims of Crime: The Dimensions of
Risk. Home Office Research Study
No.81

M R Gottfredson
Home Office
1984

The Attitude of Ethnic Minorities.
Home Office Research Study No.80

S Field
Home Office
1984

White Man's Country: Racism in British
Politics

R Miles and A Phizacklea
Pluto
1984

Black Power: The Politics of Liberation

S Carmichael and C Hamilton
Penguin
1986

Police Racism: Some Theories and Their
Policy Implications in R Mathews and J
Young (eds.). Confronting Crime

J Lea
Sage
1987

Policing and the Community

P Wilmott
Policy Studies Institute
1987

Crime and Racial Harassment in Asian-run Small Shops: The Scope for Prevention	P Ekblom and F Simon with the assistance of S Birdi Home Office 1988
The Victim in Court - Report of a Working Party	National Association of Victims Support Schemes 1988
Communities and Crime Reduction	Edited by T Hope and M Shaw Home Office 1988
Aide Memoire for Senior Investigating Officers	Home Office 1989
Race, Community Groups and Service Delivery. Home Office Research Study 113	H Jackson and S Field Home Office 1989
Racially Motivated Incidents Reported to the Police. Research and Planning Unit Paper 54	J Seagrave Home Office 1989
Murder in the Playground. Report of the Macdonald Inquiry into Racism and Racial Violence in Manchester Schools (The Burnage Report)	I Macdonald QC 1989
The Response to Racial Attacks and Harassment: Guidance for the Statutory Agencies. Report of the Inter-Departmental Racial Attacks Group	Home Office 1989
London Racial Harassment Action Guide	Metropolitan Police Service 1989
The Politics of Race and Residence: Citizenship, Segregation and White Supremacy in Britain	S Smith Policy 1989
Victim Support and Crime Prevention in an Inner-City Setting. Crime Prevention Unit, Paper 21	A Sampson and G Farrell Home Office 1990
Victim's Charter	Home Office 1990

The Institutionalization of Racism in Housing in S Smith and J Mercer (eds.) New Perspectives on Race and Housing in Britain	D Phillips Routledge 1990
Education, Racism and Reform	B Troyna and B Carrington Routledge 1990
Setting the Standards for Policing: Meeting Community Expectation. ACPO Strategic Policy Document	Association of Chief Police Officers 1990
Victim Support Racial Harassment Project Final Report.	J Kimber and L Cooper Community Research Advisory Centre, The Polytechnic of North London 1991
Lessons from a Victim Support Crime Prevention Project. Crime Prevention Unit, Paper 25	A Sampson Home Office 1991
The Victim/Witness in Court Project. Report of the Research Programme Victim Support	J Raine and R Smith University of Birmingham. 1991
Supporting Families of Murder Victims. Guidelines on Planning a Service for Families of Murder Victims and the Selection, Training, Support and Supervision of Volunteers	Victim Support Training 1991
The Response to Racial Attacks: Sustaining the Momentum. The Second Report of the Inter-Departmental Racial Attacks Group	Home Office 1991
Report of The Committee of Inquiry into the Death of Orville Blackwood	Professor H Prins 1991/1992
Report of the Independent Commission on the Los Angeles Police Department	W Christopher City of Los Angeles 1991
White Policing of Black Populations in E Cashmore and E McLaughlin. (eds), 'Out of Order: Policing Black People'	H Hawkins and D Thomas Routledge 1991

Racial Justice at Work: Enforcement of the Race Relations Act 1976 in Employment

C McCrudden, D Smith and C Brown with the assitance of J Knox
Policy Studies Institute
1991

Chief Constables: Bobbies, Bosses or Bureaucrats

R Reiner
Oxford University Press
1991

Working Together – You and Your Police: Police and Community Consultation

Home Office
1991

Seeds of Hope: Report of a Survey on Combating Racism in the Dioceses of the Church of England

The General Synod of the Church of England
Rapier Press Ltd
1991

Recruiting a Multiracial Police Force

S Holdaway
HMSO
1991

A Question of Judgement: Race and Sentencing

R Hood
Commission for Racial Equality
1992

Multiple Victimisation: Racial Attacks on an East London Estate. Police Research Group Crime Prevention Unit Series Paper 36

A Sampson and C Phillips
Home Office
1992

Race and the Criminal Justice System

Home Office
1992

Focusing on Fair Treatment For All. A Handbook to Support Learning in the Area of Equal Opportunities in Metropolitan Police Probationer Training

Metropolitan Police Training School Hendon
1992

Public Satisfaction with Police Services. Research and Planning Unit Paper 73

P Southgate and D Crisp
Home Office
1992

Equal Opportunities in the Police Service

Her Majesty's Inspectorate of Constabulary
1992

Investigative Interviewing - A Guide to Interviewing. National Investigative Interviewing Research and Development Project Team under the direction of a joint Association of Chief Police Officers/Home Office Steering Group

Home Office Central Planning and Training Unit
1992

Safer Cities and Community Safety Strategies. Police Research Group, Crime Prevention Unit Series Paper No 38

N Tilley
Home Office
1992

The Administration of Justice in a Multi-Cultural Society. 1993 Kapila Lecture

Mr Justice Brooke
1993

The Long Term Needs of Victims: A Review of the Literature. Research and Planning Unit Paper 80

T Newburn
Home Office
1993

The Criminal Justice System in England and Wales

G Barclay
Home Office
1993

The Royal Commission on Criminal Justice: Ethnic Minorities and the Criminal Justice System. Research Study No. 20

M FitzGerald
HMSO
1993

Inside the British Police

S Holdaway
Blackwell
1993

Policing and Racial Equality, A Practical Guide to the Association of Chief Police Officers Strategic Policy Document, "Setting Standards for Policing: Meeting Community Expectation"

Association of Chief Police Officers/Commission for Racial Equality
1993

Police Reform White Paper. The Government's Proposals for the Police Service in England and Wales

Home Office
1993

Third Report on Racial Attacks and Harassment

Home Affairs Committee
1993/1994

Once Bitten, Twice Bitten: Repeat Victimisation and its Implications for Crime Prevention. Police Research Group Crime Prevention Unit Series Paper 46

G Farrell and K Pease
Home Office
1993

Race and Racism in Contemporary Britain (2nd edition)	J Solomos Macmillan 1993
Police Training Concerning Migrants and Ethnic Relations Practical Guidelines	Council of Europe 1994
Colour and Spice: Gudiance on Combating Racism in Church Schools	Southwark Diocesan Board of Education 1994
Witness Intimidation, Strategies for Prevention. Police Research Group Crime Detection and Prevention Series Paper 55	W Maynard Home Office 1994
Inter-Agency Crime Prevention: Further Issues. Police Research Group, Supplementary Paper to Crime Prevention Unit Series Paper No 52 and 53	A Liddle and L Gelsthorpe Home Office 1994
Inter-Agency Crime Prevention: Organising Local Delivery. Police Research Group. Crime Prevention Unit Series paper No 52	A Liddle and L Gelsthorpe Home Office 1994
Crime Prevention and inter-Agency Co-operation. Police Research Group Crime Prevention Unit Series Paper No 53	M Liddle and L Gelsthorpe Home Office 1994
Race and the Criminal Justice System	Home Office 1994
Racial Attacks and Harassment. The Government Reply to the Third Report from the Home Affairs Committee Session 1993-94, Cm 2684	HMSO 1994
Racially Motivated Crime: A British Crime Survey Analysis. Research and Planning Unit Paper 82	N Aye Maung and C Mirrlees-Black Home Office 1994
The Ethnic Origins of Prisoners	Home Office 1994
Case Screening by the CPS: How and Why Cases are Terminated. Home Office Research Study 137	D Crisp and D Moxon 1994

Using Surveys: A Guide for Managers. Police Research Group	M Hibberd Home Office 1994
Black Children and Underachievement in Schools	F Benskin Minerva Press 1994
Monitoring the Police Initial Recruitment Test. Police Research Group Paper No. 2	P Smith, R Feltham and C Fernandez Home Office 1994
Contacts Between Police and Public: Findings from the 1992 British Crime Survey. Research Study 134	G Stogan Home Office 1994
The Code for Crown Prosecutors	Crown Prosecution Service 1994
Democracy and Policing	T Jones, T Newburn and D Smith Policy Studies Institute 1994
Tackling Racism in Europe: An Examination of Anti-Discrimination Law in Practice	M MacEwen Berg 1995
Intelligence, Surveillance and Informants: Integrated Approaches. Police Research Group Crime Detection and Prevention Series Paper 64	M Maguire and T John Home Office 1995
Policing a Multi-Cultural Society (Police, Ethnic Relations and Discrimination). First Association of European Police Colleges Conference	Police Research Group Home Office 1995
Reducing Repeat Racial Victimisation on an East London Estate. Police Research Group Crime Detection and Prevention Series Paper 67	A Samson and C Phillips Home Office 1995
Young People and Crime, Research Study Paper 145	J Graham and B Bowling Home Office 1995
Race and the Criminal Justice System	Home Office 1995
Tackling Racial Harassment - a Caseworker's Handbook	Commission for Racial Equality 1995

Action on Racial Harassment: A Guide for Multi-Agency Panels	Commission for Racial Equality 1995
The Rights of Victims of Crime: A Policy Paper	Victim Support 1995
Young People, Victimisation and the Police: Summary Findings. Home Office Research and Statistics Department, Research Findings No. 17	N Aye Maung Home Office 1995
Community Policing	N Fielding Clarendon 1995
The OFSTED Framework: Framework for the Inspection of Schools	Office for Standards in Education Stationery Office 1995
Ethnic Minorities in Great Britain	Ethnic Minorities Advisory Committee of the Judicial Studies Board Home Office 1995/1996
Policing and the Public: Findings from the 1994 British Crime Survey. Home Office Research and Statistics Department, Research Findings No. 28	T Bucke Home Office 1995
Racial Equality Means Business	Commission for Racial Equality 1995
Racial Equality Means Quality	Commission for Racial Equality 1995
Black People in Magistrates' Courts	Justices' Clerks' Society 1995
The Criminal Justice System in England and Wales	G Barclay Home Office 1995
Review of Police Core and Ancillary Tasks. Final Report, and Appendices	Home Office 1995
Developing Diversity in the Police Service: Equal Opportunities Thematic Inspection Report 1995	Her Majesty's Inspectorate of Constabulary Home Office 1996

Witnesses, Victims and the Criminal
Trial. Address by Lord Chief Justice

The Rt. Hon. Lord Taylor of Gosforth
Victim Support
1996

The Passing Winter: A Sequel to Seeds
of Hope

The General Synod of the Church of
England
Church House Publishing
1996

Ethnic Minorities: Victimisation and
Racial harassment. Findings from the
1988 and 1992 British Crime Surveys.
Home Office Research Study 154

M FitzGerald and C Hale
Home Office
1996

Evaluating Joint Performance
Management Between the Police and the
Crown Prosecution Service. Home
Office Research and Statistics
Department, Research Findings No 40

A Hooke, J Knox and D Portas
Home Office
1996

Supporting Victims of Racial
Harassment: Guidelines

Victim Support
1996

Taking Steps: Multi-Agency Responses
to Racial Attacks and Harassment. The
Third Report of the Inter-Departmental
Racial Attacks Group

Home Office
1996

The Victim's Charter

Home Office
1996

Ethnic Minorities, Victimisation and
Racial Harassment: Home Office
Research and Statistics Directorate,
Research Findings, No. 39

M FitzGerald and C Hale
Home Office
1996

Evaluating Joint Performance
Management Between the Police and the
Crown Prosecution Service: Home
Office Research and Statistics
Directorate, Research Findings No. 40

A Hooke, J Knox and D Portas
Home Office
1996

Race and Equal Opportunities in the
Police Service

Commission for Racial Equality
1996

It's Good to Talk: Lessons in Public
Consultation and Feedback. Police
Research Group Paper No 22

R Elliott and J Nicholls
Home Office
1996

Racial Attacks and Harassment: The
Response of Social Landlords

Y Dhooge and J Barelli
Department of Environment
1996

Streetwise: Effective Police Patrol - National Report. Audit Commission	HMSO 1996
Review of Ethnic Minority Initiatives - Final Report	Ministry of Defence 1996
International Action Against Racial Discrimination	M Banton Clarendon Press 1996
Dictionary of Race and Ethnic Relations (4th Edition)	E Cashmore 1996
The Racialisation of British Policing	S Holdaway Macmillan 1996
Policing for a Multi-Ethnic Society	Rotterdam Charter Rotterdam Conference 1996
The Bradford Commission Report	Stationery Office 1996
Winning the Race - Policing Plural Communities. Her Majesty's Inspectorate of Constabulary. Thematic Inspection Report	Her Majesty's Inspectorate of Constabulary 1997
Tackling Racist and Xenophobic Violence in Europe: Case Studies	Dr R Oakley Council of Europe 1997
Resigners? The Experience of Black and Asian Police Officers	S Holdaway and A Barron Macmillan 1997
Your Right to Know: The Government's Proposals for a Freedom of Information Act	HMSO 1997
Policing and the Public: Findings from the 1996 British Crime Survey. Home Office Research and Statistics Directorate, Research Findings No. 60	C Mirrlees-Black and T Budd Home Office 1997
Probationer Training Programme: Professional Development Portfolio	National Police Training Home Office 1997
Equal Opportunities and Community and Race Relations: Minimun Effective Training Levels	National Police Training Home Office 1997

Police Complaints and Discipline - Deaths in Police Custody	J Cotton and D Povey Home Office 1997
The Perpetrators of Racial harassment and Racial Violence. Home Office Research Study 176	R Sibbitt 1997
Ethnicity and Contacts with the Police: Latest Findings from the British Crime Survey. Home Office Research and Statistics Directorate, Research Findings No. 59	T Bucke Home Office 1997
Policing Racially Motivated Incidents. Police Research Group Crime Detection and Prevention Series Paper 84	W Maynard and T Read Home Office 1997
Policing Local Communities - The Tottenham Experiment. Haringay Community and Police Consultative Group	NACRO 1997
Racial Violence and Harassment - A Consultation Document	Home Office 1997
Ethnic Monitoring in Police Forces: A Beginning. Home Office Research Study 173	M Fitzgerald and R Sibbitt Home Office 1997
Aide Memoire for Senior Investigating Officers	Home Office National Crime Faculty 1997
Race and the Criminal Justice System	Home Office 1997
Disclosure in Criminal Proceedings	J Niblett Blackstone Press 1997
Racist Violence in the United Kingdom.	Human Rights Watch Helsinki 1997
Equal Opportunites and Social Policy	B Bagilhole Longman 1997
Changing Police Culture: Policing in a Multicultural Society	J Chan Cambridge University Press 1997

Police Disciplinary and Complaints Procedures: Report and Procedings of the Committee	Home Affairs Committee Stationery Office 1997
Ethnic Minorities in Britain: Diversity and Disadvantage. The Fourth National Survey of Ethnic Minorities	T Modood, R Berthoud, J Lakey, J Nazroo, P Smith, S Virdee, S Beishon Policy Studies Institute 1997
First Aid for the Police Officer	St John Ambulance and Home Office National Police Training 1997
Violent Racism: Victimisation, Policing and Social Context. Clarendon Studies in Criminology	B Bowling Oxford University Press 1998
Human Rights and Policing: Standards for Good Behaviour and a Strategy for Change	R Crenshaw, B Devlin and T Williamson Kluwer 1998
Criminal Justice Consultative Council: Summary of Activities 1997-1998	Home Office 1998
Entry into the Criminal Justice System: A Survey of Police Arrests and Their Outcomes. Research Study Paper 185	C Phillips and D Brown Home Office 1998
Deaths In Police Custody: Learning the Lessons. Police Research Group Paper 26	A Leigh, G Johnson and A Ingram Home Office 1998
Tackling Street Robbery: A Comparative Evaluation of Operation Eagle Eye. Police Research Group Paper 87	J Stockdale and P Gresham Home Office 1998
Public Expectations and Perceptions of Policing. Police Research Series Paper 96	R Bradley Home Office 1998
Manual of Murder Investigation	Association of Chief Police Officers 1998
Victims in Criminal Justice. Report of the Justice Committee.	Justice 1998
Home Affairs Committee, Inquiry into Police Training and Recruitment: Evidence to the Committee	Home Office 1998
Statistics on Race and the Criminal Justice System	Home Office 1998

Evaluation of the 'One Stop Shop' and Victim Statement Pilot Projects	C Hoyle, E Cape, R Morgan and A Sanders Home Office 1998
Speaking Up For Justice: Report of the Interdepartmental Working Group on the Treatment of Vulnerable or Intimidated Witnesses in the Criminal Justice System	Home Office 1998
Review of the Crown Prosecution Service (the Glidewell Report) CM3960	HMSO 1998
Informing: The Community	Informant Working Group Metropolitan Police, Police Complaints Authority, Representatives of Community Police Consultative Groups 1998
Good Practice Guide for Police Response to Racial Incidents	Association of Chief Police Officers 1998
Ethnicity and Victimisation: Findings from the 1996 British Crime Survey. Home Office Statistics Bulletin, Issue 6/98	A Percy Home Office 1998
From Murmur to Murder: Working With Racially Motivated and Racist Offenders	Association of Chief Officers of Probation/Midlands Probation Training Consortium 1998
Crime and Disorder Act 1998 - An Introductory Guide	Judicial Studies Board 1998
Stop and Search: Renewing the Tactic, Interim Report	Metropolitan Police Service 1998
Entry into the Criminal Justice System: a survey of police arrests and their outcomes. Home Office Research Study No. 185	Home Office 1998
Liaison Between Police and Schools	Association of Chief Police Officers/Society of Education Officers Undated
Custody Officer Training: Investing in Safety	Police Complaints Authority Undated

Printed in the UK for the Stationery Office Limited
on behalf of the Controller of Her Majesty's Stationery Office
Dd 5068604 2/99 61743 Job No. J0072405